The DevelopMentor Series
Don Box, Editor

Addison-Wesley has joined forces with DevelopMentor, a premiere developer resources company, to produce a series of technical books written by developers for developers. DevelopMentor boasts a prestigious technical staff that includes some of the world's best-known computer science professionals.

*"Works in **The DevelopMentor Series** will be practical and informative sources on the tools and techniques for applying component-based technologies to real-world, large-scale distributed systems."*
—Don Box

Titles in the Series:

Essential XML
Beyond Markup
Don Box, Aaron Skonnard, and John Lam
0-201-70914-7

Programming Windows Security
Keith Brown
0-201-60442-6

Advanced Visual Basic 6
Power Techniques for Everyday Programs
Matthew Curland
0-201-70712-8

Transactional COM+
Building Scalable Applications
Tim Ewald
0-201-61594-0

Debugging Windows Programs
Strategies, Tools, and Techniques for Visual C++ Programmers
Everett N. McKay and Mike Woodring
0-201-70238-X

Watch for future titles in The DevelopMentor Series.

Debugging
Windows Programs

Strategies, Tools, and Techniques
for Visual C++ Programmers

Everett N. McKay
Mike Woodring

Addison-Wesley

Boston • San Francisco • New York • Toronto • Montreal
London • Munich • Paris • Madrid
Capetown • Sydney • Tokyo • Singapore • Mexico City

The publisher offers discounts on this book when ordered in quantity for special sales. For more information, please contact:

Pearson Education Corporate Sales Division
One Lake Street
Upper Saddle River, NJ 07458
(800) 382-3419
corpsales@pearsontechgroup.com

Visit us on the Web at www.awl.com/cseng/

Library of Congress Cataloging-in-Publication Data

McKay, Everett N.
  Debugging Windows programs : strategies, tools, and techniques for Visual C++
programmers / Everett N. McKay, Mike Woodring.
    p. cm.
  ISBN 0-201-70238-X
  1. Debugging in computer science. 2. Microsoft Visual C++. Microsoft Windows
(Computer file) I. Woodring, Mike. II. Title.

QA76.9D43 M38   2000
005.1'4--dc21

                                                    00-0441637

ISBN 0-201-70238-X

Text printed on recycled paper.
1 2 3 4 5 6 7 8 9 10 – MA – 04 03 02 01 00
First printing, August 2000

*To my wife, Marie Séguin; my children, Philippe Mathieu
and Michèle Audrey; and my parents,
George and Irma Jo.*

— ENM

*To Sheila, Jake, Emma, and Bailly. I can never be
poor with a family like you.*

— MW

Contents

Answers to Frequently Asked Questions

Preface

Debugging Windows programs is a large, complex subject. A book that covered all possible aspects of Windows debugging could easily be twice the size of this book. The problem with such a comprehensive approach to the subject is that the results would be so large and intimidating that few people would want to read it. Consequently, we had to draw the line somewhere and focus on some aspects of Windows debugging at the exclusion of others. Let's start by explaining how we chose to draw that line.

The fundamental motivation behind this book is the belief that programmers' debugging skills could be much improved if they had access to better debugging information. Although plenty of debugging information is available, it is not currently in a form that a programmer can read and then have mastery of the subject. Too often the information is vague and incomplete, or the focus is on debugging tools instead of debugging concepts. The ultimate debugging tool is the programmer's mind, and too often that tool has been neglected. Mastering fundamental Windows debugging concepts will help you prevent many bugs and find the remaining bugs more efficiently, even if you are the most gung ho tool user.

This book identifies the fundamental debugging skills required for effective Windows debugging. Once you have read a chapter, you should have that chapter's subject wired. Part I of the book focuses on debugging strategies to help you understand the debugging process and how to use the C++ language, assertions, trace statements, and exceptions to prevent, reveal, diagnose, and remove bugs. Part II focuses on debugging tools included in Visual C++ as well as Windows. Part III focuses on debugging techniques to help you get the most out of Visual C++ debugging tools, with special attention to debugging memory-related problems, multithreaded programs, and COM.

Some subjects addressed here straddle the border between programming skills and debugging skills. However, since bug prevention is very much a part of debugging, you need to know the common programming mistakes in order to avoid making them. Most programming texts avoid the subjects of debugging and bug prevention, so these subjects need to be addressed.

What's missing in the presentation is also notable. We have largely avoided discussing third-party debugging tools or any Microsoft debugging tools that are not part of Visual C++ (such as WinDbg) or Windows. There are several motivations for this decision. The obvious motivation is to stay focused on debugging concepts and not get side tracked by documenting tools. Another strong motivation is that Visual C++ programmers need better information on how to use the tools they already have. Finally, we doubt that we could say anything about these other tools that would be more helpful than the information provided by the tool vendors themselves.

But I Use BoundsChecker . . .

Some readers are now thinking, "But I use BoundsChecker, so why should I read this book?" Excellent question. Debugging tools, such as Compuware NuMega's BoundsChecker and Rationale Software's Purify, do an excellent job of finding many types of runtime errors—bad pointers and handles, memory corruption and leaks, bad Windows API parameters, and so on. What they don't do is help you understand the debugging process, including how to use the C++ language, assertions, trace statements, and exceptions to prevent and remove bugs, how to take full advantage of the debugging tools that are part of Visual C++ Windows, or how to debug multithreaded programs and COM—all of which this book does.

Furthermore, these tools certainly do not detect all bugs, and they do nothing to help you prevent bugs. If you are totally dependent on debugging tools, you will be helpless when presented with bugs these tools don't find. In addition, using these tools requires you to perform an extra development step, and they can have a significant impact on runtime performance, whereas many of the bug-detection techniques described in this book happen automatically whenever you run the debug build and have a minimal impact on performance. Debugging is a complex puzzle, but these debugging tools will help you with only one piece.

How to Read This Book

Although our hope is that you will read this book from cover to cover, we realize that many readers are in a hurry and won't have the time to read a whole book in order to track down a bug. Consequently, each chapter is largely self-contained so you should be able to read only the chapters you need in the order you want. This self-containment approach means there are some bits of redundant material that apply to more than one chapter, although we tried to keep such redundancy to a minimum. We hope you will agree that this approach makes the book a much more useful reference.

After the Contents, there is a list of answers to frequently asked questions, which can quickly guide you to solutions to many common debugging problems. Chapter 8 is also organized in this way, and either the FAQ list or the chapter can help you quickly find an answer to a specific debugging question.

There are many different types of Windows programs, so there are many different types of debugging techniques. Debugging is presented from the point of view of the Windows API, as well as the MFC and ATL application frameworks. We have clearly identified the material that is specific to MFC and ATL; so if you're not using these frameworks, feel free to skip over those sections if you are in a hurry. If you're not in a hurry, you might want to read them because it is often useful to look at debugging from other points of view.

Finally, each chapter contains key points of advice about debugging, which are presented in a special format as shown here.

> **TIP** These tips highlight the most useful debugging ideas, make the text easier to scan, and will help you locate important debugging topics quickly.

Windows Versions and Hardware

To simplify the presentation, we refer primarily to the current versions of Windows, which at the time of this writing are Windows 2000 and Windows 98. Almost everything said here about Windows 2000 applies to Windows NT 4.0, and nearly everything said about Windows 98 also applies to Windows 95. We mention Windows NT 4.0 and Windows 95 only when referring to those specific versions of Windows.

To further simplify the presentation, we assume you are using Windows on an Intel x86 central processing unit (CPU). Although most of this book is CPU independent, the specific CPU becomes a factor when you are reading hex dumps or debugging at the assembly-language level. For those of you doing assembly-level debugging on a non-Intel platform, you have our sympathy, but not much else.

Who Is "I"?

Although there are two names on the cover, we wrote this book using the first person. Each chapter tells its story from the point of view of a single author. Mike Woodring wrote Chapter 10, Debugging Multithreaded Programs, and Chapter 11, COM Debugging, whereas Everett McKay wrote the remainder. Consequently, the "I" in Chapters 10 and 11 refers to Mike Woodring, whereas the "I" in the other chapters refers to Everett McKay.

For Updated Information

The information in this book is based on Microsoft Visual C++ version 6.0. If you are using a later version of Visual C++, chances are the majority of this book is still accurate but a few details related to the compiler or debugger have changed. To help keep this book's information fresh, we will post any updates or corrections at *www.windebug.com,* along with selected debugging tools. Should you find any errors or out-of-date information, please let us know by sending an e-mail message to *corrections@windebug.com.*

Acknowledgments

This was a very difficult book to write—not because there isn't any good information about debugging out there, but because there is so much. There are bits and pieces of useful debugging information all over the place. To a large degree, the job was to gather them, assimilate them, and describe them in a logical presentation. Many of the ideas in this book are original, but they are in the minority. I wish I could give credit to everyone who originated every debugging technique mentioned in this book, but in most cases, there is no way of knowing who they are.

One cannot write a book about debugging without being influenced by the heavy hitters in the Windows and C++ debugging world. I would like to thank

John Robbins, Matt Pietrek, and Paul DiLascia for their many years of excellent Windows debugging articles in *Microsoft Systems Journal*. I would also like to thank Steve Maguire for his inspirational *Writing Solid Code: Microsoft's Techniques for Developing Bug-Free C Programs* and Steve McConnell for his equally inspirational *Code Complete: A Practical Handbook of Software Construction*. Thanks go to Scott Meyers, Tom Cargill, and Bjarne Stroustrup for their excellent writings on the proper use of the C++ language.

I would also like to thank the pioneers of debugging: Glenford J. Myers, Brian W. Kernighan, and P. J. Plauger, whose early works are still helpful today. Finally, I would like to thank Robert M. Pirsig, whose *Zen and the Art of Motorcycle Maintenance: An Inquiry into Values* has helped to crystallize my understanding of quality. Creating quality software is fundamentally what this book is all about.

In researching this book, I spent a great deal of time monitoring the debugging discussions on various newsgroup forums, particularly *microsoft.public.vc. debugger*. I would like to thank all those newsgroup participants who either knowingly or unknowingly helped me fill in the details of many debugging subjects. Thanks to Jay Bazuzi, Bruce Dawson, Raj Rangarajan, Scott McPhillips, Tomas Restrepo, Katy Mulvey, Doug Harrison, and Joseph Newcomer, whose postings were always a worthwhile read.

I am indebted to all those at Addison-Wesley Professional who had the faith that I could write this book. I would like to thank former acquisitions editor Gary Clarke and his assistant Rebecca Bence for getting this project off the ground and for their extraordinary job of assembling an all-star cast of reviewers. Special thanks to Kristin Erickson, my other editor, for her excellent work in seeing this project through to the end. Thanks also go to Sherri Dietrich, Connie Leavitt of Bookwrights, Joan Kocsis, Marilyn Rash, Angela Stone, and Judy Strakalaitis for their excellent editorial, production, and typesetting work.

This book would not be what it is without the insightful feedback I received from the reviewers. Many thanks to Mike Woodring, Eugène Kain, Christophe Nasarre, David Schmitt, and Robert Ward for their excellent work.

Writing a book requires one to make literally thousands of decisions. Without a doubt, my best decision was bringing Mike Woodring on board as my co-author. Mike wrote Chapter 10, Debugging Multithreaded Programs, and

Chapter 11, COM Debugging. He was able to present these difficult debugging subjects at a level of expertise well beyond what I was capable of doing.

Finally, I give special thanks to my wife, Marie, and my children, Philippe and Michèle, who have had to endure my being attached to a computer for so many months. I could not have finished this project without their support. Now a new adventure awaits us all.

Everett N. McKay

I would like to join Everett in thanking those authors who have consistently put forth the considerable effort it takes to describe in print the techniques and insights that each chose to share. Thank you for not jealously keeping your knowledge to yourselves. I would especially like to thank Matt Pietrek for writing *Windows Internals* and *Windows 95 System Programming Secrets*. Those works sparked an interest in debugging and crash analysis that I am still a slave to today.

I am also grateful for the years I spent working at Intel. I would especially like to thank Jim Held and Kim Toll, with whom I had the opportunity to work on many debugging firefights. I was also fortunate to have worked for Nate LeSane, who allowed me the opportunity to spend many happy hours exercising and honing my software forensics skills. Although it's been a few years since I left Intel, Intel has never left me.

More recently, I've had the great fortune to work with some truly amazing people at DevelopMentor. DevelopMentor has given me the opportunity to humble myself in front of large numbers of students on a regular basis. I can only hope that my students take as much away from their classroom experiences with me as I do from them.

I am especially indebted to Everett for bringing me on board to contribute in some small way to a book on one of my favorite topics. When I reviewed Everett's original book proposal, I knew right away that he would put together a more complete, high-quality book than any I could have offered on the subject. Any errors, omissions, or failures to seamlessly blend Chapters 10 and 11 into Everett's very eloquent story are mine alone.

Mike Woodring

Introduction

Bugs happen. There are many reasons why programs have bugs and many strategies, tools, and techniques to prevent, detect, and remove them. As software development technology has improved, these advances have led to more complex software that is increasingly difficult to debug. Although programmers strive to develop bug-free software, we know that this goal is rarely obtainable in practice.

Complexity is the primary enemy of bug-free software. It is not possible to write even the most trivial program and be certain that it doesn't have bugs without careful testing and debugging. The craft of creating large, complex programs is a highly error-prone activity and programming is possibly *the* human activity that is least tolerant of error or imprecision. Consider how difficult it is to write even a small program that is syntactically perfect without the help of a compiler. Now consider the fact that obtaining correct syntax is much easier than obtaining correct semantics. This implies that developing software of any complexity requires debugging. If you are writing software with enough functionality that people want to buy and use, debugging is a way of life.

Innovation is another enemy of bug-free software. As soon as we are close to discovering the key to removing the bugs from a certain type of program, somebody changes the lock. Both the look and design of today's state-of-the-art program are fundamentally different from those of five years ago. Many debugging techniques that are effective in C-based Windows API programs do little for C++ Microsoft Foundation Class (MFC) Library programs. Similarly, Component Object Model (COM), Distributed COM, Active Template Library (ATL), and multithreaded Windows programs present a whole new set of debugging challenges. Ironically, the continued existence of buggy software can be considered an achievement of the innovation of our rapidly developing profession. The day we start routinely developing bug-free software is the day we will have run out of new things to do. This observation is not a cop-out but an acknowledgment that rapid innovation means that our ability to create bugs tends to exceed our ability to remove them.

Tight development schedules are also an enemy of bug-free software. Although, ideally, we want our programs to not have bugs, we also want to ship them within a reasonable schedule. Managers put far more emphasis on maintaining schedules than on quality, and this emphasis isn't entirely unreasonable. The ideal bug-free program is likely to take too much time to create in a competitive commercial environment and customers don't want to wait. You can make money from a buggy program that is delivered at the right market opportunity, but you can't make money on a perfect program that is never shipped. Software tends to have a limited shelf life, so the later a program is delivered, the less time there is to recoup the investment. Furthermore, it is extremely difficult to make money on a product delivered after the market opportunity has closed and the market leaders are well established. You can always fix bugs later, but you can never get back lost marketing opportunities. Not surprisingly, there are many examples of successful programs that are far from bug free.

A Definition of Debugging

Before going any further, now is an excellent time to establish what debugging means and to contrast debugging to the related activity of testing.

A *bug* is an implementation defect—an error in the code. A program is said to have a bug when it doesn't behave as intended. Clearly, a crash is a bug, as is any feature that doesn't work as it should. But what if a program runs slowly or one of its windows flashes unnecessarily when it is drawn? For all practical purposes, any such suboptimal performance can be considered a bug as well. I like to refer to such problems as "buglettes" to suggest that, although the problem is undesirable and should be corrected, it may not be serious enough to keep the program from shipping.

What about design defects? For example, what about a usability problem such as an interface that is difficult to use or requires unnecessary repetition? This type of problem wouldn't be considered a bug by our definition if the program behaves as intended. Such a problem is the result of bad design, not of a defect in the program's implementation. Although one could argue that design defects are bugs, the process for removing design defects is entirely different from the process of removing implementation defects. After all, you cannot remove a design defect by setting breakpoints or looking at call stacks. So, even though a design defect may be considered a bug by users and testers and is likely to be reported in a bug report, the solution to such problems is to change the design, not to remove an implementation defect from the source code.

Debugging is the process of preventing, revealing, diagnosing, and removing implementation defects. You can prevent bugs by taking full advantage of your compiler, linker, and other development tools and by writing your code in a way that makes certain types of bugs impossible. You can reveal bugs by writing debugging statements in your code (such as assertions) that force bugs to expose themselves when the program is executed. You typically diagnose bugs by gathering all the information you can about a bug and using the debugger to find the problem and its root cause. The debugging process is finished when the defect is successfully removed from the source code in a way that doesn't introduce additional defects. As this definition shows, there are many facets to debugging: Debugging can be proactive (before a bug is discovered), reactive (after a bug is discovered), static (from analyzing the source code), and dynamic (from executing the program).

The process of debugging encompasses the entire implementation defect removal process except for one critical step, which is where testing comes in. *Testing* is the process of actively detecting the existence of a bug. Testing involves either manually running the program with the purpose of uncovering bugs or creating and running automatic procedures to automate the bug-detection process. The testing process may require the development of code specifically for testing. However, unlike debugging code that intends to reveal bugs, such as assertions and trace statements, test code is never an integral part of the program's source code. Rather, test code is separate and is "bolted on" only during the testing process.

To compare these processes, testing occurs when you do not know if a bug exists and you are trying to discover one, whereas debugging is writing the code so as to prevent bugs or trying to remove known bugs. Debugging is almost always performed by a programmer and it requires access to source code, whereas anyone can test a program and source code isn't required. Although debugging and testing are tightly coupled, the processes behind them are completely different. This book focuses on the process of debugging and discusses testing only as it relates to debugging.

The Goals of Debugging

The various ways to accomplish the goals of debugging are the theme throughout this book. The obvious goal of debugging is to remove bugs, but obtaining excellent debugging skills requires one to be a bit more ambitious. At its best, debugging is crucial to software development productivity and software quality. Therefore, from the point of view of the software development process, debugging has the following goals.

- **Productivity** To develop code in a way that prevents bugs and helps you find the bugs that do occur as quickly as possible. Effective bug prevention, detection, and removal are a must for minimizing wasted effort.
- **Quality** To find the actual cause of bugs and correct them without introducing new bugs. Effective bug prevention, detection, and removal are a must for achieving software quality, and therefore reliability.

Effective debugging can improve software development productivity in many ways, but the most significant improvement occurs when you become proficient at preventing, detecting, and removing your own bugs. Many companies have dedicated testing and QA teams who are responsible for finding the bugs that programmers miss. In terms of productivity, the biggest mistake you can make is to become dependent on others to find your bugs. Rather, your goal should be to find and remove as many bugs as you can on your own. Your testing team can then be used to find just the few bugs that you somehow overlook.

To see how finding your own bugs affects productivity, let's compare the two processes. You use the following process when you find and remove your own bugs.

- You do a test and find a bug.
- You track down the bug, remove the bug, and verify the fix.

By comparison, when a tester finds a bug, your development team uses a variation of the following process.

- A new version of a program is released.
- Testing installs the program.

- Testing applies a test plan to find bugs.
- Testing finds a bug.
- Testing creates a bug report and submits it to management.
- Management reviews the bug report and assigns it to the appropriate programmer, which in this case happens to be you.
- You review the bug report, possibly asking testing for additional information.
- You reproduce the bug.
- You track down the bug, remove the bug, and verify the fix.
- You update the bug report database to describe the fix.
- You update the program and send it back to testing.
- Testing installs the updated program and reviews the bug report.
- Testing confirms that the bug has been removed and that nothing else is broken.
- Testing updates the bug report database.
- [*Optional*] Even though the bug has been removed, every week until the program is shipped you will attend a bug status meeting at which management will ask you if the bug is really fixed.

This, of course, is the procedure when things go perfectly, that is, the testing team is able to find the bug and you are able to reproduce the bug and remove it on the first try. The process gets much worse when things don't go well. Both processes require you to reproduce the bug and remove it, but the process using testing involves more people, which in turn requires much more time, communication, and management input. A dysfunctional debugging process is characterized by the fact that it takes forever to get anything done. Now you know why.

Some have argued that debugging really doesn't play a role in software quality. They believe that software quality is something that must be built into a program from the start. However, this rhetoric only gets you so far. A perfect design followed by a bug-riddled implementation and sloppy maintenance is of poor quality by anyone's definition.

Assuming your software is unlikely to be completely bug free, how should your program behave when faced with residual bugs? This question suggests two more goals from the point of view of the software itself. Given the existence of a bug, your program should be able to accomplish the following.

- **Prevent the trashing of data.** If by continuing to run the program, you run the risk of harming data or external hardware controlled by that data, the process should be shut down in an orderly manner, leaving the data untouched.
- **Keep running.** If continuing to run the program doesn't risk harming data or external hardware, the process should continue to run (possibly in a degraded state), and if the problem is significant, the user should be notified. The user can then decide to shutdown the program or keep it running.

Failing to achieve both of these goals compounds the severity of the initial bug. The second goal is in sharp contrast to what you see in most example programs, which usually terminate whenever an error is detected. Note that automatically shutting down isn't in the user's best interest if that means losing salvageable work. If the program is unable to determine the state of the data and its ability to save the data, it can compromise by saving the data to a temporary file and letting the user decide if the data is worth keeping.

The Need for Better Debugging Skills

Debugging is clearly an important programming skill. Programmers spend up to half their development time testing and debugging their code, yet they spend very little effort to improve their debugging skills. In this sense, debugging is like the weather—everybody talks about it, but nobody does anything about it. Let's face it, every programmer's debugging skills could be better. Considering the amount of time programmers spend debugging, it's surprising that more effort isn't made to improve those skills.

One explanation for this lack of effort is that debugging skills are hard to learn. This doesn't mean that there isn't enough information on debugging. Quite the contrary—if anything, there is an overwhelming amount of information about debugging, ranging in quality from extremely helpful to totally useless. For example, in researching for this book, we referred to more than 40 books; nearly 100 magazine articles; dozens of MSDN articles, online articles, newsletter articles, and conference notes; three videotapes; and hundreds of newsgroup discussions. The typical debugging information consists of only a few pages, giving either a superficial description of a debugging process or an in-depth treatment of a narrow debugging topic in isolation from all other development and debugging concerns. Sorting through all this information takes a lot of time and motivation, as we can well attest. Given this lack of a coherent source of information, debugging traditionally hasn't been a skill one deliberately sets out to master but, rather, is a collection of skills one gathers along the way.

Strategic Debugging

The primary objective in writing this book was to acknowledge the debugging problem and to present the essential information you need to know to be able to effectively and efficiently debug Windows programs using Microsoft Visual C++. The focus here is on practical solutions that you can actually use in commercial software development. The ultimate goal of this book is to make your programming efforts more productive and the resulting software more reliable.

We have tried to present the fundamental debugging techniques with a strategic focus. That is, rather than just describing a debugging technique and saying something silly like "this technique works really well, so use it liberally," we have presented a strategic approach that discusses not only how to use a debugging technique but also why to use it, when to use it, and how it fits in with other debugging and development concerns. We believe that you will get better results in your debugging efforts by using a systematic approach rather than random application of debugging techniques.

Although we have chosen to focus on debugging using the Visual C++ environment and its MFC and ATL application frameworks, much of the material in this book is general enough to apply to other Windows C++ development environments, or even other Windows programming languages. However, because it is better to do one thing well than many things poorly, we prefer to focus on one specific environment and leave any translation to other environments and languages as an exercise for the reader. Most of the time such translations should be fairly simple. We know this from experience because only three of the more than 40 books researched for this book were specifically about debugging with Visual C++.

PART I

Debugging Strategies

Chapter 1

The Debugging Process

Even though there are an infinite number of possible bugs, and thus potentially an infinite number of debugging strategies, most bugs can be removed using a fairly standard debugging process. This chapter presents that process.

The Five (Wrong) Stages of Debugging

Let's start off by looking at a debugging process that doesn't work well. Like the five stages of grief described by Elisabeth Kübler-Ross in her book *On Death and Dying* (Collier Books, 1997), the stages in this ineffective process are denial, anger, bargaining, depression, and acceptance. Let's look at these stages and see why they should not be part of your debugging process.

1. **Denial** The programmer refuses to believe the bug exists or that it is caused by his code. The pathology: "That bug simply isn't possible," "That bug must be in another part of the system—it can't be in my code," or "This is obviously a bug in Windows or the compiler."

2. **Anger** The programmer gets angry at the person who found the bug. The pathology: "Why do those testers always pick on my code? Why don't they find bugs in other parts of the program for a change?" or "Don't those QA guys have anything better to do than to find minor problems like this? They obviously don't know what a *real* bug looks like."

3. **Bargaining** The programmer is so desperate to find the bug that he becomes delirious to the point of promising to break all bad programming habits in the future. The pathology: "If I just find this bug, I promise I will always use assertion statements from now on." Of course, these promises aren't kept once the bug is found.

4. **Depression** The programmer becomes depressed and considers a career change. The pathology: "I knew I should have become a tech writer. At least they don't have to debug anything."

5. **Acceptance** The programmer accepts the fact that he can't remove the bug. The pathology: "OK, let's just document it and say it's a feature. Having a few outstanding bugs isn't so bad since it encourages users to upgrade."

This approach represents a breakdown of the debugging process, where each step undermines the programmer's ability to remove bugs. Becoming angry with those who help you by finding your bugs is especially destructive. Unfortunately, this process is used all too often by programmers with weak debugging skills, resulting in nothing but grief.

> **TIP**
>
> Avoid the five stages of grief in your debugging process.

The Five Stages of Debugging

Now let's look at the five stages of an effective debugging process to see how debugging really should be performed.

1. **Determining that a bug exists** Someone (a programmer, a tester, or a user) determines that a bug exists. The existence of a bug may be determined by testing, running debug code, using development tools, or reviewing the source code.

2. **Gathering bug information** The person reporting the bug and the programmer work together to gather additional information to help analyze the bug. Information is gathered by running the program, checking the source code, and using debugging tools. Among the information gathered is whether the bug is reproducible, the steps required to reproduce the bug, the data and program settings required to reproduce the bug, and the system and hardware configurations required to reproduce the bug.

3. **Analyzing the bug information** By analyzing the information, the programmer determines the problem in the code, its root cause, and the changes to the source code necessary to remove the bug.

4. **Removing the bug** The programmer removes the bug from the source code by changing the code that caused the malfunction.

5. **Verifying the change** The programmer verifies that new code removes the defect without creating any new bugs. The programmer also looks for related code that may have similar problems.

The remainder of this chapter examines each step in more detail and presents some tips to help you improve the debugging process.

Determining That a Bug Exists

As defined in the Introduction, a *bug* is an implementation defect and *testing* is the process of actively detecting the existence of a bug. Not surprisingly, most bugs are discovered as the result of testing by programmers, by in-house quality assurance testers and alpha testers, or by external beta testers. I strongly believe that the most effective way to achieve bug-free software is for programmers to make the best effort they can to find their own bugs. Unfortunately, bugs can slip through the process, so bugs are detected by end users as well. If you don't find the bug yourself, you generally receive notification of the existence of a problem with a bug report.

In addition to testing, bugs can be determined directly by the debugging process itself because this process includes bug prevention and reveals bugs through debugging code. You can often prevent bugs from happening by taking full advantage of the C++ compiler and avoiding language pitfalls that are a common source of bugs (see Chapter 2, Writing C++ Code for Debugging). The most common debugging techniques used to reveal bugs are assertions (see Chapter 3, Using Assertions), trace statements (see Chapter 4, Using Trace Statements), exceptions (see Chapter 5, Using Exceptions and Return Values), and techniques for detecting resource leaks (see Chapter 9, Debugging Memory). Of course, you can also detect bugs by directly examining the source code, either on your own or in code reviews.

Gathering Bug Information

Finding that a bug exists is the critical first step in the debugging process, but detecting a bug is analogous to finding the tip of an iceberg: What you see at first is hardly the whole story because there is a lot going on underneath. To successfully remove a bug, you usually need to gather much more information. Of course, the amount of information you need depends on the nature of the bug itself. Although you often need quite a lot of information to debug a program malfunction, by contrast you need very little information to debug a typo in the user interface. Obtaining good bug information is the key to successful, productive debugging.

TIP

Obtaining good bug information is the key to successful, productive debugging.

Crashes are often the hardest type of bug to analyze, so they typically require the most information. Consequently, this section is largely focused on gathering the information required to debug a crash. You should adjust the amount of information you need for simpler bugs accordingly.

Tester-supplied Information (Bug Reports)

If someone other than you finds a bug in your program, most likely you will receive the bug information through some kind of bug report. In addition to supplying testers with bug report forms, the variations in the amount of information required to analyze the different types of bugs suggests that you should also supply detailed instructions on how to fill out a bug report form. After all, testers shouldn't have to guess what specific information you want to receive.

TIP

Supply testers with both a bug report form and detailed instructions on how to use it.

You need to impress on your testers that they must make an extra effort to provide useful information in their bug reports. Many testers incorrectly believe that their only goal is to find bugs. In reality, their goal is to find bugs and provide enough information for the programmers to reproduce the bug and ultimately remove it. Bug detection not followed up by bug removal is pretty much a waste of time. Vague bug reports that read like "the program crashes after I click on it" or "the program occasionally exhibits bizarre behavior" aren't likely to result in bug removal.

Bug Reproduction

The first step in preparing a bug report for nontrivial bugs is for the tester to reproduce the bug and try to determine the specific circumstances in which the bug does and does not occur. (In this context, a "nontrivial" bug could be defined as a bug whose reproducibility is questionable. Trivial bugs tend to be easy to reproduce.) The tester should first try to reproduce the bug as it originally occurred, then try to find the simplest test case that reproduces the bug. This simplest test case is rarely the same test that first revealed the bug. The tester should also try variations of the simplest test case to look for different behavior, that is, to find similar test cases in which the bug doesn't happen. This information helps you understand the specific circumstances in which the malfunction occurs.

This might seem like a lot of information and perhaps too much to hope for in a bug report, especially a bug report coming from a customer. Perhaps so— don't be too surprised if you don't receive all this information. But testers need to play an active role in reproducing bugs. After all, if the tester can't reproduce a bug immediately after discovering it, it is unlikely that you will be able to either. The steps required to reproduce a bug are easily the most important information in a bug report and carefully determining them is well worth the extra effort.

> **TIP**
>
> Testers need to play an active role in reproducing the bug.

Testers must understand the importance of reproducing a bug immediately on detection. When it comes to reproducing bugs, there's no better time than the present. The longer a tester waits to reproduce the bug, the more likely the tester will forget how. If your testers have persistent trouble reproducing bugs, you might want to recommend that they videotape their testing sessions to document their exact steps.

Bug Report Form Information

Preparing a good bug report form is essential to obtaining good bug information. At the very least, a bug report form should contain the following entries:

- **Today's date**

- **Tester name, company, and contact information**

- **Program name and version** May need to include versions of dependent Dynamic Link Library (DLL) files.

- **System configuration information** Supply both hardware and system software, including the Windows version and service pack.

- **Problem type** Types to list include system crashes, program crashes, program malfunctions, usability problems, installation problems, documentation and help problems, product production problems, and suggestions.

- **Problem description** Describe the symptoms of the observed problem and any other related information. If the program has a user interface, include a description of the window that has the problem and what was on the screen. The specific text of any error messages, assertion failed message boxes, or Windows crash dialog boxes must be included.

- **Steps to reproduce** Include a description of program settings and data required to reproduce the problem. It should be noted if the problem wasn't reproducible or if it is inconsistent.

- **Instructions on how to include attachments** Such attachments include screen shots, Dr. Watson files, test data files, and the like.

Interestingly, a common entry on most bug report forms is a severity rating, although the rating typically isn't set by testers. I prefer to not use a severity rating, but I am in the minority with this opinion. My observation is that far too much time is spent arguing about the rating. The simpler the bug, the more time that seems to be wasted arguing about its rating. For simple bugs, I find it easier to just fix the bug and be done with it. This keeps the list of outstanding bugs smaller and easier to manage. However, this approach works well only if you maintain a small bug list. It is clearly not practical if you have hundreds or even thousands of outstanding bugs. As an alternative, consider a simple Care/Don't Care rating, where you assign a Don't Care rating if you don't care if the bug is fixed in the next release. If you do care, there is no reason not to remove the bug sooner rather than later.

TIP

Reconsider the need for a severity rating on your bug report forms.

Bug Report Form Instructions

Your bug report forms need to be supplemented with detailed instructions on how you want testers to fill them out. These instructions should help testers understand the information you expect beyond what can be inferred from the bug report form itself. A good set of instructions contains the following information.

• **Describe the specific information you want to see, broken down by problem type.** For example, give guidelines for when you really need the steps to reproduce a problem and when you need the detailed system information.

• **Encourage testers to find the simplest activity that reproduces the problem.** Point out that not only does this help the programmer debug the problem, but it also requires less for the tester to document in the bug report.

• **Give advice on providing specific information, with both good and bad examples.** At the very least, the steps to reproduce the problem should include a description of the task the tester was trying to perform, the specific data and program options the tester had selected, and the exact program interaction that caused the problem. For example, if the problem was the result of giving a command, how was the command given? Was it given from the menu bar, the toolbar, a context menu, or the keyboard? Point out that such details can make a big difference in locating the problem. Also, point out that providing specific information doesn't mean the report has to be lengthy. If the tester can clearly describe the problem in a single sentence, that's fine.

• **Give advice on the procedure to follow to reproduce the problem.** Describe what you want the tester to do immediately when the bug is discovered, then give steps to reproduce the problem. For example, should the tester restart the program and try again? Should the tester restart Windows and try again?

• **Give specific instructions on what to do if the program crashes with an unhandled exception.** At the very least, the tester should document the specific type of unhandled exception (such as access violation, stack overflow, integer divide by zero) and the crash address. If the program crashed in Windows 98, the tester should click the **Details** button, copy the details text (not manually, but using the **Select All** and **Copy** commands in the context menu), and include the text in the bug report.

• **Give specific instructions on what to do when an assertion fails.** Should testers write down what the message box says? What button should they choose? To obtain the most information, typically you should recommend that the tester click **Ignore** to see what happens and stop testing only after crashing or receiving the same assertion failure several times in a row.

- **Give specific instructions on how to use Dr. Watson for Windows 98 and Windows 2000.** Give instructions on the specific Dr. Watson options you want to use, what to enter in the problem description box (if anything), and how to attach a Dr. Watson log file to a bug report. For Windows 98 users, describe how to have Dr. Watson launch automatically at startup by creating a shortcut to the Dr. Watson executable in the Startup group. For Windows 2000 users, also indicate if you want them to attach a compressed *User.dmp* that is also created by Dr. Watson. Unless you have an excellent reason not to, you should always instruct testers to test with Dr. Watson running. Note that for each version of Windows Dr. Watson behaves differently and has different options. (Using Dr. Watson is described in Chapter 6, Debugging with Windows.)

- **Give specific instructions on what testers should do if they receive the Windows 2000 Blue Screen of Death (BSOD).** Should they at least write down what it says at the top of the screen? Should they write down any other information? Should they attach a *Minidump* or *Memory.dmp* file? You can enable saving the blue screen information to *Minidump* or *Memory.dmp* by running the System Control Panel, clicking the **Advanced** tab, clicking **Startup and Recovery**, and selecting either **Small Memory Dump (64 KB)** or **Complete Memory Dump**. You can then obtain a dump file when you restart after a Blue Screen of Death. Generally, you should choose the small memory dump option; the complete memory dump files tend to be huge because they are literally a memory dump (although they compress well). Alternatively, you can save just the information on the blue screen using the BlueSave utility from Systems Internals (*www.sysinternals.com*).

- **Give one or more examples of correctly filled out bug report forms.**

One interesting problem to be aware of is that sometimes testers report possible solutions instead of problems. Possible solutions can be helpful if they supplement the problem but are harmful if they replace the problem. For example, instead of reporting that a feature doesn't work, testers might report how they think the problem should be corrected. This approach can be confusing, especially if the suggested solution isn't very good or the underlying problem is not obvious. You can help prevent this situation by making sure that the bug report forms are clearly focused on reporting problems. The bug report form should include specific problem-focused sections, such as Problem Description, and the instructions should clearly indicate that you are more interested in problems than solutions.

TIP

Make sure the bug report forms are clearly focused on reporting problems. Discourage testers from reporting possible solutions in lieu of problems.

Terminology Problems

One of the most frustrating realizations in debugging is discovering that you have wasted several hours tracking down the wrong bug. There are many ways this problem can happen, but the classic scenario results from someone using incorrect terminology in the bug report.

Many terminology problems could lead you to look for the wrong bug. For example, some testers refer to any dialog box that looks abnormal as a crash (perhaps they use some other word, such as trap, bomb, or fault). Such testers describe assertion message boxes or possibly any message box with a stop sign icon and **Abort, Retry**, and **Ignore** buttons as a crash. Failed assertions are definitely not crashes, and they are debugged in a completely different way. Some testers confuse disk space with memory. They may report something like "I ran the program, then ran out of memory," but by "memory" they really mean disk space.

To see how such confusion can lead to wasted time, let's look at a recent example of mine. Someone had reported a crash that I had to debug remotely. I added some strategically placed assertion statements to the code to provide additional information and asked the tester to try the program again. The tester said the program still crashed—definitely not what I was expecting. Fortunately, I didn't panic. Instead, I then asked the tester to read what was on the screen; and the tester read: "Debug Assertion Failed!"

The first solution to this problem is to make sure testers report exactly what is on the screen. If you plan to have a long-term relationship with the tester, you might make an effort to educate the tester about such terminology problems. But while you want to encourage testers to supply accurate bug reports, you must recognize that sometimes they won't. Consequently, the ultimate solution is to understand that testers are typically not as computer literate as you are and are likely to use misleading terminology in their bug reports. If you are not sure about the language in a bug report, don't hesitate to ask the tester for a confirmation.

Be aware that testers may use misleading terminology in their bug reports.

Programmer-supplied Information

Once you receive a bug report, you gather additional information by reproducing the bug yourself, verifying the bug report, filling in any missing information, possibly reducing the number of steps to reproduce the problem, and finding clues to help diagnose the problem. You might also review the source code and run the program using debugging tools to look for additional clues. If you are not able to reproduce the bug, you may request that the tester resubmit the bug report with additional information. If possible, you might ask the tester to reproduce the bug in front of you or walk through the problem over the phone.

Analyzing the Bug Information

Once you have finished gathering information, you are now ready to analyze it and determine the code that needs to be changed to remove the bug. In this analysis, you need to discover three additional pieces of source code–related information beyond the bug itself. The information you need breaks down as follows.

- **The bug** The malfunction the tester sees, as reported in the last step
- **The symptom** The specific code that fails, resulting in the observed failure
- **The cause** The underlying cause of the symptom
- **The solution** The specific code that needs to be changed to remove the bug without adding new bugs

When one speaks of isolating a bug, in effect one is referring to obtaining all this information.

As you can see, there are several steps to get from the bug itself to the ultimate code change. For simple bugs, the symptom, the cause, and the solu-

12   DEBUGGING STRATEGIES

tion are often the same code or clearly related code. For the most insidious bugs, the symptom is only the bearer of bad news and those three pieces of code are only remotely related. In such cases, if you attempt to remove the bug by changing the symptom code, the real bug remains and you have only masked the symptom. To really remove the bug, you have to trace back in the code to determine what really caused things to go wrong. In such cases, finding the true cause of a bug can be much more difficult than finding the bug itself.

TIP

The symptom of a problem is the cause of a problem for only the simplest bugs. For more difficult bugs, you have to trace back to find the underlying cause.

For a typical example, suppose a program crashes because a function is passed a null object pointer as a parameter. The bug would be an access violation exception. The symptom code would be the function that received the invalid parameter, but the symptom isn't the cause. You need to figure out why the object pointer is incorrectly set to null. For a simple bug, the cause might be that you simply forgot to set the object pointer or you somehow set the wrong variable. For a more difficult bug, you might have set the pointer correctly, but somehow the pointer was changed before the problem function was called. This accidental change could be the result of calling a function with an unintended side effect or having a memory buffer overwritten.

Performing the Analysis

There are two ways to perform the analysis of the bug information: with the debugger and with your head.

Using the Debugger

The Visual C++ debugger is easy to use, efficient, and quite productive. This makes the debugger the first choice for analyzing most bugs. With a few exceptions (often related to the Heisenberg Uncertainty Principle, as discussed later in this chapter), using the debugger is the best way to understand exactly what is going on in your code using direct observation. You typically track down the symptom, cause, and solution by setting breakpoints, watching the execution flow (especially the call stack), checking variable values, and checking thread information (for multithreaded programs). Using the Visual C++ debugger is discussed in detail in Chapter 7, Debugging with the Visual C++ Debugger.

> **TIP**
>
> Using the debugger helps you understand what is going on in your code using direct observation.

Using Your Head

In his classic book *The Art of Software Testing*, Glenford Myers prefers thinking through bugs over using a debugger. He states, "The general problem with these brute-force methods is that they ignore the process of *thinking*. . . . An efficient program debugger should be able to pinpoint most errors without going near a computer." Obviously, Myers had never programmed Windows using C++ when he wrote this advice. Modern programs developed using these technologies are too complex to analyze without a debugger, so using a debugger is likely to be your first choice for most bugs.

> **TIP**
>
> Some bugs are difficult to reproduce in the debugger. For such bugs, it is more productive to instrument your program with debugging aids, such as assertions, trace statements, and log files, and then use your head and think through the problem.

The biggest problem with using the debugger is that you can become overly dependent on it. This problem becomes significant when you are faced with a bug that is difficult to reproduce in the debugger or, worse, impossible to reproduce at all. In these situations, trying to track down the cause of a bug in the debugger can be more trouble than it is worth. The alternative is to use your head and think through the problem. After all, you have the source code and you know how it is supposed to work (don't you?), so you can determine how the code really works by executing it in your head. Instead of directly witnessing the crime with the debugger, it can be more productive to reconstruct the crime scene using circumstantial evidence. Of course, you can supplement your

DEBUGGING STRATEGIES

circumstantial evidence by instrumenting your program with debugging aids such as assertions, trace statements, and log files.

It is important to use your head even if you are using the debugger. To successfully get from the symptom to the cause to the solution, you need to know what is going on in the code. If you don't understand the code, it is unlikely you will be able to correctly identify when the problem first appears.

Drawing Conclusions

Whereas the solution to simple bugs is often obvious by inspection or plain common sense, for more complex bugs, you usually have to use some form of logic to draw correct (or at least reasonable) conclusions. In this section, I review the two classic forms of logic: deductive logic and inductive logic. I will also review several puzzle-solving strategies that can be effective in unraveling the most difficult debugging puzzles.

Deductive Logic

Deductive logic asserts that conclusions follow necessarily from the truth of the premises. For example, given the premise "It is always cold in Vermont in the winter," if you are in Vermont in the winter, you can deduce that it must be cold. If the premise is true, then the conclusion must be true. In fact, in deductive logic, the conclusion is nothing more than a more specific restatement of the premise.

Deductive logic is often referred to as going from the general to the specific (to *deduce* is to lead away from). You use deductive logic to apply existing, general knowledge about the world (based on facts and rules) to specific cases to draw conclusions or make predictions. In terms of debugging, you can use knowledge about the bug, Windows, C++, Microsoft Foundation Class (MFC), Access Template Library (ATL), and such to make conclusions. For example, to receive an integer divide by zero exception, you must have executed code with integer division with a zero denominator. Alternatively, if you didn't receive an integer divide by zero exception, you know that no denominator could have been zero. Although such individual conclusions are hardly profound, combining several such deductions with knowledge of your source code and the bug itself can get you a long way in tracking down the problem.

The Process of Elimination

The process of elimination is a well-known method of drawing conclusions based on deductive reasoning. The process of elimination uses the following steps.

1. Gather relevant facts.
2. Determine possible explanations.
3. Eliminate explanations inconsistent with facts.
4. Refine remaining explanations.
5. Prove remaining explanations with experimentation.
6. Concluded remaining explanations are true.

The process of elimination is a form of deductive logic since it derives conclusions based on existing knowledge. This process should look familiar because it is the problem-solving technique used by most criminal detectives, from Sherlock Holmes to Joe Friday. As noted by Sherlock Holmes author Sir Arthur Conan Doyle in *Sign of Four,* "When you have eliminated the impossible, whatever remains, however improbable, must be the truth." If a bug has only a handful of possible explanations, the process of elimination can help you quickly determine the problem—even without using the debugger.

Inductive Logic

The problem with deductive logic is that all conclusions are based on existing knowledge (since all the knowledge is in the premise itself), so you can't derive new knowledge. Inductive logic allows you to derive new knowledge with the help of experimentation, which is why it is used so often by scientists. Inductive logic asserts that conclusions follow probably from the truth of the premises. For example, given the premise "It is always cold in Vermont in the winter," then if it is winter and it is cold, you can induce that you are in Vermont. This conclusion cannot be logically deduced from the premise, but it can be induced with the help of experimentation. The more conclusive the experimentation, the more confidence you can have in the correctness of the conclusion. To continue the example, if you are driving down the highway and you see many mountains and notice that most of the license plates are green (Vermont is the Green Mountain State) and realize that there are no billboards along the roads (billboards are illegal in Vermont), there is a high probability that you are in fact in Vermont (assuming you are in the United States to begin with). But note that given only deductive logic, such a conclusion from this premise would be nonsense.

Inductive logic is often referred to as going from the specific to the general (to *induce* is to lead to). You use inductive logic to derive general knowledge about the world from specific premises (based on facts, rules, or experience) to draw conclusions or make predictions. In terms of debugging, you can generalize knowledge learned in specific instances to more general instances. For example, you can use the Spy++ utility to observe the messages received by a correctly working dialog box as it is being created to induce that all correctly working dialog boxes receive roughly the same sequence of messages during creation. Again, note that there is a probability that such conclusions are wrong. Induction is a powerful technique to help you create knowledge where none previously existed. This is especially useful when debugging programs that use poorly documented technology.

The Scientific Method

The scientific method is a well-known method of drawing conclusions based on inductive logic. The scientific method uses the following steps.

1. Observe facts and look for patterns.
2. Develop a testable hypothesis that explains the observed facts.
3. Based on the hypothesis, predict new facts that have not yet been observed.
4. Perform experiments to observe the new facts.
5. If the new facts are observed, the hypothesis is assumed to be true. If the new facts are not observed, modify the hypothesis to explain the new facts and continue from step 3. Alternatively, reject the hypothesis and continue from step 2.

The scientific method is a form of inductive logic since it derives general knowledge based on specific premises, although the facts you induce while debugging are often quite specific. For example, suppose while debugging you discover a variable that appears to have an incorrect value. You hypothesize that if the variable were to have what you believe is the correct value, the bug would go away. You perform an experiment within the debugger of changing that variable's value and observing the results. If the bug disappears, then you can have confidence that your hypothesis is correct. Alternatively, if the bug remains, either that variable wasn't the problem or there are additional problems. Although scientific research typically strives to find a single true hypothesis using the scientific method, in debugging you often find that multiple hypotheses prove true if there are multiple bugs.

Making Hypotheses

When you are making a hypothesis using the scientific method or any other method, note that the better you understand the problem domain (the program's goals, the source code, Windows, C++, MFC, ATL, and so forth), the better you will be at making a good hypothesis. Furthermore, a hypothesis about a bug based on watching controlled execution of the code within a debugger is more likely to be right than one based on examining the source code alone. Also note that if you are performing your analysis within the debugger, you can often quickly prove or disprove hypotheses within the debugger itself, avoiding the need for a complete debugging cycle.

> **TIP**
>
> Having a good understanding of the problem domain will help you make better hypotheses.

Deductive Logic versus Inductive Logic—Which to Use?

The primary factor in determining which form of logic to use is the nature of the problem at hand. Neither form of logic is better or preferable on its own. Note that although conclusions based on deductive logic are considered certain and inductive conclusions are merely probable, in reality there isn't that much of a distinction. The problem with deductive logic is that it relies on premises whose correctness is taken for granted. There aren't that many certain premises in the real world, especially in the field of debugging.

Using Puzzle-solving Strategies

Although you want your conclusions to be logical, all the logic in the world isn't going to help you when you haven't a clue what to do next. Analyzing a bug is often like solving a puzzle, so it shouldn't be surprising that puzzle-solving techniques are useful. These same techniques are also used to promote creative thinking. Here are some puzzle-solving strategies that I find useful in debugging.

- **Simplify the problem.** Reduce the problem to the relevant information. Don't be misled by irrelevant information. Find the simplest test case that reproduces the bug. Find the simplest code fragment that reproduces the bug. Eliminate all that isn't essential to the problem.

- **Don't overlook the obvious.** I once read of a highly skilled programmer diagnosing a problem with a user's floppy disk drive. The programmer spent more than an hour having the user run diagnostic programs, tracing through the device driver code, and doing memory dumps. Then the programmer asked the user to check the floppy drive data cable to make sure it was securely attached. It was partially unplugged, so the user reconnected the cable and the drive worked fine. Moral: Don't overlook the obvious. Try the simplest things first. Another moral: Don't be too smart. Use your head, but don't use it more than you have to.

- **Watch out for false assumptions.** Often good logic puzzles lead you to make a false assumption, which in turn makes the right solution appear wrong or makes you focus on obvious solutions that are incorrect. Usually the trick to solving such puzzles is to simply realize that you have made a false assumption. For example, suppose you have a bug that appears on one computer and not another. You might assume that the problem was related to the configuration of the computer or perhaps the hardware itself. However, it is also possible that the program on the computer with the problem has different settings or is using different data. For another example, suppose you make a change to some code and a bug appears. You might assume that the bug is in the new change and wrack your brain trying to find it. However, the bug may have already been there and the change simply exposed it.

- **Look at the problem from other points of view.** Sometimes it is easy to get stuck simply by looking at a problem from the wrong perspective. Try creative solutions to the problem: Try new or unusual things. There are many logic puzzles in which the solution lies in looking at the problem from another point of view.

- **Do the opposite.** If what you are doing isn't working, do the opposite. For example, if you can't figure out what the problem is, try to figure out what the problem isn't. Use techniques such as the process of elimination or binary searches (divide and conquer).

- **Remember that no information is information.** Sometimes having no information is enough information to solve the problem. If things you expect to happen don't happen, that should tell you something. There are many logic puzzles in which the solution arises from the lack of information or from expected events that didn't happen.

• **Don't prefer solutions.** Although some solutions are more likely than others, this situation changes once you have eliminated all the likely solutions. In this case, instead of trying to find *the* solution, find *a* solution—any solution that is consistent with the facts. Fixating on favored solutions prevents you from seeing the alternatives. If you're stuck, the bug probably isn't where you think it is or you would have found it there already.

• **Consider using sample cases.** Some problems are so complex you really can't think them through in general, whereas other problems are difficult to grapple with in abstract terms. In such cases, the best approach is to work through some sample cases. Try some normal cases and boundary conditions. For example, you can easily detect the classic off-by-one bug simply by working through a single example. It is typically easier to find an off-by-one bug with a specific case than through abstract thinking.

• **Take a break.** Sometimes it pays to clear your mind by taking a break and thinking about something else for a while. Gazing off into space seems to be particularly effective. This strategy is especially effective when you are overlooking something simple. Taking a break allows you to attack the problem from a fresh point of view. To paraphrase Robert M. Pirsig in *Zen and The Art of Motorcycle Maintenance,* debugging Windows programs requires great peace of mind.

• **Be persistent.** Taking a break can be helpful, but many good puzzles make you want to give up too soon—sometimes just before you solve them. The same is often true for difficult bugs. Often I find that when I'm just about to give up, if I just keep at the problem a bit longer and try a few more approaches, the solution is close at hand. Some problems require a lot of hard work to figure out.

I find these puzzle-solving strategies really help me get out of difficult situations. Other techniques are discussed in Chapter 12, Desperate Measures.

Removing the Bug

If you have performed careful analysis, removing the bug from the source code should be relatively simple. But whenever you remove a bug from source code, especially code you are not overly familiar with, it is important to "cover your assets" (CYA). Consider the possibility that when you verify your changes in the next stage, you will determine that you completely blew it: Either the problem isn't fixed or the change introduced new bugs that are worse than the original bug. In this case, you need to restore the code to its original state and start over.

The possibility of making a bad change means you need to have a backup of the original code. If you are using a source code control system, you can get back the original code as long as all the files were checked in, so you should be in the habit of checking in files before making risky bug fixes. If you aren't using a source code control system or you can't check in your files because they don't satisfy your check-in criteria, you need to make backup copies of all the files you are going to change. Often the simplest approach is to make a temporary copy of the source code directory. If the project has many files, it may be preferable to compress them into a single archive. One way or another, make sure that you can get the original code back if necessary.

Don't live dangerously. Cover your assets before making risky bug fixes.

Verifying the Change

The remaining debugging challenge is to verify the change to make sure the defect has been successfully removed. Specifically, you need to verify that

- The original problem has been removed.
- New problems have not been introduced.
- Similar bugs do not exist elsewhere in the program.

Use a file comparison utility to locate and review all the source code changes. Then set breakpoints and witness the execution of the changed code from within the debugger.

One way to verify that the bug has been successfully removed is to try to reproduce the bug and see what happens. If you can't reproduce the bug, you can assume the problem has been fixed. However, I use this technique only for trivial bug fixes. A safer and ultimately more productive approach (since you will waste less time later) is to use a file comparison utility, such as the WinDiff utility included with Visual C++, and determine all the code changes. You should carefully review all the changes within the utility to verify that they really do make sense. You should then set breakpoints, run the program, and witness the execution of the changed code from within the debugger. If the code works the way you expect it to and the problem is gone, you can have confidence that the change is successful. If not, you have more work to do.

Note that although this approach to verifying changed code may seem like a lot of work, it really isn't. The WinDiff utility allows you to compare directories, so if you made a backup of your source code directory, you can find all the changes in a matter of seconds. The process of watching the execution of the changed code typically requires only a few additional minutes. In fact, of all the steps required by this procedure, setting the breakpoints is by far the hardest.

This review process is also effective in making sure you haven't introduced any new bugs. Ideally, your testers should also verify that the bug has been removed and perform some regression testing to make sure new bugs haven't been introduced.

Don't stop with finding the first bug. If you find one bug, there are probably more. In this sense, software bugs are like their insect counterparts. Since similar code is most likely to have similar bugs, you should focus on looking for similar code. You should first check the code near the original bug for problems, then check the entire project source code using the Visual C++ **Find in Files** command. Try searching for similar variable names, function names, and language features. You can even search for comment text. Then review all the matches for similar problems.

> **TIP**
>
> If you find one bug, there are probably more. Similar code is likely to have similar bugs.

Debug Smarter, Not Harder

Debugging is often hard work, but it doesn't always have to be. Here are some bonus tips to help you make the debugging process easier.

Fix Bugs as Soon as Possible

Try to fix bugs as soon as possible, ideally immediately after you find them or they are reported to you. This approach has several advantages.

- You start debugging when the bug is well understood and (hopefully) reproducible. Both the knowledge about the bug and its reproducibility fade with time.
- The process of fixing bugs helps you learn from your mistakes. Learning earlier rather than later keeps you from repeating the same mistakes over and over.
- Keeping the list of outstanding bugs small makes it easier to add new features and diagnose other bugs since you aren't constantly running into known problems. It also makes it easier for you to determine if a change has introduced new bugs.
- Keeping the list of outstanding bugs small makes the program easier to test, since testers don't have to report the different symptoms of the same bug. Having dozens of bug reports for the same bug creates unnecessary work for everyone.
- Keeping the list of outstanding bugs small helps make a project easier to manage since the true state of the project is easier to determine.

In short, the software development process is more productive when there are fewer outstanding bugs. Bugs, unlike fine wine, don't get better with age; so make an effort to remove bugs quickly.

Also, believe what you see when testing your program. If something looks like a bug, then it's a bug. Don't go into denial and treat a bug you just witnessed as if it were some sort of mirage. Go after it now. It isn't going to go away by itself.

Prevent Bugs from Happening in the First Place
You can often prevent bugs from happening by taking full advantage of the compiler, linker, and language features that reveal bugs when building a program. Such measures include

- Compiling without warnings at the highest warning level
- Using type-safe linkage
- Using specific data types instead of generic types (such as `void *`)
- Using C++ language features instead of the preprocessor
- Using type-safe C++-based casting instead of generic C-based casting

These techniques are discussed in detail in the next chapter.

Learn from Your Mistakes to Prevent Future Bugs

The process of detecting and removing bugs provides an excellent opportunity for you to learn from your mistakes and prevent future bugs. Glenford Myers in *The Art of Software Testing* and Steve Maguire in *Writing Solid Code* recommend that you ask yourself variations of the following questions whenever you find a bug.

- Why was the mistake made?
- How could I have prevented the bug?
- How could I have detected the bug earlier?
- How could I have detected the bug automatically?
- How can I prevent the same mistake in the future?

Every bug you find is an opportunity to learn something new. (Although you shouldn't go out of your way to write buggy code just for the learning experience; after all, the goal of this learning is to prevent bugs.) Bugs don't always happen randomly, so there are patterns; and these patterns suggest ways for you to improve your programming skills and your development process. By asking yourself these questions and devising practical answers, you can learn how to write better, more reliable software.

Assume It Has Bugs

Suppose you have written a function to perform some task. You have just finished typing in the code, and you got it to compile and link. Now what? Here are your choices.

- (a) Mentally walk through the code to find as many problems as you can.
- (b) Walk through the code using the debugger to check its behavior as well as boundary conditions and error handling.
- (c) Just let 'er rip and hope for the best.
- (d) Both *a* and *b*.
- (e) None of the above.

If you like to live dangerously, then *c* is definitely the way to go. What you will soon discover is that the fact that code compiles and links isn't proof that it actually works. Running the code and noting that it appears to work doesn't prove much either. Neither does not crashing. To really know if the code works, you need to carefully review it both in your head and with the debugger. With the debugger you can also change variable values and execution paths to test boundary conditions and error handling.

I believe you don't need to test new code to determine that it has bugs. Rather, it is easier just to take it for granted that new code has bugs. The more complex the code, the more likely this is true. On occasion, I do decide to live dangerously and let it rip to quickly check the code's behavior (or, rather, mis-behavior). However, I don't do this because I think the code doesn't have bugs. Rather, I assume the code is incorrect but I want to quickly see how it fails. This approach helps me understand what to look for in the debugger, especially in complex code.

> **TIP** You don't have to test new code to determine that it has bugs—just take it for granted.

Although this technique may seem like a lot of work, remember that the alternatives take much longer. This doesn't really require hard work as much as it requires discipline. Note that reviewing the code both mentally and with the debugger takes only a small fraction of the time it takes to write the code in the first place, so the overall effect of this technique isn't so significant.

Develop Incrementally

The debugging process is simplified if you develop incrementally. That is, try to add one significant feature or make one significant change at a time and verify that it works before moving on. That way, if problems appear, you know the problem is related to the code you just changed. If you make several changes at a time, you've got a lot more work to do to isolate and diagnose the cause of the bug.

Don't Play the Blame Game

As suggested by the denial phase [see The Five (Wrong) Stages of Debugging earlier in this chapter], some programmers are too eager to blame their colleagues, their compiler, or Windows itself for their bugs. These programmers have a talent for discovering a new compiler bug every week. They also find that their coworkers seem to make a lot of mistakes. Somehow bugs are never their fault. Although it is possible that these factors are the cause of the problem, it is more courteous and productive to assume that the problem is in your code and to suspect others only after finding compelling evidence that the problem isn't in your code. Until then, save yourself some embarrassment and keep your suspicion of other factors to yourself. Note that your inability to find the bug in your code after a quick check isn't compelling evidence.

TIP

Avoid blaming your coworkers and your tools for your bugs. Blame your code first.

This is not to say that Windows and compiler bugs don't happen, because they most definitely do. There are hundreds of bugs in Visual C++ (more than 400 are documented in MSDN) and thousands reported in some versions of Windows itself. The magazine *Windows Developer's Journal* has had a monthly column called "Bug++ of the Month" for years. For compilers, you are more likely to find a bug if you are using new or obscure language features. You are especially likely to find compiler bugs when porting code from other C++ compilers because different compilers are likely to have trouble with different language features. But under normal circumstances, your chance of stumbling across a compiler or operating system bug is fairly remote. Rather, the problem is more likely to be a bug in your code. For example, consider the following code, which attempts to set *m_Size* to the size value set by the dialog box:

```
CSizeDialog dialog;
dialog.m_Size = m_Size;
if (dialog.DoModal() == IDOK) {
    int tempVar1, tempVar2, tempVar3, tempVar4,
    m_Size = dialog.m_Size;
    ...
    // use temp variables here
}
if (newBlock) {
    // value of m_Size appears to be reset here
    ...
}
```

This code seems simple enough; yet no matter what value the user enters in the dialog box, the size value is unchanged. The debugger shows that the value of *m_Size* is getting reset once the program enters the second `if` block. A compiler bug? Not quite—there is a comma instead of a semicolon after the declaration of *tempVar4*, so the *m_Size* variable in the first `if` block is local to that block, hiding the class member variable of the same name.

Understand the Heisenberg Uncertainty Principle

The Heisenberg Uncertainty Principle was discovered by the physicist Werner Heisenberg, the founder of quantum mechanics. It states that "the more precisely the position is determined, the less precisely the momentum is known in this instant, and vice versa." A more practical translation into plain English is that the more accurately you try to observe something, the more you disturb what you are measuring. This principle indicates that perfect observation or measurement of certain phenomena is impossible, thus leading to the uncertainty.

This principle is clearly a concern in debugging because compiling a debug build and running a program from an interactive debugger clearly changes the way the program behaves. Most of the time this isn't a problem because debugger designers go out of their way to make sure it isn't. However, certain behaviors are difficult to debug in Windows because the presence of the debugger disturbs those behaviors. These behaviors include the following:

- Window drawing (particularly when the window being drawn is overlapped when the debugger activates)
- Window activation
- Input focus
- Keyboard input
- Mouse input, movement, and capture
- Memory allocation
- Thread synchronization

The act of debugging changes the outcome of these activities. For example, consider the difficulty in debugging a WM_MOUSEMOVE message. If you set a breakpoint on code that handles this message, the debugger activates once you move the mouse within the corresponding window. Most likely you will then move the mouse to interact with the debugger, making the future WM_MOUSEMOVE messages different from what they would be without the presence of the debugger. Consequently, WM_MOUSEMOVE messages are very difficult to debug. I present several techniques for debugging these activities in Chapter 8, Basic Debugging Techniques. Trace statements (see Chapter 4) can be particularly effective at bypassing the Heisenberg Uncertainty Principle.

> **TIP**
>
> Be aware that compiling a debug build and running a program from a debugger changes the way the program behaves.

Know Your Tools—RTFM

If you are developing programs that use complex technologies you don't understand well, your code is going to have a lot of bugs. Guaranteed. For example, it is unlikely that you can handle Windows paint messages correctly if you don't understand how paint messages are created, how window validation works, and how the graphics device interface (GDI) works. When learning a new technology, you can reduce the number of bugs by making a sincere effort to read the documentation. Be sure to "read the fine manual" (RTFM) to know your tools. Don't try to program without understanding what you are doing.

Understand the Problem Domain—RTFC

Similarly, if you are debugging code you don't understand well, your source code modifications are likely to be buggy. When changing code, be sure that you have a good understanding of what the program is doing and how the code implements it. If you can't figure it out, consider discussing the change with someone who understands it. Be sure to "read the fine code" (RTFC) to understand what you are doing. Avoid debugging by trial and error.

Use Defensive Maintenance

Although most of your debugging effort takes place during the implementation phase of the development process, a significant amount of debugging occurs during the maintenance phase as well. When maintaining code, be sure to practice defensive maintenance. That is, use self-restraint when maintaining code to defend against accidentally adding new bugs, but try to improve code when you have to make changes. To summarize, the rules of defensive maintenance are as follows.

1. If it ain't broke, don't fix it.
2. If it is broken, fix it and make it better.

The first rule requires that you not change code unless there is a real problem. You shouldn't make trivial changes to code just because you don't like the way it looks. Don't change variable names, function names, code formatting, and such for correctly working code, no matter how hideous these details may be. Just *don't* do it. Resist the urge—sit on your hands if necessary. If you make a change, even an apparently trivial change, you run the risk of adding bugs. That risk may seem small, but the risk-reward ratio can be infinite. Rather, you should follow a previous tip: Assume that all new code has bugs. Never change any code unless you are willing to carefully test the code as well—an unlikely event during drive-by maintenance.

There is often a reason why code is the way it is; and, unfortunately, code that is intentionally "special" isn't always documented. By making a seemingly harmless change you can easily introduce bugs, especially if you don't completely understand the code. (Documenting "special" code reduces this risk.) Consider the following MFC window painting functions:

```
void CMyWindow1::OnPaint () {
    CPaintDC dc(this);   // necessary code that appears unnecessary
}

void CMyWindow2::OnPaint () {
    CPaintDC dc(this);
    CPen grayPen (PS_SOLID, 1, GetSysColor(COLOR_3DSHADOW));
    dc.SelectObject(&grayPen);
    // do some drawing with the pen
    dc.SelectStockObject(BLACK_PEN); // necessary code that
                                     // appears unnecessary
}
```

These painting functions are correct, yet they appear to have unnecessary code. In the first *OnPaint*, a paint device context is declared but never used. However, the destructor of a paint device context has the side effect of validating the update region, which in turns keeps Windows from sending further paint messages. If you were to remove this "unnecessary" code, the program would get stuck in a loop processing the same paint message over and over again. In the second *OnPaint*, the device context selects a black pen that it never uses just before it goes out of scope. If you were to remove this "unnecessary" code, the program would continue to function as before, except there would be a GDI resource leak. The problem is that Windows doesn't allow a program to delete a GDI object that is in use, and selecting a stock object is a common method for removing an object from use.

Of course, everything changes when you really do need to modify the code, which is where the second rule comes in. When you have to make a fix, try to make the code better than it was before the fix. Don't just sloppily patch the code; make the code cleaner and easier to understand if it needs improvement. If the code is so bad it is beyond hope, completely rewrite it. (Note that such code may be cleanly implemented, but implemented the wrong way.) After all, you've got to test the code anyway, so there's no harm in improving code that you have to change as long as you understand what you are doing. The difference isn't all that significant for a single bug fix, but consider what happens over the lifetime of the program. If you practice this technique, over time the quality of the code slowly improves. By contrast, if you don't practice this technique, the quality of the code slowly degrades with time, making future bugs more likely.

Take a Responsible Attitude

In the beginning of this chapter, I outlined an ineffective debugging process based on the five stages of grief. All these undesirable behaviors stem from one problem: having a poor, immature attitude about debugging. They reveal a lack of concern about quality and an eagerness to weasel out of a programmer's ultimate responsibility of delivering correctly working code. Doing things like assuming there aren't bugs without checking or getting upset with testers for finding bugs undermines this responsibility.

Although our ideal goal as programmers is to develop bug-free software, we know that there are many practical problems that make this goal difficult to obtain. Some people believe that it is better to ignore reality and pretend that we can routinely deliver bug-free software. I disagree. I don't see how being delusional about what is possible improves anything. If you believe bug-free software is possible but are never willing to declare your software bug free, then you're being delusional. It is always healthier to assume your code has bugs than pretend that it doesn't.

The best approach to developing bug-free software is to have a responsible attitude. If you wrote it, it's your code and you're responsible for it. It's your job to prevent, detect, and remove as many bugs as you can as soon as you can. The fact that someone else may find or fix your bugs doesn't change anything. You shouldn't depend on this happening, and it's your fault if it doesn't. Delivering bug-free software is unlikely, but delivering nearly bug-free software is an obtainable goal if you take full responsibility for your work.

> **TIP**
>
> The best approach to developing bug-free software is to have a responsible attitude. It's your job to prevent, detect, and remove as many bugs as you can.

How should you feel if someone finds a bug in your code? I think the answer depends on the bug itself. If someone finds a bug in my code that is obvious or could have been found with simple testing, I am embarrassed and I try not to repeat that mistake. In this case, I made a stupid error and failed to take responsibility for my code. On the other hand, I feel no embarrassment at all when someone finds a bug in my code that was difficult to find and not obvious at all. Although I would prefer to find the bug myself and I do try to find all of them, the reality is that I occasionally let such bugs slip through. I just try to make sure it doesn't happen often.

As this chapter has shown, there are many types of bugs; but most bugs can be removed using variations of a fairly standard process. As you become more experienced in debugging, you will acquire a deeper understanding of this process and create many debugging techniques of your own. The remainder of this book is largely an elaboration of the processes and tips presented in this chapter.

Recommended Reading

Badger, Terry M. *Puzzles and Games in Logic and Reasoning*. Mineola, NY: Dover, 1996.   An excellent collection of logical and spatial puzzles to help exercise your logical reasoning, creative thinking, and problem-solving skills.

Kernighan, Brian W., and Rob Pike. *The Practice of Programming*. Reading, MA: Addison-Wesley, 1999.   Chapter 5, Debugging, gives a comprehensive yet concise overview of the debugging process with a strong slant toward using your head instead of a debugger. Chapter 6, Testing, is also worthwhile reading that covers topics I consider debugging related, such as assertions and defensive programming.

Maguire, Steve. *Writing Solid Code: Microsoft's Techniques for Developing Bug-Free C Programs*. Redmond, WA: Microsoft Press, 1993.   Maguire presents a system for dealing with bugs and the debugging process. The most notable ideas are that programmers are responsible for finding and fixing their own bugs, that bugs should be fixed as soon as they are found and that waiting to fix bugs later wastes time, that fixing bugs is a negative feedback process that keeps sloppy programmers in check, and that maintaining a low bug count greatly simplifies determining the status of a project.

McConnell, Steve. *Code Complete: A Practical Handbook of Software Construction*. Redmond, WA: Microsoft Press, 1996.   Chapter 26, Debugging, presents an alternative explanation of the debugging process, complete with a work-through example. An excellent summary of debugging.

Myers, Glenford J. *The Art of Software Testing*. New York: Wiley, 1979.   Chapter 7, Debugging, of this classic testing book gives an excellent overview of the debugging process. The presentation is insightful and, given its age, remarkably current. The chapter focuses on using your head to remove bugs, especially using inductive and deductive processes. Although I strongly disagree with his belief that you should avoid using a debugger and that programmers shouldn't test their own code, the remainder of this concise chapter is filled with many useful ideas.

Pirsig, Robert M. *Zen and the Art of Motorcycle Maintenance: An Inquiry into Values*. New York: William Morrow, 1974.   This philosophical exploration of logic, values, and quality uses motorcycle maintenance as a practical example. Although this may seem like an unlikely source of information for debugging Windows programs, almost every high-level aspect of the debugging process is examined in some detail, including an excellent description of deductive and inductive logic and the scientific method. Essential reading if your debugging process in any way resembles the five stages of grief.

Rosenberg, Jonathan B. *How Debuggers Work: Algorithms, Data Structures, and Architecture*. New York: Wiley, 1996. Chapter 1, Introduction, discusses the basic principles of debugger design, including avoiding problems related to the Heisenberg Uncertainty Principle.

von Oech, Roger. *A Whack on the Side of the Head: How You Can Be More Creative*. New York: Warner Books, 1998. A classic book to help promote creative thinking. It presents ten effective techniques for opening mental locks that can help you improve your puzzle-solving skills.

Chapter 2

Writing C++ Code for Debugging

When writing C++ code, undoubtedly you have several things on your mind. Will the code do the job? Will it be fast enough? Will it be reliable? Will it be easy to maintain? Will the project be finished on time? Will people like the results? Your ability to debug the code you are writing should also be among these concerns.

C++ is an extraordinary programming language, with enormous potential both to create bugs and to prevent bugs. In this chapter, I present several techniques to help you use C++ strategically for debugging. These techniques help you prevent and remove bugs by letting you take full advantage of the C++ compiler, avoid language pitfalls that are a common source of bugs, and adopt a programming style that facilitates debugging with the Visual C++ debugger. When properly used, your programming language and its compiler are the most powerful debugging tools you have.

Design

Since your code is the implementation of your design, your ability to write code that prevents bugs starts with creating a good design. Clearly, a well-designed program is easier to debug than a poorly designed one. Although there are many important design attributes, simplicity and coupling are the two that are most relevant to debugging.

Simplicity

To say that your program design should be simple might seem a bit, well, simplistic, but easily the most common design mistake I see is unnecessary complexity. A good design should reflect the requirements of the problem at hand, that is, the solution should match the problem and not have unnecessary features. Often, the justification for overly complex designs is the desire to handle future, unknown requirements. I have found, however, that simple, elegant designs are much better at adapting to future requirements than "kitchen sink" designs. Furthermore, speculation about future requirements tends to be wrong. A good example of this principle is the evolution of the C++ programming language itself, starting with the original simple C. There's a reason we don't program using Ada++.

Coupling

Coupling is a measurement of the dependence between objects. The less dependence the better so, the objects in a program that can be independent should be independent. This *decoupling* makes the program easier to understand, implement, test, and maintain. Such programs are less likely to have bugs, and the bugs they have are easier to find and remove. In object-oriented designs, derived classes are coupled to their base classes, so such "vertical" coupling can be desirable. What is undesirable is "horizontal" coupling, in which otherwise independent objects are made dependent in order to get them to work together. Having a decoupled design is especially important in testing since it allows you to test the objects individually—perhaps with the aid of some kind of test harness.

C++ Programming Style

In this section, I examine several issues of programming style. These issues relate to the presentation of the code, but not to any specific C++ language-features. In fact, you can use these presentation styles with any programming language. One could argue that programming style is mostly a matter of personal preference and therefore largely arbitrary. Often that is true. In fact, the more arbitrary the issue, the more fervent people seem to get about their preferred approach. For several programming styles, however, that arbitrariness disappears when you look at style from the point of view of debugging. A good programming style makes the code easy to read and understand as well as easy to manipulate with the debugger. Considering how much time is spent reading and rereading source code when debugging, this is not an insignificant issue.

TIP

Programming style matters in debugging.

Write Clearly

In their classic book *The Elements of Programming Style,* Brian Kernighan and P. J. Plauger start with these two basic rules.

- Write clearly—don't be too clever.
- Say what you mean, simply and directly.

These rules are a good place to start here as well. Any code that is difficult to understand is difficult to debug. Clean, well-written code is less likely to have bugs, and any bugs it does have are likely to be easy to find and remove.

In terms of not being too clever, C++ offers a wide range of features, including many advanced features that are not well understood by the typical programmer. Some programmers avoid this problem by using a "sane" subset of the language that is familiar to most programmers and less prone to error. Others believe that the whole language should be used. My advice is that you should feel free to use advanced language features when really necessary. In addition, consider documenting what you are doing with these features to make it clear. Use advanced language features because you need them, not because they are there.

TIP

Use advanced language features because you need them, not because they are there.

Use Well-Structured Code

The most basic debugging information you typically receive when a program crashes is the source code file and line number where the problem occurred and a call stack. A call stack is one of the most helpful pieces in the debugging puzzle because it gives you the context in which the error occurred; namely, the function call sequence with parameter values. The better the code is structured, the more informative the call stack will be. For example, consider two equally buggy implementations of a complex algorithm. One is well structured; the other is a single giant function. The call stack of the well-structured algorithm provides useful information, but the call stack of the poorly structured algorithm is unlikely to have any information at all.

> **TIP**
> Well-structured code provides more useful call stacks.

Use Good Identifier Names

Using good identifier names for classes, functions, variables, and constants makes your code easier to understand and therefore less prone to error. This is especially true during maintenance, when poor variable names are more likely to cause confusion. The most important idea to consider is that the audience for your source code is you, other programmers, and the compiler. Compilers can understand any names you choose equally well, but humans can't. Write your code so that it can be easily read by humans.

> **TIP**
> The audience for your source code is you, other programmers, and the compiler; so write your code so that it can be easily read by humans.

Here are some of the rules I use when selecting variable names.

• **Use brief, descriptive names.** A good identifier name briefly summarizes what the identifier represents. The meaning should be self-evident. The reader should have a good idea what the identifier does without having to read a comment, but keep the names short because unnecessarily long names are cumbersome. Long identifier names are desirable only when they add needed clarity.

• **Avoid abbreviations.** The practice of using abbreviations in variable names started decades ago, when storage was expensive and keyboards were of poor quality. Programming languages at that time were often limited to eight-character identifiers. Times have changed, but unfortunately this practice continues. Although truncating long words doesn't harm readability much, dropping letters does. For example, *pos* is a good name for a position variable, but *pstn* (obtained by dropping all the vowels) is not. Dropping letters is a poor practice that makes identifiers difficult to read and remember. Abbreviations to save a character or two are especially silly. Prefer mixed-case, full words.

- **Avoid similar names.** There should be enough "psychological distance" between names to avoid confusion. *Psychological distance* is how much distinction there is between two things in one's mind. For example, the name *count* is fine on its own, but *count* combined with *Count, cnt*, or *count2* creates confusion. Adding a numeric suffix to a variable creates only a small psychological distance.

- **Avoid generic names.** Programming texts (such as this book) often use generic names in examples when the identifier doesn't refer to anything in specific. For example, the name *CMyDocument* is a good class name for sample code because it is general and clearly derived from *CDocument*. Such a name would be a poor choice for production code, however, since it tells you nothing about the specific document class. Other poor examples are identifiers that use the company name (again, what does this tell you?), variable names using articles or pronouns (such as *theObject, anObject,* or *itsObject*), or variable names such as *foo* or *bar*. Variable names based on *foobar* are particularly inappropriate because the real meaning is an obscenity (something similar to "fouled up beyond all recognition.")

- **Avoid random names.** I remember a study used to help justify the horrible naming conventions used by UNIX. In this study, test subjects were asked to use state names in place of commands, such as "California" for a directory listing or "Mississippi" to copy a file. They found that the test subjects had no trouble performing simple tasks using this naming convention. However, this study is nonsense because it ignores the difference between short-term and long-term memory and the fact that people shouldn't have to create mental maps to understand simple things when they don't have to.

- **Avoid joke names.** Sorry, poorly written code isn't very funny.

In Chapter 9, The Power of Data Names, of *Code Complete,* Steve McConnell gives a whole chapter of guidelines for choosing identifier names. You might want to refer to this book for additional information.

The bottom line is that using plain language makes the best identifier names. In *The Elements of Programming Style,* Kernighan and Plauger recommend using the "telephone test" for readability, that is, "If someone could understand your code when read aloud over the telephone, it's clear enough. If not, then it needs rewriting." If your code can't pass the telephone test, then it's not readable.

Reconsider Hungarian Notation

By now you may have surmised that my failure to recommend Hungarian notation is not accidental. In case you're not familiar with it, Hungarian notation combines (encrypts?) the meaning of an identifier with its representation; so that instead of using the variable name *count,* someone using Hungarian notation would use *nCount,* where *n* represents an integer data type. Although many Windows programmers love Hungarian notation and swear by it, I prefer to swear at it. It has done more to undermine the readability of Windows programs than anything else I can think of.

Hungarian notation became popular in the early days of Windows programming, and at that time it actually made sense. Remember that the first Windows programs were written before ANSI C, so back then functions didn't have prototypes. Furthermore, these programs were typically developed using the 16-bit medium model (in which function pointers were far by default but data pointers were near) to create a single data segment so that users could run multiple instances of a program. In these conditions, the statement

```
Messageox(hWnd, (LPSTR)"Help! My program has bugs!"
    lpszAppName, MB_OK);
```

would crash without an explicit LPSTR cast because the compiler had no way of knowing that a far pointer was required and would use a near pointer by default. In this environment, the programmer effectively had to act as a human compiler, manually scouring the code line by line to make sure that all functions were passed parameters with the right data types and pointer lengths. Failing to do so led to much grief. Given this unfortunate situation, I too would use Hungarian notation.

Times have changed. A modern C++ compiler armed with prototypes and strong type checking is able to report most type mismatches. (There are exceptions, such as generic types like `void *`, WPARAM, and LPARAM and variable parameter functions like *wsprintf*.) The fact that code compiles tells you a great deal about the code itself. For example, given the fact that the following code compiles

```
firstName = name.Left(FirstNameSize); list->Add(firstName);
```

we know that *firstName* and *name* are strings and that *list* is a pointer to a list object from context. Program context usually provides enough information to determine variable types from the code, just as sentence context provides enough information to interpret prose. Letting the compiler deal with type checking is a better solution because modern compilers are certainly much more effective at finding such data type mismatches than programmers are.

The most significant problem with Hungarian notation is that the resulting code is usually difficult to read (although some may argue that the biggest problem is that bolting the representation to the variable name seriously violates the concept of data abstraction.) Although using the Hungarian prefixes doesn't force you to choose bad variable names, that is typically the result. Programmers who use Hungarian notation seem to fixate on the prefix and don't seem too concerned about the resulting readability. As a result, Hungarian notation names tend to be gibberish. So although one could use Hungarian notation to name a pointer to tooltip text *lpszToolTipText,* for some reason Hungarian notation aficionados find the urge to name the variable *lpszttt* irresistible.

Another serious problem with Hungarian notation is that it makes maintenance difficult. Since Hungarian notation combines meaning with representation, if the representation changes, the identifier name needs to change as well. Unfortunately, once a prefix becomes established (such as with a published API function), it is very difficult to change later. For example, WPARAM and LPARAM variables are now both 32-bit, but their obsolete prefixes suggest they are different sizes. Similarly, the *l* in any *lp* prefix is for far (long) pointers, yet far pointers are meaningless in 32-bit Windows. Even though these prefixes are wrong and misleading, they are firmly established and unlikely to change. Using Hungarian notation in function names is especially troublesome when the function return type changes because your only options are to leave the incorrect prefix or change the function name and risk breaking a lot of code.

The last problem with Hungarian notation is that it simply isn't very informative. To completely understand a variable, you need to know more than its type. What is the variable's scope? Is it global, local, or member data? Is the variable a scalar or an array? If an array, what are the array's dimensions? Is the variable `const`? Is it `static`? Is it `volatile`? All this information can be just as important as the data type, but it isn't always encoded into the Hungarian prefix. Consequently, it should be clear that any conclusion based solely on a Hungarian prefix is likely to be a bad one. Note that, aside from scope, all this information is readily obtained using the datatip feature in the Visual C++ source code editor when you aren't running the debugger. These datatips are *very* cool.

The problem of incomplete information suggests a better solution to variable naming. A good naming convention should indicate the variable's scope so that you can easily check its declaration when necessary. Your naming convention should make it obvious whether a variable is global, local, or member data. Referring to a variable's declaration is always more useful and trustworthy than relying on its Hungarian prefix.

Hungarian notation can be useful in limited doses. In fact, certain Hungarian prefixes are so standard in Windows programming that it would be confusing not to use them, as in the following examples.

m_	for data members
p	for pointers
h	for handles
C	for classes
I	for COM interfaces

For example, the conventional name for a device context handle is *hDC*; using any other name would be confusing, so please don't name it *device ContextHandle*. Hungarian notation is also useful when you have an object, a pointer to an object, and a handle to an object all within the same scope, which is common in Windows programs.

Despite all its problems, Hungarian notation remains surprisingly popular. Of course, if your programming team uses Hungarian notation, you should follow the established coding standards because consistency can be as important as clarity. I know that it's unlikely that I have changed your opinion if your mind is already made up. (Wait—let me give it one more shot. What is the Hungarian prefix for an integer? Is it *n* or is it *i*? What does the *f* prefix stand for? Is it `float` or is it BOOL (flag)? If you don't know, you have some thinking to do.) If you haven't decided yet, please don't use Hungarian notation because you have been led to believe it is *the* correct way to write Windows programs—it isn't. You can do many things to improve the readability of your code and make it less error prone, but using Hungarian notation isn't one of them.

> Although using Hungarian notation made sense at one time, times have changed. Hungarian notation is difficult to read, difficult to maintain, and often misleading.

Use Simple Statement Lines

The C++ language makes it easy to combine several statements on a single line, and its heritage of succinct expression encourages this practice. When choosing what to put on a single line, keep in mind that debugging is a line-oriented activity unless you debug at the assembly code level. Debugging features, such as breakpoints; commands, such as **Step Into**, **Step Over**, **Set Next Statement**, and **Run to Cursor**; assertions; trace statements; and MAP files are all based on source code lines. Using overly complex lines makes it difficult to take full advantage of these features by making it harder to set breakpoints, trace into functions, or determine the specific code that crashed or had a failed assertion. Consider each statement line a separate atomic unit from the point of view of debugging.

> Overly complex statement lines make it difficult to take full advantage of debugging features.

Use Uniform Alignment

Some programmers meticulously align their code, whereas others leave the code in its "natural" state. Not surprisingly, I believe that uniformly aligned code is preferable. Not only does the code look better, but the alignment makes patterns easier to identify, and code that doesn't follow the pattern suggests a bug. For example, try to spot the bugs in the following code:

```
// save values if change
if (location != savedLocation &&
    displayMode = savedDisplayMode &&
    size != savedSize &
    colorScheme != savedColorScheme)
    SaveValues();
```

Such unaligned code is difficult to scan quickly. Now try to spot the bugs in the aligned version:

```
// save values if change
if (location    != savedLocation    &&
    displayMode  = savedDisplayMode &&
    size        != savedSize         &
    colorScheme != savedColorScheme)
    SaveValues();
```

Uniform alignment clearly makes a difference—the errors jump right out at you (in this case, "=" was mistakenly used instead of "!=" and "&" was mistakenly used instead of "&&".) Note that uniform alignment doesn't mean you have to make all statements line up exactly or go to ridiculous extremes. Using two or three different alignments also works well, as with this example:

```
// save values if change
if (location != savedLocation &&
    size        != savedSize         &
    displayMode  = savedDisplayMode &&
    colorScheme != savedColorScheme)
    SaveValues();
```

Consider using uniform alignment to reveal patterns for class and function declarations; variable declarations; and `if`, `switch`, `for`, and `while` statements. To preserve that alignment, always use spaces instead of tab characters to make the alignment independent of the tab settings. In Visual C++, you can make this setting using the **Options** command in the **Tools** menu by selecting the **Insert spaces** option on the **Tabs** tab. (If you have ever tried to maintain code written using different tab settings, you know what I mean.)

Use Parentheses to Make It Clear

I first learned how to program C by reading *The C Programming Language* by Brian Kernighan and Dennis Ritchie. After a while, if you were to lay my copy of the book flat on a desk (or even throw it across the room), chances are it would open on page 49, which contains the C precedence and associativity table. I referred to this table often to make sure I was writing correct C code because these rules tell you when you must use parentheses.

I haven't looked at this table in years. It isn't because I have the table memorized or because it's now available on line. Rather, it is because I am now following Steve Maguire's advice in *Writing Solid Code* (Microsoft Press, 1993), where he says "Don't look it up!" Why is this good advice? Remember that the audience for your source code is you, other programmers, and the compiler. Although the compiler has the precedence and associativity rules wired, most programmers do not. So if you're not sure whether or not you need to use parentheses, then you need to use parentheses. Go ahead and use them, even if they aren't really necessary. The reader should not have to consult the precedence and associativity table to understand your code, nor should the reader have to consult this table to determine if there's a bug. Using this strategy saves you time, prevents bugs, and makes your code easier to understand. Best of all, unnecessary parentheses carry no performance cost because they have absolutely no impact on the compiled code (unless, of course, there would be a bug without the parentheses.)

> **TIP**
>
> If you're not sure whether or not you need to use parentheses, then you need to use parentheses. Don't look it up.

Use Good Comments

Using good comments makes your code less error prone and therefore less likely to have bugs, especially bugs due to bad maintenance. Again, it helps to remember that the audience for your source code is you, other programmers (including maintenance programmers), and the compiler; and although the compiler won't understand the comments, programmers will. Make sure to give comments that others will need and understand because it is likely that someone else will be maintaining the code in the future. Always provide comments that explain what the classes, structures, and functions are for and any assumptions you make in the code.

It is especially important to provide good comments that explain confusing, tricky, or unusual code. One might argue that such code should be rewritten instead of documented, but sometimes such code is necessary. If you need to explain something and can't explain it clearly in the code itself, explain it with comments. One event that should always result in a comment is whenever you make a bad code change during development. For example, if you make a change that you assumed would improve the code but that actually resulted in a bug, be sure to document the bad change and the nature of the problem. Otherwise, it is likely that someone else (perhaps even you) will make the same "improvement" in the future. For more information, see Chapter 19, Self-Documenting Code, of Steve McConnell's *Code Complete*.

> **TIP**
>
> Write comments with maintenance in mind.

The C++ Language

Here are some ways to prevent bugs using the C++ language itself by taking advantage of the C++ language and compiler and avoiding common C++ pitfalls.

Prefer C++ to C

Consider using the following techniques to take full advantage of the C++ compiler.

1. Use `const` instead of `#define` to create constants.
2. Use `enum` instead of `#define` to create a set of constants.
3. Use `inline` functions instead of `#define` macros.
4. Use `new` and `delete` instead of `malloc` and `free`.
5. Use iostreams instead of stdio.

The first three techniques use the C++ language instead of the C preprocessor. The problem with using the preprocessor is that the compiler knows nothing about what the preprocessor does, so it can't check for problems and inconsistencies with data types. Preprocessor names aren't in the symbol table, so you can't use the debugger to check preprocessor constants. Similarly, preprocessor macros are compiled away, so you can't use the debugger to trace into macros. Preprocessor macros are notoriously buggy due to precedence problems and passing parameters with side effects. By contrast, the compiler is fully aware of `const`, `enum`, and `inline` statements and can warn you of any problems at compile time. Since `inline` functions are compiled as normal functions in debug builds, you can trace into them with the debugger; whereas it is impossible to trace into preprocessor macros.

There is one glaring exception to the principle of preferring the language to the preprocessor: The preprocessor is a critical player in most debugging code. The reason is that debugging code often needs to have different behavior from nondebugging code, and the most efficient way to obtain this different behavior is to have the preprocessor create different code for debug builds. Consequently, this book contains a lot of preprocessor-based debugging code.

TIP

Prefer the C++ language to the C preprocessor, but understand that debugging code requires using the preprocessor.

It is better to use `new/delete` instead of `malloc/free` for object construction, type safety, and flexibility. Whereas `malloc` just allocates memory, `new` allocates memory (always the right amount of an object) and calls the object's constructor. Similarly, `free` only deallocates memory, whereas `delete` calls the object's destructor and then deallocates memory. In fact, you can't create a C++ object using `malloc` because you can't call constructors directly. For safety, you can have `new` throw exceptions on failure using `_set_new_handler` whereas `malloc` returns 0 by default—although you can use `_set_new_mode` to have `malloc` behave the same way as `new` does on failure. (See Chapter 5 for example code.) Using `new` also has the advantage of type safety, which makes it impossible to assign the resulting pointer to an incompatible pointer type. By contrast, `malloc` returns `void *`, so it always requires a cast. Additionally, the `new` operator can be overloaded by a class, thus providing flexibility. Because Visual C++ `malloc` uses the same core memory management routines as `new` (and therefore has the same diagnostic support), there is never an advantage to using `malloc` and `free` in C++ programs.

Finally, consider using the C++ iostreams (that is, `operator>>` and `operator<<`) instead of the C stdio library (that is, `printf`/`sprintf` and `scanf`/`sscanf`) for type safety and extensibility. From the point of view of debugging, the biggest problem with the stdio functions is that the compiler is unable to perform any type checking on the control string arguments. In fact, the compiler knows so little about these functions that it can't even warn you if you don't pass pointers to `scanf`. By contrast, any problems with iostreams are detected at compile time. Furthermore, you can supply iostream operators for any C++ class, whereas stdio works only with built-in data types. For additional information on this subject, see Scott Meyers' *Effective C++, Second Edition,* Items 1, 2, and 3.

Using Header Files

Use header files for all declarations that are shared across files. Using header files ensures that all your declarations are exactly the same for all compilation units. Note that C++ mangles external symbols to ensure type-safe linking, which prevents most declaration mismatches. However, mismatches are always possible in situations in which casting, generic pointers, or functions declared using `extern` `"C"` are involved. In addition, arrays and pointers receive the same decoration, so the following code will link:

```
int Fibonacci[] = {1,1,2,3,5,8,13,21};   // definition in
                                          // File1.cpp
extern int * Fibonacci;                   // declaration in
                                          // File2.cpp
```

However, note that accessing `Fibonacci[0]` in *File2.cpp* crashes with an access violation exception. Why fool around? Place all shared declarations in header files. You don't want to see the `extern` keyword in your .cpp files.

By the way, always leave the parameter names in the header file function prototypes. Although the compiler doesn't care, having the parameter names makes the code much easier to read and use.

TIP

Declare all shared external symbols in a header file, and always leave the parameter names in the function prototypes.

Initializing Variables

Always initialize variables before using them. Failing to initialize a variable before using it is certainly a bug. (However, an uninitialized variable that is immediately passed to a function as an out parameter should be considered initialized.) This idea is simple enough and fairly obvious, but the details behind variable initialization are surprisingly complicated. Variables of built-in (or intrinsic) data types (such as `char`, `int`, and `float`) are automatically initialized to zero when a program is loaded if the variable is global, but they are not initialized if the variable is automatic (a local on the stack) or allocated using `new` (on the heap). (Actually, automatic variables are initialized in debug builds if you use the /GZ compiler option, which I discuss later in the chapter.) Objects are initialized by their constructor no matter where they are stored. Since most constructors initialize their objects to a well-defined state (after all, that is what constructors are for), you usually don't have to initialize objects. For example, the following Microsoft Foundation Class (MFC) initialization code generated by the Visual C++ ClassWizard isn't necessary because *CString* objects are initialized to empty strings at construction:

```
CExampleDialog::CExampleDialog(CWnd* pParent)
   : CDialog(CExampleDialog::IDD, pParent)
{
   //{{AFX_DATA_INIT(CExampleDialog)
   m_String = _T("");
   //}}AFX_DATA_INIT
}
```

Unfortunately, there are exceptions, and not all objects are initialized at construction. For example, the MFC *CRect, CPoint,* and *CSize* objects are not initialized by their default constructors, so you always have to initialize these objects explicitly. This is clearly a bug in MFC, although I assume it was done intentionally to make these objects behave like their RECT, POINT, and SIZE API counterparts. You should always initialize data members in a constructor. After all, the data members have to be initialized somehow; so it is better to give the constructor that responsibility.

TIP

Always initialize all data members in a constructor.

You must explicitly initialize arrays and data structures allocated on the stack or the heap. Although the `memset` library function can be used for initialization, the *ZeroMemory* API function is a bit more convenient for Windows programs. Never use these functions to initialize objects, however, since such an initialization may destroy the work of base class or data member constructors. For example, never do this:

```
CDisasterApp:: CDisasterApp () {
    ZeroMemory(this, sizeof(this));   // bad idea - living very
                                      // dangerously
}
```

Rather, individually initialize each data member that needs to be initialized.

Finally, the Visual C++ compiler can detect the use of an uninitialized local variable, but it does a much better job at this detection with release builds than with debug builds because variable use is checked by the optimizer. This fact suggests that it is a good idea to perform release builds occasionally, especially when you are faced with tracking down a difficult bug.

Occasionally create release builds to help detect uninitialized variables.

Using Bit Masking

Bit masking can be prone to error if any bit masks are zero or not a power of two. If each bit mask is a power of two, each bit in an integer represents a distinct state. For example, the following bit masks can be used as expected.

```
#define WS_EX_DLGMODALFRAME      0x00000001L
#define WS_EX_NOPARENTNOTIFY     0x00000004L
#define WS_EX_TOPMOST            0x00000008L
#define WS_EX_ACCEPTFILES        0x00000010L
#define WS_EX_TRANSPARENT        0x00000020L

if ((extendedStyle & WS_EX_TOPMOST) == WS_EX_TOPMOST)...;// works
if (extendedStyle & WS_EX_TOPMOST)...;    // works as expected
if (extendedStyle == WS_EX_TOPMOST)...;   // doesn't work -

// never use
```

Unfortunately, not all the bit masks used by Windows are nonzero powers of two, which allows more information to be packed into an integer. Consider the following bit mask usage:

```
#define SS_LEFT             0x00000000L
#define SS_CENTER           0x00000001L
#define SS_RIGHT            0x00000002L
#define SS_ICON             0x00000003L
#define SS_BLACKRECT        0x00000004L


// doesn't work - statement is always true
if ((controlStyle & SS_LEFT) == SS_LEFT) ...;
// doesn't work - if statement is true, style could be SS_CENTER
//    or SS_ICON
if ((controlStyle & SS_CENTER) == SS_CENTER) ...;
```

Both of these bit mask statements are incorrect. This type of bug can be very difficult to track down because the code looks right. There is a good chance the code will behave right most of the time as well. For example, if you write code that processes static control text, you won't realize that your code confuses centered text with icons until someone tests your text code with an icon—not an obvious test to make. These bit mask statements are correctly written as follows:

```
#define SS_TYPEMASK        0x0000001FL
// works as expected
if ((controlStyle & SS_TYPEMASK) == SS_LEFT) ...;
// works as expected
if ((controlStyle & SS_TYPEMASK) == SS_CENTER) ...;
```

Unfortunately, this problem means that you cannot use bit masks abstractly. The only way you can determine how to write the bit masking statements correctly is to look at the bit mask value declarations. In fact, this type of bit mask bug is impossible to figure out without knowing the specific bit mask values. To prevent problems when writing bit mask code, be sure to check the declarations and use the necessary masking macros (such as HRESULT_CODE()) or subfield masks (such as SS_TYPEMASK).

TIP

Check the bit mask values of unfamiliar bit masks. When necessary, use masking macros or subfield masks.

Using Boolean Variables

Although C++ now has a built-in Boolean type (specifically `bool`, which has values of `true` or `false` and a size of 1 byte), Windows programs typically still use the BOOL type, which has the following definition:

```
typedef int          BOOL;
#define FALSE         0
#define TRUE          1
```

In C++, a Boolean expression is considered false if it has a value of 0 and true if it has any other value. This means that the following innocent-looking statements are actually bugs:

```
if (booleanValue == TRUE) ...;
if (booleanValue != TRUE) ...;
```

The problem, of course, is that these Boolean tests behave incorrectly when *booleanValue* has a value other than 0 or 1. Note that many Windows API functions that return BOOL values return values other than 0 or 1. (The *IsWindow* API function is a good example.) In fact, the Windows API documentation is always written in terms of zero and nonzero return values. If *booleanValue* is set to 2 once in a thousand times, you'll have a very difficult bug to catch.

Clearly, Boolean expressions should never test against true but should test against false instead. Here are the previous statements written correctly:

```
if (booleanValue != FALSE) ...; or even better if (booleanValue) ...;
if (booleanValue == FALSE) ...; or even better if (!booleanValue) ...;
```

TIP

Boolean statements should never test against true but should test against false instead.

Using Integer, Character, and Floating Point Variables

Using integer variables in C++ is usually straightforward, but there are a few classic mistakes to watch out for.

- **The off-by-one bug** A common bug is for an integer value to be off by one, especially in loop indices. An easy way to detect this problem is to work through a single test case, typically the first or last index value. If the test case is right, all other cases will be right as well.

- **Dividing by zero** Performing division with a zero denominator results in an integer divide by zero exception. When performing division, either make it impossible for the denominator to be zero or handle the resulting exception.

- **Overflow** Integer variables have a limited size and will eventually overflow if their value is too large. Although integer overflow is less likely in 32-bit Windows programs than in 16-bit programs, it is still a problem you need to check for when dealing with large positive or negative numbers for signed integers or negative numbers for unsigned integers. Either prevent or handle the overflow. Also, be sure to use the minimum and maximum value constants defined in *Limits.h* for the integer data type representation limits.

- **Testing unsigned values against signed values** Obviously, signed and unsigned variables have different minimum and maximum values. For example, an unsigned integer can never have a value of -1, so the statement

```
if (unsignedInt == -1) ...;
```

won't work as expected. The Visual C++ compiler is good at complaining about signed or unsigned mismatches for variable comparisons, but it says nothing about comparing variables to constants that are out of range; so don't expect the compiler to warn you about such statements. (Be very careful with mismatched comparisons. If you compare a signed value to an unsigned value, the compiler converts the signed value to an unsigned value—probably not what you expect. The previous statement will be true if *unsignedInt* has a value of 0xFFFFFFFF.) If the compiler does give you a warning, don't be in too much of a hurry to use casting to get the warning to go away. Think through what you are doing first. In this case, an alternative to casting is not to mix signed and unsigned variables and use only signed variables instead. Although this may seem like a draconian solution, keep in mind that the benefit of using unsigned variables is greatly reduced if they are constantly mixed with signed variables.

Character variables have the same problems as integer variables, with two additional considerations.

- **The `char` data type is signed** Character variables in Visual C++ are signed, which is an often unexpected detail that is easy to overlook. For example, don't expect a character to have a value of 255. Sign extension may also give you unexpected results.

- **Overflow** Since characters have a range of -128 to 127, they are easy to overflow if you aren't thinking. The following code is an example of an infinite loop.

```
for (char ch = 0; ch < 200; ch++)
    array[ch] = 0;
```

Interestingly, the compiler doesn't complain about such errors.

Floating point variables have similar opportunities for blunder.

- **Dividing by zero** As with integers, performing division with a 0.0 denominator results in problems. Unlike integers, floating point division by zero doesn't result in an exception by default but assigns the rather bizarre "1.#INFO" value. If you prefer, you can have floating point errors result in exceptions with the following code:

```
#include <float.h>
int cw = _controlfp(0, 0);
cw &= ~(EM_OVERFLOW | EM_UNDERFLOW | EM_INEXACT | EM_ZERODIVIDE |
        EM_DENORMAL | _EM_INVALID);
_controlfp(cw, MCW_EM);
```

When performing division, either make it impossible for the denominator to be 0.0 or handle the resulting exception.

- **Overflow or underflow** It is difficult to imagine overflowing a `double`, but it is relatively easy to overflow or underflow a `float`. Either prevent or handle the overflow or underflow. Also, be sure to use the minimum and maximum value constants defined in *Float.h* for the floating point data type representation limits.

- **Testing floating point values** Floating point values do not have an exact binary representation, so you should never expect them to have an exact value. Consequently, you should never compare floating point values for equality. For example, to check a variable for "equality" to 42.0, use the following code:

```
#include <float.h>
if (fabs(floatValue - 42.0) < FLT_EPSILON) ...;
```

where FLT_EPSILON is the maximum representation error for `float` values and DBL_EPSILON is the maximum representation error for `double` values.

Using Pointers and Handles

Pointers are notorious for causing problems in C++ code, but there are a couple steps you can take to eliminate some of these problems. The first step relates to how you initialize pointers and destroy objects with pointers. A pointer should be initialized either to a valid memory address or to zero (a null pointer) to indicate that the pointer isn't pointing to valid memory. This seems obvious enough, but a common mistake is not to reinitialize a pointer once its object has been destroyed. Consider the following code:

```
CObject *pObject1, *pObject2, *pObject3;

// initialize pointers to point to valid objects
...

// destroy the objects
delete pObject1;
delete pObject2;
pObject2 = 0;
if (pObject3 != 0)
    delete pObject3;
pObject3 = 0;
```

In this example, *pObject1* points to invalid memory once its object is destroyed. This dangling pointer is likely to result in a bug unless *pObject1* immediately goes out of scope or it is a data member and the code is in a destructor. Both *pObject2* and *pObject3* are correctly reinitialized after their objects are destroyed. However, C++ guarantees that `delete 0` is harmless, so you don't need to clutter your code to prevent deleting a null pointer, as done with *pObject3*.

The second step in eliminating pointer problems relates to how you handle the possibility that a pointer might be null. Consider the following three approaches:

```
// approach 1
if (p1->p2->p3->fn()) ...; // living dangerously

// approach 2
try {
    if (p1->p2->p3->fn()) ...;
}
catch (...) {
    // handle access violation exception, but how?
}

// approach 3
if (p1 == 0 || p1->p2 == 0 || p1->p2->p3 == 0)
    ...; // handle error
else if (p1->p2->p3->fn()) ...;
```

The first approach is risky because the code clearly assumes that the pointers are never null. If they are, you've got a serious bug. The second approach is robust because it handles the possibility of an access violation exception. It is also simple code to write since you don't have to worry about checking all the possible error conditions. The question left unanswered is how to handle this exception, especially given that you don't know exactly what failed, assuming there is much more code within the `try` block that could result in an access violation. The third approach, although it is also robust, requires more code but has the advantage of clarifying exactly what the problem is. Which approach should you choose? That question is answered in detail in Chapter 5, Using Exceptions and Return Values.

When dereferencing pointers, the ultimate question is this: Can you be certain the pointer is pointing to valid memory? Unless you have already checked the pointer value (perhaps earlier in the code), the answer is no. To prevent bugs, your code needs to handle this possibility.

TIP

To prevent bugs, reinitialize a pointer to null once its object has been destroyed and handle the possibility that a pointer might be null before dereferencing it.

Handles are roughly analogous to pointers, so they have roughly the same problems. Always reinitialize a handle to null after freeing its object, and always handle the possibility that it might be null.

Using Data Structures

Many Windows data structures use a technique you should consider using for your data structures. Specifically, they set the first data member in the structure to the size of the structure in bytes. Here's a typical example:

```
struct OPENFILENAME
{
   DWORD  lStructSize;      // size of structure in bytes
   ...
};
```

There are two benefits to this approach. The first is that this value acts as a kind of structure version ID, so you can add data members to the structure in the future and have a convenient way to distinguish the different structure versions. The second benefit is that this value acts as a structure signature, which makes it easy to determine if the structure has been corrupted. For example, if you expect this value to be 20 and it really is 0x4F98D638, then you can be certain you have a bad structure, regardless of the other structure values. You can check this value in debugging code and before saving the structure to storage.

If you use this technique, be sure to assert the reasonableness of this value to make it obvious if there is a problem. Unfortunately, the Windows API functions that use this type of structure require the value to be correct, otherwise they fail to work without displaying an assertion. It can be easy to forget to initialize these values, and failing silently can lead to bugs that waste a lot of time to track down.

By the way, you can prevent initialization problems with this type of structure by declaring the following template:

```
template <class T> class SizeStruct : public T
{
public:
    SizeStruct () {
        memset(this, 0, sizeof(T));
        lStructSize = sizeof(T);
    }
};
```

You can then use the template to declare the structure variables, as shown here:

```
SizeStruct<OPENFILENAME> openFile;
```

Now *openFile* is guaranteed to be correctly initialized.

Prefer Reference Parameters to Pointer Parameters

C++ allows you to pass large objects to functions efficiently, either as pointers or as references. Each of these techniques has its advantages. Consider the following function declarations:

```
void PointerFunction (CObject *pObject = 0);
void ConstPointerFunction (const CObject *pObject = 0);
```

```
void ReferenceFunction (CObject &object);
void ConstReferenceFunction (const CObject &object);
```

The pointer functions have two advantages. The first is that you can pass a null pointer to the function, as suggested by the default parameter values. In the case of *PointerFunction*, the other advantage is that the presence of the address operator makes it easier to tell that the parameter can be changed by the function:

```
PointerFunction(&object);   // address operator suggests object
                            // will be changed
```

That benefit is lost if you are already dealing with a pointer.

```
PointerFuncion(pObject);   // object is changed, but without a
                           // visible clue
```

The last example reveals the pitfall of relying on the presence of an address operator to determine if a variable can be modified. The C++ approach is to look for the `const` attribute in the function prototype.

By contrast, a reference is an alias to an object, so it must refer to a valid object. There is no such thing as a null reference or an uninitialized reference. Consequently, when you receive a reference parameter in a function, you can safely assume the object is valid. You don't have to check it for validity before you can use it. From the debugging perspective, this advantage makes reference parameters more robust than pointer parameters, albeit at the cost of some flexibility because you can never have a null reference.

For additional information on this subject, see Scott Meyers' *More Effective C++,* Item 1.

Using Casts

A *cast* is a C++ expression that explicitly converts one data type into another data type. The actual effect of a cast on the compiled code depends on the data types involved. Casting one object to another creates a temporary variable of the new object type by calling the appropriate constructor or conversion function. Casting a reference to an object has the same effect, whereas casting a pointer from one type to another type doesn't change the pointer but eliminates a compiler error (or creates one, if done incorrectly). There are some types of casting that the compiler simply cannot do, such as converting a function pointer to a data pointer and vice versa or converting one data type to another without the required constructor or conversion function. Such casts always result in compiler errors.

The following code illustrates what really happens when you cast.

```
class CDoubleClass {
public:
    CDoubleClass (double data)   { m_Data = data; }
    operator double ()           { return m_Data; }
private:
    double m_Data;
};
main ()
{
    double         doubleData = 5.0;
    CDoubleClass doubleObject(6.0);
    int            intData = 7;
    // cast calls constructor
    doubleObject = (CDoubleClass)doubleData;
    // cast calls conversion function
    doubleData   = (double)doubleObject;
    // cast creates temp double variable
    doubleData   = (double)intData / 2;
}
```

Although casts aren't necessary in theory, they are quite necessary in practice. This is especially true in Windows programs, which tend to use many polymorphic data types. Unfortunately, casting is a hazardous activity that tends to result in bugs. The problem is that casts subvert the compiler's ability to perform type checking, which is one of the compiler's best mechanisms for finding bugs. If the compiler can do the cast, it will do the cast—without warning. Each cast places an additional burden on you to perform manual type checking to guarantee the safety of the cast. Consequently, you should never be in a hurry to cast, and use a cast only if there isn't a better alternative.

TIP

Don't be in a hurry to cast. Each cast places an additional burden on you to perform manual type checking to guarantee the safety of the cast.

Perhaps the most hazard-prone cast is the dreaded downcast, which converts a base class pointer into a derived class pointer. Here is a typical example.

```
class CBase {
public:
virtual ~CBase () {}    // a virtual function is required for
                        // dynamic_cast
};

class CDerived1 : public CBase {
public:
    double m_Data;
};

class CDerived2 : public CBase {
public:
    int m_Data;
};

CBase * SomeFunction ();

main ()
{
    CBase     *pBase = SomeFunction ();
    CDerived1 *pDerived = (CDerived1 *)pBase;
    pDerived->m_Data = 5.0;
}
```

This code behaves perfectly as long as *SomeFunction* always returns pointers to *CDerived1* objects. Given the code, there is no way to guarantee that this will always be true. If it isn't true, for all practical purposes *pDerived* points to corrupted memory because its object isn't valid. Setting *m_Data* can then result in an access violation exception. If a program crashes soon after a downcast, chances are an invalid downcast is to blame.

TIP

Casting creates maintenance problems.

Casting in general and downcasting in particular create maintenance problems. In this example, even if you could prove right now that *SomeFunction* always returns pointers to *CDerived1* objects, the circumstances that led to that conclusion may change in the future. A small change to *SomeFunction* can easily break this code without any warning from the compiler.

Prefer C++ Casts

While casting can be a necessary evil, using the new C++ casts can make it less hazardous. Here is a summary of the C++-style casts.

- `static_cast` has similar behavior to the C-style cast with a different syntax, except that it can't convert between pointers and nonpointers and it can't remove the `const` or `volatile` attribute from a type. Most importantly, it verifies at compile time that the variable being cast is type compatible with the target type (expressed in angle brackets). If the conversion isn't sensible, the cast results in a compile-time error. This cast is preferred for most casting operations because it is safe and performs no run-time checking. It is not recommended for downcasts because they require run-time checking to be performed safely.

- `dynamic_cast` performs run-time checking on the cast. It returns zero for an invalid pointer cast or throws a `bad_cast` exception for an invalid reference cast (remember, there is no such thing as a null reference). This cast is recommended for downcasts.

- `const_cast` removes the `const` or `volatile` attribute from a type. Typically, it is used to remove `const` from a function parameter that isn't modified but (incorrectly) isn't declared as `const`.

- `reinterpret_cast` converts incompatible data types. Typically, it is used to convert between pointers and nonpointers, such as when passing a pointer to a polymorphic LPARAM parameter.

Note that `dynamic_cast` requires C++ Run-time Type Information (RTTI), which in turn requires a vtable. This means you cannot use `dynamic_cast` for downcasting objects without virtual functions (doing so results in a compiler error.) Although this may seem like an unfortunate restriction, chances are that if your class doesn't have any virtual functions, you won't need to do much downcasting because it probably isn't a base class. Applying a `dynamic_cast` to the previous example results in the following code:

```
pDerived = dynamic_cast<CDerived1 *>(pBase);
// need to check - can no longer assume a valid pointer
if (pDerived != 0)
   pDerived->m_Data = 5.0;
```

The C++-style casts are safer, more specific, and easier to locate in the source code than their C-style counterpart.

Using `dynamic_cast` makes downcasting safe at the cost of some performance overhead. By being more specific, C++ casts make the resulting code easier to understand and maintain since they make it clear what you are trying to do. Being more specific also contributes to safety by making it impossible to make the wrong type of cast accidentally. For example, you can't accidentally remove a type's `const` attribute. Also, the C++-style casts look quite different from the C-style casts, and that difference is intentional. Their syntax makes them easier to find in source code because you can find all such casts by searching for "_cast". C-style casts are very simple in appearance, but they are unlike any other C++ language feature in that they are impossible to search for with the **Find in Files** command. Although searchability might not seem significant at first, remember that the **Find in Files** command is an important debugging tool because it helps you search code for similar bugs.

> **TIP**
>
> Prefer C++-style casts to C-style casts.

C++-style casts eliminate many problems, but often the best solution is to not use a cast at all. Here are some preferred alternatives to casting.

- **Avoid using polymorphic data types.** Polymorphic data types require casting. Often, you are required to use such types when dealing directly with the Windows API, but you have more options when choosing among classes in a C++ class library. For example, template-based collections provide type safety where pointer-based collections require casting.

- **Use broader base classes.** C++ programs achieve polymorphic behavior by providing virtual functions in base classes. You can often eliminate casting by moving behavior from derived classes to base classes. Special handling of specific data types (often implemented with `if` statements combined with casting) can frequently be eliminated by adding a virtual function to the base class (although this approach may be impractical for generic classes, such as MFC's *CObject* or classes you cannot change). Note that special case type handling harms the extensibility of a class because creating new derived classes requires adding more special cases.

- **Provide specialized access functions.** You can eliminate the need for casting by providing specialized functions that perform the necessary casting. In MFC, for example, *CView*-derived classes always provide a specialized *GetDocument* function that returns the appropriate *CDocument*-derived object.

- **Let the compiler handle type conversions implicitly.** C++ can perform many type conversions implicitly, thereby eliminating the need for casts. You can help the compiler perform implicit type conversions by providing the appropriate conversion functions. (Unfortunately, such implicit type conversions have their own problems that you must be aware of; for details see Scott Meyers' *More Effective C++,* Item 5.) For example, given the class declarations presented earlier, the following type conversions do not require casts:

```
// compiler calls constructor without a cast
doubleObject = doubleData;
// compiler calls conversion function without cast
doubleData = doubleObject;
// can assign derived to base class without a cast
pBase = pDerived;
```

One more way to eliminate casting is to use C++ covariant return types. A covariant return type is when a base class virtual function returns a base-class type but a derived class override of the virtual function returns a derived-class type. Unfortunately, the Visual C++ compiler does not currently support this standard feature, thus eliminating it as an option.

Now, the ultimate question: If C++-style casts are so much better than C-style casts, why don't you see them often in Windows code? They are noticeably absent from MFC code, which commonly uses downcasts, as with

```
CEdit   *pEdit;
if ((pEdit = (CEdit *)GetDlgItem(IDC_INPUTBOX)) != 0)
    pEdit->GetLine(lineNumber, lineBuffer);
```

Force of habit is one explanation. The fact that C++ casts aren't used by the most popular Windows programming books is another. (Note that such sample code is rarely concerned with preventing bugs. Debugging is typically left as an "exercise for the reader.") But the ultimate reason is that using `dynamic_cast` in this situation will fail. The *CDialog::GetDlgItem* function always returns pointers to *CWnd* objects and never pointers to derived class objects, such as *CEdit*. The *CDialog::GetDlgItem* simply calls the Windows *::GetDlgItem* API function, which returns a generic window handle, and then wraps the result in a *CWnd* object. Since the Run-time Type Information indicates that the returned object is a *CWnd*, a `dynamic_cast` always returns a null pointer when cast to a derived type. Note that unlike a normal incorrect downcast, calling a member function such as *CEdit::GetLine* on a non-*CEdit* control, such as a *CStatic* control, is harmless because the function is simply a *::SendMessage* wrapper sending a message that is safely ignored. Although a `static_cast` works fine in this situation, it provides no type safety.

If you use `dynamic_cast` in Visual C++, be sure that you select the **Enable Run-time Type Information** option in your project settings. If you fail to do so, any `dynamic_cast` you make will result in an exception. The compiler will give you the obscure warning "warning C4541: 'dynamic_cast' used on polymorphic type 'class CBase' with /GR-; unpredictable behavior may result." The "unpredictable behavior" is that your program is going to crash.

If you use `dynamic_cast`, be sure to enable Run-time Type Information in your project settings.

If you are using MFC, note that *CObject*-derived classes don't use Run-time Type Information, but use their own run-time class information (RTCI)—although enabling RTTI in an MFC project allows you to use both. The MFC version of `dynamic_cast` using RTCI is the DYNAMIC_DOWNCAST macro, which returns a null pointer for invalid casts. There is also a STATIC_ DOWNCAST macro; it returns a null pointer and displays an assertion for a bad cast in debug builds but simply does the cast in release build. Unfortunately, this odd tradeoff allows you either to have robust code or to have cast bugs reveal themselves, but not both. You can eliminate this tradeoff by creating your own custom MFC cast macro as follows.

```
#define SAFE_DOWNCAST(class_name, object) \
    (class_name *)SafeDownCast(RUNTIME_CLASS(class_name), object)
CObject* SafeDownCast (CRuntimeClass *pClass, CObject *pObject) {
    ASSERT(pObject == 0 || pObject->IsKindOf(pClass));
```

```
    if (pObject != 0 && pObject->IsKindOf(pClass))
        return pObject;
    else
        return 0;
}
```

Using `const`

In one sense, using `const` is the opposite of using casts. Whereas casts remove the compiler's ability to find problems using strong type checking, using `const` adds to it. When you use `const`, you are in effect saying to the compiler "this variable isn't supposed to be modified, so make sure it isn't." The `const` attribute is best regarded as an extension to the type, making `char *` and `const char *`, for example, related but different types. Using `const` carefully throughout a program is a good way to help the compiler help you find bugs at compile time, which is far preferable to finding them the hard way at run time.

> **TIP**
>
> Using `const` carefully throughout a program is a good way to help the compiler help you find bugs at compile time.

If you have much experience using `const`, you know there is one important detail. Since you can't pass a `const` variable to a non-`const` parameter, if your program doesn't use `const` correctly (that is, if it doesn't declare all parameters that aren't modified as `const`) and you introduce one `const` variable, the impact can ripple throughout the entire program. You will then have to change many function declarations and add many `const` operators to your classes. Using `const` tends to be an all-or-nothing deal. This problem can be largely eliminated by playing by the rules and using `const` correctly from the start. Adding `const` support after the code is already written can be a real pain in the neck.

> **TIP**
>
> Using `const` is much easier if you do it from the start.

Using Loop Statements Correctly

Everyone knows what a `for` statement is and what a `while` statement is and their differences. Even so, it is not unusual to find `while` loops used where `for` loops should be used. The problem is that where

```
for (int i = 0; i < count; i++) {
  ...
}
```

is computationally equivalent to

```
int i = 0;
while (i < count) {
  ...
    i++;
}
```

that equivalence ends as soon as a `continue` statement is added to the loop because the `for` statement guarantees that the increment expression will be executed, but the `while` statement does not. Consequently, adding `continue` statements to such `while` loops is a hazardous activity because it is easy to forget to perform the increment expression. Such bugs can be especially difficult to detect if the `continue` statement is rarely executed. In my experience, `while` loops are most often used incorrectly when the initialization, test, or increment expressions are complex or the "increment" expression isn't an increment operator but some kind of *GetNextObject* function. Neither situation is a good reason to avoid using a `for` loop.

The same principle applies when more than one variable is incremented in the `for` loop, as in the following code.

```
POSITION pos;
int  line;
for (line = 0, pos = lineList.GetHeadPosition();
     pos != 0;
     line++, lineList.GetNext(pos)) {
  ...
}
```

> **TIP**
>
> Always use a `for` statement instead of a `while` statement whenever a loop has an increment expression that must be executed for each iteration.

Using Constructors and Destructors

After memory has been allocated for an object, a constructor is called to put the object in a well-defined state. Similarly, a destructor is called to perform the inverse of a constructor, typically by freeing any allocated resources before memory for an object is deallocated. Both operations present an opportunity for bugs if done incorrectly.

Constructors

You can prevent bugs in constructors by doing the following.

- Consolidate similar constructor code.
- Properly handle constructors that fail.
- Understand how virtual functions work in a constructor.

A class often has several versions of a constructor, such as a default de-structor (with no parameters), a copy constructor (with a single parameter of the same type), and possibly many other constructors with different parameters. Because the code for these constructors tends to be similar, you can eliminate the duplication and the potential for maintenance problems by calling a single protected or private helper function that does most of the work. For example, the MFC *CString* class has seven constructors, all of which call a protected *CString::Init* function.

A more difficult problem is handling constructors that can fail. Often constructors need to allocate memory, create resources, or open files, and there is no guarantee that such operations will succeed. Furthermore, constructors don't have return values, so there is no direct way to indicate their failure. One common approach (used by many MFC classes) is to break the object construction process into two steps: The first step is for the constructor to initialize the object in a way that cannot fail, and the second step is for some initialization function (such as *Init* or *Open*) to finish the job and it may fail. For example, the MFC *CFile* default constructor simply sets a file handle to zero and a status Boolean to false. The *CFile::Open* function then really opens the file but may fail.

An alternative approach is to use exceptions and have the initialization process happen in three phases, all within the constructor. The first phase is to initialize the object to a known state in a way that cannot fail. The second phase is to initialize the object using code that can fail within a `try` block. The last phase is to handle the exception in a `catch` block, if one occurs, clean up any resources allocated within the constructor, and rethrow the exception. Note that destructors are called only when an object is successfully constructed, so you cannot expect a destructor to clean up an object whose constructor throws an exception. The following is a typical example of a constructor that uses exception handling.

```
CMyObject::CMyObject (const CString &resource1,
    const CString &resource2) {
    // do safe initialization first
    m_pResource1 = 0;
    m_pResource2 = 0;

    // now do initialization that can fail
    try {
       m_pResouce1 = CreateResource(resource1)
       m_pResouce2 = CreateResource(resource2)
    }
    catch (...) {
       // Must clean up here, since destructor won't be called.
       //    Note that these delete statements would not be safe
       //    unless the pointers were initialized to 0 in the
       //    beginning of the constructor
       delete m_pResouce1;
       delete m_pResouce2;
       m_pResource1 = 0;
       m_pResource2 = 0;
       throw;       // rethrow exception to caller
    }
}
```

TIP ──

Try to handle constructors that can fail consistently throughout your program.

───

Yet another alternative is to use the C++ `auto_ptr` smart pointer template class or an equivalent, which relies on the C++ language to clean up resources instead of programmer discipline. This approach is discussed in Chapter 9, Debugging Memory. All these constructor techniques work well, so you can choose the approach that works best for you. However, your object construction will be easier to understand if you use one technique for constructors that can fail exclusively throughout your program.

You need to know that virtual functions do not behave like virtual functions within a constructor. That is, if the constructor of the base class calls a virtual function, the base class version of that function is called, not the overriding derived class version. Were this not the case and the base class called the derived class override, this would most likely lead to an access violation exception because no derived class data members would have been constructed yet. If your construction process really needs to have virtual functions act as virtual functions, using a separate initialization function is the way to go.

Destructors

Similarly, you can prevent bugs in destructors by doing the following.

- Properly handle destructors that fail.
- Make base class destructors virtual.
- Understand how virtual functions work in a destructor.

One key detail of exception handling is that an exception thrown during a stack unwind will terminate the program. Because destructors are often called while an exception is being handled, they are especially prone to this problem. An exception in a destructor that isn't handled within the destructor itself will terminate the program if called from an exception handler. Consequently, it is important to make sure that destructor exceptions are handled within the destructor, as follows:

```
CMyObject::~CMyObject () {
    // do safe destruction first
    delete m_pResource1;
    delete m_pResource2;

    // now do destruction that can fail
    try {
        FunctionThatCanThrowException();
    }
    catch (...) {}
}
```

Note that you don't have to do anything beyond catching the exception. For additional information on this subject, see Scott Meyers' *More Effective C++,* Item 11.

> **TIP**
>
> Make sure destructor exceptions are handled within the destructor.

Finally, you need to make sure that base class destructors are virtual. Doing so guarantees that the derived class's destructor is called even if the object exists as a pointer to a base class. Not making a base class destructor virtual can lead to resource leaks. As with constructors, virtual functions do not behave like virtual functions within a destructor.

Using Copy Constructors and Assignment Operators

If a base class constructor allocates resources, the class obviously needs a virtual destructor. What is less obvious is that the class also needs a copy constructor and an assignment operator as well. Marshall Cline first made this observation in the Law of the Big Three, which states that "if a class needs a destructor, or a copy constructor, or an assignment operator, it needs all three of them." The reasoning behind this rule is straightforward. The C++ compiler automatically writes a copy constructor and an assignment operator if they are not provided by a class. If the class constructor allocates resources, the compiler implementation of these functions is certain to be wrong. The need for a virtual destructor is a clear sign of this. If you don't want the class to have these functions, you can prevent the compiler from writing them automatically by declaring them in your class as `private` but not implementing them. Any use of these functions will then be reported as an error at link time.

For more information on this subject, see Chapter 30, The Big Three, in *C++ FAQs* by Marshall Cline, Greg Lomow, and Mike Girou.

> **TIP**
>
> If your class needs a virtual destructor, either provide a copy constructor and assignment operator or prevent them from being automatically generated.

The Visual C++ Compiler

The simplest way to remove bugs from a program is to have the compiler find them for you. Nothing beats having the compiler find your bugs. This section presents techniques to improve the compiler's ability to find bugs.

TIP

Prefer compile-time checking to run-time checking.

Always Use the /W4 Warning Level

Many of the programming issues presented in this chapter affect the compiler's ability to find bugs; for example, programming style is a factor. Consider the following statement:

```
if (x = 2) ...;
```

Visual C++ happily compiles this statement without warning by default. The problem with this statement is that the C++ equality operator (==) is easily confused with the C++ assignment operator (=). Without knowing the program context, it is safe to assume that the programmer actually meant

```
if (x == 2) ...;
```

To prevent this problem, many programmers use the following style:

```
if (2 == x) ...;
```

The advantage to this somewhat awkward style is that since constants are not l-values, they cannot be assigned, making the following statement result in the "error C2106: '=' : left operand must be l-value" compiler error:

```
if (2 = x) ...;
```

Of course, this style doesn't work if the left-hand operand is a non-const variable. You might want to consider using this style, but I prefer a more elegant solution, which is to use the highest compiler warning level (/W4) instead of the default warning level (/W3). If you use /W4, then the statement

```
if (x = 2) ...;
```

results in the "warning C4706: assignment within conditional expression" warning. If that statement is what you really want, you can rewrite the statement as follows to prevent the warning:

```
if ((x = 2) != 0) ...;
```

You also receive this warning if both operands are variables, as with

```
if (x = y) ...;
```

The /W4 warning level gives you the following useful warnings that the /W3 warning level does not:

warning C4100: 'id' : unreferenced formal parameter
warning C4127: conditional expression is constant
warning C4189: 'id' : local variable is initialized but not referenced
warning C4245: 'conversion' : conversion from 'type1' to 'type2', signed/unsigned mismatch
warning C4701: local variable 'name' may be used without having been initialized
warning C4705: statement has no effect
warning C4706: assignment within conditional expression
warning C4710: 'function' : function not inlined

Consequently, it is a good idea to always use the /W4 warning level.

TIP

Always use the /W4 warning level.

Always Use the /GZ Compiler Option in Debug Builds

The /GZ compiler option was introduced in Visual C++ 6.0 to help catch bugs that were often found in release builds but not in debug builds. This compiler option does the following.

- It initializes all automatic (local) variables with a 0xCC byte pattern.
- It validates the stack pointer to check for function calling convention mismatches when functions are called through function pointers.
- It checks the stack pointer at the end of a function to make sure it hasn't been changed.

The /GZ compiler option is discussed in more detail in Chapter 9, Debugging Memory.

TIP

Always use the /GZ compiler option in debug builds.

Suppressing Bogus Warning Messages

Unfortunately, using the /W4 warning level has a downside. Along with the helpful warnings, you may receive a blizzard of completely bogus warning messages as well. Many standard Windows header files result in /W4 warnings because they use nonstandard language features. Certain types of programs, such as those using Standard Template Library (STL), are especially prone to such warnings when compiled using /W4. Constant sifting through such messages can be a waste of time, and they have a tendency to hide the warning messages that are truly important. Because you want to use the highest warning level to find bugs in your code and not deal with insignificant details or problems in the standard Windows header files (which you should never change anyway), you may need to suppress certain warnings. If you are using MFC, the *Afx.h* header file largely takes care of this problem for you.

The first warning message to deal with is "warning C4100: 'id' : unreferenced formal parameter." It is quite common not to use all the function parameters in Windows programs, as in

```
void CMyView::OnMouseMove (UINT nFlags, CPoint point)
{
    // nFlags is unused, resulting in a /W4 warning
    ...
}
```

One solution to this problem is to remove the parameter name from the function declaration, which has the side effect of suppressing the warning. Some examples:

```
void CMyView::OnMouseMove (UINT, CPoint point)
void CMyView::OnMouseMove (UINT /* nFlags */, CPoint point)
```

The first version simply removes the parameter, which makes the code harder to understand, whereas the second version is better but awkward. MFC provides what I believe is a better solution (which you can easily adapt to non-MFC programs) with the following macros:

```
#ifdef _DEBUG
#define UNUSED(x)
#else
#define UNUSED(x) x
#endif
#define UNUSED_ALWAYS(x) x
```

The UNUSED macro is used when a variable is not used in the release build, whereas UNUSED_ALWAYS is employed when a variable is not used at all. These macros "touch" the variable so that the compiler considers them used, as in the following example:

```
void CMyView::OnMouseMove (UINT nFlags, CPoint point)
{
    // suppresses "unreferenced formal parameter"
    UNUSED_ALWAYS(nFlags);
    ...
}
```

The #pragma warning Compiler Directive

You can use the #pragma warning compiler directive to suppress specific warnings for your entire program, specific header files, specific code files, or specific lines of code, depending on where you put the #pragma directive. This directive is quite flexible, so you might want to refer to the Visual C++ documentation for the many ways you can use it. For example, you can suppress specific warnings for your entire project by adding a #pragma to the *StdAfx.h* file:

```
#pragma warning(disable: 4511)  // private copy constructors are OK
```

Alternatively, you can disable warnings for specific lines of code using the following technique:

```
// unreachable code caused by optimizations
#pragma warning(disable: 4702)
...
#pragma warning(default: 4702)  // restore the warning
```

As a final example, if you are including a library that doesn't cleanly compile using /W4, you can temporarily compile with /W3 using the following technique:

```
#pragma warning(push, 3)    // temporarily revert to /W3
#include "BogusLibrary.h"    // doesn't cleanly compile using /W4
#pragma warning(pop)        // revert back to previous settings
```

Because such `#pragma` directives aren't exactly self-explanatory, always give a comment that explains what a `#pragma` does and why it is necessary, as with the previous examples.

 TIP

> Always give a comment that explains what a `#pragma warning` directive does and why it is necessary.

The Compile Without Warning Rule

Many software development teams adopt a "compile without warning" rule, in which code is not considered acceptable unless it compiles without warning. (There is no such thing as a "compile without error" rule, because code with errors never compiles.) Of course, this rule is applied after the bogus warnings have been eliminated as necessary. Requiring you to remove all warnings has two advantages. It forces you to look at all compiler warnings, and it makes it obvious when a code change introduces warnings. This rule is sensible and well intentioned, but it creates two problems to be aware of:

1. Removing a compiler warning is not necessarily the same as removing a problem in the code.
2. Prematurely removing legitimate compiler warnings is a bad idea.

The first problem relates to the fact that it is easy to remove a compiler warning in a way that simply suppresses the warning but doesn't address the underlying problem in the code. Got pointers to incompatible data types? Just cast it to get the compiler to shut up. Got a signed/unsigned mismatch? Again, just cast it. Casting is the duct tape of compiler warnings, allowing you to fix just about anything. Although casting might be the right thing to do in many circumstances, you shouldn't cast without first carefully analyzing the particular code in question. By automatically casting to suppress a warning, you may be simply masking a significant problem.

> **TIP**
>
> Carefully review all compiler warnings before removing them.

The second problem is that the compiler warning may be legitimate. For example, you may receive a "warning C4100: 'id' : unreferenced formal parameter" or "warning C4101: 'id' : unreferenced local variable" warning simply because you haven't finished writing the code. Immediately changing your code just to suppress such error messages undermines the value of the warnings.

The fundamental problem with a "compile without warning" rule is that compiler warnings are desirable in helping you find bugs, so you shouldn't be in a hurry to get rid of them. The focus of handling compiler warnings should be to find problems, not to suppress the warning itself. Of course, you should immediately fix the code if you can or do something to suppress a useless warning; but if the warning identifies a legitimate problem that you will fix in the future, leave the warning alone. Consequently, I don't recommend using the /WX compiler option (which treats all warnings as errors) because it forces you to suppress all warnings immediately regardless of the circumstances.

> **TIP**
>
> Compiler warnings are a good thing. It is better to have residual compiler warnings than residual bugs in your code.

The bottom line is that a "compile without warning" rule can be helpful, especially for large programming teams, but only if the rule allows for exceptions. The ultimate goal is to remove bugs, not warnings.

Recommended Reading

Cargill, Tom. *C++ Programming Style*. Reading, MA: Addison-Wesley, 1992.   By examining some C++ programs in need of improvement, Cargill derives a small set of C++ style guidelines. The *style* Cargill refers to is not the presentation style of the code but the usage of the most fundamental features of the language, such as abstraction, inheritance, virtual functions, and operation overloading.

Cline, Marshall, Greg Lomow, and Mike Girou. *C++ FAQs,* 2nd ed. Reading, MA: Addison-Wesley, 1999.   Answers many frequently asked questions about C++ program design and implementation. The FAQ presentation style helps you find information quickly. Chapter 9, Error Handling Strategies; Chapter 10, Testing Strategies; Chapter 14, Const Correctness; Chapter 30, The Big Three; and Chapter 32, Wild Pointers and Other Devilish Errors are especially relevant to this chapter.

Kernighan, Brian W., and Rob Pike. *The Practice of Programming.* Reading, MA: Addison-Wesley, 1999.   Chapter 1, Style, consolidates the most important ideas of *The Elements of Programming Style* into a single chapter and updates them to use C/C++.

Kernighan, Brian W., and P. J. Plauger. *The Elements of Programming Style,* 2nd ed. New York: McGraw-Hill, 1978.   Although this book is old, the fundamental programming style analysis is still valuable to the modern reader. Sure, tips like "Avoid the Fortran arithmetic IF" and "Use statement labels that mean something" are pretty much useless, but by my count more than two-thirds of the tips are still relevant, especially with respect to preventing bugs. The tips warning against shortsighted efficiency improvements are particularly interesting. All the examples are in Fortran and PL/1.

McConnell, Steve. *Code Complete: A Practical Handbook of Software Construction.* Redmond, WA: Microsoft Press, 1996.   It covers practically everything related to programming, and it has a comprehensive, detailed analysis of programming style not found in any other book. Topics include function design, data design, variables naming, using fundamental data types, code organization, using conditional statements and loops, program structure, program complexity, layout and style, and documentation. Note that the examples are in C and Pascal—C++ is not covered.

Meyers, Scott. *Effective C++, Second Edition: 50 Specific Ways to Improve Your Programs and Designs.* Reading, MA: Addison-Wesley, 1998.   The ultimate resource for learning how to program correctly using C++, focusing on the fundamentals. Essential reading.

Meyers, Scott. *More Effective C++: 35 New Ways to Improve Your Programs and Designs.* Reading, MA: Addison-Wesley, 1996.   This book supplements *Effective C++*, focusing on more advanced C++ techniques.

Chapter 3

Using Assertions

In Chapter 2, Writing C++ Code for Debugging, I described what debugging was like in the early days of Windows programming. Before ANSI C, the C programming language was weakly typed and didn't support function prototypes. Windows programs were typically developed using the 16-bit medium model, in which function pointers were far by default but data pointers were near. Programmers effectively had to act as human compilers, manually scouring the code line by line to make sure that all functions were passed parameters with the right data types and pointer lengths, applying casts when necessary. Failing to find such problems invariably led to program crashes and, even worse, having to program with Hungarian notation.

Today, the situation is greatly improved. C++ is now a strongly typed language, and modern C++ compilers do an excellent job at finding such data type errors. The fact that a well-written C++ program compiles and links successfully suggests that data type errors are unlikely. Now imagine the next step: A compiler of the future that could find almost any type of programming error, anything from invalid parameter values to logic errors. Such a compiler would help make programmers much more productive and the resulting software much more reliable.

Unfortunately, it is doubtful that such a compiler will ever exist. The problem is that although compilers can statically analyze the source code for many types of problems, there are many other types of problems that require dynamic analysis. To find these bugs you have to run the program. You can't have the compiler automatically find such problems at compile time, but you can add information to your code to have the program itself automatically detect many types of run-time errors. You accomplish this goal using assertions.

> **TIP**
>
> Use assertions to detect many types of run-time errors automatically.

Here is a typical assertion statement:

```
_ASSERTE(count >= 1 && count <= MAXCOUNT);
```

This statement indicates that if the code is working correctly, the *count* variable must have a value greater than or equal to 1 and less than or equal to MAXCOUNT. If *count* has any other value, there is a bug in the code and a message box displays to inform you of the problem.

The *Microsoft Press Computer Dictionary, Third Edition* (Microsoft Press, 1997), defines an assertion as "a Boolean statement used in a program to test a condition that, if the program is operating correctly, should always evaluate as true." The characteristics of an assertion are as follows.

- An assertion is used to find run-time bugs. Assertions find program implementation errors but not other types of errors, such as user input errors, resource allocation errors, file system errors, and hardware errors.
- An assertion has a Boolean statement that indicates that an object or state is valid but not necessarily correct (more on this later).
- An assertion is conditionally compiled to exist only in the debug build, not in the release build. Specifically, assertions compile only when the _DEBUG symbol is defined (or in the case of ANSI C assertions, when the NDEBUG symbol is *not* defined). Because assertions have no overhead in the release build, they can be used aggressively without a performance penalty.

- An assertion must not contain program code or have side effects, so that the program has equivalent behavior in the release build. Assertions must not modify program variables or call functions that modify program variables.
- An assertion is intended to provide information to the programmer, not to the user.

In short, assertions are Boolean debug statements that make bugs reveal themselves to the programmer during run time.

TIP

Assertions are Boolean debug statements that make bugs reveal themselves to the programmer during run time.

Here's an interesting question: Are assertions really necessary when developing software in a protected-memory operating system such as Windows? After all, if a program has a bad pointer and it tries to dereference the pointer, the program crashes with an access violation exception. Access violation exceptions are a handy way to have bugs reveal themselves to the programmer during run time, and they don't require any additional programming effort.

TIP

Use assertions to find problems early. Try to detect problems close to their cause.

Having a program crash with an unhandled exception is certainly one way to make a bug reveal itself, but assertions have many advantages that make them well worth the extra effort. One advantage is that you can use assertions to detect a wide variety of bugs. A simple logic error does not result in an access violation exception unless things have really gone awry, but you can detect just about any type of logic error using assertions. The most important advantage of assertions, however, is that if your program makes good use of them, the detection of a bug is more likely to be closer to its cause, thus making the problem easier to understand and the correct solution easier to find. A logic error may eventually lead to an access violation exception, but there may be quite a distance in time and code between the cause and its effect. By contrast, you can pinpoint the cause of a logic error using assertions with great accuracy. The key to debugging is to know where to look to find the bug's cause. Once you know where to look, it is usually easy to fix the problem. To make your job easier, you want to find problems sooner rather than later.

The Limitations of Assertions

Although adding assertions to your code can be a powerful technique for finding bugs, it is important to understand their limitations. Let's review the definition of an assertion carefully: An assertion is a Boolean statement used in a program to test a condition that, if the program is operating correctly, should always evaluate as true. There is an important loophole in this definition that requires careful interpretation. An assertion is always true if a program is working correctly, but what happens when the program isn't working correctly? Ideally, an assertion should fail, but there is no guarantee that this will happen. An assertion failing indicates that a problem was found, but the absence of assertions failing does not indicate the absence of problems. Consequently, you can use assertions to determine that a program is incorrect, but you can't use assertions to show that a program is correct because an incorrect program can have all its assertions evaluate as true.

> **TIP**
>
> Use assertions to verify that your program state is valid, but understand that being valid is not the same as being correct.

Doesn't this fact limit the value of assertions? Fortunately, this is the way it should be. The goal of using assertions isn't to test your program or to prove that it is correct. It simply isn't practical to assert every possible condition that may go wrong. Rather, the goal of using assertions is to make sure that the program's state is valid but not necessarily correct. For example, consider a date object. If you add 10 days to January 22 and get January 32, the object state is invalid because January 32 isn't a valid date. This type of problem can be caught with an assertion. If you add 10 days to January 22 and get February 2, the object state is valid because February 2 is a valid date, but the state is not correct. This type of problem cannot be easily caught with an assertion because you would have to determine the correct value using an independent means. Similarly, a pointer is considered valid if it points to memory that can be accessed by a process, but that doesn't mean that it points to the correct memory address.

The typical assertion is a simple statement that is both easy for the programmer to write and efficient for the program to evaluate. Assertions are different from test code, and using assertions is not a substitute for careful testing, although assertions can facilitate testing by allowing you to focus on higher-level tests and help your tests reveal more bugs. Although checking for valid values is less ideal than checking for correctness, incorrect values tend to be invalid as well, especially when the code is run enough times. Consequently, assertions can find many bugs, but they can't find all bugs.

TIP

Assertions are not a substitute for careful testing.

Checking for validity instead of correctness suggests that it is not necessary to use overly complex assertions and that such assertions can even be counter-productive. Since it is impossible to prove that a program is correct using assertions, there is no real benefit to trying. Instead, think of assertions as a simple way to create barriers that bugs have difficulty crossing without revealing themselves. Use assertions to contain bugs within a limited scope. The goal of containment requires good coverage, so it is far better to have many simple assertions than a few complex ones. Since it is easier and more efficient to write code to check for validity than for correctness, not trying to prove correctness allows you to keep your assertions simple and easy to write.

TIP

Keep your assertions simple. Good coverage is more important than complex checking.

Types of Assertions

Several types of assertions are available through Visual C++. In this section, I review the assertions provided by ANSI C, the Visual C++ C Run-time Library, and the Microsoft Foundation Class (]) and Active Template Library (ATL) application frameworks.

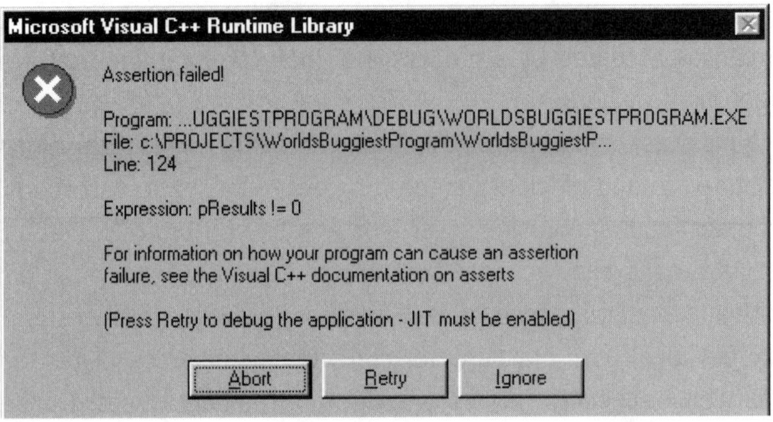

Figure 3.1   The ANSI C `assert` function displays this message box when the assertion is false.

ANSI C Assertions

The first assertion you can use is the ANSI C `assert` function, which requires you to include *assert.h* and link with the C Run-time Library:

void assert(int *expression* **);**

This type of assertion is the most portable because it is part of the standard ANSI C Run-time Library included with all C++ compilers. The Visual C++ implementation of this function displays the message box shown in Figure 3.1 when the assertion expression is false. Note how displaying a message box with options for how to proceed is vastly superior to the common technique of outputting the assertion text to `stderr` and immediately terminating the program. The assertion failed message box is much less hostile to the programmer and to those using the debug build of the program, such as testers. Always terminating the program is a severe penalty for bug detection, making widespread use of such assertions less appealing.

In the message box shown in Figure 3.1, clicking **Abort** exits the program, whereas clicking **Ignore** allows the program to continue. If you are running from the Visual C++ debugger, clicking **Retry** activates the debugger and displays the source code with the failed assertion. If you are not running from the Visual C++ debugger but have Just-in-time (JIT) debugging enabled,[1] clicking **Retry**

---

[1] To enable JIT debugging, give the **Options** command from the **Tools** menu. From the Options dialog box, select the **Debug** tab and the **Just-in-time debugging** option.

launches Visual C++, loads the program into the debugger, and displays the offending code. Either way, by giving the **Call Stack** command and examining the calling context on the stack, the values of a few relevant variables, and the contents of the **Debug** tab of the Output window, you can often readily determine what caused the assertion to fail.

One drawback to the ANSI C `assert` function provided by Visual C++ is that it may truncate the file name if the path is too long, making it difficult to tell which file had the failed assertion. Another drawback is that it is driven from the ANSI C NDEBUG symbol (specifically, it is removed when NDEBUG is defined) instead of the _DEBUG symbol used by all other Visual C++ debug code. Additionally, the `assert` function lacks the flexibility of the other assertions that are implemented using _CrtDbgReport, which allows you to redirect assertion messages. Because of these problems, this type of assertion is my last choice of the various alternatives.

C Run-time Library Assertions

You can use either the _ASSERT macro or the _ASSERTE macro. Both macros require you to include *crtdbg.h* and link with the C Run-time Library.

   _ASSERT(*booleanExpression* **);**
   _ASSERTE(*booleanExpression* **);**

Like the `assert` function, these assertion macros are also part of the C Run-time Library but are specific to Visual C++ (hence the leading underscore) and therefore not automatically portable. The _ASSERT macro displays the message box shown in Figure 3.2 when the assertion expression is false. The _ASSERTE macro displays the message box shown in Figure 3.3 when the assertion expression is false. Oddly, the _ASSERTE macro doesn't support Unicode.

To compare these assertion message boxes, note that _ASSERT and _ASSERTE versions don't truncate the file name, as the `assert` function does. Also note that the _ASSERTE macro, like the `assert` function, displays the text of the failed expression in the message box.

TIP

The _ASSERTE macro displays the failed expression, making it more convenient and providing extra protection against accidentally debugging the wrong problem.

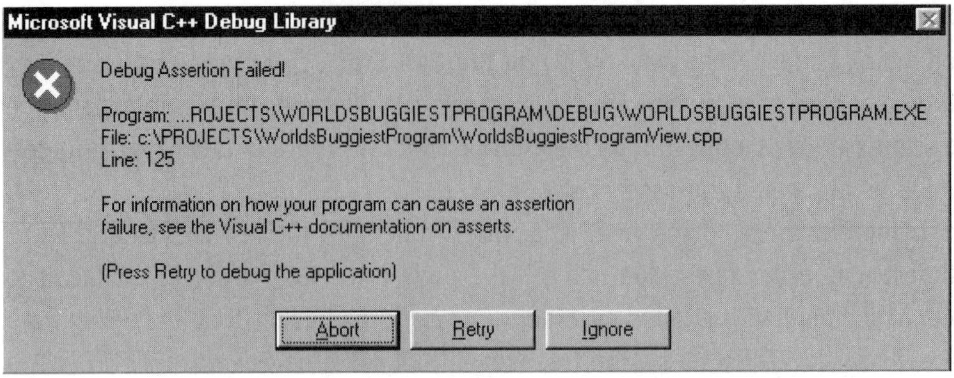

Figure 3.2 The _ASSERT macro displays this message box when the assertion is false.

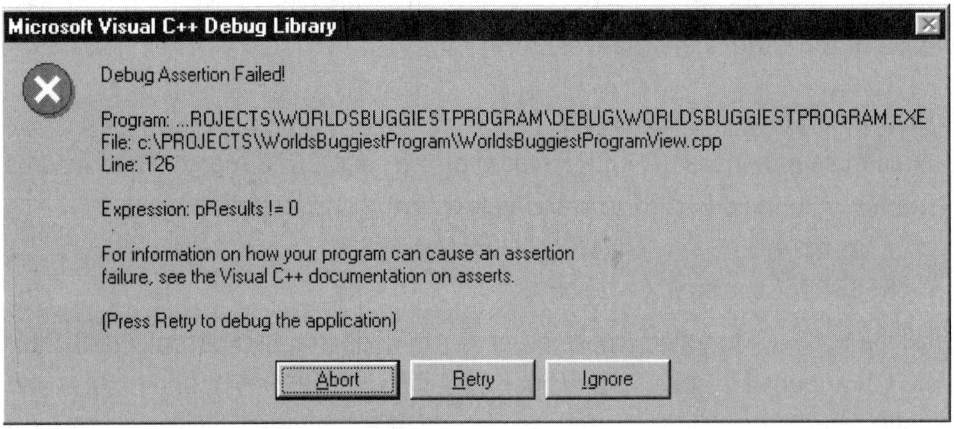

Figure 3.3 The _ASSERTE macro displays this message box when the assertion is false.

Displaying the failed expression makes the _ASSERTE macro more convenient than the _ASSERT macro. True, storing the failed expression strings in a program does make the program size larger (for example, a program with 1,000 assertions with an average expression length of 32 characters would be 32 KB larger), but keeping a program's size small isn't especially significant in 32-bit Windows (unlike in 16-bit Windows, where these strings would be stored in the default data segment). Consequently, the extra convenience of the _ASSERTE macro makes it the preferred choice among C Run-time Library assertions. Although you can easily obtain the failed expression text by locating the source code with the reported file and line number, the redundant information provides extra protection against accidentally debugging the wrong problem. For this reason, I use the _ASSERTE macro in all code examples in which the specific assertion used doesn't matter.

MFC Library Assertions

If you are using the Microsoft Foundation Class Library, you can use the ASSERT macro:

ASSERT(*booleanExpression* **);**

The ASSERT macro displays the same message box as _ASSERT when the assertion expression is false. MFC also provides several variations of the ASSERT macro and other debugging functions that are useful as assertion Boolean expressions. These MFC debugging routines are presented later in this chapter.

ATL Assertions

If you are using Active Template Library, the *ctrdbg.h* file is included by default in *Atlbase.h,* so you can immediately use the _ASSERT and _ASSERTE macros. However, if you review any ATL code, you will quickly discover that ATLASSERT is the assertion macro of choice. It is defined as follows in *AtlDef.h*:

```
#ifndef ATLASSERT
#define ATLASSERT(expr) _ASSERTE(expr)
#endif
```

As you can see, ATLASSERT is nothing but an alias for _ASSERTE. So why bother with it? Because ATL is designed so that you can easily use your own custom assertion code. For example, suppose you are debugging an ATL system component that doesn't have a user interface. For such a component, having a failed assertion display a message box might be inconvenient because it would lock up the system until someone dismissed the message box. By defining your own ATLASSERT, you can have the assertion do anything you want, such as calling the *OutputDebugString* API function or writing a message to a log file in a thread-safe manner. Note that since ATL is template based all the ATL code is compiled directly into the program so that all the ATLASSERT macros call your custom assertion. This feat is not possible in a precompiled nontemplate library, such as MFC.

TIP

Using ATLASSERT in ATL programs allows you to use custom assertions.

Assertion Source Code

Let's now take a look at the assertion source code. Here is the C Run-time Library assertion source code:

```
// from assert.h
#undef  assert
#ifdef NDEBUG
#define assert(exp) ((void)0)
#else
#ifdef __cplusplus
extern "C" {
#endif
_CRTIMP void __cdecl _assert(void *, void *, unsigned);
#ifdef __cplusplus
}
#endif
#define assert(exp) (void)( (exp) || (_assert(#exp, __FILE__,\
    __LINE__), 0) )
#endif /* NDEBUG */

// from Crtdbg.h
#ifndef _DEBUG
#define _ASSERT(expr) ((void)0)
#define _ASSERTE(expr) ((void)0)
#else   /* _DEBUG */
#define _ASSERT(expr) \
    do { if (!(expr) && \
    (1 == _CrtDbgReport(_CRT_ASSERT, __FILE__, __LINE__, NULL, \
    NULL))) \
    _CrtDbgBreak(); } while (0)
#define _ASSERTE(expr) \
    do { if (!(expr) && \
    (1 == _CrtDbgReport(_CRT_ASSERT, __FILE__, __LINE__, NULL, \
    #expr))) \
    _CrtDbgBreak(); } while (0)
#endif   /* _DEBUG */
```

Here is the assertion source code used by MFC:

```
// from Afxver_.h
#define AfxDebugBreak() _CrtDbgBreak()

// from Afxasert.cpp
BOOL AFXAPI AfxAssertFailedLine(LPCSTR lpszFileName, int nLine)
{
    // we remove WM_QUIT because if it is in the queue then the
    // message box won't display
    MSG msg;
    BOOL bQuit = PeekMessage(&msg, NULL, WM_QUIT, WM_QUIT,
        PM_REMOVE);
    BOOL bResult = _CrtDbgReport(_CRT_ASSERT, lpszFileName, nLine,
        NULL, NULL);
    if (bQuit)
        PostQuitMessage(msg.wParam);
    return bResult;
}

// from Afx.h
#ifdef _DEBUG
#define ASSERT(f) \
    do \
    { \
    if (!(f) && AfxAssertFailedLine(THIS_FILE, __LINE__)) \
        AfxDebugBreak(); \
    } while (0)
#else    // _DEBUG
#define ASSERT(f)              ((void)0)
#endif // !_DEBUG
```

A quick scan of the source code reveals why the different Visual C++ assertions are so similar: They are all basically the same code. The MFC ASSERT macro has an important advantage in its ability to display the assertion failed message box even when a WM_QUIT message has been posted. Note that a WM_QUIT message can be posted by Windows for a variety of reasons, such as when Windows is unable to create a program's main window, so the user doesn't have to quit the program for the WM_QUIT message to be a problem. Another small advantage is that it uses the THIS_FILE variable, which is defined only once per file, instead of __FILE__ symbol, which generates a copy of the file name string every time the ASSERT macro is used (although this advantage is eliminated if you use the /Gf or /GF compiler options). For these reasons, I recommend using the ASSERT macro when you are using MFC.

More MFC Assertion Macros

MFC provides several variations of the ASSERT macro and other debugging functions that are useful as assertion Boolean expressions. The VERIFY macro is a good example:

VERIFY(*booleanExpression* **);**

The VERIFY macro allows you to put program code (as opposed to debugging code) in its Boolean expression. The difference between VERIFY and ASSERT is that the Boolean expression is preserved in the release build, so only the assertion code itself is removed. The VERIFY macro is designed to simplify checking a function's return value, so that instead of writing

```
CString str;
int retVal = str.LoadString(IDS_STRING);
ASSERT(retVal);
```

you can write

```
CString str;
VERIFY(str.LoadString(IDS_STRING));
```

The VERIFY macro is typically used to check the return value of Windows API functions such as *SendMessage*, *PostMessage*, *GetMessage*, *DefWindowProc*, *ShowWindow*, *SetWindowPos*, *LoadString*, *LoadBitmap*, *GetObject*, *ReleaseDC*, and *CloseHandle*. You should never use the VERIFY macro for statements that don't contain program code because the ability to preserve program code is the only reason to use this macro in the first place. Consequently, please never do this:

```
VERIFY(count >= 1 && count <= MAXCOUNT);   // never do this
```

Here is the VERIFY macro source code:

```
// from Afx.h
#ifdef _DEBUG
#define VERIFY(f)          ASSERT(f)
#else   // _DEBUG
#define VERIFY(f)          ((void)(f))
#endif // !_DEBUG
```

Using the VERIFY macro is riskier than using other assertions. Consequently, I recommend against using the VERIFY macro for the following reasons.

- The worst mistake you can make with an assertion is to put program
  code in its Boolean expression because that code will be removed from
  the release build. Using both the ASSERT macro and the VERIFY macro
  makes it harder to build the discipline required to prevent this mistake.
  I don't want to have to debug my debugging code. I especially want to
  avoid debugging my debugging code with the release build.
- Assertion macros provide a complete separation between the program
  code and the debugging code. I find that this separation makes the code
  easier to read and understand.
- The VERIFY macro tends to interfere with defensive programming. As
  shown later in this chapter, defensive programming using an if statement together with an assertion is usually a better approach. After all, the
  VERIFY macro provides absolutely no protection against a function failing
  in the release build.

All told, I think the VERIFY macro is more trouble than it is worth.

TIP

Avoid using the VERIFY macro. Use an assertion macro instead.

Another variation of the ASSERT macro is the MFC ASSERT_VALID macro,
which is used to determine if a pointer to an object derived from *CObject* is
valid.

ASSERT_VALID(*pObjectDerivedFromCObject* **);**

Remember that being valid is not the same as being correct, so it is possible
for an incorrect object to be found valid. ASSERT_VALID determines that a
CObject-derived object is valid by calling the override of the *AssertValid* function. Although you could bypass the macro and call *AssertValid* directly, the

ASSERT_VALID macro performs several other checks as well, making it far more robust. Here is its source code:

```
// from Afx.h
#ifdef _DEBUG
#define ASSERT_VALID(pOb)  (::AfxAssertValidObject(pOb, \
    THIS_FILE, __LINE__))
#else  // _DEBUG
#define ASSERT_VALID(pOb)  ((void)0)
#endif // !_DEBUG

// from Objcore.cpp
#ifdef _DEBUG
void AFXAPI AfxAssertValidObject(const CObject* pOb,
    LPCSTR lpszFileName, int nLine)
{
  if (pOb == NULL)
  {
    TRACE0("ASSERT_VALID fails with NULL pointer.\n");
    if (AfxAssertFailedLine(lpszFileName, nLine))
      AfxDebugBreak();
    return;    // quick escape
  }
  if (!AfxIsValidAddress(pOb, sizeof(CObject)))
  {
    TRACE0("ASSERT_VALID fails with illegal pointer.\n");
    if (AfxAssertFailedLine(lpszFileName, nLine))
      AfxDebugBreak();
    return;    // quick escape
  }

  // check to make sure the VTable pointer is valid
  ASSERT(sizeof(CObject) == sizeof(void*));
  if (!AfxIsValidAddress(*(void**)pOb, sizeof(void*), FALSE))
  {
    TRACE0("ASSERT_VALID fails with illegal vtable pointer.\n");
    if (AfxAssertFailedLine(lpszFileName, nLine))
      AfxDebugBreak();
    return;    // quick escape
  }

  if (!AfxIsValidAddress(pOb, pOb->GetRuntimeClass()-
    >m_nObjectSize, FALSE))
  {
    TRACE0("ASSERT_VALID fails with illegal pointer.\n");
```

```
        if (AfxAssertFailedLine(lpszFileName, nLine))
            AfxDebugBreak();
        return;      // quick escape
    }
    pOb->AssertValid();
}

void CObject::AssertValid() const
{
    ASSERT(this != NULL);
}
#endif // !_DEBUG
```

As this code suggests, the problem with calling the *AssertValid* function directly is that it requires a valid *CObject* pointer to make the call successfully. The ASSERT_VALID macro makes sure its given object is a valid *CObject* pointer before calling *AssertValid* by checking the object for a null pointer, making sure it has a valid address, checking the object size, making sure its vtable pointer is valid, and checking the MFC run-time class object. Whenever you obtain an object derived from *CObject*, you should always call the ASSERT_VALID macro before doing anything with the object, including making any other assertions with that object.

TIP

Always call ASSERT_VALID before using a *CObject*-derived object.

Yet another variation of the ASSERT macro is the MFC ASSERT_KINDOF macro.

ASSERT_KINDOF(*className, pObjectDerivedFromCObject* **);**

Again, this macro applies only to *CObject*-derived objects. Here is the source code:

```
// from Afx.h
#define ASSERT_KINDOF(class_name, object) \
    ASSERT((object)->IsKindOf(RUNTIME_CLASS(class_name)))
```

This macro is used to verify that a pointer to a *CObject*-derived object derives from the specified class. ASSERT_KINDOF performs a run-time check similar to that performed by the C++ dynamic_cast, which is discussed in

Chapter 2. Since the *IsKindOf* function requires the class to have run-time class support (note that MFC doesn't use C++ run-time type information (RTTI)), the class must be declared with the DECLARE_DYNAMIC, DECLARE_DYNCREATE, or DECLARE_SERIAL macros for the ASSERT_KINDOF macro to work. Note that ASSERT_KINDOF does not call ASSERT_VALID, so you should always call ASSERT_VALID before ASSERT_KINDOF.

> **TIP**
>
> Always call ASSERT_VALID before ASSERT_KINDOF.

Use ASSERT_KINDOF when you obtain a *CObject*-derived object of a general type but your code requires a specific type. For example, let's look at the typical *CView::GetDocument* function:

```
class CView : public CWnd
{
    ...
protected:
    CDocument* m_pDocument;
    ...
};

CMyDocument* CMyView::GetDocument() {
    // ASSERT_VALID should be performed first
    ASSERT_VALID(m_pDocument);
    ASSERT_KINDOF(CMyDocument, m_pDocument);
    return (CMyDocument*)m_pDocument;
}
```

Given the implementation of the *CView* base class, the compiler would be happy to return any type of *CDocument* pointer from the *CMyView::GetDocument* function (after using the appropriate cast); but only a *CMyDocument* object is acceptable, and ASSERT_KINDOF enforces this restriction. In theory, you could check the type of every *CObject*-derived object to protect against invalid casts (such as all *CObject*-derived function parameters), but I prefer to leave such routine type checking to the compiler. ASSERT_KINDOF is best used for problems that the compiler will miss, such as in the previous example and with generic object collections, such as *CObList*, *CObArray*, *CMapWordToOb*, and *CMapStringToOb*. Consequently, I find that I use ASSERT_KINDOF only in unusual circumstances.

There are two more undocumented variations of the ASSERT macro:

ASSERT_POINTER(*pointer, pointerType* **);**
ASSERT_NULL_OR_POINTER(*pointer, pointerType* **);**

Here is their source code:

```
#define ASSERT_POINTER(p, type) \
    ASSERT(((p) != NULL) && AfxIsValidAddress((p), sizeof(type), \
        FALSE))
#define ASSERT_NULL_OR_POINTER(p, type) \
    ASSERT(((p) == NULL) || AfxIsValidAddress((p), sizeof(type), \
        FALSE))
```

As you can see, these assertion macros are simply convenient wrappers for asserting the MFC *AfxIsValidAddress* function. Use ASSERT_POINTER when a pointer can't be null; otherwise, use ASSERT_NULL_OR_POINTER. Note that unlike using undocumented Windows API functions, there is no risk in using undocumented assertion macros because you can always define them yourself if necessary.

Although you can put any Boolean expression in an assertion statement that doesn't contain program code or have side effects, MFC provides two functions that are ideal for assertions:

BOOL AfxIsValidAddress(const void **memoryAddress*, **UINT** *memoryBytes*,
  BOOL *isWritable* = **TRUE);**
BOOL AfxIsValidString(LPCSTR *string*, **int** *stringLength* = **-1);**

The *AfxIsValidAddress* function determines if the calling process has read access to a block of memory of the specified size (use 1 if the size is unknown) and write access if *isWritable* is true. The *AfxIsValidString* function determines if the calling process has read access to the given string of the specified length (use the default value of −1 if the string is null terminated). The following is the source code for these functions:

```
BOOL AFXAPI AfxIsValidAddress(const void* lp, UINT nBytes,
    BOOL bReadWrite /* = TRUE */)
{
    // simple version using Win32 APIs for pointer validation.
    return (lp != NULL && !IsBadReadPtr(lp, nBytes) &&
        (!bReadWrite || !IsBadWritePtr((LPVOID)lp, nBytes)));
}
BOOL AFXAPI AfxIsValidString(LPCSTR lpsz, int nLength /* = -1 */)
{
    if (lpsz == NULL)
        return FALSE;
    return ::IsBadStringPtrA(lpsz, nLength) == 0;
}
```

These functions are simply convenient wrappers for the *IsBadReadPtr, IsBadWritePtr,* and *IsBadStringPtr* API functions. Alternatively, you can use these API functions directly in assertion statements as well as the *IsBadCodePtr* API function. You can also use the Visual C++ C Run-time Library *_CrtIsValid-Pointer* function, which is nearly identical to *AfxIsValidAddress* except that it exists only in the debug build.

Custom Assertions

You may find yourself in a situation where none of the standard Visual C++ assertions quite does the job. There are several reasons why you may choose to create your own custom assertions:

- To provide portability with different types of Visual C++ programs, such as Windows API, MFC, and ATL programs
- To explain the problem by providing a problem description
- To simplify postmortem debugging by providing a call stack (you can obtain a call stack using the *StackWalk* API function)
- To have the option of throwing an exception so that the program can continue to run correctly (possibly in a degraded state) in the presence of bugs

Reviewing the previous assertion source code reveals an important fact: Writing custom assertion code is easy because the Visual C++ C Run-time Library *_CrtDbgReport* and *_CrtDbgBreak* functions do all the hard work. For example, the following custom assertions provide portability (within Visual C++), problem descriptions, and optional exceptions:

```
#ifndef _DEBUG
#define MCASSERT(expr, description) ((void)0)
#define MCASSERTX(expr, description) \
    do { if (!expr) throw exception;} while (0)
#else
#define MCASSERT(expr, description) \
    do { if (!(expr) && \
        (1 == _CrtDbgReport(_CRT_ASSERT, __FILE__, __LINE__, NULL, \
            #expr ## "\n\nProblem: " ## description))) \
        _CrtDbgBreak(); } while (0)
#define MCASSERTX(expr, description) \
    do { if (!(expr)) { \
        if (1 == _CrtDbgReport(_CRT_ASSERT, __FILE__, __LINE__, \
            NULL, #expr ## "\n\nProblem: " ## description)) \
            _CrtDbgBreak(); throw exception; } } while (0)
#endif
```

Both the MCASSERT and MCASSERTX macros allow you to supply a description of the problem. This description serves to document the problem and make it easier to understand without access to a debugger or the source code, which is especially helpful when debugging remotely. These macros display the message box in Figure 3.4 when the assertion expression is false.

The MCASSERTX macro is interesting because it throws an exception in both the debug and release builds. Throwing an exception when detecting a bug

Figure 3.4 The custom MCASSERT and MCASSERTX macros display this message box when the assertion is false.

is an interesting idea since it makes it easier to write code that is well behaved in the presence of bugs, that is, as long as the code is exception] safe. However, this macro violates one of the fundamental characteristics of an assertion, which is that it exists only in the debug build and therefore has no overhead. I leave it up to you to decide if the benefits of throwing an exception in an assertion exceed the drawbacks.

Portable Assertions

When writing portable code, you can feel free to use nonportable assertions since they are so simple to port. For example, if you are writing portable code for an MFC program and think you might need to port the code to a non-MFC environment, don't avoid the VERIFY, ASSERT_POINTER, and ASSERT_NULL _OR_POINTER macros based on their portability. You can easily port these routines or even create your own custom versions of them. For example, you can port the various types of assertion macros to any Windows C++ compiler or framework using the following macros:

```
#ifdef _DEBUG
#define _ASSERT(expr)        assert(expr)
#define _ASSERTE(expr)       assert(expr)
#define ASSERT(expr)         assert(expr)
#define VERIFY(expr)         assert(expr)
#define ASSERT_POINTER(p, type) \
   assert(((p) != 0) && _CrtIsValidPointer((p), sizeof(type), \
      FALSE))
#define ASSERT_NULL_OR_POINTER(p, type) \
   assert(((p) == 0) || _CrtIsValidPointer((p), sizeof(type), \
      FALSE))
#define ASSERT_STRING(s) \
   assert(((s) != 0) && !IsBadStringPtr((s), 0xffffffff))
#define ASSERT_NULL_OR_STRING(s) \
   assert(((s) == 0) || !IsBadStringPtr((s), 0xffffffff))
#else   // _DEBUG
#define _ASSERT(expr)        ((void)0)
#define _ASSERTE(expr)       ((void)0)
#define ASSERT(expr)         ((void)0)
#define VERIFY(expr)         ((void)(expr))
#define ASSERT_POINTER(p, type)         ((void)0)
#define ASSERT_NULL_OR_POINTER(p, type) ((void)0)
#define ASSERT_STRING(s)                ((void)0)
```

```
#define ASSERT_NULL_OR_STRING(s)          ((void)0)
#endif  // !_DEBUG
```

When porting code, don't remove nonportable assertions. Rather, port the assertion code as well.

TIP

When porting code, port the assertion code as well.

Assertion Strategy

The proper use of assertions requires a strategy. You can't just sprinkle assertions randomly throughout your code and expect them to make your program automatically reveal its bugs. Using a systematic approach leads to superior results, much better than the vague "use assertions liberally" advice that you may have seen elsewhere. While it is doubtful that I would ever recommend doing anything liberally, I find that using an assertion strategy makes it much easier to write assertion code because it allows you to follow established patterns. Don't try to make it up as you go.

TIP

The effective use of assertions requires a strategy. Don't sprinkle assertions randomly throughout your code. Instead, follow established patterns.

Consider the MFC source code itself. By my count, MFC has well over 7,500 assertions. If you have used MFC extensively, you know how effective these assertions are. Not only have these assertions helped the MFC developers find bugs within MFC itself, they are also extraordinarily effective in revealing bugs resulting from using MFC incorrectly. For example, if you have ever tried to use an MFC *CScrollView* object using an isotropic mapping mode, you have discovered immediately that mapping mode isn't allowed. Checking the source for *CScrollView::SetScrollSizes* shows why:

```
void CScrollView::SetScrollSizes(int nMapMode, SIZE sizeTotal,
    const SIZE& sizePage, const SIZE& sizeLine)
{
    ASSERT(sizeTotal.cx >= 0 && sizeTotal.cy >= 0);
    ASSERT(nMapMode > 0);
```

```
ASSERT(nMapMode != MM_ISOTROPIC && nMapMode != MM_ANISOTROPIC);
...
}
```

If you examine the MFC source code, you find that the assertions tend to follow regular patterns. The assertion strategy I propose roughly follows these patterns.

Assert the World

How do you determine exactly what to assert? After all, if you knew what bugs you were going to have in order to make the assertions necessary to find them, you probably wouldn't have made the mistakes in the first place. In his book *No Bugs! Delivering Error-Free Code in C and C++* (Addison-Wesley, 1992), David Thielen recommends that you "assert the world." I believe this is good advice as long as you interpret it correctly. You could interpret "assert the world" to mean that you should assert practically anything you can possibly think of. Taken to a ridiculous extreme, this would result in bloated, hard-to-maintain code in which every other line is an assertion, as with

```
DoTrivialAction();
_ASSERTE(TrivialActionReallyHappened);
```

For such assertions, their cost well exceeds their benefit. Again, remember that assertions are not a substitute for testing and they cannot be used to prove that a program is correct.

I have a different interpretation of "assert the world." I believe it means that you shouldn't try to predict what bugs you are going to have. You shouldn't try to select which assertions are going to find bugs; rather, just assert everything according to your assertion strategy. For example, suppose you have a date class and you determine that it is impossible for the month value ever to be greater than 12 or less than 1. You could argue that there is no need to make this assertion since the problem simply isn't possible. Even so, make the assertion anyway. Consider the following possibilities.

- A date member function is called with unanticipated input, resulting in an invalid month.
- There is a bug in the leap year logic that causes the 366th day to be in a thirteenth month.

- The date object's memory is corrupted by an error in pointer arithmetic.
- A different type of object was incorrectly cast to a date object.
- A date object is a data member of an object that was incorrectly down-cast from a base class pointer.
- While maintaining the code, you or someone else makes a programming error.
- You are wrong, and the bug is possible.

Assert the world. That is, don't try to select which assertions are going to find bugs, just assert everything according to your assertion strategy.

What to Assert

As noted earlier, I find it useful to think of assertions as a simple way to create barriers that bugs have difficulty crossing without revealing themselves. Such assertions accomplish the following.

- They check the input to a function. They validate the parameters, relevant data members, and relevant global variables. They also validate variables derived from other variables, such as dialog box controls obtained from the parent dialog box.
- They check the output of a function, especially if the output is the result of a complex process or computation. Trivial output doesn't benefit much from assertions.
- They check the current state of an object. For example, they determine if an object has been properly initialized and if the given function call or input is permitted for the current object state.
- They check logic variables by testing them for reasonableness and consistency. Such checks include checking counter and offset variables, loop invariants (which must be true for loop logic to be correct), impossible values (such as values that are illegal or out of valid range), impossible conditions (such as impossible `switch` statement cases), and variables that have a fixed relationship with other variables or constants. Any assumptions about the data and program state are also checked.
- They check class invariants, which are statements that must be true for an object of a class to be valid (more on this later in this chapter).

What Not to Assert

There are several specific situations where assertions should never be used. These situations include the following.

- Assertions must not be used to check for conditions that may be wrong but could be correct. Given the definition of an assertion, it is clear that a correctly functioning program shouldn't have any assertions fail. If an assertion fails, there should be a bug, not a potential bug. Use trace statements for potential bugs, as described in the Chapter 4.
- Assertions are not a substitute for defensive programming. Assertions do not prevent the release build of a program from crashing.
- Assertions must not be used to check for errors that are not implementation errors. Such nonimplementation errors include user input errors, resource allocation errors, file system errors, and hardware errors. Assertions are not a substitute for exception handlling, return values, or other forms of error handling.
- Assertions must not be used to report errors to the user. Assertions provide information to the programmer, not to the user. Since you ship the release build, the user never sees any assertions. Assertions are not a substitute for error messages.

As noted previously, assertions must not contain program code or have side effects so that the program has equivalent behavior in the release build. Assertions must not modify program variables or call functions that modify program variables.

Invariants

Although you can find many types of bugs by making simple assertions (such as checking a pointer parameter for null), the most powerful assertions compare fixed relationships between variables. These relationships are called *invariants*, of which class invariants and loop invariants are the most common. A *class invariant* is a fixed relationship of a data member to other data members and constants. An invalid class invariant at the end of a public member function indicates a bug in the member function's logic. Similarly, a *loop invariant* is a fixed relationship of a loop variable to other variables and constants. An invalid loop invariant at the end of a loop indicates a bug in the loop logic.

The class constructors establish the class invariant, and all other public member functions must maintain it. Clearly, the class invariant can't be valid at the beginning of a constructor or at the end of a destructor. Continuing with the date class example, the following function checks simple date class invariants:

```
void CDate::CheckInvariants () const {
    // 100 is the first valid year given the representation
    _ASSERTE(m_Year >= 100);
    _ASSERTE(m_Month >= 1  && m_Month <= 12);
    _ASSERTE(m_Day >= 1    && m_Day <= 31);
    _ASSERTE(m_Hour >= 0   && m_Hour <= 23);
    _ASSERTE(m_Minute >= 0 && m_Minute <= 59);
    _ASSERTE(m_Second >= 0 && m_Second <= 59);
}
```

In this example, all the data members are compared to constants. Note how it is better to assert the invariants individually within the *CheckInvariants* function than to have the function return a Boolean and assert the function, as with `_ASSERTE(date.CheckInvariants())`. This is because asserting the invariants individually indicates exactly which invariant failed in the assertion message box.

The problem with these invariants is that they don't check the relationship between the data members, thereby incorrectly making February 31 a valid date. You could fix this problem by adding the following code to *CheckInvariants*:

```
int daysInMonth = DaysInMonth(m_Month, m_Year);
_ASSERTE(m_Day <= daysInMonth);
```

where *DaysInMonth* returns the number of days in any month, with logic to handle leap years. This extra check might not seem like a big deal, but it is probably worth the extra effort since leap year dates are more likely to have bugs than other dates. Note that if *CDate* were derived from the MFC *CObject* base class, the *CheckInvariants* function would be named *AssertValid*. Guidelines for implementing *AssertValid* are presented later in the chapter.

Although class invariants are typically based on existing data members, sometimes it is worth adding more data members that contain redundant information specifically for invariant checking. Common examples are class signatures, such as data members that contain the size of a structure in bytes (as described in Chapter 2), and checksums, which are values calculated from the other data members to detect errors.

Class invariants are sometimes called representation invariants. The two concepts are essentially the same, but the definition of a representation invariant is a bit more precise. A *representation invariant* is a restriction on the specific *concrete* data representation necessary to correctly implement the *abstract* data type. The idea is that all classes are represented in terms of more fundamental data types. For example, the *CDate* class is represented by six integers. So whereas an integer is a concrete representation of an integral value between INT_MIN and INT_MAX (as defined in *limits.h*), the data abstraction of a month requires a value between 1 and 12, making any other value an invalid representation of a month. For another example, you could use a *CStringList* as a concrete representation of a contact name list class. The representation invariants might require that the name list be sorted, the entries unique, and the names case insensitive, all of which are not constraints of a *CStringList* object. The representation invariant concept helps you determine the class invariants by examining each data member of the representation and determining what restrictions are required for that data member to represent a valid object correctly.

Compared to class invariants, loop invariants are very simple. For example, suppose you are writing a function to add a name to a sorted contact name list. A good loop invariant is that the list must remain sorted after the new name has been added, as in this example:

```
CString itemName, prevItemName, nextItemName;
int itemCount;

// add new name
for (int item = 0; item < itemCount; item++) {
    . . .
    if (insertItem) {
        // insert item
        . . .
        // loop invariants - make sure list is still sorted
        _ASSERTE(item == 0 || prevItemName < itemName);
        _ASSERTE(item == itemCount - 1 || itemName < nextItemName);
        break;
    }
}
```

Establish invariants while you are designing your programs. Document them in your code, and be aware of them when you implement and maintain the code. In fact, it is difficult to write code correctly without understanding the invariants. Invariants are an integral part of the code's design, not something you make up just for assertions. By asserting invariants, you are simply enforcing the design constraints.

TIP

Design invariants when you design your program. Understand and document them before you write the code.

Public versus Private Functions

Your assertion strategy must vary depending on the type of function you are writing. Public member functions need to have more thorough assertions than private and protected member functions. This difference is out of necessity, not convenience. The problem, simply enough, is that whereas class invariants are valid at the beginning and end of all public member functions (with the obvious exceptions of constructors and destructors), class invariants are not necessarily valid in the middle of a public member function while the object is in the process of changing. Consider the following *CDate* public member function:

```
void CDate::SomePublicFunction (int input) {
   CheckInvariants();    // the object is now valid
   ASSERT(input <= MaxInput);

   // perform some sort of state change
   // the object may temporarily be invalid
   PrivateMemberFunction1(input);
   PrivateMemberFunction2(input);
   PrivateMemberFunction3(input);

   CheckInvariants();    // now the object is valid again
}
```

While the object is undergoing its state change, it may become temporarily invalid. If any of the private member functions were to call *CheckInvariants*, an assertion might fail. However, these private member functions can assert anything specifically required by the function, such as the validity of the parameters, the validity of relevant data members, and the validity of its assumptions. Consequently, when you use assertions to create bug-exposing barriers, erect the full barriers at the public functions and do the minimum checking at the private and protected functions.

TIP

Public member functions need to have more thorough assertions than private and protected member functions.

Assertion Patterns

The following assertion patterns show the most common forms of assertions used in Windows programs, along with the general context in which they are used. These patterns show several forms of assertions, but typically you use only the assertion that best applies to your situation, which is often the most powerful assertion that matches your data. For example, you could use the assertions

```
void ExampleFunction (CMyObject *pObject, MyStruct *pStruct,
     LPCTSTR string) {
  _ASSERTE(pObject != 0);
  _ASSERTE(pStruct != 0);
  _ASSERTE(string != 0);
  ...
}
```

but the following is a better approach

```
void ExampleFunction (CMyObject *pObject, MyStruct *pStruct,
     LPCTSTR string) {
  ASSERT_VALID(pObject);
  ASSERT_POINTER(pStruct, MyStruct);
  ASSERT_STRING(string);  // this is a custom assertion
  ...
}
```

TIP

Use the most powerful assertion that matches your data.

As in this example, I freely use the MFC-based macros I defined in Portable Assertions earlier in this chapter because they are so easy to port.

DEBUGGING STRATEGIES

Function Parameter Assertions

By far the most common assertions check the validity of function parameters. You can make the same checks for global variables that act as implicit parameters. Here are the common assertion patterns used for function parameters (the "need to document" comments are explained in the next section):

```
void FunctionWithParams (int value, int flagOrMode, BOOL boolean,
    LPTSTR string, HANDLE handle, char *pointer, MyStruct *pStruct,
    CMyObject *pObject, CNonMFCObject *pOtherObject, FARPROC
    lpfnCallback)
{
    // assertions for integers
    _ASSERTE(value <= maxValue); // need to document
    _ASSERTE(value >= minValue); // need to document
    _ASSERTE(value >= minValue && value <= maxValue); // document
    _ASSERTE(value == redundantValue); // need to document
    _ASSERTE(value == requiredValue);  // need to document
    _ASSERTE(value != illegalValue);   // need to document

    // assertions for flags or modes
    _ASSERTE(flagOrMode & REQUIRED_FLAG_OR_MODE);        // document
    _ASSERTE((flagOrMode & ILLEGAL_FLAG_OR_MODE) == 0); // document

    // assertions for Booleans
    _ASSERTE(boolean); // need to document
    _ASSERTE(!boolean);// need to document

    // assertions for strings
    ASSERT_STRING(string);          // this is a custom assertion
    ASSERT_NULL_OR_STRING(string);  // this is a custom assertion
    // use if string buffer must be a certain size
    _ASSERTE(_CrtIsValidPointer(string, charsInString, FALSE));
    // use if string is uninitialized and buffer size is unknown
    ASSERT_POINTER(string, char);

    // assertions for handles
    _ASSERTE(handle != 0);
    _ASSERTE(::IsWindow(handle));    // for window handles
    _ASSERTE(::IsMenu(handle));      // for menu handles
    _ASSERTE(GetObjectType(handle)); // for GDI handles

    // assertions for pointers
    _ASSERTE(pointer == 0); // need to document
    ASSERT_POINTER(pointer, pointerType);
```

```
        ASSERT_NULL_OR_POINTER(pointer, pointerType);
        // use 1 when size is unknown
        _ASSERTE(_CrtIsValidPointer(pointer, 1, FALSE));

        // assertions for structs
        ASSERT_POINTER(pStruct, MyStruct);
        ASSERT_NULL_OR_POINTER(pStruct, MyStruct);

        // assertions for objects derived from CObject
        ASSERT_VALID(pObject);

        // assertions for objects not derived from CObject
        _ASSERTE(pOtherObject != 0);

        // assertions for callback functions
        _ASSERTE(!IsBadCodePtr(lpfnCallback));
    }
```

CObject Function Assertions

Here are assertion patterns for objects derived from the MFC *CObject* base class:

```
    void CMyObject::PublicFunction ()
    {
        // Use only for public member functions, since private and
        // protected member functions may be called while the class
        // invariant is temporarily invalid.
        ASSERT_VALID(this); // make this assertion first
        ...
    }

    void CMyObject::PrivateFunction ()
    {
        // For private and protected member functions, assert only the
        // data members that are used by the function, not the whole
        // object.
        ASSERT_VALID(m_pUsedMemberData1);
        _ASSERTE(m_pUsedMemberData2 != 0);
        ...
    }
```

```
void CMyObject::ComplexStateChange ()
{
    // This is a complex function that is likely to have bugs.
    ASSERT_VALID(this); // make this assertion first
    ...
    // perform complex change
    ...
    ASSERT_VALID(this); // make sure object is still valid when done
}

void CMyObject::SomeOperation (CMyObject *pObject)
{
    ASSERT_VALID(this);      // make this assertion first
    // use if can't perform operation on itself
    _ASSERTE(pObject!= this);
    ...
}
void CMyObject::AssertValid ()
{
    // check the immediate base class first
    CMyObjectBaseClass::AssertValid();

    // check the data members not in the base class
    ASSERT_VALID(m_pObject1);
    ASSERT_VALID(m_pObject2);

    // now check the class invariants not checked by the base class
    // be sure to document the class invariants
    _ASSERTE(m_Value != illegalValue);
    _ASSERTE(m_Object1.GetSize() == m_Size);
    ...
}
```

Derivative Data Assertions

These MFC assertion patterns are for derivative data (that is, data derived from other data). You can use similar assertions for non-MFC derivative data.

```
void CMyObject::MFCFunctionWithDerivativeData ()
{
    CWinApp  *pApp     = AfxGetApp();
    CWnd     *pMainWnd = AfxGetMainWnd();
    CDoc     *pDoc     = GetDocument();
    CView    *pView    = GetActiveView();
```

```
        // check derivative data
        ASSERT_VALID(pApp);
        ASSERT_VALID(pMainWnd);
        ASSERT_KINDOF(CFrameWnd, pMainWnd); // use ASSERT_VALID first
        ASSERT_VALID(pDoc);
        ASSERT_VALID(pView);

        // then check data derived from the derivative data
        CFont *pFont = 0;
        if (pView != 0)
           pView->GetFont();
        ASSERT_VALID(pFont);
        . . .
    }

    void CMyDialog::TypicalDialogBoxFunction ()
    {
        CButton    *pButton;
        CEdit      *pEdit;

        // check dialog box control pointers
        pButton = (CButton *)GetDlgItem(ID_BUTTON);
        pEdit = (CEdit *)GetDlgItem(ID_EDIT);
        ASSERT_VALID(pButton);
        ASSERT_VALID(pEdit);
        . . .
    }
```

Logic Assertions

Here are assertion patterns for checking function logic and memory corruption:

```
    BOOL FunctionWithLogic ()
    {
        . . .
        switch (value)
        {
           case ImpossibleCase:    // often the default case
              _ASSERTE(FALSE);      // need to document
              return FALSE;
           . . .
        }
        . . .
        while (someLoop)
        {
```

```
    . . .
    _ASSERTE(loopInvariant); // check loop invariant
  }
  . . .

  // after a complex calculation, assert the results
  _ASSERTE(results > 0);
  _ASSERTE(results == 0);
  _ASSERTE(results <= maxValue); // need to document
  _ASSERTE(results >= minValue); // need to document
  _ASSERTE(results >= minValue &&
    results <= maxValue);       // need to docment
  _ASSERTE(results == redundantValue); // need to document
  _ASSERTE(results == requiredValue);  // need to document
  _ASSERTE(results != illegalValue);   // need to document
  . . .
  return TRUE;
}

void FunctionMessingWithMemory ()
{
  . . .
  // assert memory check if concerned about memory corruption
  _ASSERTE(_CrtCheckMemory());
}
```

Windows API Assertions

Here are assertion patterns for programming the Windows API directly. When handling messages in a window procedure, you should apply the relevant assertions when cracking messages. That is, make assertions for parameters derived from *wParam* and *lParam*.

```
LRESULT CALLBACK MyWndProc (HWND hWnd, UINT msg, WPARAM wParam,
    LPARAM lParam)
{
  _ASSERTE(IsWindow(hWnd));

  switch (msg)
  {
    case MyMessage1:
    {
       HWND hChildWnd = (HWND)wParam;
       _ASSERTE(IsWindow(hChildWnd));
```

```
        LPSTR string = (LPSTR)lParam;
        ASSERT_STRING(string);   // this is a custom assertion

        ...
        break;
    }
    case MyMessage2:
    {
        HDC hDC = (HDC)wParam;
        _ASSERTE(GetObjectType(hDC) == OBJ_DC);

        BYTE *buffer = (BYTE *)lParam;
        ASSERT_POINTER(buffer, BYTE);

        ...
        break;
    }
    ...
    }
    return DefWindowProc(hWnd, msg, wParam, lParam);
}
```

Assertion Strategy Summary

To summarize the assertion strategy, apply these assertion patterns as needed. Try to follow established patterns—don't try to make it up as you go. Select the most powerful forms of the assertions that match your data. Many types of assertions exist, but function parameter assertions are the most common, and invariant-based assertions are often the most powerful. Assert everything according to your strategy. Don't try to select which assertions are going to find bugs.

Document Your Assertions

Several of the assertions just presented have the comment "need to document." Some specific assertion statements, such as ASSERT_VALID(pObject) and ASSERT_POINTER(pointer, pointerType), are self-documenting, but the more general assertions are not. For example, if an assertion verifies an assumption or requirement, you must make sure that the assumption or requirement is clear. Consider the following code from a Windows 98 program:

```
void CExampleClass::DrawObject (CDC dc, int x, int y) {
    ASSERT(x >= -32768 && x <= 32767);
```

```
    ASSERT(y >= -32768 && y <= 32767);
    . . .
}
```

Think of how confused you might be if one of these assertions were to fail. Why are the coordinates restricted to these arbitrary limits? These coordinate range limits seem arbitrary unless you understand that unlike Windows 2000, the Windows 98 GDI coordinate system is limited to 16-bit values. Documenting the assertion solves the mystery.

```
void CExampleClass::Draw (CDC dc, int x, int y) {
    // Win 98 requires 16-bit coordinates
    ASSERT(x >= -32768 && x <= 32767);
    ASSERT(y >= -32768 && y <= 32767);
    . . .
}
```

Better yet, if you are using custom assertions that have an explanation feature (such as the custom assertions described earlier in this chapter), you can document the assertion directly in the assertion statement.

In the assertion patterns, I have identified the assertions that typically require documentation. Always document unclear assertions. After all, you know better than anyone else what the assertions mean. If there is a simple solution to the problem, document that as well. Give your coworkers (and yourself) a clue what is going on.

TIP

Always document unclear assertions. Give your coworkers (and yourself) a clue what is going on.

Implementing *AssertValid*

The MFC ASSERT_VALID macro can be much more powerful than a normal assertion, but only if you make an effort to write good *AssertValid* functions for your *CObject*-derived classes. If you use the generic code generated by the MFC ClassWizard shown below, you won't get very far.

```
void CExampleClass::AssertValid() const
{
    CObject::AssertValid();
}
```

Recall the implementation of *CObject::AssertValid()*:

```
void CObject::AssertValid() const
{
    ASSERT(this != NULL);
}
```

In short, without a good implementation of *AssertValid,* ASSERT_VALID (pObject) is the same as ASSERT(pObject != 0).

TIP Fully implement the *AssertValid* function. Don't use the default implementation provided by the MFC ClassWizard.

The *AssertValid* function is the ideal place to check an object's class invariants. The MSDN documentation suggests that the *AssertValid* function should perform a "shallow check." Specifically, it states, "if an object contains pointers to other objects, it should check to see whether the pointers are not null, but it should not perform validity testing on the objects referred to by the pointers." The goal behind this recommendation is to prevent a cascade of assertion checking that could bring the performance of the debug build of your program to its knees. For example, suppose you have a data member that is a collection of other objects and that the collection typically contains several hundred objects. Performing a "deep check" of such an object could result in thousands of assertions every time you call a function that performs an ASSERT_VALID. Such a cascade of assertions adversely affects performance, making your program harder to debug.

Although you definitely want to avoid this problem, I don't think performing a shallow check is good practice in general. Specifically, if a data member is not a collection, performing an ASSERT_VALID on it won't affect performance significantly. In addition to using ASSERT_VALID for simple *CObject*-derived data members, I would recommend using more powerful assertions for other types of pointers, such as ASSERT_POINTER and ASSERT_NULL_OR_POINTER, instead of just checking for null. Save the shallow checks only for data members that are collections. After all, *AssertValid* is your best opportunity to validate your *CObject*-derived objects; don't squander it because of misguided performance fears. You certainly shouldn't have fewer assertions in this function than any other function. Keep in mind that you can always scale back your assertion checking if the *AssertValid* functions really become a performance bottleneck. If performance is a problem, it is better to have powerful *AssertValid* functions for general usage and to use simple assertions in time-critical routines.

I recommend using the following pattern for the *AssertValid* function:

```
void CMyObject::AssertValid ()
{
    // check the immediate base class first
    CMyObjectBaseClass::AssertValid();

    // check the data members not in the base class
    ASSERT_VALID(m_pObject1);
    ASSERT_VALID(m_pObject2);

    // now check the class invariants not checked by the base class
    // be sure to document the invariants
    ASSERT(m_Value != illegalValue);
    ASSERT(m_Object1.GetSize() == m_Size);
    ...
}
```

The first step is to perform an *AssertValid* on the object's immediate base class. Doing so validates all the data members provided by the base class, so you don't need to validate them here as well. Consequently, the next step is to validate all the data members unique to the derived class. Finally, make the class invariant assertions specific to the derived class that are relatively efficient to perform. For example, if the class contains a list of values, you might want to check the size of the list and compare it to other data members. You might also want to check the head and the tail of the list to make sure they conform to the invariant. You probably shouldn't check all the items in the list unless the list is small, nor should you check the order of the items in the list because such checks are likely to take too much time.

A few additional details to consider:

- The order of the assertion checking in the *AssertValid* function is important. Make sure that a data member is valid before checking it for details.
- Programmers do not expect assertions to throw exceptions, so the *AssertValid* function must not throw exceptions. (Clearly, this is another problem with the MCASSERTX macro presented earlier.) If you must call a function within *AssertValid* that may throw an exception, handle the exception within the *AssertValid* function itself.
- Be sure to document the class invariant (even the invariants you don't check) and any assertions that may be unclear.
- As discussed in Chapter 2, some objects are constructed in two steps, in which the constructor creates a valid but basically empty object and an initialization function (such as *Init* or *Open*) creates the real object. In this case, make sure the *AssertValid* function reflects the two steps because the object is valid in either case. For example, review the following approach:

```
void CMyWindow::AssertValid () {
    // check the immediate base class first
    CWnd::AssertValid();

    // check the data members not in the base class
    ASSERT_VALID(m_pObject);

    if (::IsWindow(m_hWnd)) {
        // object has been fully constructed - now check the
        // class invariants not checked by the base class
        ...
    }
}
```

In this code, the class invariant is checked only if the actual window has been created.

Defensive Programming

Assertion statements help reveal run-time errors during debugging, but they do nothing to protect a program from run-time errors. Consider the following code to regulate the core temperature of a nuclear reactor:

```
HRESULT CReactorCore::RegulateTemperature (
        int currentTemperature) {
    if (currentTemperature < MaximumDesiredTemp)
        RemoveCoolingRods(); // remove rods - no longer necessary
    else if (currentTempurature < MaximumAllowedTemp) {
        InsertCoolingRods(); // insert rods to cool down core
        return S_HOTCORE;
    }
    else
        _ASSERTE(FALSE);       // reactor out of control
    return S_OK;
}
```

Although this code may have worked perfectly during development and testing and it may even work well in the field under normal conditions, it is a disaster waiting to happen. Were the core temperature to exceed the maximum allowed temperature during development, the assertion would indicate a problem to the programmer. However, were the core temperature to exceed the maximum allowed temperature during actual usage, the program would not do anything to address the problem. It wouldn't even notify the operators. Worse yet, if the debug build were mistakenly shipped and the assertion had the standard behavior of terminating the program on failure (an approach not used by Visual C++), the program wouldn't even run when it is most needed.

The real problem with this code is that an assertion shouldn't be used here at all. Assertions should be used to test for conditions that should never happen if the program is operating correctly. In this case, the program is operating correctly, but the reactor is not. This overheating problem must be handled; the fact that it is inappropriately "handled" with an assertion is the real bug. Assertions should be used to reveal bugs, not to handle run-time errors.

TIP

Inappropriately used assertions can result in bugs. Assertions should be used to reveal bugs, not to handle run-time errors.

Sure, this is a contrived example, and I know you would never do such a thing. But how many times have you seen code that looks like the following?

```
char * strcpy (char *dest, char *source) {
    _ASSERTE(source != 0);
```

```
        _ASSERTE(dest != 0);
        char *returnString = dest;
        while ((*dest++ = *source++) != '\0')
            ;
        return returnString;
    }

    void CExampleDialog::SetEditBoxText (const CString &caption) {
        CEdit *pEdit = (CEdit *)GetDlgItem(ID_EDITBOX);
        ASSERT_VALID(pEdit);
        pEdit->SetWindowText(caption);
    }
```

In these examples, assertions are used to notify the programmer of a bug in the program. Unfortunately, they do nothing to handle the error in the release build and result in access violation exceptions when given unexpected data. What these examples lack is defensive programming.

Defensive programming is constructing a program in such a way that it continues to function when something that isn't supposed to happen actually happens. Defensive programs protect themselves from receiving unexpected or invalid data, running in unexpected circumstances, having system failures, or even having bugs. Such programs are also described as being robust. I have often seen assertions described as a method of defensive programming. As the previous examples demonstrate, this is clearly not the case. Assertions make bugs reveal themselves to the programmer during run time while debugging (using the debug build), whereas defensive programming allows a program to continue to function in unexpected situations when run by the user (using the release build). The two concepts go together, but they are not the same.

In practice, defensive programming requires functions to detect unexpected situations and handle them by returning a "safe" value (such as false for a Boolean function or null for a function that returns a pointer or a handle), by returning an error code, or by throwing an exception. (These alternatives are discussed in detail in Chapter 5, Using Exceptions and Return Values.) Regardless of the technique used, garbage in should not result in garbage out. Specific defensive programming techniques include handling invalid function parameters and data, having a function fail gracefully when a problem is detected, checking error codes returned by critical functions, and handling exceptions. Typical problems that require defensive programming include bad input data, running out of memory or disk space, not being able to open a file, having an inaccessible peripheral device or network connection, or even having residual bugs in the program. The goal is to keep the program running, notify the user of the problem if it is significant, and continue to function, possibly in a degraded state.

TIP

> Garbage in should not result in garbage out. Rather, keep the program running, notify the user of the problem if it is significant, and continue to function, possibly in a degraded state.

Of course, programs crash for a reason, and some problems are so serious that the best thing to do is to shut down the program. For example, consider a word processing program. Suppose the user gives a command to display the About Box, and the About Box displays the user name and licensing information. Now suppose for some reason the licensing information string cannot be created. This is a trivial problem, so the About Box code should handle the problem gracefully by simply displaying the dialog box without the licensing text. Such a simple problem doesn't even require an error message. The user should continue to use the program and certainly should not lose the document. On the other hand, suppose the program detects that the document has been corrupted. This is a serious problem, and the user shouldn't be allowed to continue to edit the document or save it to an existing document file. Rather, the program should alert the user of the problem and shut down gracefully.

In his book *Writing Solid Code,* Steve Maguire stresses that defensive programming hides bugs. Although this problem is possible, it doesn't have to be that way. After all, there is nothing about defensive programming that requires you to hide bugs. If you program defensively, don't forget to use assertions. If you use assertions, don't forget to program defensively. Make the two techniques go together.

TIP

> If you program defensively, don't forget to use assertions. If you use assertions, don't forget to program defensively. Make the two techniques go together.

When combining defensive programming with assertive programming, I find that I tend to use _ASSERTE(FALSE) quite often. For example, instead of writing

```
_ASSERTE(complexExpression);
if (!complexExpression) {
    // handle error
    ...
}
VERIFY(!FAILED(retVal = SomeFunction()));
if (FAILED(retVal)) {
    // handle error
    ...
}
```

I prefer to write

```
if (!complexExpression) {
    // handle error
    _ASSERTE(FALSE);
    ...
}
if (FAILED(SomeFunction())) {
    // handle error
    _ASSERTE(FALSE);
    ...
}
```

Asserting false in such cases is easy to write and very easy to maintain because it eliminates the need for asserting complex statements with duplicate code or using cumbersome and risky VERIFY statements. The downside to asserting false is that if you are using the _ASSERTE macro or the assert function, the failed expression in the assertion failed message box provides next to no information. To get useful information, you can use one of the following approaches:

```
_ASSERTE("This object requires the MM_TEXT mapping mode." == 0);
_ASSERTE(!"This object requires the MM_TEXT mapping mode.");
```

These assertions evaluate to false but display a more descriptive message.

TIP

Consider using ASSERT(FALSE) to simplify the combination of defensive programming and assertions. For more descriptive assertion messages, consider using _ASSERTE("Problem description." == 0).

Error Handling

Assertions are not a substitute for defensive programming, but neither are they a substitute for error handling. Assertions should not be used in situations that may occur in a correctly functioning program. For example, you should never write the following code:

```
// read file
CFile file;
CString  pathName;
...    // set pathName somehow
if (!file.Open(pathName, CFile::typeText | CFile::modeRead))
    _ASSERTE(FALSE);
...
```

Failing to open a file is a problem, but it is certainly not a bug. It should not be considered unexpected, and it must be handled by the program.

> Assertions are not a substitute for error handling.

Note that if you handle such a problem with an error message, you don't need to use an assertion to locate the problem in the source code of a single-threaded program. To determine why you received an error message, just give a **Break Execution** command from the debugger or press the F12 key from the program itself (in Windows 2000 only).

Miscellaneous Tips

The following tips will help you get the most out of assertions.

Release Build Problems

There are several differences between a debug build and a release build, assertions being just one. (The specific differences are discussed in detail in Chapter 7, Debugging with the Visual C++ Debugger.) If your debug build works correctly but the release build does not, it is possible that some assertion statements have side effects. To quickly rule out assertions as a problem, try redefining the assertion macros as follows and add this code to the end of *StdAfx.h*:

```
#ifndef _DEBUG
#undef ASSERT
#undef _ASSERT
#undef _ASSERTE
#define ASSERT (expr)        ((void)(expr))
#define _ASSERT (expr)       ((void)(expr))
#define _ASSERTE (expr)      ((void)(expr))
#endif // !_DEBUG
```

If the program behavior changes, you've got an assertion with a side effect.

Always Use the /W4 Warning Level

Always use the /W4 warning level to prevent assertion errors. For example, the following statement compiles without warning with the /W3 warning level:

```
_ASSERTE(i = 42);
```

The /W4 warning level gives the message "warning C4706: assignment within conditional expression." (The implications of using the /W4 warning level are discussed in detail in Chapter 2.)

Assertions Are Code

Assertion statements are code, and they must be maintained. They also occasionally need to be debugged. As your code changes, the assertion statements and their documentation may change as well. Of course, assertions must not fail in correct code, so you must modify or remove such assertions. If a different team of programmers maintains the code, make sure they understand that they need to maintain the assertions as well.

Keep It Simple

Try to keep your assertion statements simple. Don't be too clever by doing things like placing assertions in unusual locations. Instead, try to keep the debug code separate from the program code. Remember that the more complex your assertion statements are, the more likely you will have to spend time debugging your debug code.

Don't combine unrelated checks into a single assertion statement unless you are certain you will always be able to break into the debugger (which is unlikely). If you can't use the debugger, you won't be able to tell from the file name and line number which check caused the assertion to fail. For example, note that

```
_ASSERTE(value != illegalValue);
_ASSERTE((flagOrMode & ILLEGAL_FLAG_OR_MODE) == 0);
```

is preferable to

```
_ASSERTE(value != illegalValue && (flagOrMode &
    ILLEGAL_FLAG_OR_MODE) == 0);
```

because the problem will be clearly identified by the assertion failed message.

Sometimes assertion statements (as well as any other kind of Boolean statement) can be simplified by using DeMorgan's theorem, which states that A && B is the same as !(!A || !B) and that A || B is the same as !(!A && !B).

As previously noted, complex assertions can be simplified when programming defensively by using the _ASSERTE(FALSE) statement. For example, note that

```
_ASSERTE(complexExpression);
if (!complexExpression) {
    . . .
}
```

can be replaced with

```
if (!complexExpression) {
    _ASSERTE(FALSE);
    . . .
}
```

On the other hand, try to keep the assertion logic within the assertion statement and not in the program code. Instead of

```
if (x > 0)
    _ASSERTE(y > 0);
if (x == 0)
    _ASSERTE(this);
else
    _ASSERTE(that);
```

use

```
_ASSERTE(x <= 0 || y > 0);
_ASSERTE((x == 0) ? this : that);
```

Consider Using _CrtSetReportMode and _CrtSetReportFile

The C Run-time Library and MFC assertion macros display an assertion failed message box, but this default behavior can be changed. You can use the _CrtSetReportMode function to make assertions output messages to message boxes, to the Output window, to a file, or to any combination of these options. The _CrtSetReportFile function is used to set the output file.

In some circumstances, changing the output destination is useful. For example, you can choose to have assertions both display a message box and output to a log file for testing. Log files help your testers provide accurate information in their bug reports. If you perform automated testing and want to test the debug build (since it has all those assertion statements to help you find bugs), you should direct the assertions to a file or debugger output window. This is helpful because automated testing scripts don't handle assertion message boxes well. Also, you might want to redirect assertion output when testing system components that don't have a user interface because a failed assertion would lock up the system until someone dismissed the message box.

You can also use the _CrtSetReportMode function to selectively prevent the assertion failed message box from displaying. For example, suppose you make a change to your program that results in a flurry of hundreds of failed assertions. Instead of clicking the **Ignore** button hundreds of times, call _CrtSetReportMode(_CRT_ASSERT, _CRTDBG_MODE_DEBUG) to output the assertions to the debugger output window and restore the message box output once you have fixed the problem. Since you can double-click the assertion failed messages in the **Debug** tab of the Output window, it is still easy to find the offending code. The only downside is that you can't get a call stack.

Alternatively, suppose you have failed assertions in window painting code. Having a message box display over a window while it is being painted can make drawing code difficult to debug since the window will be constantly invalidated. In this case, you can use the following technique:

```
void CMyView::OnDraw (CDC* pDC) {
    int previousReportMode = _CrtSetReportMode(_CRT_ASSERT,
        _CRTDBG_MODE_DEBUG);
    CMyDoc* pDoc = GetDocument();
    ASSERT_VALID(pDoc);
    ... // draw the window
```

```
    if (previousReportMode != -1)
        _CrtSetReportMode(_CRT_ASSERT, previousReportMode);
}
```

This approach allows you to review the code that caused the failed assertions at any time after the window is drawn without disrupting the window drawing.

Using Assertions in Library Code

The MFC library provides an excellent example of how to use assertions. If you make a mistake using MFC, there is a good chance the problem will be caught by an assertion. Clearly, there are significant benefits to using a good assertion strategy in library code. However, note that standard assertion failed message boxes display source code file names and line numbers, and MFC ships with the source code. What should you do if you want to create a debug build of your library but don't want to ship the source code?

The simplest approach is to use the _ASSERTE macro instead of the other assertions in order to provide the failed expression. Alternatively, you could combine assertions with trace statements to provide additional information, as in this example:

```
if (!string.LoadString(promptID)) {
    TRACE1("Error: Failed to load string %d.\n", promptID);
    _ASSERT(FALSE);
}
```

Clearly, the best solution is to create custom assertion macros (such as the MCASSERT and MCASSERTX macros presented earlier in this chapter) that display a complete description of the problem in the assertion failed message box itself. It is also possible to create a custom assertion macro that displays a call stack in the message box using the *StackWalk* API function. For a bonus, the custom assertion failed message box could have a **Save** command so that library users won't have to write down all the information in the message box. Not providing the source code makes assertions less effective, but you can use custom assertions to provide enough information to at least make them usable.

Checking Correctness

Although you shouldn't use assertions to check for correctness in general, there may be specific circumstances in which it makes sense to perform an algorithm two different ways and compare the results in an assertion. For example, suppose you have a very complex, highly optimized algorithm that may have bugs. You can make the following assertion:

```
result = ComplexHighlyOptimizedGoryAlgorithm(input);
_ASSERTE(result == SimpleAlgorithm(input));
```

Of course, you must make sure that calling *SimpleAlgorithm* has no side effects. Consider writing specialized, debug-only functions to perform more complicated assertions whenever necessary.

Using *GetObjectType*

You can use the *GetObjectType* API function to assert that a handle is a valid GDI object (by looking for a nonzero return value) or a specific type of GDI object (by looking for a specific return value). For example, you can assert that a brush is valid as follows:

```
_ASSERTE(GetObjectType(hBrush) == OBJ_BRUSH);
```

However, be aware that *GetObjectType* may return some surprising results. For example, the following assertion does not fail:

```
HBRUSH hBrush = CreateSolidBrush(RGB(0,0,0));
DeleteObject(hBrush);
_ASSERTE(GetObjectType(hBrush) == OBJ_BRUSH);
```

Why? Because a black brush is a stock object (which can't be deleted), so the *DeleteObject* call has no effect.

MSDN Documentation Errors

The MSDN documentation states that the *IsBadCodePtr*, *IsBadReadPtr*, *IsBad-StringPtr*, and *IsBadWritePtr* API functions cause an assertion in the debug build if given a bad pointer. This statement is incorrect. You must wrap these functions in assertion statements, as shown throughout this chapter.

Learn from Your Mistakes

Adapt your assertion strategy to match your bugs. Although the assertion strategy described in this chapter works well in general, your programs may be different. Whenever you find a bug that was not revealed by an assertion (especially a bug that was difficult to track down), ask yourself if there is a way to add or change an assertion so that the code could have revealed the bug automatically. If so, add that assertion to your code and consider modifying your assertion strategy.

Unstable Programs

If your program is unstable and it doesn't use assertions or it has a random sprinkle of assertions, stop everything and spend a day going through all the code to add assertions as described in this chapter. You'll be glad you did.

Assertions are a simple, effective, practical technique for making bugs reveal themselves during run time. They help you find problems early and easily, making the entire debugging process more productive. To be most effective, using assertions requires a strategy. Don't sprinkle assertions randomly throughout your code. Instead, follow an established pattern. You will find that the benefits are well worth the effort.

Recommended Reading

Bates, Rodney. "Debugging with Assertions." *C/C++ Users Journal,* January 1992.
A good general overview of using assertions. The description of the history of assertions is especially interesting.

Fong, Earl. "Being Assertive in C/C++." *C/C++ Users Journal,* June 1997. A good, concise overview of how to use assertions, including a summary of the various uses of assertions. His discussion of using assertions in defensive programming is especially good.

Maguire, Steve. *Writing Solid Code: Microsoft's Techniques for Developing Bug-Free C Programs.* Redmond, WA: Microsoft Press, 1993. Chapter 2, Assert Yourself, gives an excellent presentation on how to use assertions, with many practical examples. Highly recommended.

Robbins, John. "Bugslayer." *Microsoft Systems Journal,* February 1999. The custom SUPERASSERT macro, which displays the failed expression, the last error value, and a call stack.

Rosenblum, Bruce D. "Improve Your Programming with Asserts." *Dr. Dobb's Journal,* December 1997. Ten easy rules for using assertions to create more reliable software, with particular attention paid to how assertions should not be used.

Stout, John W. "Front-End Bug Smashing in Visual C++ and MFC." *Visual C++ Developers Journal,* November 1996. An excellent overview of using assertions in Visual C++ and MFC. Highly recommended.

Chapter 4

Using Trace Statements

The C Programming Language was developed in the mid-1970s as a low-level, general-purpose programming language. Although I don't know what the first significant C program was, I can tell you with confidence that it had bugs and that those bugs were debugged using `printf` statements. Similarly, Microsoft Windows was developed in the mid-1980s as a graphical user interface for IBM personal computers. While I don't know what the first significant Windows program was, I can tell you with confidence that it had bugs and that those bugs were debugged using *MessageBox* API statements.

Today, debugging a Windows program using trace statements is the modern equivalent to debugging with `printf` and *MessageBox* statements, the only significant difference being how the output is displayed. The trace statement is a primordial debugging device that has largely defied evolution. Its simplicity, flexibility, and power make it the debugging tool of choice in the most dire circumstances.

Trace statements make the execution of a program and variable values visible to the programmer. They are a way to instrument a program for observation independent of an interactive debugger, but typically they are used to supplement the information provided by a debugger. Here is a typical trace statement:

```
TRACE(_T("Warning (FunctionName): Object %s not found.\n"),
    objectName);
```

This statement indicates that a specific event happened in the code; in this case the program tried to find an object but failed. In Visual C++, trace messages are usually output to the **Debug** tab of the Output window. They can also be redirected to a file.

Use trace statements to make the program internals visible.

The characteristics of a trace statement are as follows.

- A trace statement is used to report a significant run-time event in the code. The event isn't necessarily a bug, but it could be. (Events that are certain bugs are reported using assertions.) The event might be a symptom of a bug or information useful for tracking down a bug. In addition to tracing program execution, trace statements are also used to dump variable values and call stacks.
- A trace statement is usually conditionally compiled to exist only in the debug build, not in the release build. Specifically, the *OutputDebugString* API function, the MFC *AfxOutputDebugString* macro, and the MFC *AfxDumpStack* function are compiled in all builds, but all other trace statements compile only when the _DEBUG symbol is defined. Because conditionally compiled trace statements have no overhead in the release build, they can be used aggressively without a performance penalty.
- A trace statement must not contain program code or have side effects, so that the program has equivalent behavior in the release build. Trace statements must not modify program variables or call functions that modify program variables.
- A trace statement is intended to provide information to the programmer, not to the user. They are not a substitute for error messages.

Trace statements are debug statements that make program execution and variable values visible to the programmer during run time.

DEBUGGING STRATEGIES

In short, trace statements are debug statements that make program execution and variable values visible to the programmer during run time.

In theory, trace statements aren't necessary when you are using a modern interactive debugger, but they are useful for making particularly significant code visible, such as process startup and shutdown, function failure, program warnings, and unexpected behavior. Trace statements are especially valuable when interactive debuggers don't work well, such as when debugging across machines (as with Distributed Component Object Model (DCOM)), across processes, or across programming languages (as with C++ and Visual Basic); when debugging server code that has no user interface; and when debugging remotely. Trace statements are effective for debugging program behaviors that are difficult to debug with interactive debuggers due to the Heisenberg Uncertainty Principle (see The Heisenberg Uncertainty Principle in Chapter 1, The Debugging Process), such as window activation and mouse movement messages. Finally, trace statements are also helpful in situations where using an interactive debugger simply requires too much effort, such as when tracing a specific set of Windows messages or monitoring exception handling.

To understand trace statements fully, it is important to compare them to assertions. Although their characteristics and implementation are similar, their usage is completely different. Trace statements differ from assertions in the following ways.

- **Trace statements are unconditional.** Assertions are conditional Boolean statements, but trace statements are always executed.

- **Trace statements don't directly reveal bugs.** Assertions are used to reveal bugs, but trace statements are used to reveal program execution and variable values.

- **Trace statements can be easily ignored.** By default, assertions stop program execution with a message box and require a response; trace statements are output to a debug window or file and can be easily ignored. This property makes trace statements ideal for general program instrumentation and program warnings. A good analogy is that assertions are to compiler errors as trace statements are to compiler warnings.

Although assertions and trace statements have some similarities, they are used to report completely different types of information, so they shouldn't be considered interchangeable.

Types of Trace Statements

Several types of trace statements are available through Visual C++. In this section, I review the trace statements provided by the Windows API, ANSI C++ Run-time Library, the Visual C++ C Run-time Library, and the MFC and ATL application frameworks.

Windows Trace Statements

The most basic trace statement you can use is the Windows *OutputDebug-String* API function:

void OutputDebugString(LPCTSTR *traceText* **);**

This function outputs *traceText* to the **Debug** tab of the Output window if the debugger is running or does nothing if the debugger is not running. This function is not conditionally compiled, so it is used in both debug and release builds. It is part of Windows, so it is always available, thus making it a good choice for tracing during program startup and shutdown. By contrast, the Visual C++ C Run-time Library and MFC trace statements are not a good choice for tracing program startup and shutdown because they are available only when their DLLs are loaded.

If you want to use *OutputDebugString* only for debug builds, you can accomplish this goal by using the following macros:

```
#ifdef _DEBUG
#define OutputTraceString(text)    OutputDebugString(text)
#else   // _DEBUG
#define OutputTraceString(text)    ((void)(0))
#endif // !_DEBUG
```

ANSI C++ Run-time Library Tracing

The ANSI C++ Run-time Library does not have trace statements, but it has standard character-mode output streams for tracing, specifically, the C `stderr` stream and the C++ `cerr` and `clog` streams. Two of these streams use minimal buffering to reduce the need for constant flushing. Specifically, `stderr` is unbuffered; `cerr` uses unit buffering, in which the characters are flushed after each insertion operation; and `clog` uses full buffering. Because buffered output that hasn't been flushed is lost when a program crashes, using minimal buffering is important for debugging.

Note that because these standard output streams are not designed for graphical user interfaces, they have no effect in normal Windows programs, but you can use them in console-based Windows programs. Because of this important limitation, I don't discuss these streams any further in this chapter.

Visual C++ C Run-time Library Trace Statements

The ANSI C Run-time Library doesn't have a trace statement, but the Visual C++ C Run-time Library does. You can use either _RPTn or _RPTFn debug report macros (the leading underscores indicate that these macros are Visual C++ specific), which require you to include *crtdbg.h* and link with the C Run-time Library:

_RPT0(*reportType, format* **);**
_RPT1(*reportType, format, arg1* **);**
_RPT2(*reportType, format, arg1, arg2* **);**
_RPT3(*reportType, format, arg1, arg2, arg3* **);**
_RPT4(*reportType, format, arg1, arg2, arg3, arg4* **);**
_RPTF0(*reportType, format* **);**
_RPTF1(*reportType, format, arg1* **);**
_RPTF2(*reportType, format, arg1, arg2* **);**
_RPTF3(*reportType, format, arg1, arg2, arg3* **);**
_RPTF4(*reportType, format, arg1, arg2, arg3, arg4* **);**

These macros use a `printf`-style format string and a variable number of format arguments, in which the number appended to the macro name indicates the number of format arguments. The *reportType* parameter indicates the type of report. The report type options are _CRT_WARN, _CRT_ERROR, and _CRT_ASSERT, where _CRT_WARN is for trace statements. The _RPTFn macros report the source code file name and line number where the macro was called, so you should use these versions in situations where the source code information is meaningful, which I assume is most of the time. These macros are conditionally compiled to exist only in the debug build. Interestingly, unlike *OutputDebugString*, the _RPTn macros don't support Unicode.

By default, these macros output the formatted text to the **Debug** tab of the Output window if the debugger is running; if the debugger is not running, they do nothing. However, you can change this default output behavior using the *_CrtSetReportMode* function. You can use the *_CrtSetReportMode* function to have trace messages output to the debugger Output window, to a file, to message boxes, or to any combination of these. The _CrtSetReportFile function indicates which file to output the report to. Trace messages redirected to a file are effectively a log file, which can be particularly helpful when debugging server code. Figure 4.1 shows what a trace message looks like when redirected to a message box. You don't want to redirect too many trace messages to message boxes because they quickly become annoying.

MFC Trace Statements

If you are using MFC, you can use the TRACE and *AfxOutputDebugString* macros, the *CObject::Dump* virtual functions, and the *AfxDumpStack* function. The *AfxOutputDebugString* macro and *AfxDumpStack* function are compiled in all builds, whereas the remaining routines are conditionally compiled to exist only in the debug build.

The TRACE macro has the following variations:

TRACE(*format...* **);**
TRACE0(*format* **);**
TRACE1(*format, arg1* **);**
TRACE2(*format, arg1, arg2* **);**
TRACE3(*format, arg1, arg2, arg3* **);**

Like the _RPTn and _RPTFn macros, the TRACE macros use a `printf`-style format string and a variable number of format arguments. The TRACEn versions of the macro require you to give the specified number of arguments,

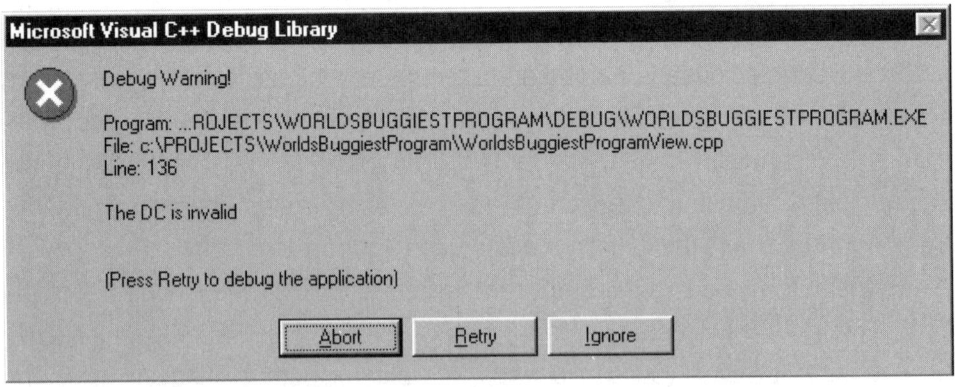

Figure 4.1   An _RPTFn trace message redirected to a message box

DEBUGGING STRATEGIES

whereas the TRACE macro allows you to use any number of arguments, as with

```
TRACE(_T("window rect l: %d r: %d t: %d b: %d\n"), rect.left,
    rect.right, rect.top, rect.bottom);
```

It is often recommended that you use the TRACEn macros instead of the TRACE macro and the MFC source code does so exclusively. The difference is that when using the TRACE macro you need to use the _T macro for the *format* parameter to handle Unicode correctly (as shown in the previous example), whereas you must not use this macro for the TRACEn versions. Since this difference is trivial, feel free to use the version you prefer.

Ironically, although MFC provides a *CString* class to handle strings of practically any length, internally these tracing functions use a fixed buffer size of 512 characters. Giving the TRACE macro parameters that require a text buffer longer than 512 characters causes an assertion to fail.

Using the Tracer Utility

The output of the TRACE macro can be turned on or off by changing the *TraceEnabled* setting in the *Diagnostics* section of the *Afx.ini* file. MFC tracing output is enabled by default. However, instead of editing this file directly, the standard way to change this value is to run the Visual C++ Tracer utility, as shown in Figure 4.2. Selecting the **Enable tracing** option turns on the tracing output.

If you do not see TRACE macro output, most likely tracing has been disabled. Run the Tracer utility, and verify that tracing is enabled.

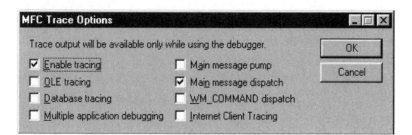

Figure 4.2   The Visual C++ Tracer utility

As you can see, many other trace options are available to control the trace messages output by MFC itself. For example, if you select the **Main message dispatch** option, MFC traces all window messages using the following code:

```
// from Wincore.cpp
#ifdef _DEBUG
    if (afxTraceFlags & traceWinMsg)
        _AfxTraceMsg(_T("WndProc"), &pThreadState->m_lastSentMsg);
#endif
```

These trace options can be very useful, such as using the **WM_COMMAND dispatch** option to trace through the MFC command message routing. The simplest way to understand what these options do is to turn them all on and see what happens. However, remember that Tracer affects only MFC trace statement output.

Use Tracer to control the trace statements output by MFC itself.

Using AfxOutputDebugString

The *AfxOutputDebugString* macro uses the same syntax as *OutputDebugString*, but internally it is implemented with the _RPT0 macro in debug builds and with *OutputDebugString* in release builds. It also handles Unicode by translating Unicode characters to single-byte characters. Disregarding Unicode string handling, the *AfxOutputDebugString* macro has the following definition in debug builds:

```
#define AfxOutputDebugString(lpsz) _RPT0(_CRT_WARN, lpsz)
```

This makes the *AfxOutputDebugString* a convenient way to use Visual C++ C Run-time Library trace statements in MFC programs.

Using CObject::Dump

All the trace statements I have presented so far are primarily for tracing program execution. The *CObject* class has a dump virtual function, so all *CObject-*

derived classes can output their values by overriding this function. For example, you can output the value of a *CObject*-derived *pObject* using any of the following statements:

```
#ifdef _DEBUG
AfxDump(pObject);
pObject->Dump(afxDump);
afxDump << pObject;
#endif
```

where *afxDump* is a predefined global *CDumpContext*. Note that *CDumpContext* supports the insertion operator (<<) for the most common built-in data types and *CObject* pointers and references. Several classes not derived from *CObject* also have insertion operators defined, specifically *CPoint*, *CSize*, *CRect*, *CString*, *CTime*, and *CTimeSpan*. Consequently, of these three dump statements, the insertion operator version is most versatile since you can supplement the output with additional text and other data, such as

```
afxDump << _T("Warning: This object doesn't seem right:\n")
    << pObject;
```

As shown in Chapter 7, Debugging with the Visual C++ Debugger, one cool thing you can do is call program functions from the Watch window. For example, you can dump an object directly from the debugger by entering the following expression in the Watch window:

```
{,,mfc42d.dll}AfxDump((const CObject*){*}this)
```

See Chapter 7 for more information on how Watch window expressions work.

For complex objects with a lot of data, such as collections, you might want to use the *CDumpContext::GetDepth* function to control the amount of data that is output. By convention within MFC, the dump virtual function does a shallow dump if the depth is set to zero or a deep dump if the depth is greater than zero. For example, the *CObList* class implements its dump function as follows:

```
void CObList::Dump(CDumpContext& dc) const {
    CObject::Dump(dc);
    dc << "with " << m_nCount << " elements";
    if (dc.GetDepth() > 0) {
        POSITION pos = GetHeadPosition();
```

```
        while (pos != NULL)
            dc << "\n\t" << GetNext(pos);
    }
    dc << "\n";
}
```

What you do with the dump virtual function largely depends on your trace statement strategy. If you primarily use an interactive debugger and use trace statements for supplemental information, you probably won't need to dump objects very often. On the other hand, if you are using trace statements in place of interactive debugging, you will probably dump objects quite often. However, as discussed in Chapter 9, Debugging Memory, you can set up the debug heap so that *CObject* memory leaks are reported using the dump virtual function, making memory leaks much easier to track down. This capability gives you extra incentive to implement the dump virtual function for your classes.

Using AfxDump

As the previous example suggests, *afxDump* is the MFC equivalent of the `cerr` stream for trace statements, so you can output trace messages directly to it. Like iostreams, it has the advantages of type safety and extensibility. Unlike iostreams, it lacks the advantage of portability. While you can port the other types of MFC trace statements to a non-MFC program simply by defining suitable macros, using the insertion operator will require you to rewrite all the trace statements. This makes the *afxDump* and insertion operator combination the least portable of the different types of trace statements.

The TRACE macros are implemented using *afxDump,* which in turn is implemented using *AfxOutputDebugString,* which in turn is implemented using the _RPTO macro in debug builds. This means you can use the _CrtSetReport-Mode function to have these trace messages output to the debugger Output window, to a file (using _CrtSetReportFile to set the specific file), to message boxes, or to any combination. You can also redirect *afxDump* directly using the following technique:

```
#ifdef _DEBUG
CFile dumpFile;    // must be a global variable
dumpFile.Open(_T("dump.log"), CFile::modeWrite |
    CFile::modeCreate);
```

```
afxDump.m_pFile = &dumpFile;
#endif
```

Alternatively, you can create another global *CDumpContext* object (such as *afxFileDump*) using this technique and use that object when you want specific trace messages to be output to a file.

Using AfxDumpStack

You can use the *AfxDumpStack* function to output a call stack:

void AFXAPI AfxDumpStack(DWORD *dwTarget* = **AFX_STACK_DUMP_
TARGET_DEFAULT);**

where the *dwTarget* parameter allows you to determine where the output is sent in debug and release builds. Output can be sent to the TRACE macro, to *OutputDebugString,* or to the clipboard. You probably want to use the AFX _STACK_DUMP_TARGET_TRACE option, which outputs to the TRACE macro in debug builds and has no output in release builds. Alternatively, if you want trace output for release builds, you can use the AFX_STACK_DUMP_TARGET_ODS option. Note that for this function to work you must have the *Imagehlp.dll* file in the path.

If you use this function, be sure to change your project settings to link using both the Microsoft format and Common Object File Format (COFF) debug information (from the Project Settings dialog box, select the **Debug Category** on the **Link** tab, and then select the **Both formats** debug information option). The COFF debug information is necessary to get debugging symbols in the call stack. Obviously, release build call stacks will not have debugging symbols unless you include COFF format debug information, which you probably won't do to keep the executable sizes small.

> **TIP**
>
> If you use the *AfxDumpStack* function, link debug builds using both the Microsoft format and COFF format debug information.

If you are not using MFC and want to output a call stack, you can write your own stack dump function using the *StackWalk* API. Using *StackWalk* is not particularly easy, so you might want to consult the MFC *AfxDumpStack* source code (in *Mfc\Src\Dumpstak.cpp*) to see how it's done.

ATL Trace Statements

ATL supports a variety of trace statements, the most basic being the *AtlTrace* function:

> **inline void _cdecl AtlTrace(LPCTSTR** *format,...* **);**
> **ATLTRACE(** *format...* **);**

As usual, this function uses a `printf`-style format string and a variable number of format arguments. Like the MFC TRACE macro, it uses a fixed buffer size of 512 characters, and giving it parameters that require a text buffer longer than 512 characters causes an assertion to fail. Internally, it is implemented using the *OutputDebugString* API function, so its output cannot be redirected. Oddly, this function is compiled to exist in all builds, but it has no effect in release builds since it compiles to an empty function. Consequently, the ATLTRACE macro is usually used in its place, which has exactly the same behavior, except it exists only in debug builds.

The ATL trace statement of choice is the *AtlTrace2* function:

> **inline void _cdecl AtlTrace2(DWORD** *category,* **UINT** *level,* **LPCTSTR**
>   *format,...* **);**
> **ATLTRACE2(** *category, level, format...* **);**

This function adds a trace category, such as *atlTraceCOM*, *atlTraceWindowing*, and *atlTraceControls*, and a severity level. Since ATL programs generally have a lot of tracing, the category and level parameters allow you to display only the trace messages you are really interested in and filter out the rest. The category values are bit masks, so you can assign a trace statement to more than one category by ORing the category bit masks. You can use any value for the severity level, but values between 0 and 4 are recommended, with 0 being the most severe. ATL itself uses levels between 0 and 2. Like the *AtlTrace* function, *AtlTrace2* compiles to an empty function in release builds, so the ATLTRACE2 macro is usually used in its place. This macro is used exclusively within ATL itself for its internal tracing.

Using ATL_TRACE_CATEGORY and ATL_TRACE_LEVEL

You determine which *AtlTrace2* messages are displayed by defining the ATL _TRACE_CATEGORY and ATL_TRACE_LEVEL preprocessor constants. All categories are output by default, but you can filter the category by defining the ATL_TRACE_CATEGORY constant using the *atlTrace* bit masks. Note that you can choose to display multiple categories by ORing these values. For example, to display all the COM method and reference count trace messages, make the following definition:

```
#define ATL_TRACE_CATEGORY   (atlTraceCOM | atlTraceRefcount)
```

By defining ATL_TRACE_LEVEL, you can set the minimum severity level that is output. Only the most severe warning level (level 0) is output by default, so most likely you will want to set this value to the least severe warning level (that is, the highest level number) you can stand. For example, to see all but the least severe of the standard levels, make the following definition:

```
#define ATL_TRACE_LEVEL   3
```

You can set the category and severity level for your entire program by defining these symbols at the top of *StdAfx.h* (before `#include <atlbase.h>`). However, note that the *AtlTrace2* function is inline, so you can redefine the symbols for an individual file or even a section of code for more precise control.

Using _ATL_DEBUG_QI and _ATL_DEBUG_INTERFACES

You can use the built-in support for tracing *QueryInterface* calls by defining the _ATL_DEBUG_QI preprocessor constant at the top of *StdAfx.h* (before `#include <atlcom.h>`). This setting traces all the *QueryInterface* calls by displaying the class name, the name of the interface being queried, and whether the query succeeded or failed.

Similarly, you can use the built-in support for tracing *AddRef* and *Release* calls by defining the _ATL_DEBUG_INTERFACES preprocessor constant at the top of *StdAfx.h* (before `#include <atlcom.h>`) instead of _ATL_DEBUG_QI. This setting traces all the *AddRef* and *Release* calls by displaying the current reference count, the class name, and the name of the interface being referenced.

The Visual C++ Message Pragma

The message pragma is essentially a compile-time trace statement that you can use to warn about potential build problems found during preprocessing. Here is a typical example:

```
#if (WINVER >= 0x0500)
#pragma message ("NOTE: WINVER has been defined as 0x0500 or ")
#pragma message ("greater which enables features that require ")
#pragma message ("Windows 2000 or Windows 98.")
#endif
```

The message pragma can be very useful, especially with complex builds. However, if you detect a situation that is a certain problem instead of a potential problem, use the #error preprocessor directive instead to stop the compilation.

Trace Statement Source Code

Let's now take a look at the trace statement source code. Here is the Visual C++ C Run-time Library assertion source code for the _RPT4 and _RPTF4 macros:

```
// from Crtdbh.cpp
#ifndef _DEBUG
#define _RPT4(rptno, msg, arg1, arg2, arg3, arg4)
#define _RPTF4(rptno, msg, arg1, arg2, arg3, arg4)
#else    /* _DEBUG */
#define _RPT4(rptno, msg, arg1, arg2, arg3, arg4) \
    do { if ((1 == _CrtDbgReport(rptno, NULL, 0, NULL, msg, arg1,\
        arg2, arg3, arg4))) \
        _CrtDbgBreak(); } while (0)
#define _RPTF4(rptno, msg, arg1, arg2, arg3, arg4) \
    do { if ((1 == _CrtDbgReport(rptno, __FILE__, __LINE__, NULL, \
        msg, arg1, arg2, arg3, arg4))) \
        _CrtDbgBreak(); } while (0)
#endif   /* _DEBUG */
```

Of course, the other _RPTn macros have the same implementation but with fewer arguments. As you can see, the implementation of the _RPT macros is nearly identical to the implementation of the _ASSERT macros, the only significant difference being that assertions have Boolean expressions where the trace statements have strings.

Here is the trace statement source code used by MFC:

```
// from Afx.h
#ifdef _DEBUG
#define TRACE                    ::AfxTrace
#define TRACE0(sz)               ::AfxTrace(_T("%s"), _T(sz))
#define TRACE1(sz, p1)           ::AfxTrace(_T(sz), p1)
#define TRACE2(sz, p1, p2)       ::AfxTrace(_T(sz), p1, p2)
#define TRACE3(sz, p1, p2, p3)   ::AfxTrace(_T(sz), p1, p2, p3)
#else    // _DEBUG
inline void AFX_CDECL AfxTrace(LPCTSTR, ...) { }
#define TRACE                    1 ? (void)0 : ::AfxTrace
#define TRACE0(sz)
#define TRACE1(sz, p1)
#define TRACE2(sz, p1, p2)
#define TRACE3(sz, p1, p2, p3)
#endif // !_DEBUG


#ifdef _DEBUG
#ifdef _UNICODE
#define AfxOutputDebugString(lpsz) \
    do \
    { \
       USES_CONVERSION; \
       _RPT0(_CRT_WARN, W2CA(lpsz)); \
    } while (0)
#else
#define AfxOutputDebugString(lpsz) _RPT0(_CRT_WARN, lpsz)
#endif
#else    // _DEBUG
#define AfxOutputDebugString(lpsz) ::OutputDebugString(lpsz)
#endif // !_DEBUG

// from Dumpout.cpp
#ifdef _DEBUG    // entire file
void AFX_CDECL AfxTrace(LPCTSTR lpszFormat, ...)
{
#ifdef _DEBUG // all AfxTrace output is controlled by
              // afxTraceEnabled
   if (!afxTraceEnabled)
      return;
#endif
```

```
va_list args;
va_start(args, lpszFormat);

int nBuf;
TCHAR szBuffer[512];
nBuf = _vsntprintf(szBuffer, _countof(szBuffer), lpszFormat,
          args);
// was there an error? was the expanded string too long?
ASSERT(nBuf >= 0);
if ((afxTraceFlags & traceMultiApp) && (AfxGetApp() != NULL))
    afxDump << AfxGetApp()->m_pszExeName << ": ";
afxDump << szBuffer;
va_end(args);
}
#endif //_DEBUG
```

Note that the weak link in the MFC TRACE macros is that the *AfxTrace* function uses a fixed 512-character buffer, making them useless for tracing large strings. This limitation is puzzling, given that stack space is cheap.

Here is the trace statement source code used by ATL:

```
// from Atlbase.h
#ifndef ATL_TRACE_CATEGORY
#define ATL_TRACE_CATEGORY 0xFFFFFFFF
#endif

#ifdef _DEBUG
#ifndef ATL_TRACE_LEVEL
#define ATL_TRACE_LEVEL 0
#endif

#ifndef ATLTRACE
#define ATLTRACE        AtlTrace
#define ATLTRACE2       AtlTrace2
#endif
#else // !DEBUG
inline void _cdecl AtlTrace(LPCSTR , ...){}
inline void _cdecl AtlTrace2(DWORD, UINT, LPCSTR , ...){}
#ifndef ATLTRACE
#define ATLTRACE        1 ? (void)0 : AtlTrace
#define ATLTRACE2       1 ? (void)0 : AtlTrace2
#endif //ATLTRACE
#endif //_DEBUG
```

```
#ifdef _DEBUG
inline void _cdecl AtlTrace2(DWORD category, UINT level, LPCSTR
    lpszFormat, ...)
{
    if (category & ATL_TRACE_CATEGORY && level <= ATL_TRACE_LEVEL)
    {
        va_list args;
        va_start(args, lpszFormat);

        int nBuf;
        char szBuffer[512];
        nBuf = _vsnprintf(szBuffer, sizeof(szBuffer), lpszFormat,
                args);
        ATLASSERT(nBuf < sizeof(szBuffer)); //Output truncated
        OutputDebugStringA("ATL: ");
        OutputDebugStringA(szBuffer);
        va_end(args);
    }
}
#endif //_DEBUG
```

The *AtlTrace* function implementation is exactly the same as *AtlTrace2* except that it doesn't filter by category and level. Like the *AfxTrace* function, the *AtlTrace* functions use a fixed buffer size of 512 characters. Unlike *AfxTrace*, the *AtlTrace* functions output using *OutputDebugString,* so their output cannot be redirected.

Custom Trace Statements

Even though there are several types of trace statements to choose from, you may find yourself in a situation where none of the standard Visual C++ trace statements quite does the job. There are several reasons for creating your own custom trace statements.

- To provide portability with different types of Visual C++ programs, such as Windows API, MFC, and ATL programs
- To output the source code file name and line number
- To filter out undesired trace statements and be able to change the filters without recompiling
- To be able to redirect trace message output to the debugger Output window, to a file, to message boxes, or to any combination, ideally using the *_CrtSetReportMode* and *_CrtSetReportFile* functions
- To handle text of any length

The _RPTFn macros have all these capabilities except filtering, so the easiest way to implement such a custom trace statement would be to add a filter to these macros. Here is one possible implementation:

```
int CategoryFilter = 0xffffffff;
int DetailLevelFilter = 0xffffffff;
#ifdef _DEBUG
#define OutputTraceString(category, detailLevel, text) \
    do { if (((category) & CategoryFilter) && \
        ((detailLevel) <= DetailLevelFilter)) \
        _RPTF0(_CRT_WARN, text); } while (0)
#else   // _DEBUG
#define OutputTraceString(category, detailLevel, text) \
    ((void)0)
#endif // !_DEBUG
```

This custom *OutputTraceString* macro adds filtering similar to *AtlTrace2* except that it uses variables instead of preprocessor constants, so you can change the filters while the program is running, using either code or the debugger. For more flexibility, you could read the initial filter values from an INI file or the registry. You could improve this routine further by making it a function and handling `printf`-style arguments. You could also improve your ability to debug multithreaded programs by including a timestamp, process ID, and thread ID with each output string.

Trace Statement Strategies

I believe the proper use of trace statements requires a strategy. Compared to assertions, trace statements are very simple (you simply output a diagnostic string), so what can go wrong? The problem with trace statements is that you can have too much of a good thing. Although very little can go wrong with an individual trace statement, the more trace messages a program outputs, the less effective they become. Suppose you are working on a project with several other programmers and each programmer adds many trace statements to help debug various problems. Furthermore, suppose these trace statements are left in the program once the problem has been solved. There aren't any problems with this approach at first, but over time the program will output thousands of trace messages, almost all of them useless. Most of these trace statements provide information to track down bugs that have already been removed. Having the program output so much useless diagnostic information slows it down notice-ably and makes finding the useful trace messages difficult. You are much less likely to notice a significant warning if it is mixed in with hundreds of insignifi-cant messages. By contrast, it's easy to find a needle in a haystack if you start with a very small stack.

There are two fundamental trace statement strategies:

- Use trace statements to supplement the information provided by an inter-active debugger.
- Use trace statements in place of an interactive debugger.

I refer to the first strategy as the Debugger Supplement Strategy; it is most effective when there are few trace statements. I refer to the second strategy as the Debugger Replacement Strategy. It is more effective when there are many trace statements, but the trace statements need to be filterable so that you can focus specifically on what you are interested in. You can combine these strate-gies in a single program by using the Debugger Supplement Strategy for general debugging and the Debugger Replacement Strategy only for situations where interactive debugging is not effective.

Debugger Supplement Strategy

The Debugger Supplement Strategy is similar to the diagnostic strategy used by your family doctor. Whenever you visit the doctor's office, he performs a stan-dard set of general diagnostics regardless of your problem (such as taking your temperature and blood pressure), and then a specific set of diagnostics for your particular ailment (such as an X-ray, blood test, or throat culture.) The general diagnostics are always useful since they can change the interpre-tation of other information if they are out of the ordinary. Once your ailment has been cured, in future visits the general diagnostics continue, but the specific diagnostics do not. At this point, the specific diagnostics are unlikely to have any value.

General Diagnostics

The Debugger Supplement Strategy works well when you are primarily using an interactive debugger, which lets you easily trace through the code and watch the program execution and variable values. Certain general diagnostics ("vital signs") can help you get a good understanding of what is really going on in the program. Such general diagnostics include

- Premature program termination
- DLL loading and unloading
- Process startup and termination
- Thread startup and termination
- Exception handling
- Function failure
- Incorrect but usable function input
- Program warnings
- Unsupported features or modes
- Unexpected program behavior

All these general diagnostics make the most notable events in your program visible. If any of these general diagnostics are out of the ordinary, you probably want to know about it—especially if you are tracking down a bug. For example, how do you debug a program that terminates while it is loading? In such a case, the program might not even get to *WinMain,* thereby making it difficult to track down the problem by setting breakpoints in the debugger. This problem can be very easy to find if all premature program termination code has a trace statement that gives the reason for termination and the source code file name and line number.

Use general diagnostic trace statements to make the most notable events in your program visible.

For an example of tracing incorrect function input, suppose you call a function that assigns text to an HTML control. HTML text is often usable even if it has several tagging errors, so tagging errors usually don't result in function failure or even an error message. Most likely you want the control to accept and display the text if it can, but you might want to know that the text has errors.

Trace statements are the perfect way to make such feedback visible. Note that while having HTML text with tagging errors could be a bug in the code, it doesn't have to be. It could be the result of an error in a file or in user input, so asserting the correctness of the tagging would be inappropriate.

For an example of tracing function failure, there are many ways in which a function can fail that aren't necessarily bugs. A function could fail if the resources required to perform the function have been exhausted or couldn't be found. A function could fail given bad user input. These problems could be bugs, but clearly they don't have to be. Again, reporting these problems with trace statements is appropriate, but using assertions is not.

Specific Diagnostics

At times you may be tracking down a specific problem that is just too difficult to find manually with an interactive debugger. Often you track down the cause of the problem by doing some type of binary search, using trace statements to help determine what to rule out. These types of specific diagnostic tracing include

- Tracing when a specific function is called
- Tracing a specific part of program execution, such as program initialization
- Tracing a specific variable value or state
- Tracing message routing for a specific message

TIP

Use specific diagnostic trace statements to track down a specific problem.

Using trace statements to track down a specific problem is best illustrated with an actual debugging example. I was developing a control that could display text using either plain text or HTML. The program was a combination of Windows API code and MFC code. The control worked fine in Windows 98, but the code that determined the size of the text had an assertion failure in Windows 2000. Here is the specific code that failed:

```
textExtent = pDC->GetTextExtent(token);
```

The *CDC::GetTextExtent* function is a wrapper for the *GetTextExtentPoint32* API function, and it fires an assertion if *GetTextExtentPoint32* fails. Checking the value of *token* in the debugger showed that it was a valid string. The value of the device context pointer also looked valid, but apparently it was not since the function failed. (What else could cause it to fail?) Interestingly, the code nearby performed other graphics device interface (GDI) operations using the same device context without a problem. Since you don't have access to the internal data structures of a device context, it is impossible to determine what is going wrong by directly examining a device context handle with the debugger. All I knew was that sometimes the device context was valid, and other times it was not. Reviewing the source code itself didn't reveal any obvious problems. Since I didn't have a clue how to find this problem directly with the debugger, it was time to do some tracing.

The first thing I wanted to determine was if the CDC device context pointer or its internal HDC handle were somehow getting corrupted and then perhaps trace back to where the corruption first occurred. I accomplished this goal with the following trace statement:

```
_RPTF2(_CRT_WARN, "TEMP: CDC: %x, HDC: %x\n", pDC,
    pDC->m_hAttribDC);
```

By placing this trace statement before and after the relevant code where the device context was used, I determined that these values weren't getting clobbered. This test ruled out simple memory corruption. Something was wrong with the device context internally. (Note that instead of using trace statements, I could have looked for memory corruption using data breakpoints, as described in Chapter 7.

I then wanted to see the extent to which the device context was corrupted, which I did with the following trace statement:

```
_RPTF0((GetObjectType(pDC->m_hAttribDC) == OBJ_DC) ?
    "TEMP: The DC is valid\n" : "TEMP: The DC is corrupted\n");
```

The *GetObjectType* API function returns the type of a GDI object after checking it for validity. Placing this trace statement throughout the relevant code showed that the device context was valid most of the time and was only invalid after calling a specific function. Here is an excerpt of that function:

```
void DrawControlText (HDC hDC, LPCTSTR text, int textLength,
        RECT *pRect, int style)
{
    CRect extentRect(*pRect);
    if (IsHTMLText(text)) {
        CDC        dc;
        CPtrList textList, formatList;
        int        lines;

        dc.Attach(hDC);
        ScanHTMLText(text, textList, style);
        FormatHTMLPage(&dc, extentRect, textList, formatList, lines);
        if (style & DT_CALCRECT) {
            ClearHTMLTextList(textList);
            ClearHTMLList(formatList);
            *pRect = extentRect;
            return;
        }
        . . .
    }
    else
        . . .
}
```

As this excerpt shows, if the text is HTML text and the *style* parameter indicates to just calculate the text rectangle (which is determined in *Format HTMLPage* by calling *GetTextExtent*), then the function sets *pRect* to the resulting extent rectangle and immediately returns. What the function doesn't do before returning is call `dc.Detach()`, so the input *hDC* device context is destroyed as soon as the *dc* variable goes out of scope. The purpose of the *CDC::Detach* function is to prevent this destruction. (Yes, it was a dumb mistake, but there was so much code involved that the problem wasn't as obvious as the excerpt suggests.) The fact that the code worked at all with Windows 98 is the only remaining mystery.

The most significant detail in using trace statements for specific diagnostics is that they are temporary. I prefixed the text of these trace statements with "TEMP:" to clearly document that fact. (Better yet, you can use "TEMP (bug ID):" to associate the trace statement with a specific bug report.) Once the problem has been solved, you should remove these temporary trace statements to prevent having useless diagnostics in the future. You don't have to remove them the minute the bug has been removed because vestiges of the bug may remain or there may be similar bugs that can use the same diagnostics. But once you are confident that the bug and all its friends have been removed, you should remove these trace statements as well.

TIP

Remove trace statements used for specific diagnostics once you are confident that the bug has been removed.

Debugger Replacement Model

An interactive debugger is the most productive tool for finding most bugs in most programs, but in some situations using an interactive debugger isn't the best approach. Such situations may include

- Debugging servers
- Debugging across machines (as with DCOM)
- Debugging across programming languages (as with C++ and Visual Basic)
- Debugging across processes
- Debugging threads
- Debugging remotely
- Debugging program behaviors that are difficult to debug due to the Heisenberg Uncertainty Principle

TIP

When necessary, use trace statements to track down a problem without a debugger.

In these situations, the best approach often is to debug using trace statements. Trace statements are effective in such situations because they don't require a debugger, they can output more information than can be produced manually, and they don't affect the execution of the program significantly, thus bypassing problems related to the Heisenberg Uncertainty Principle. (As shown in Chapter 10, Debugging Multithreaded Programs, trace statement output is serialized, so using trace statements can affect the relative timing between

DEBUGGING STRATEGIES

threads. Consequently, multithreaded programs with trace statements behave differently when run with a debugger.) Note that these trace statements differ from the specific diagnostics just discussed in that they are general in nature, so they should not be removed from the program.

The first key to success in the Debugger Replacement Model is to output as much useful information as you can for the types of problems in which an interactive debugger falls short. For example, transaction-based servers typically trace when a transaction starts, when a transaction ends, and when and why a transaction fails. Since this is likely to be an overwhelming amount of information, the second key to success is to be able to filter the trace messages so that you can focus specifically on what you are interested in. The filtering mechanisms used by the *AtlTrace2* function or the custom *OutputTraceString* macro presented earlier are ideal.

Since the ATL trace statements support filtering, perhaps the best example of the Debugger Replacement Model is ATL itself. Whereas MFC is used to create Windows programs with full user interfaces, ATL is used to create COM components. Typically, these components provide some kind of service and have little or no user interface. These COM components can use multiple threads, multiple processes, and multiple programming languages. They can also be distributed across multiple machines using DCOM.

Analyzing the source code, it is interesting to note that where MFC has more than twelve assertions for every one trace statement, ATL has less than two assertions for every trace statement. These trace statements are used to trace the execution of significant events (such as getting and setting properties, destroying windows, and creating database sessions) and to trace when a function fails. Many situations that return an E_FAIL, E_OUTOFMEMORY, E_INVALIDARG, or E_UNEXPECTED result code are made visible with a trace message. Consider how impractical it would be to set a breakpoint on every function failure using an interactive debugger.

Miscellaneous Tips

The following sections discuss tips that will help you get the most out of trace statements.

Get a DBWIN-Like Utility

The 16-bit versions of Visual C++ had a handy utility called DBWIN that allowed you to view trace statements independently of a debugger. This utility was especially useful when debugging remotely because it allowed users to capture your program's trace statement output and send it to you. The bad news is that the way Windows handles *OutputDebugString* internally has changed so much that the original DBWIN utility no longer works for 32-bit programs. The good news is that there are several 32-bit utilities that provide similar capabilities. Perhaps the best is a program called DebugView from Systems Internals, which works for both Windows 2000 and Windows 98. You can download this program from *www.sysinternals.com*. The only caveat is that this program does not appear to handle the output of *AfxDumpStack* well.

Consider Providing a Redirection Setting

Perhaps a better alternative to using a DBWIN utility is to have users of the debug build redirect the trace messages to a file, which you can do if you are using the Visual C++ C Run-time Library _RPTn and _RPTFn macros and the MFC TRACE macro. By putting a trace statement redirection setting for your program in an INI file or the registry, you can have users redirect the trace messages as needed.

Handling Long Strings

The MFC TRACE macro and the ATL ATLTRACE macros use a fixed buffer size of 512 characters. Normally this is not a problem, but in some circumstances you need to dump very long strings, such as Structured Query Language (SQL) statements. As I mentioned previously, one approach is to use a custom trace statement. However, you can dump long strings using standard trace statements as well. When using MFC, the easiest approach is to trace directly using *afxDump* and the insertion operator:

```
TRACE(longString);      // asserts if _tcslen(longString) > 511
#ifdef _DEBUG
afxDump << longString; // doesn't assert for long strings
#endif
```

When using ATL, the easiest approach is to trace directly using *OutputDebug String*.

```
ATLTRACE(longString);      // asserts if _tcslen(longString) > 511
#ifdef _DEBUG
OutputDebugString(longString); // doesn't assert for long strings
#endif
```

In both cases you need to conditionally compile the trace statements for debug builds only, as shown.

Handling Large Trace Output

The Visual C++ Output window has a limited buffer size, so if trace message data comes in faster than it is processed, the buffer becomes full and data is lost. A simple way to avoid this problem is to call the *Sleep* API function (such as `Sleep(100)`) in code that dumps a lot of data, such as object dump functions.

Making Debug Reports

The _RPTn macros are called *debug report* macros. I find it useful to think of trace statements as a way to create debug reports, which means that the presentation of trace messages is important. You can improve the readability of trace messages by using tab characters to show the relationship between message lines. You can also improve the searchability of trace messages by consistently using prefixes that indicate the type of trace message. For example, you can prefix all trace messages used to supplement function failures with "Error (function name):", all warnings with "Warning (function name):", and so on. This way you can quickly filter out the trace messages you aren't interested in with a text processing tool such as the Visual C++ **Find in Files** command.

Output Individual Lines and Don't Forget the Newline Characters

Trace statements are like `printf` statements in that their output is appended to the current line. Consequently, you might be tempted to use multiple trace statements to compose a single line instead of formatting the text using an intermediate string, as in the following example.

```
OutputDebugString(_T("The variable name is "));
OutputDebugString(variableName);
OutputDebugString(_T("\n"));
```

This approach turns out to be a bad idea for two reasons. The first is that, although this technique works well for single-threaded programs, the output can become garbled in multithreaded programs. The output of *OutputDebugString* is serialized between multiple threads, guaranteeing correct output for individual statements but not for multiple statements. The second problem with this approach is that some DBWIN-like utilities prefix each output string with timestamps and process and thread IDs, thereby garbling strings that are output in pieces.

Also, remember that to create a new line, you must output a newline character. While this idea is simple enough, I find this is the mistake I make most often with trace statements.

Don't Forget to Check the Trace Statements

The good news about trace statements is that they can make the most notable events in your program visible in an unobtrusive way that is easy to ignore. The bad news is that trace messages are too easy to ignore. In fact, trace messages are so easy to ignore that you can easily get into the habit of not looking at them at all. Although your program's trace messages are not useful for every type of bug, you need to get in the habit of reviewing the trace messages whenever you have a bug that requires more information. Often that extra information is right there in the trace messages—all you have to do is look.

> **TIP**
>
> Be sure to check the trace messages whenever you have a bug that requires more information.

Recommended Reading

DiLascia, Paul. "C++ Q & A." *Microsoft Systems Journal,* April 1997. Presents TRACEWIN, a DBWIN-like DLL specifically for tracing MFC programs.

Plooy, Ton. "A dbwin Utility for Win95." *Windows Developer's Journal,* December 1996. Presents dbwin32, a DBWIN-like utility for Windows 98/95 that uses a virtual device driver and a console program.

Robbins, John. "Bugslayer." *Microsoft Systems Journal,* June 1999. Presents LIMODS, a utility that allows you to control trace statement output by limiting *OutputDebugString* output on a source code file basis. This utility works for Windows 2000 only.

Robbins, John. "Bugslayer." *Microsoft Systems Journal,* December 1997. Presents TraceSrv, a DBWIN-like program what works in 32-bit Windows. It outputs all trace statements of a program to a single window, even if the program is distributed across several machines. Clearly valuable for debugging DCOM programs. The version in this article works for Windows 2000 only.

Tucker, Andrew. "A DBWin32 Debugger for Windows." *C/C++ Users Journal,* October 1996. Presents DBWin32, a DBWIN-like utility for Windows 2000 and Windows 98.

Chapter 5

Using Exceptions
and Return Values

To return status information in a C++ program, you can use either exceptions or return values. In the early days of C programming, the best way to return a function's status was through its return value. The programmer using the function then had to check the return value to determine if the function behaved as expected. The Windows API, being C based, uses a variation of this technique in which an API function returns a special value to indicate an error and the specific error code is obtained by calling the *GetLastError* API function.

This status-handling mechanism is simple enough, but it has two glaring problems. The first problem occurs when programmers don't bother to check the return values. For example, consider the following code:

```
_tprintf(_T("This program might fail without warning!\n"));
```

Of course, the _tprintf function formats the input text and then writes it to the standard output stream. What if the standard output stream is full and can't accept any more input? The _tprintf function handles this situation by returning the number of characters it has written or a negative value to indicate an error. But when was the last time you saw code that checked _tprintf (or any other form of printf) for its return value? The problem rarely happens, so programmers just don't bother. I certainly don't.

You might argue that _tprintf is a relatively trivial function and most of the time you don't care too much if the function fails. That's a good excuse, but what about the Windows API? Certainly there are many Windows API functions that present real problems if they fail. Now review a typical Windows program and see how consistently API return values are checked. (Technically, you should check all Windows APIs that don't return void for error.) Then review how frequently *GetLastError* is called. Considering that most Windows API functions can fail (only a few cannot), you should find these results disturbing.

The second problem with return values is when programmers *do* bother to check them. For example, consider the following code:

```
if (_tprintf(_T("This code checks all return values, \n")) < 0) {
    // handle problem
    ...
}
else if (_tprintf(_T("but most of it is error handling!\n")) < 0) {
    // handle problem
    ...
}
```

The problem with this approach is that the program becomes cluttered with error-handling code, often to the point where most of the code is actually for handling errors. This makes the code more complex and difficult to understand and maintain and, therefore, more susceptible to bugs. It also relies completely on strict programmer discipline, in which any accidental slips can undermine the integrity of the error-handling mechanism. The programmer must constantly check for exceptional conditions everywhere they might occur, even if they almost never happen.

TIP

Using return values for error handling requires strict programmer discipline, which is undesirable whether programmers have that discipline or not.

Enter exceptions. C++ exceptions allow you to solve both problems grace-fully using the following mechanism:

```
try {
    // code that may fail
}
catch (...) {
    // handle the failure
}
```

One clear benefit of exceptions is that they allow a complete separation of pro-gram code from error-handling code, thereby simplifying the program code be-cause you don't have to constantly check function return values. Another benefit of exceptions is that they don't require strict programmer discipline. Exceptions signal errors in a way that a program can't ignore.

> Exceptions allow a complete separation of program code from error-handling code by signaling errors in a way that a program can't ignore.

Incorrect Error Handling Results in Bugs

So what does all this have to do with debugging? After all, unlike assertions and trace statements, which are clearly related to debugging, error handling is more of a C++ programming issue than a debugging issue, isn't it? These questions are best answered by looking at a real-world example.

On June 4, 1996, the maiden flight of the Ariane 5 launcher ended in cat-astrophic failure. Here is an excerpt from the European Space Agency (ESA)/Centre National d'Etudes Spatiales (CNES) joint press release for Ariane 501 that reported the cause of the failure (with emphasis added):

> Only about 40 seconds after initiation of the flight sequence, at an altitude of about 3700 m, the launcher veered off its flight path, broke up and exploded. The origin of the failure was rapidly narrowed down to the flight control system and more particularly to the Inertial Reference Systems (SRI), which obviously ceased to function almost simultaneously at around H0 + 36.7 seconds.
>
> Based on the extensive documentation and data on the Ariane 501 failure made available to the Board, the following chain of events, their inter-relations and causes have been established, starting with the destruction of the launcher and tracing back in time toward the primary cause.

- The launcher started to disintegrate at about H0 + 39 seconds because of high aerodynamic loads due to an angle of attack of more than 20 degrees that led to separation of the boosters from the main stage, in turn triggering the self-destruct system of the launcher.
- This angle of attack was caused by full nozzle deflections of the solid boosters and the Vulcain main engine.
- These nozzle deflections were commanded by the On-Board Computer (OBC) software on the basis of data transmitted by the active Inertial Reference System (SRI 2). Part of these data at that time did not contain proper flight data, but showed a diagnostic bit pattern of the computer of the SRI 2, which was interpreted as flight data.
- The reason why the active SRI 2 did not send correct attitude data was that the unit had declared a **failure due to a software exception.**
- The OBC could not switch to **the back-up SRI 1** because that unit **had already ceased to function** during the previous data cycle (72-millisecond period) **for the same reason as SRI 2**.
- **The internal SRI software exception was caused during execution of a data conversion from 64-bit floating point to 16-bit signed integer value.** The floating point number which was converted had a value greater than what could be represented by a 16-bit signed integer. This resulted in an Operand Error. **The data conversion instructions (in Ada code) were not protected from causing an Operand Error, although other conversions of comparable variables in the same place in the code were protected.**
- The error occurred in a part of the software that only performs alignment of the strap-down inertial platform. **This software module computes meaningful results only before lift-off. As soon as the launcher lifts off, this function serves no purpose.**
- The alignment function is operative for 50 seconds after starting of the Flight Mode of the SRIs which occurs at H0 −3 seconds for Ariane 5. Consequently, when lift-off occurs, the function continues for approximately 40 seconds of flight. **This time sequence is based on a requirement of Ariane 4 and is not required for Ariane 5.**
- **The Operand Error occurred due to an unexpected high value** of an internal alignment function result called BH, Horizontal Bias, related to the horizontal velocity sensed by the platform. This value is calculated as an indicator for alignment precision over time.
- The value of BH was much higher than expected because the early part of the trajectory of Ariane 5 differs from that of Ariane 4 and results in considerably higher horizontal velocity values.

To summarize briefly, the Inertial Reference System used to control the rocket flight failed because it had an unhandled exception in its diagnostic software, a subsystem that had no purpose during flight. Furthermore, the diagnostic operation being performed wasn't even required by this version of the rocket. (This was a bad day for code reuse.) To prevent failure, the rocket had two SRI systems, but since they both had the same input data and the same software, they both failed in the same way.

(By the way, if you ever need to write test code for flight control software, you might consider running it in a separate process. That way, even if the test process terminates, the flight control process itself continues to run. Using multiple processes provides protection to critical systems that multithreaded software cannot.)

Exceptions solve the fundamental problems caused by using return values for status handling, but they present a significant problem of their own. Specifically, any exception thrown in a process must be handled or the process will terminate. An unhandled exception will crash your process, no matter how insignificant the cause. This is a very real example that shows exactly why exceptions are a debugging issue.

Error handling in general and exception handling in particular are a common source of program bugs. Depending on how they are used, exceptions can either improve the reliability of a program or destroy it. Well-designed and well-implemented error handling can prevent bugs where incorrect error handling results in bugs. Further complicating matters, error handling typically occurs when a program is most vulnerable to problems.

Given this reality, you may be tempted to conclude that return values are the safer way to go. After all, for a return value to crash a program would really take some doing, whereas an unhandled exception can do it effortlessly. There are several problems with this logic. For starters, not all C++ functions can have return values, and using such functions (such as constructors and overloaded operators, like *operator=*) is essential to object-oriented programming in C++. Using return values also poses problems, as we have already seen. Furthermore, library code (such as MFC and STL) and even C++ itself throws exceptions, so your program needs to deal with exceptions whether it throws them or not. Consequently, proper exception handling is a C++ fact of life.

The Need for a Strategy

This situation suggests the need for a project-wide status-handling strategy. Exceptions can go a long way in helping to prevent bugs, but using exceptions without an established, understood strategy is just as likely to cause bugs as it is to remove them. If some team members aren't throwing exceptions for errors, most likely those programmers aren't handling exceptions either because they don't expect them. The worst situation is for programmers not to understand exceptions in an environment that uses exceptions.

For a common example of this problem, consider how you would react if you found the following code in your program:

```
CSomeVarType *pSomeVar;
if ((pSomeVar = new CSomeVarType) == 0)
    return -1;
```

What do you think of this code? The correct answer is that you don't know because it depends on whether new is set to throw an exception or return a null pointer on failure. By default in Visual C++, new returns a null pointer on failure, but you can have new throw an exception instead by installing a handler using _set_new_handler (which is done by default in MFC). If new throws an exception, checking its return value for a null pointer accomplishes nothing; so this code will most likely result in the program crashing with an unhandled exception. The real issue, however, is that all programmers on the team must know which error-handling method is being used. If they don't, your program has bugs.

> **TIP**
>
> All the programmers on your team must know the error-handling methods being used. If they don't, your program has bugs.

Your status-handling strategy should have the following goals:

- To design the status handling (Usually status handling isn't designed at all.)
- To determine when your program should use exceptions and when it should use return values

- To make the program exception safe and determine the level of exception safety you need to support (A program is *exception safe* when it works correctly in the presence of exceptions.)
- To determine when and how the program throws exceptions
- To determine when and how the program catches exceptions
- To prevent a process from crashing unnecessarily with an unhandled exception
- Not to use exception handling to mask unrecoverable bugs
- To make sure everyone on the programming team understands and follows the strategy

The goal of this chapter is to help you develop such a strategy.

Using Exceptions

Now is a good time to explore the circumstances in which exceptions should be used. In the previous examples, exceptions were always used for error handling—that usage was deliberate. Let's start by looking at the fundamental characteristics of C++ exceptions.

- Exceptions are raised and handled on a per-thread basis.
- Exceptions cannot be ignored by a thread and must be handled.
- Unhandled exceptions terminate the process, not just the thread.
- Exception handling prevents resource leaks by destroying all stack objects when performing a stack unwind.
- Exception handling requires a fair amount of overhead, making it unsuitable for code that is run often. To be more specific, a `catch` block has some overhead, but a `try` block has minimal overhead; so most exception-handling overhead is incurred only when exceptions are thrown.
- You can throw any type of exception object, not just integers.

Exceptions are for error handling.

Given these characteristics, it should be clear that you shouldn't use exceptions for just any type of status information. Rather, exceptions are best used for error-handling code because other types of status information can usually be safely ignored, should definitely not terminate the process if unhandled, and don't warrant the overhead of exceptions. A function should either perform its task as expected or throw an exception, but an exception shouldn't occur as the result of normal behavior.

OK, great—so what's an error? An *error* is a condition under which a thread cannot continue to execute normally without some special handling. Consider the following hardware/operating system type exceptions.

- **Access violation** The thread can't continue because a virtual memory address is invalid.
- **Stack overflow** The thread can't continue because there is no more stack space.
- **Illegal instruction** The thread can't continue because the current CPU instruction isn't valid.
- **Integer divide by zero** The thread can't continue because it has an integer value that isn't meaningful.
- **Floating point overflow** The thread can't continue because it has a floating point value that isn't meaningful.

Clearly, a thread cannot continue to execute in any of these conditions unless the problem is handled in some way. However, by default these specific exceptions are handled by Windows Structured Exception Handling (SEH), not by C++ exceptions. I explain exactly what this means a bit later.

Programs have other conditions that may be considered errors. Here are some typical examples.

- File system errors, such as not finding a disk drive, folder, or file or there is no free disk space
- Memory errors, such as being out of heap space or virtual memory
- Network errors, such as being unable to make a network connection
- Peripheral errors, such as a printer off line or out of paper
- Data errors, such as input data that is invalid or missing
- User errors, such as a user entering invalid input into a dialog box

In all these cases, the thread cannot continue executing as expected without the problem being addressed in some way.

When properly performed, exception handling has the following characteristics.

- **Exceptions are exceptional.** Exceptions should not result from normal program execution. Conditions that happen often are most likely not really an error.

Unexpected or unusual conditions that don't prevent normal execution aren't errors either.

- **Exceptions are used when using a return value is impossible.** Such conditions include errors in constructors and operators without return values, such as *operator=* and reference casts. Note that although destructors don't have return values, destructors should never throw an exception.

- **Exceptions are reliable.** When properly used, exceptions are the most reliable way to communicate error information in an exception-safe program because they cannot be ignored.

- **Exceptions simplify error handling.** Exceptions allow you to create a clear separation between normal program logic and error-handling logic, thus simplifying the program code. They also make error handling more convenient.

Using Return Values

As valuable as they are, exceptions are not appropriate for all situations. For starters, you are forced to use return values when programming the Windows API or with COM because these technologies don't use exceptions. Not surprisingly, return values are best used when exceptions are inappropriate. Here are the fundamental characteristics of return values.

- Return values indicate normal or unusual function execution but not a condition that would prevent the thread from executing normally.
- Return values can be easily ignored.
- Return values are typically an integer, usually mapped according to a predefined scheme.
- Return values are efficient to pass and receive.

Consequently, return values are best used in the following situations:

- **For status information that isn't an error** All nonerror status information should use return values.

- **For errors that can be safely ignored most of the time** In this case, return values are likely to be more convenient because you don't want to have to catch unimportant errors to prevent them from crashing your process.

- **For errors that are likely to occur during a loop** In this case, the error handling must be fast. The overhead of exceptions makes return values a better choice to obtain better performance. In this case, if you really want to use exceptions, you can create a wrapper function that converts the return value into an exception.

- **For errors in language-neutral modules** One problem with using C++ exceptions is that they tie the module to a specific programming language. Language-neutral modules, such as COM components, must use return values instead of exceptions.

> **TIP**
>
> Return values are for status information that isn't an error as well as error conditions in which using exceptions wouldn't be appropriate.

If you choose not to use exceptions for error handling, you can use the same error-handling scheme used by the Windows API with your own code. That is, you can have your functions return a special value to indicate abnormal execution, and then set the error code using the *SetLastError* API function. The calling function would check for a special return value and then obtain the error code using *GetLastError*. You can also use the Windows error code mapping scheme. Both the use of *GetLastError* and *SetLastError* API functions and the Windows error code mapping are discussed in Chapter 6, Debugging With Windows. I prefer not to use this approach because I find the two-step error-handling technique inconvenient.

When using return values, make an effort to design the values to convey as much information as you can. The Windows error code mapping scheme is a good model, whereas returning −1 for all problems doesn't help much. Try to give specific codes for specific conditions.

> **TIP**
>
> Design the return values you use. Returning −1 for all problems doesn't help much.

Exceptions and Bugs

I have defined an error as a condition under which a thread cannot continue to execute normally without some special handling. A program bug certainly meets that definition; but a bug is caused by a defect in the code, whereas an error is caused by some problem external to the code itself, such as being out of heap space. The Ariane 5 crash was certainly caused by a program bug. So what about bugs? From the point of view of C++ exception handling, should bugs be considered errors? The correct answer is yes—but with a catch.

From the point of view of C++ exception handling, bugs are considered errors.

Later in this chapter, I make the case that a program should handle recoverable bug-related exceptions whenever possible in release builds to keep the process running but should not use exceptions to mask bugs in debug builds. In this section, my goals are to present the bug-related exception issue and to describe how bug-related exceptions need to be handled in Visual C++. To this end, what do you think will happen when the following function is executed?

```
void TestBugException () {
    try {
        int *pInt = 0;
// set address 0 to 42, causing an access violation
*pInt = 42;
    }
    catch (...) {
        MessageBox(0, _T("Exception caught!"),
            _T("Exception Test"), MB_OK);
    }
}
```

The possible answers are

  (a) The access violation exception is handled.
  (b) The access violation exception is not handled.
  (c) Depending on the circumstances, the access violation exception may or may not be handled.

The obvious answer is *a*, but actually the correct answer is *c*. In fact, by default in Visual C++, the exception is handled in the debug build but not in the release build.

The problem is that as far as Visual C++ is concerned, a C++ exception can be caused only by code that has a `throw` statement or that calls a function (which could potentially have a `throw` statement). Any other code can't receive a C++ exception, so the compiler optimizes away the unnecessary exception-handling code in release builds but not in debug builds. But wait—

doesn't this code clearly have an exception? It in fact does. It has a *structured exception*, which is an operating system feature, not a C++ exception, which is a C++ language feature. A C++ exception can occur only as the result of a `throw` statement, in accordance with the optimization, whereas a structured exception can result from an access violation, division by zero, stack overflow, and such. An ellipsis catch handler catches any type of exception, including system-generated and program-generated exceptions.

What I have just described is referred to as the synchronous exception model, which is set using the /GX compiler option and is the default behavior starting with Visual C++ 6.0. You can choose to use the asynchronous exception model, which assumes that any instruction can result in an exception; this is the correct assumption for all types of exceptions. You can obtain this behavior using the /EHa compiler option instead of /GX. The synchronous exception model is used because C++ exception handling requires some extra code to track object lifetimes for stack unwinding, so eliminating such code when unnecessary can make executables smaller and somewhat faster. Any programmer who doesn't completely understand this behavior is in for a big surprise when some exception handlers disappear in the release build. This compiler behavior really is considered a feature, but it is not an obvious feature. I think it would be safer if Visual C++ used the asynchronous exception model by default, on the assumption that programmers won't change the exception model unless they know what they are doing.

> **TIP**
>
> You must use the /EHa compiler option to catch operating system exceptions using C++ exception handling.

C++ Exceptions versus Windows Structured Exception Handling

While we're on the subject, now is a good time to compare C++ exceptions to Windows structured exceptions and show how to combine them in a C++ program.

Let's start by looking at Windows Structured Exception Handling, which has the following characteristics.

- It uses _try, _except, _finally, and _leave keywords and the
  RaiseException API function.
- It is supported by Windows, so it isn't portable to other operating sys-
  tems, but you can use it with any language (in theory), including C.
- It doesn't handle C++ object destruction.
- It throws unsigned integer values. The exception codes use the same
  rules as Windows error codes, which are presented in Chapter 6.
- It is thrown as a result of a hardware exception (such as an access viola-
  tion or divide by zero) or operating system exception (such as when an
  API function is passed an invalid handle). It can also be thrown as the
  result of a *RaiseException* function.

By contrast, C++ exception handling has the following characteristics.

- It uses `try`, `throw`, and `catch` keywords.
- It is supported by C++.
- It handles C++ object destruction.
- It throws any C++ object. Exception objects can be derived from the
  standard *exception* base class or any other class, or they can be built-in
  types.
- It is thrown as the result of a `throw` statement.

Interestingly, Visual C++ implements C++ exceptions using the Structured
Exception Handling mechanism.

By the way, MFC presents a third exception-handling mechanism. MFC has
its own exception-handling macros because it was created before exception
handling was added to Visual C++. These macros now compile down to C++
exceptions, so there is absolutely no reason to use them in new code. Consequently, the only differences in programming exceptions in MFC are that all
MFC exception objects are derived from the *CException* base class (which has
the convenient *GetErrorMessage* and *ReportError* member functions), that most
MFC exception objects are dynamically allocated and must be deleted when
caught, and that uncaught MFC exceptions are caught and deleted by MFC
itself in *AfxCallWndProc*.

Structured Exception Handling doesn't handle object destruction, therefore you should always use C++ exceptions in C++ programs. However,
because C++ exceptions don't normally handle hardware and operating system exceptions, your program needs to translate structured exceptions to C++

exceptions. While you probably won't use structured exceptions directly in your C++ program, it is helpful to understand how they work. Jeffrey Richter has an excellent description of structured exceptions in his book *Programming Applications for Microsoft Windows*.

Translating Structured Exceptions to C++ Exceptions

You can catch structured exceptions using C++ exceptions by using an ellipsis catch handler. Unfortunately, this approach loses all the information contained in the structured exception, including the exception code, the exception address, and the CPU register values. Furthermore, you want to avoid using the ellipsis catch handler to prevent masking bugs. Fortunately, Visual C++ allows you to translate structured exceptions into C++ exceptions using the _set_se_translator function, as shown here:

```
#include <eh.h>  // exception handling header file

// a C++ exception class that contains the SEH information
class CSEHException {
public:
    CSEHException (UINT code, PEXCEPTION_POINTERS pep) {
        m_exceptionCode   = code;
        m_exceptionRecord = *pep->ExceptionRecord;
        m_context         = *pep->ContextRecord;
        _ASSERTE(m_exceptionCode ==
            m_exceptionRecord.ExceptionCode);
    }
    operator unsigned int () { return m_exceptionCode; }

    // same as exceptionRecord.ExceptionCode
    UINT m_exceptionCode;
    // exception code, crash address, etc.
    EXCEPTION_RECORD m_exceptionRecord;
    // CPU registers and flags
    CONTEXT m_context;
};
// the SEH to C++ exception translator
void _cdecl TranslateSEHtoCE (UINT code, PEXCEPTION_POINTERS pep) {
    throw CSEHException(code, pep);
}

int APIENTRY WinMain(HINSTANCE hInstance, HINSTANCE hPrevInstance,
                LPSTR lpCmdLine, int nCmdShow) {
```

```
    // install the translator
    _set_se_translator(TranslateSEHtoCE);
    ...
}
```

This code installs the *TranslateSEHtoCE* exception translator, which throws a C++ exception using a *CSEHException* object, which in turn contains all the useful structured exception information. Exception translators work on a per-thread basis, so you need to install a translator for each thread. Note that you can create any exception class you like for this purpose; you can even just throw the exception code integer. As a side effect of this exception translation, you see two first-chance exception trace messages in the **Debug** tab of the Output window: one for the original structured exception and one for the translated C++ exception.

> **TIP**
>
> To handle hardware and operating system exceptions properly, create your own exception class and install a structured exception to C++ exception translator using the _set_se_translator function.

With this code in place, you can now catch structured exceptions as C++ exceptions, as in the following example.

```
void TestBugException2 () {
    try {
        int *pInt = 0;
        *pInt = 42;
    }
    catch (CSEHException &bug) {
        switch (bug) {
            case EXCEPTION_ACCESS_VIOLATION:
                MessageBox(0,
                    _T("Access violation exception caught!"),
                    _T("Exception Test"), MB_OK);
                break;
            case EXCEPTION_INT_DIVIDE_BY_ZERO:
                MessageBox(0,
                    _T("Integer divide by zero exception caught!"),
                    _T("Exception Test"), MB_OK);
                break;
            case EXCEPTION_STACK_OVERFLOW:
```

```
            // stack overflow is unrecoverable, so rethrow
            throw;
        }
    }
}
```

You need to know a few details when handling translated structured exceptions. The first is that you should attempt to recover only from the following exceptions:

- EXCEPTION_ACCESS_VIOLATION
- EXCEPTION_INT_DIVIDE_BY_ZERO
- EXCEPTION_FLT_DIVIDE_BY_ZERO
- EXCEPTION_FLT_OVERFLOW
- EXCEPTION_FLT_UNDERFLOW

You shouldn't catch the other exceptions because they aren't likely to be problems from which you can recover. For example, stack overflow exceptions are unrecoverable because the reserved stack space has been exhausted. (If a thread has a stack overflow, however, the thread can still use the stack—for a while. The reason is that the stack is protected by a 4 KB guard page, so when a thread runs out of stack space, Windows converts the guard page to usable stack space and throws an EXCEPTION_STACK_OVERFLOW exception. The thread can continue to run, but it should shut down immediately. The mechanics of thread stacks are described in more detail in Chapter 9, Debugging Memory.) Consequently, you shouldn't install a default exception handler by adding a `default` case to the catch block in the previous *TestBugException2* example. Note that if you want to handle all exceptions (even the unrecoverable ones) by, for example, writing an entry to a log file and then shutting down the program, you should install a crash handler with the *SetUnhandledException Filter* API function. Again, remember that to catch structured exceptions, you need to use the /EHa compiler option whether you translate the exceptions or not.

TIP
Don't catch translated structured exceptions that result from problems from which you can't recover.

Finally, to help distinguish between translated structured exceptions that you can handle from those you can't, you can change the exception translation code as follows:

```
class CRecoverableSEHException : public CSEHException {
public:
    CRecoverableSEHException (UINT code, PEXCEPTION_POINTERS pep) :
        CSEHException(code, pep) {}
};

class CUnrecoverableSEHException : public CSEHException {
public:
    CUnrecoverableSEHException (UINT code,
            PEXCEPTION_POINTERS pep) :
        CSEHException(code, pep) {}
};

// the SEH to C++ exception translator
void _cdecl TranslateSEHtoCE (UINT code, PEXCEPTION_POINTERS pep) {
    if (code == EXCEPTION_ACCESS_VIOLATION    ||
        code == EXCEPTION_INT_DIVIDE_BY_ZERO  ||
        code == EXCEPTION_FLT_DIVIDE_BY_ZERO  ||
        code == EXCEPTION_FLT_OVERFLOW        ||
        code == EXCEPTION_FLT_UNDERFLOW)
        throw CRecoverableSEHException(code, pep);
    else
        throw CUnrecoverableSEHException(code, pep);
}
```

Exception Performance

You shouldn't choose your exception strategy based on performance alone, but it is important to remember that exception handling isn't free. In fact, it can be very expensive if misused. However, there is a cost to not using exceptions, which is the need for significantly more error-handling code in your program.

Let's start by reviewing where the exception overhead originates. When a C++ exception is thrown, the function call chain is searched backward for a handler that can deal with the type of exception that was thrown. Of course, if no matching handler is found, the process is terminated. If a handler is found, the call stack is unwound, all automatic (local) variables are destroyed, and the stack is cleaned up to the context of the exception handler. Consequently, the exception overhead results from maintaining an exception handler list and a table of active automatic variables (which requires extra code, memory, and processing whether an exception is thrown or not) plus the function call chain search, automatic variable destruction, and stack adjustment (which requires processing only when an exception is thrown).

Let's proceed by checking the performance of code that is clearly a misuse of exceptions.

```
int ReturnValueFunction (int i) {
    if (i % 2 == 0)
        return i;
    else
        return 0;
}

int TestReturnValue () {
    int i, result = 0;
    for (i = 0; i < 100; i++) {
        result += ReturnValueFunction(i);
    }
    return result;
}

int ExceptionFunction (int i) {
    if (i % 2 == 0)
        return i;
    else
        throw 0;
}

int TestException () {
    int i, result = 0;
    for (i = 0; i < 100; i++) {
        try {
            result += ExceptionFunction(i);
        }
        catch (...) {
        }
    }
    return result;
}
```

Here *TestReturnValue* sums the values of even integers between 0 and 100 using return values, whereas *TestException* calculates the same sum using

DEBUGGING STRATEGIES

exceptions. In this case, *TestException* is about 8000% slower than *TestReturn Value*. Clearly, using exceptions for nonerror conditions is a really bad idea.

A more interesting test is to compare the performance of exceptions when used properly.

```
class CIntObject {
public:
    CIntObject (int arg) { m_data = arg; }
    operator int () { return m_data; }
private:
    int m_data;
};

int DereferenceWithPointerCheck (int *pInt1, int *pInt2,
        int *pInt3) {
    if (pInt1 != 0 && pInt2 != 0 && pInt3 != 0) {
       CIntObject int1(*pInt1), int2(*pInt2), int3(*pInt3);
       return int1 + int2 + int3;
    }
    else
       return -1;
}

int TestWithPointerCheck () {
    int i, result = 0, data1 = 1, data2 = 2, data3 = 3;
    int *p1 = &data1, *p2 = &data2, *p3 = &data3;
    for (i = 0; i < 100; i++)
        result += DereferenceWithPointerCheck(p1, p2, p3);
    return result;
}

int DereferenceWithException (int *pInt1, int *pInt2, int *pInt3) {
    try {
       CIntObject int1(*pInt1), int2(*pInt2), int3(*pInt3);
       return int1 + int2 + int3;
    }
    catch (...) {
       return -1;
    }
}

int TestWithException () {
    int i, result = 0, data1 = 1, data2 = 2, data3 = 3;
    int *p1 = &data1, *p2 = &data2, *p3 = &data3;
```

```
    for (i = 0; i < 100; i++)
        result += DereferenceWithException(p1, p2, p3);
    return result;
}
```

Here both *TestWithPointerCheck* and *TestWithException* add the values of 1, 2, and 3 together 100 times by dereferencing pointers. *TestWithPointer Check* performs the calculation by checking the pointers for null, whereas *TestWithException* doesn't check the pointer values but uses asynchronous exception handing to deal with possible access violation exceptions. Since much of the overhead in exception handling relates to keeping track of automatic variables, the *CIntObject* objects are used in the calculations to ensure that there are variables for the exception handling to track. Finally, the code was compiled with the /EHa compiler option to handle access violations and optimized with the /O2 compiler option.

Surprisingly, the *TestWithException* version is actually 4% *faster* than the *TestWithPointerCheck* version, which suggests that the exception-handling overhead that occurs when an exception isn't thrown can be less than the overhead of checking the pointer values for null. The results are the same with *TestWithPointerCheck* compiled with /GX instead of /EHa. Although different code will have different results, this test indicates that the performance overhead of using exceptions isn't significant when they are rarely thrown and that using such exceptions may actually improve performance by eliminating the need to execute code to handle circumstances that aren't likely to happen.

 TIP

It isn't expensive to use exceptions that are rarely thrown, and doing so may actually improve performance.

It is interesting to see how adding exception handling affects executable size. By checking a variety of smaller programs (in the 150 KB range), I found that using synchronous exceptions (with the /GX compiler option) added between 8% and 20% to the executable size, whereas using asynchronous exceptions (with the /EHa compiler option) added between 13% and 22% to the executable size. Put another way, using asynchronous instead of synchronous exceptions added between 2% and 5% to the executable size. Of course, the results are totally dependent on the program in question, but larger programs should tend to have less additional overhead, so these figures should be close to the worst case.

Exception Strategy

The strategy presented here for both throwing and catching exceptions primarily focuses on preventing bugs. Although there are many opportunities to introduce bugs in both exception throwing and catching, the greatest opportunity for bugs occurs when your exception-handling strategy isn't designed, when it isn't well understood by all the programmers on your team, and when it isn't applied consistently. Consequently, the most important part of an exception strategy is actually having a strategy. Don't make it up as you go.

TIP

> The most important part of an exception strategy is actually having a strategy. Don't make it up as you go.

When to Throw

At this point, it should be clear when to throw exceptions. An exception should be thrown when a function detects an error condition that prevents it from continuing to execute normally without some special handling that it cannot perform itself. Exceptions should also be thrown by functions that fail when using a return value is impossible. When done properly, such conditions should be exceptional. By contrast, return values should be used for status information that isn't an error, for errors that can be safely ignored most of the time, for errors that are likely to occur during a loop (thus making the performance of exceptions unacceptably slow), and for programming language–neutral modules.

What to Throw

A C++ exception can throw any object, but some objects are much better to throw than others. When designing what to throw, consider how the exception is handled. Sample code you find in textbooks often throws objects such as integers and strings, but such objects are very difficult to handle.

Now is a good time to review the rules for catching exceptions. The following rules determine how an exception is caught.

- The catch handlers are applied in order.
- The exception is caught if the catch handler catches the same type or a reference to the type of the thrown object.
- The exception is caught if the catch handler catches a public base class or a reference to a public base class of the thrown object.
- An ellipsis catch handler catches any type of exception, so it is always placed last.

The `const` and `volatile` attributes don't affect these rules, so *CMyException* can be caught by `CMyException &` or `const CMyException &`.

When an exception is caught, the catch handler must have the following format:

```
catch (someType &exceptionParam) {
    . . .
}
```

where the exception parameter is optional but everything else is required. That is, each handler must have a single object type and a compound statement (with parentheses). Furthermore, there is no way to combine different types of exceptions in the same handler unless they share a common base type.

The last concern is that the handler must figure out what to do with the exception once caught. This requires the exception object to contain enough information about the error to make that decision properly.

To address all these concerns, the best solution is to design a hierarchy of exception classes, all with a common base class. Using different exception types for different exceptions makes it easy to identify the specific problem using the exception type alone. Using a well-designed hierarchy allows you to handle related problems in a single handler, and the handler code won't have to be changed as you add more exception types. The exception object should contain information about the specific problem so that it can be properly handled.

TIP

Using a well-designed hierarchy of exception classes allows you to handle related problems in a single handler.

DEBUGGING STRATEGIES

The C++ `exception` class makes an excellent base class for your program's exceptions unless you are using Unicode. Here is its class definition (from *Stdexcpt.h*):

```
typedef const char *__exString;

class exception {
public:
    exception();
    exception(const __exString&);
    exception(const exception&);
    exception& operator= (const exception&);
    virtual ~exception();
    virtual __exString what() const;
private:
    __exString _m_what;
    int _m_doFree;
};
```

However, because these exceptions are also thrown by C++ itself, you should create another base exception class specifically for your program, as with the following:

```
class CProgramException : public exception {
public:
    CProgramException (const __exString &_what_arg) :
        exception(_what_arg) {}
};
```

Using the *CProgramException* class makes exception handling easier because you can catch all your program's exceptions by handling this base class. You can also use additional data members to fully describe the specific problem as needed.

TIP

Define an exception base class to handle exceptions thrown by your program code.

When to Catch

When should a function catch an exception? Determining when to catch an exception is a challenging problem because it often requires you to balance several conflicting issues.

- The current function may be better able to determine exactly what the problem is but may not know how to handle the error.
- The higher-level functions may not know what the problem is (this is certainly true if there is information hiding), but they may know how to handle the error.
- An exception should be handled by the function that knows what to do with it.
- If an exception goes unhandled, the process will crash, which is the least desirable outcome for recoverable problems. You can't always assume the caller will handle the exception. To keep the process running, the buck has to stop somewhere.

Given that an exception can be thrown in the first place, here are some reasonable criteria for catching it.

- When the function knows what to do with the exception
- When the function can handle an exception reasonably and higher-level functions wouldn't know what to do with it
- When throwing an exception can potentially crash the process
- When the function can still perform its task
- When necessary to clean up allocated resources

Certainly a function should handle an exception when it knows how to handle it. If the higher-level functions also need to address the problem, a function can handle the exception and then throw the same exception or a different exception. However, there are many situations where the higher-level functions wouldn't know what to do with an exception, so a function should also handle exceptions that it can handle in a reasonable way and that higher-level functions aren't likely to expect or wouldn't be able to handle. This problem is always a concern with information hiding. For example, suppose you have a class that is implemented using a linked list, either as a private data member or using private inheritance. For true information hiding, the caller should have no clue that a linked list is being used, but any uncaught linked list–related exception may betray that fact. Also, a function should always catch exceptions whenever throwing an exception may crash the process. For example, throwing an exception from a destructor can be disastrous, as you will see shortly.

A function should also handle an exception when it can still perform its task. For example, consider the following function.

```
BOOL IsFileFound (LPCTSTR filename) {
    _ASSERTE(filename != 0);    // don't forget the assertions
    try {
        // try to find the file
        BOOL isFound = FALSE;
        ...
        return isFound;
    }
    catch (CFileException) {
        return FALSE;
    }
}
```

A variety of exceptions could be thrown while this function is trying to find the file: the file name and path could be invalid, the drive might not be accessible, and so on. Even so, if any of these problems were to result in a file-related exception, the function can still perform its task by returning false. Consequently, it is better to catch the error and return false than to make the calling function handle the problem.

One drawback to exception handling is that it creates an opportunity to leak resources. Of course, preventing resource leaks is very much a part of making a program exception safe. The problem is that the stack unwinding automatically cleans up local variables but not dynamically allocated variables. Consider the following code:

```
void LeakyFunction (int arg) {
    CMyObject *pObject = new CMyObject(arg);
    ...    // do something that throws an exception
    pObject->MemberFunction();
    delete pObject;
}
```

The problem with this function is that there will be a memory leak if an exception is thrown. One solution is to catch the exception, plug the leak, and rethrow the exception, as shown in the following code.

```
void LeakFreeFunction (int arg) {
   CMyObject *pObject = 0;
   try {
      pObject = new CMyObject(arg);
      ...    // do something that throws an exception
      pObject->MemberFunction();
      delete pObject;
   }
   catch (...) {
      delete pObject;
      throw;
   }
}
```

However, if a function handles exceptions only to free resources, a better approach is to use an `auto_ptr` or a similar smart pointer class to free the resource automatically by wrapping the dynamic allocation in a local variable:

```
void LeakFreeFunction2 (int arg) {
   auto_ptr<CMyObject> pObject(new CMyObject(arg));
   ...    // do something that throws an exception
   // can still call member functions as normal
   pObject->MemberFunction();
   // no need to delete pObject
}
```

Now the resource is freed even when an exception is thrown by changing only two lines of code from the original, thus eliminating the need to catch the exception. You can use smart pointers to protect your code against resource leaks in the presence of exceptions. Debugging memory leaks and using `auto_ptr`s are discussed in Chapter 9. Note that `auto_ptr`s work only for resources freed with `delete`. You can create similar classes to free other types of resources, such as the *CAutoPen* class discussed in Chapter 9 to delete GDI pens.

Now is the time to answer a question posed in Chapter 2, Writing C++ Code for Debugging. Consider the following code:

```
// approach 1
try {
   if (p1->p2->p3->fn()) ...;
}
```

```
catch (CRecoverableSEHException &e) {
    // handle access violation exception
}

// approach 2
if (p1 == 0 || p1->p2 == 0 || p1->p2->p3 == 0)
    ...; // handle error
else if (p1->p2->p3->fn()) ...;
```

To create robust code, is it better to write the code directly and use exception handling to take care of any unexpected problems (as in approach 1 above) or to handle explicitly any possible problems by checking all variables before using them (as in approach 2)? I believe using exception handling is the better approach for the following reasons.

• **Exception handling is simpler.** There is less code and there is a complete separation between program code and error-handling code. Being simpler also means that the code is less likely to have bugs and is easier to maintain.

• **It is more reliable.** It doesn't depend on programmer discipline, so there isn't the risk of forgetting to check a variable before using it. Furthermore, it is possible for an invalid pointer to have a value other than null, so checking for null isn't completely reliable.

• **It is efficient.** As my previous exception-handling performance tests showed, using exception handling for exceptional conditions can be as efficient or even more efficient than explicit checking.

If you use this approach, you must compile with the /EHa compiler option, as previously discussed in this chapter. Of course, keep in mind that you should use exception handling only for exceptional conditions. If you expect a pointer to be null, explicitly check for that condition in the code rather than using exceptions. Use exception handling for cases in which a null pointer should never happen.

 TIP

It is simpler, more reliable, and more efficient to use exception handling to create robust code. However, you should use exception handling only for exceptional conditions. If you expect a pointer to be null, explicitly check for that condition in the code rather than using exceptions.

How to Catch

Here are some rules for catching exceptions.

- Non-MFC C++ exceptions should be caught by reference, as shown throughout this chapter. Catching C++ exceptions by reference eliminates the need to delete the exception object (because exceptions caught by reference are passed on the stack) and it preserves polymorphism (so that the exception object you catch is exactly the exception object that was thrown). Catching an exception by pointer might require you to delete the object, whereas catching an exception by value could result in object "slicing," that is, converting derived exception objects to the caught data type. For more information on this subject, see Scott Meyers, *More Effective C++,* Item 13.
- MFC exceptions are designed to be caught by pointer. Since they are usually allocated from the heap, you need to call the *Delete* member function when you are done with the exception, as shown here:

```
catch (CFileException *e) {
   // handle file exception
   ...
   e->Delete();   // required to prevent a memory leak
}
```

Consequently, you should never catch MFC exceptions using an ellipsis catch handler because that results in a memory leak. You must delete MFC exceptions with the *Delete* member function instead of `delete` because some MFC exceptions are created as static objects. See Paul DiLascia's "C++ Q&A" column in *Microsoft Systems Journal* for a good comparison of C++ and MFC exception handling.

Once you have caught an exception, you can handle it by performing some combination of the following typical actions.

- Do nothing.
- Fix the problem and retry the code.
- Fix the problem and do not retry the code.
- Display an error message to the user if the user needs to know.
- Output a diagnostic trace message if the problem isn't a bug.
- Display an assertion if the problem is a bug.
- Log the problem in a log file.
- Shut down the process if the exception isn't recoverable.
- Clean up allocated resources.

- Rethrow the exception so that higher-level functions can handle it as well, typically when the problem can't be completely handled in the current function. You can rethrow the same exception object or throw a new exception object.

Using Ellipsis Catch Handlers

As previously mentioned, an ellipsis catch handler catches any type of exception, including system-generated and program-generated exceptions. This exception-handling mechanism is powerful and convenient, but it can also be hazardous if misused because you can't tell exactly what the problem is. All you know is that some unknown problem occurred at an unknown place. Consequently, you have no way of knowing if it is more appropriate to handle the exception in the current function or at a higher level. You also don't know if it is appropriate to handle the exception at all. Note that handling an exception inappropriately may lead to trashing your program data or other types of damage, so you want unrecoverable exceptions to result in process termination. Not only does this prevent the program from doing damage, but it also helps you debug the program. After all, a crashed program is a clear indication of a problem, whereas a buggy program that never crashes can be very difficult to debug. The bottom line is this: Don't use ellipsis catch handlers to mask bugs.

TIP

Don't use ellipsis catch handlers to mask bugs.

It is entirely appropriate, however, to use an ellipsis catch handler in two situations:

- The handler will rethrow the same exception or throw another exception. Ellipsis catch handlers are often used to clean up resources and rethrow the exception.
- The handler is going to shut down the process anyway.

When you consider using an ellipsis catch handler, assume that the problem that resulted in the exception is unrecoverable and that the process is crashing for a good reason, such as with an unrecoverable structured exception. If the ellipsis catch handler still makes sense to use in this circumstance, you should be able to use it safely. If not, try to handle the exception using a specific exception object handler instead.

Throwing an exception during exception handling will terminate the process. More precisely, throwing an exception during a stack unwind will result in process termination, but you can safely throw an exception once in an exception handler. Stack unwinding involves calling destructors, therefore exceptions should not be thrown from destructors. You may see destructor code that uses an ellipsis catch handler to prevent exceptions from escaping. This technique isn't safe in Windows because it may catch unrecoverable structured exceptions. When translating structured exceptions, use the following approach instead.

```
CSomeObject::~CSomeObject () {
    try {
        // destroy the object
        ...
    }
    catch (CUnrecoverableSEHException) {
        throw; // don't suppress unrecoverable structured exceptions
    }
    catch (...) {
        // now it's safe to suppress the exception
    }
}
```

By the way, note that throwing an exception from a destructor is bad even if it doesn't result in process termination because the exception prevents the `delete` operator from being called, resulting in a resource leak. Specifically, the statement

```
delete pObject;
```

is equivalent to

```
pObject->~CSomeObject();
operator delete(pObject);
```

so throwing an exception in the destructor skips the `operator delete` call.

You may notice that I use ellipsis catch handlers exclusively in all other chapters, even when their use is not justified. I chose not to use specific exception handlers to simplify the code because proper exception handling is complex enough to be too much of a distraction in these examples.

Using Exception Specifications

One problem with handling exceptions is knowing which types of exceptions a function can throw. The exceptions thrown by a function should be regarded as part of its interface contract, on par with its parameters and return value. Certainly you must know what exceptions a function can throw in order to use it properly.

C++ provides exception specifications for this very purpose. Consider the following function prototypes.

```
// normal C++ function, can throw any exception
void NormalFunction ();
void NoThrowFunction () throw(); // cannot throw exceptions
// can throw only CException-derived objects
void ThrowFunction () throw(CException);
```

Here, *NormalFunction* can throw any exception because it doesn't have an exception specification, whereas *NoThrowFunction* cannot throw any exceptions. (You can also indicate that a function doesn't throw exceptions in Visual C++ using the `_declspec(nothrow)` extended attribute.) Although the exception specifications for these two functions may seem backward (shouldn't the function without a `throw` not throw exceptions?), this counterintuitive approach is used to maintain backward compatibility with code without exception specifications. Finally, the *ThrowFunction* can throw any exception object derived from *CException*. Exception specifications give yet another advantage to using a hierarchy of exception classes because an overridden virtual function can throw any exception derived from the objects in the base class exception specification without a problem.

Exception specifications may seem useful, but they have several serious problems.

- **Exception specifications provide another way to crash.** If an exception is thrown that is not derived from any of the exception specification classes, the thread calls `unexpected`, which by default shuts down the process. Not good. To create a complete function specification, you need to find all the exceptions thrown directly by the function as well as all the unhandled exceptions thrown by any functions it calls.

- **They are checked at run time.** Unfortunately, exception specifications are not something that can be verified at compile time, so they must be enforced at run time. (Note that if exception specifications were checked at compile time, changing one specification might require your entire program to be recompiled.) Consequently, the following code compiles without warning.

```
void SomeFunction () throw () {
    throw CProgramException(
        "Exception specifications aren't checked at compile time.");
}
```

It is very easy to forget to add an item to an exception specification, and the only way you will find out about it is from the process crashing. It is better not to use an exception specification than to use an incorrect one.

- **They don't mix well with templates.** Because template parameters can be any type, you don't know what exceptions can be thrown by that type's member functions.

- **Structured exceptions are a problem.** If you are using the asynchronous exception model, practically any function can throw a translated structured exception.

- **They result in more exception overhead.** Exception specifications require additional overhead because the exception-handling code has to enforce the specification.

Others may disagree, but I believe that having an incorrect exception specification simply isn't worth crashing for (except, perhaps, during testing). If a function throws an unexpected exception, let the exception run its course and crash the process only if unhandled. It just seems silly to have a process crash because of an incomplete exception specification if the exception would be properly handled anyway. Although you definitely want to document the exceptions thrown by your functions, I recommend against using exception specifications as a mechanism of enforcement.

Finally, there is one more important problem with exception specifications: Visual C++ currently doesn't support them. You can put them in your code, but they are ignored by the compiler. Check compiler warning C4290 for more information. Even so, you should understand exception specifications now on the assumption that they will be supported by Visual C++ in the future.

Defensive Programming with Exceptions

In the Introduction, I stated that your software is unlikely to be completely bug free, so given the existence of residual bugs your program should do the following.

- **Prevent the trashing of data.** If by continuing to run the program, you run the risk of harming data or external hardware controlled by that data, the process should be shut down in an orderly manner, leaving the data untouched.

- **Keep running.** If continuing to run the program doesn't risk harming data or external hardware, the process should continue to run (possibly in a degraded state), and if the problem is significant, the user should be notified. The user can then decide to shut down the program or keep it running.

In Chapter 3, I defined *defensive programming* as constructing a program in such a way that it continues to function when something that isn't supposed to happen actually happens. Defensive programs protect themselves against receiving unexpected or invalid data, being run in unexpected circumstances, system failures, or even having bugs. This section presents some ideas on how to program defensively using exceptions to accomplish these goals.

Shut Down the Program Only If You Must

When faced with a bug, most programs strive to shut down gracefully by freeing allocated resources and perhaps writing some diagnostic information to a log file. This approach is safe and easy to do, and it helps you track down the bug, but it isn't necessarily in the user's best interest. In my opinion, shutting down gracefully is vastly overrated: By shutting down in this manner, the rocket still crashes or the documents are still lost. It's not clear to me how the Ariane rocket benefited from a graceful shutdown of its Inertial Reference System while it was in the process of exploding.

Furthermore, for many types of programs, ungraceful shutdowns in Windows aren't all that bad. If you do nothing at all, Windows will most likely reclaim all your program's resources anyway. Some programmers like to install custom crash handlers that do things like create a log file with the crash address, stack trace, and register values. If you do nothing, you can obtain roughly the same information from a Dr. Watson log file. I've never heard a user say: "Well, I really don't mind the program crashing all the time and losing my work as long as it shuts down gracefully. What really gets me is that standard Windows crash message box."

Sure, cleaning up allocated resources is essential to the long-term stability of the program. But if the program is going to shut down, the long term doesn't count for much. Of course, there are situations in which shutting down gracefully is critical. For example, it is clearly better for a rocket to shut down "gracefully" with a controlled midair explosion than to careen out of control into a large city. Any software that controls hardware needs to make sure that all failure modes protect life, limb, and property. It is better if a robot arm fails gracefully by stopping in place rather than crashing wildly into equipment or into the operator. Multiprocess programs need to shut down gracefully so that all the processes terminate together. Perhaps the ultimate graceful shutdown is a process that restarts itself when it crashes, which is a technique used by Windows Explorer.

> **TIP** ▸
>
> Shutting down gracefully is vastly overrated. Instead, focus on keeping the program running if you can and shutting down gracefully only if you must.

Clearly, continuing to perform the program's primary task, even in a degraded state, is far more important than performing a graceful shutdown. Instead, the focus should be on keeping your program running if you can and shutting down gracefully only if you must. Shutting down should be your second choice, not your first.

Defensive Programming Strategy

To prevent trashing data and keep the program running, we need to understand when it is really necessary to shut down a process. Consequently, we need to answer these fundamental questions:

- What bugs are recoverable?
- What bugs are unrecoverable?
- How do you handle recoverable bugs?
- How do you handle unrecoverable bugs?

To answer these questions, we need to identify the types of exceptions, the situations in which exceptions can occur, and how to determine the program state.

For the exception types, I start by assuming that your program already handles exceptions caused by errors, such as running out of disk space, and focus only on exceptions caused by bugs. We can start by classifying bug-related exceptions as expected or unexpected. One might argue that all such exceptions are unexpected, but some are clearly more expected than others. For example, in the following code

```
int MulDiv (int number, int numerator, int denominator) {
   _ASSERTE(denominator != 0);
   return number * numerator / denominator;
}
```

an integer divide by zero exception is expected if there is a bug in the code (which is why there is an assertion to check for it), whereas any other type of exception is not. A function that called *MulDiv* could handle an integer divide by zero exception and safely assume that a bug in the code somehow resulted in a zero denominator. By contrast, a function that called *MulDiv* shouldn't handle an illegal instruction exception; something is terribly wrong if it does. Consequently, a process must shut down if it receives such an unexpected exception.

We can also classify bug-related exceptions by their object type and, consequently, determine their origin. Assuming you have followed the exception strategy presented earlier and are translating structured exceptions, then all exceptions thrown by your program code are derived from *CProgramException* (which in turn is derived from exception), and all exceptions thrown by the hardware or by Windows are derived from *CSEHException*. Consequently, you can break down the exception types by their base classes as follows.

- *CProgramException* is an exception thrown by your program code. It is caused by a program error and is a bug only if uncaught. All such bugs are potentially recoverable.
- *CException* is an exception thrown by MFC or by your program code if using MFC exceptions. It is caused by a program error and is a bug only if uncaught. All such bugs are potentially recoverable.
- exception is an exception thrown by C++, including dynamic_cast (which throws bad_cast) and the Standard C++ Library (which includes STL). Exceptions derived from exception are potentially bugs and are certainly bugs if uncaught. All such bugs are potentially recoverable.
- *CSEHException* is an exception thrown by hardware or the operating system. Exceptions caused by access violations and arithmetic errors (divide by zero, overflow, and underflow) are often expected and potentially recoverable; all other exceptions (stack overflow, illegal instruction, DLL not found) are not.

Note also that the C Run-time Library functions don't throw C++ exceptions but can throw structured exceptions.

Next we can classify bug-related exceptions by where they occur in the program. Since the program may be a user application (where a user is creating or viewing documents) or a server (where the system is requesting services), I use the term *client* instead of *user* to handle both situations. I also use the term *document* to describe any internal data necessary for the program to perform its tasks, which may or may not be a document in the usual sense. Here are the times when a bug-related exception can occur.

- **Program startup and shutdown** Any bug-related exception that occurs while the process is starting up or shutting down shouldn't be considered recoverable. A bug-related exception during startup is a very bad sign, whereas a bug-related exception during shutdown isn't worth recovering from because the process is terminating anyway. Since these phases occur when the client is not depending on the program, the client has little risk of losing anything except the ability to use the program.

- **Program processing** Any bug-related exception that occurs during a program command or transaction is potentially recoverable, but the risk of that recovery depends on the task at hand. Functions that perform tasks essential to the program are critical, whereas other functions are not. For example, with a word processing program, any bug-related exception that occurs while a document is being modified is critical and should result in program termination, possibly allowing the user to save the documents to temporary files in case they are salvageable. By contrast, a bug-related exception that occurs while the user is manipulating the user interface isn't critical and shouldn't result in a loss of the documents. Low-level functions typically aren't capable of determining the significance of bugs that occur during their execution, so such functions should defer error handling to higher-level functions.

To summarize, a program can recover from a bug-related C++ exception if it is expected, if it occurs in noncritical code, and if it does not occur during program startup or shutdown or result from an unrecoverable structured exception.

TIP

A program can recover from a bug-related C++ exception if it is expected, if it occurs in noncritical code, and if it does not occur during program startup or shutdown or result from an unrecoverable structured exception.

Once your program determines that it can recover from the bug-related exception, it should then check the state of the program and its documents. If either the program or documents appear to be corrupted, the process should still shut down. Otherwise, the program needs to notify the client to determine the course of action. If the client agrees that execution should continue, the program should recover from the error and continue running.

With this strategy, there are many situations in which it is still necessary to shut down the process, but there are also many circumstances in which the program can keep running. Sometimes it can be the difference between staying aloft or going down in flames.

Defensive Programming Examples

Now it's time to put everything together by looking at some sample code from the bottom up. A typical low-level function should handle only expected error-related exceptions, as shown in the following code.

```
void LowLevelFileFunction (LPCTSTR filename) {
    _ASSERTE(filename != 0);    // don't forget the assertions
    try {
        // do something with the filename
        ...
    }
    catch (CFileException) {
        // handle expected error-related exception somehow
        // use a trace statement to make the error visible during
        // debugging
        _RPTF1(_CRT_WARN, "Couldn't do something with file %s\n",
            filename);
    }
}
```

In this function, the expected error-related exceptions are handled, but any other exceptions must be handled by higher-level functions.

Now consider a critical low-level function.

```
class CCriticalException : public CProgramException {
public:
    CCriticalException(const __exString &_what_arg) :
        CProgramException(_what_arg)) {}
};

void CriticalDocumentFunction () {
    try {
        // modify the document
    }
    catch (expectedException &e) {
        // handle somehow
    }
    catch (...) {
        // any unexpected exceptions here can't be good
        _RPTF1(_CRT_WARN,
            "Unexpected exception occurred while modifying %s\n",
            m_DocumentName);
        throw CCriticalException(
            "An unrecoverable exception may have corrupted the \
document");
    }
}
```

For this critical function, any unexpected exception that occurs while the document is being modified must be dealt with. This function throws a *CCritical*

Exception to clearly signal to the caller that the document may have been corrupted.

> **TIP**
>
> Create a special class to identify clearly any critical, unrecoverable exceptions.

Here is an example of how exceptions could be handled at the command level.

```
int NotifyUser (LPCTSTR problem = 0, UINT code = 0) {
    LPCTSTR format = _T("Can't perform the last command.\n\
%s, but the program should still run.\n\
However, to be safe you might want to save your documents to \n\
temporary files and restart the program.\n\n\
Click Abort to quit the program now or Ignore to continue.");
    LPCTSTR codeProblem = _T("A potentially recoverable exception \
0x%X was found");
    LPCTSTR genericProblem = _T("An unexpected problem was found");
    TCHAR message[LARGE_SIZE], problemBuf[LARGE_SIZE];
    if (problem == 0 || *problem == _T('\0')) {
        if (code != 0) {
            _stprintf(problemBuf, codeProblem, code);
          problem = problemBuf;
        }
        else
            problem = genericProblem;
    }
    _stprintf(message, format, problem);
    return MessageBox(0, message, AppName, MB_ABORTRETRYIGNORE |
        MB_ICONSTOP);
}

void CMyDocument::OnSomeCommand () {
    try {
        DoSomeCommand();
    }
    catch (CCriticalException &e) {
        HandleCorruptDocument(e);
    }
    catch (exception &e) {
        if (!IsValid() || NotifyUser(e.what()) == IDABORT)
            terminate();
    }
```

```
catch (CRecoverableSEHException &e) {
    if (!IsValid() || NotifyUser(0, e.m_exceptionCode) ==
        IDABORT)
        terminate();
    }
}
```

If a function at the command level fails, this code assumes that the only consequence is that the command currently can't be performed, unless a *CCriticalException* was thrown (which indicates that the command may have corrupted the document) or *CUnrecoverableSEHException* was thrown. However, programs can crash for a reason, so if this assumption proves false (if, for example, the stack has been corrupted in a way that results in an access violation exception), the next high-level function call should result in an unhandled exception. By keeping defensive exception handling at the command or transaction level, unrecoverable bugs still result in process termination.

> **TIP**
>
> By keeping defensive exception handling at the command or transaction level, unrecoverable bugs still result in process termination.

The first exception handler catches any critical exceptions that occurred during *DoSomeCommand* by calling *HandleCorruptDocument*, which probably should shut down the process. The second exception handler catches any exceptions thrown by the program code using the *CProgramException* class as well as exceptions thrown by C++ itself. The third handler catches only the translated structured exceptions that can be caused by bugs in program logic. The second and third handlers verify that the document is valid and notify the user of the problem (with a message box that could be greatly improved if message boxes had more flexibility) and allow the user to decide if the process should continue to run. If the document isn't valid or the user doesn't wish to continue, the process is terminated.

To apply this set of exception handling to all commands, you can simplify the code by using macros.

```
#ifndef _DEBUG
#define CATCH_DOCUMENT_BUG() \
    catch (CCriticalException &e) { HandleCorruptDocument(e); } \
```

```
        catch (exception &e) \
            { if (!IsValid() || NotifyUser(e.what()) == IDABORT) \
                terminate(); } \
        catch (CRecoverableSEHException &e) { if (!IsValid() || \
            NotifyUser(0, e.m_exceptionCode) == IDABORT) terminate(); }
#elif
#define CATCH_DOCUMENT_BUG() catch (...) { throw; } // don't catch
#endif

void CMyDocument::OnSomeCommand () {
    try {
        DoSomeCommand();
    }
    CATCH_DOCUMENT_BUG()
}
```

Using macros also makes it easier to perform bug-related exception catching only during release builds, thus making unhandled exceptions easier to find in debug builds. Of course, having different code between the builds requires more release-build testing.

Finally, to ensure that the document hasn't been corrupted by the command, implement an *IsValid* function to validate the document. Such an *IsValid* function should be similar to the *AssertValid* function used in MFC assertions (as described in Chapter 3, Using Assertions), except that it returns a Boolean, is compiled for all builds, and shouldn't throw exceptions. Here is what such a function might look like.

```
BOOL CMyDocument::IsValid () {
    try {
        // check the immediate base class first
        if (!CMyDocumentBaseClass::IsValid())
            return FALSE;

        // check the data members not in the base class
        if (!m_pObject1->IsValid())
            return FALSE;
        if (!m_pObject2->IsValid())
            return FALSE;

        // now check the class invariants not checked by the base
        // class be sure to document the invariants
        if (m_Value == illegalValue)
            return FALSE;
```

```
        if (m_Object1.GetSize() != m_Size)
           return FALSE;

        ...

        return TRUE;
     }
     catch (...) {
        return FALSE;
     }
  }
```

If your program has no bugs, users should never see any of this code in action. If your program has an unrecoverable bug, the process will crash with an unhandled exception, preventing further damage. If there is a recoverable bug-related exception, the program will continue to function (although with degraded performance because any buggy commands won't run) and avoid unnecessarily losing the user's work. Losing work that doesn't have to be lost is one of the worst types of bugs there is.

Debugging Exceptions

When using the Visual C++ debugger, you can debug either first-chance exceptions or last-chance exceptions. You are notified of first-chance exceptions in the **Debug** tab of the Output window. You are notified of last-chance exceptions by an unhandled exception message box if the program is run from Visual C++, as shown in Figure 5.1. If the program is run as a standalone, you will receive an exceptions message box as shown in Figure 5.2. Having a process crash with an unhandled, last-chance exception is useful when debugging because it helps you find bugs.

For starters, a first-chance exception isn't a bug or even necessarily a sign of a bug. It does not indicate that there's a problem in running your program

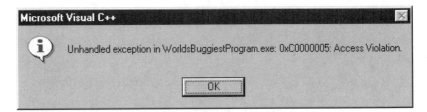

Figure 5.1 Unhandled exception message box for a program run from Visual C++

DEBUGGING STRATEGIES

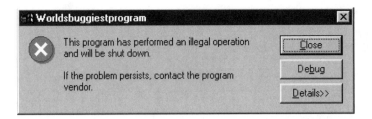

Figure 5.2   Unhandled exception message box for a program run from Windows 98.

from the debugger. Rather, a first-chance exception simply means that the debugger detected that an exception was thrown. This isn't a bug as long as the exception is eventually handled by the program. If not, the debugger will receive a last-chance exception notification and your process will crash with an unhandled exception, which is obviously a bug. By having the debugger give trace messages for first-chance exceptions, Visual C++ makes exception handling more visible. For example, suppose your program is throwing thousands of exceptions. Since exceptions are intended for exceptional conditions, such behavior most likely isn't right, even if all the exceptions are handled by the program. Since such exception handling has a high cost, handling thousands of exceptions will, at the very least, affect performance.

TIP

A first-chance exception isn't a bug or even necessarily a sign of a bug. Rather, a first-chance exception simply means that the debugger detected that an exception was thrown.

You can track down where an exception was thrown by using the following procedure. First, note the exception number given in the Output window. For example, the following first-chance exception

```
First-chance exception in WorldsBuggiestProgram.exe: 0xC0000005:
Access Violation.
```

has an exception number of 0xC0000005. Now give the **Exceptions** command in the **Debug** menu and locate that exception number in the Exceptions dialog box, as shown in Figure 5.3. Select the **Stop always** action to break on first-chance exceptions or **Stop if not handled** to break on unhandled, last-

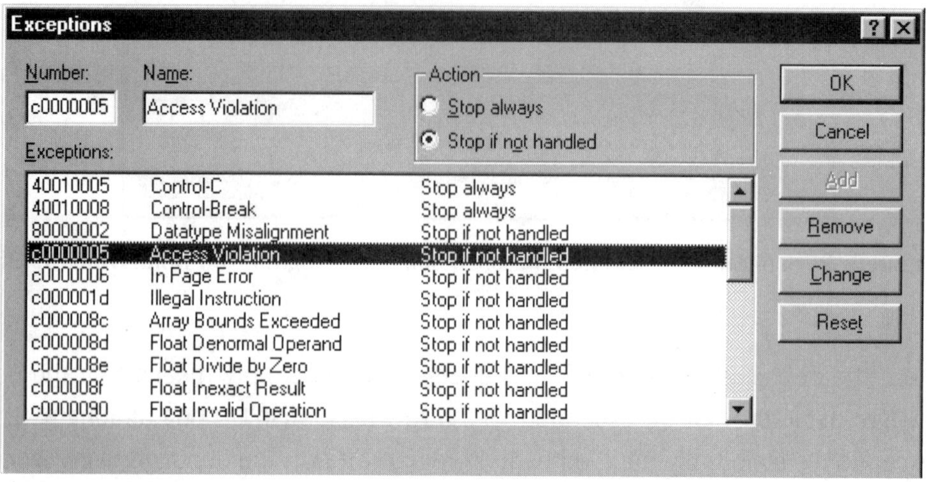

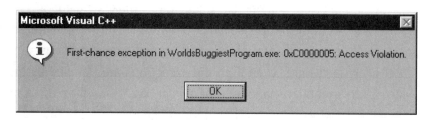

Figure 5.3   The Visual C++ exception dialog box

Figure 5.4   The Visual C++ first-chance exception message box

chance exceptions. Now to track down a first-chance exception, run the program, and wait to receive the first-chance exception message box, as shown in Figure 5.4.

Click **OK** and check the current code location and the Call Stack window to determine when and how the exception was thrown. Note that C++ exceptions are not thrown directly from your program code but from within the C++ Run-time Library, so you will need to use the Call Stack window to return back to your code.

To determine where the exception is caught (if it is caught at all), give the **Step Out** command. The pass exception message box appears as shown in Figure 5.5. Click **Yes** to pass the exception to the program (you would click **No** only if you fixed the problem from the debugger), and then continue to give the **Step Out** command until you are in the exception handler. If you get stuck at

DEBUGGING STRATEGIES

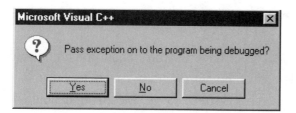

Figure 5.5 The Visual C++ pass exception message box

the first-chance exception message box and are receiving the same first-chance exception over and over again, you can proceed by changing the breakpoint setting in the Exceptions dialog box from **Stop always** to **Stop if not handled**.

Miscellaneous Tips

The following are a few miscellaneous tips that will help you get the most out of exceptions.

Correctly Enabling Exception Handling

I have already discussed when to use the /GX and the /EHa compiler options, but there is one more situation to be aware of. The opposite of asynchronous exceptions (/EHa) is synchronous exceptions (/EHs), not /GX. The /GX compiler option is actually shorthand for /EHsc, where the "c" indicates that the compiler should assume that extern "C" functions never throw C++ exceptions, so such functions are disregarded during exception optimization. This assumption is reasonable because extern "C" functions are typically written in C so they can't throw C++ exceptions. However, this assumption can be wrong, as with the following code.

```
extern "C" int CompareInt (const void *arg1, const void *arg2) {
    if (arg1 == 0 || arg2 == 0)
        throw CProgramException("Bad pointers passed to comparison \
function");
    int int1 = *(int *)arg1, int2 = *(int *)arg2;
    if (arg1 < arg2)
        return -1;
    else if (arg1 > arg2)
        return 1;
    else
        return 0;
}
```

In this case, instead of using the /GX compiler option for this function, you must use /EHs.

Fortunately, you never have to worry about forgetting to use an exception-handling compiler option if your program uses exceptions. If you do forget, you will receive a "warning C4530: C++ exception handler used, but unwind semantics are not enabled. Specify -GX" compiler warning.

Documenting Exceptions

Exceptions have two possible audiences: the user and the calling environment. Usually, the exception object type is used to communicate the problem to the calling environment, whereas a problem description string is used to communicate to the user. Exceptions that may result in error messages should contain a description of the problem within the exception object. For example, exception objects derived from the C++ exception class can describe the problem by passing a description string to the constructor. Handlers then gain access to the string using the what member function. Alternatively, the *CSEHException* class doesn't have a description string, but it contains enough information to create a description when necessary.

> **TIP**
>
> Document exceptions for both the user and the calling environment. Usually, the exception object type is used to communicate the problem to the calling environment, whereas a problem description string is used to communicate to the user.

The description string should be formatted so that it can be used directly in the error message text. For example, in this chapter I have formatted the strings starting with a capital letter and ending with no punctuation. To facilitate localization, you should use resource IDs instead of text strings. Unfortunately, the design of the exception class makes using resource IDs difficult because you can't set the description after the object has been created and you can't allocate a local variable in a constructor's member initialization list. One solution is to load the resource string in a data member, as shown here.

```
extern HINSTANCE hInst;

LPCSTR LoadResString (int resID, LPSTR buffer,
        int bufferLength) {
    if (LoadString(hInst, resID, buffer, bufferLength) == 0)
        *buffer = '\0';
    return buffer;
}

class CProgramException : public exception {
public:
    CProgramException (const __exString &_what_arg) :
        exception(_what_arg) {}
    CProgramException (int resID) :
        exception(LoadResString(resID, m_Description, LARGE_SIZE)) {}
protected:
    Tchar m_Description[LARGE_SIZE];
};
```

If you throw an exception that doesn't have a description, at least document the exception at the `throw` statement with a comment.

Making `new` and `malloc` Throw Exceptions

Neither `new` nor `malloc` throws exceptions on error by default in Visual C++. The only good reason to maintain this default behavior is for existing code that doesn't expect these functions to throw exceptions. New code should have these functions throw exceptions because memory allocation errors are errors that a program shouldn't ignore. You can have `new` throw exceptions upon failure by installing a handler using _set_new_handler. You can also have `malloc` use the same handler by calling _set_new_mode. The following code shows how it's done.

```
#include <new.h>

class bad_alloc : public exception {
public:
    bad_alloc(const __exString& what_arg) : exception (what_arg) {}
};

int NewHandler (size_t size) {
    throw bad_alloc("Operator new couldn't allocate memory");
    return 0;
}
```

```
int APIENTRY WinMain(HINSTANCE hInstance, HINSTANCE hPrevInstance,
                    LPSTR lpCmdLine, int nCmdShow) {
    _set_new_handler(NewHandler);
    _set_new_mode(1);          // use NewHandler for malloc as well
    ...
}
```

You can have `new` throw any type of exception you want, but this code uses the standard C++ `bad_alloc` exception. Interestingly, Visual C++ doesn't define the `bad_alloc` exception (but it defines the standard `bad_cast` and `bad_typeid` exceptions), so I had to define this class myself. The `new` handler can attempt to make more memory available and return a nonzero value to indicate that the allocation should be retried. Ordinarily, there isn't a simple way to make more memory available in Windows; therefore *NewHandler* throws a `bad_alloc` exception and returns zero to indicate the allocation has failed (although the `return` statement is never executed). Finally, `_set_new_handler` installs the handler and `_set_new_mode` is called with a value of 1 to indicate that `malloc` should use the `new` handler.

Unless you are maintaining existing code that assumes `new` returns null, always have `new` throw an exception on failure.

Having Floating-Point Errors Throw Exceptions

Unlike integers, floating-point division by zero doesn't result in an exception by default but assigns the rather bizarre "1.#INFO" value (which indicates that the value is not a number.) To make it easier to detect floating-point problems, you should have floating-point errors result in exceptions with the following code.

```
#include <float.h>
int cw = _controlfp(0, 0);
cw &= ~(EM_OVERFLOW | EM_UNDERFLOW | EM_INEXACT | EM_ZERODIVIDE |
        EM_DENORMAL | _EM_INVALID);
_controlfp(cw, MCW_EM);
```

A floating-point exception handler must call `_clearfp` as its first instruction to clear the floating-point exception.

Recommended Reading

Cline, Marshall, Greg Lomow, and Mike Girou. *C++ FAQs,* 2nd ed. Reading, MA: Addison-Wesley, 1999. Chapter 9, Error Handling Strategies, and Chapter 26, Exception Tactics, give practical information on error handling and exception handling in a very convenient format.

DiLascia, Paul. "C++ Q & A." *Microsoft Systems Journal,* July 1999. Presents a good comparison of C++ and MFC exception handling, focusing on details of MFC exception handling and why you need to delete MFC exceptions.

Lippman, Stanley B., and Josée Lajoie. *C++ Primer,* 3rd ed. Reading, MA: Addison-Wesley, 1998. Chapter 11, Exception Handling, is an excellent primer on exception handling. This is a good place to start if you need to brush up on the basics.

Meyers, Scott. *More Effective C++: 35 New Ways to Improve Your Programs and Designs.* Reading, MA: Addison-Wesley, 1996. Items 9 through 15 are essential reading for anyone who is programming with exceptions. Unlike most authors, Meyers warns against using exception specifications, which scores extra points in my book.

Pietrek, Matt. "A Crash Course on the Depths of Win32 Structured Exception Handling." *Microsoft Systems Journal,* January 1997. Presents the gory details of the Windows Structured Exception Handling mechanism at the system level.

Pietrek, Matt. "Under the Hood." *Microsoft Systems Journal,* October 1997. Gives a detailed description of Windows exception handling and how hardware exception codes are translated to Windows exception codes. It also presents a simple program that generates each type of exception.

Richter, Jeffrey. *Programming Applications for Microsoft Windows: Master the Critical Building Blocks of 32-Bit and 64-Bit Windows-based Applications.* Redmond, WA: Microsoft Press, 1999. Part V, Structured Exception Handling, has three excellent chapters on Windows Structured Exception Handling.

Schmidt, Robert. "Handling Exceptions." *Microsoft Developer Network.* A multi-part series on many detailed aspects of exception handling, with plenty of interesting, useful information. If you want detailed information on how exception handling is implemented in Visual C++ (as well as how it is supposed to be implemented), this is the first place to turn. Highly recommended. Do try to read the entire series, however, because some mistakes in earlier parts are corrected in later parts.

Stroustrup, Bjarne. *The C++ Programming Language,* 3rd ed. Reading, MA: Addison-Wesley, 1997. Chapter 14, Exception Handling, presents a comprehensive and authoritative summary of exception handling in C++. Gives many useful tips for developing an exception strategy.

Sutter, Herb. *Exceptional C++: 47 Engineering Puzzles, Programming Problems, and Solutions*. Reading, MA: Addison-Wesley, 2000. Everyone agrees that exception-safe code works correctly in the presence of exceptions, but Sutter focuses on what is called the strong guarantee of exception safety: If a function terminates because of an exception, the program state will remain unchanged as if the function was never called. This level of exception safety is not easy to implement, but Sutter shows you how.

PART II

Debugging Tools

Chapter 6

Debugging with Windows

Sooner or later it's going to happen to you—if it hasn't already. You give your program to someone important—your best customer or the president of your company—and it crashes on them. The person won't remember what he was doing at the time, except that it was very important and that the crash was extremely embarrassing.

In this kind of situation, you won't be able to reproduce the problem. All that's known is that the program crashed with a Windows 98 crash dialog box (sometimes referred to as the "box of death"), as shown in Figure 6.1. The following information is displayed when you click the **Details** button.

```
KILLERAPP caused an invalid page fault in module COMDLG32.DLL at
    017f:7fe14530.
Registers:
EAX=00000000 CS=017f EIP=7fe14530 EFLGS=00010246
EBX=bff520a4 SS=0187 ESP=0065f684 EBP=00000500
ECX=0065fbbc DS=0187 ESI=0065fa58 FS=0f67
EDX=00000016 ES=0187 EDI=bff54efc GS=0000
Bytes at CS:EIP:
8b 10 83 c0 04 89 11 83 c1 04 ff 4c 24 2c 75 f0
Stack dump:
0065fa58 00000000 0065f734 00000500 00000530 000000de 000000ea
0000001d 0000019b 000000da 7fe130cb 00000010 00000508 0065fcb0
0065f73c 000087aa
```

You also know one more thing: Your boss expects you to fix it—and assumes you know how.

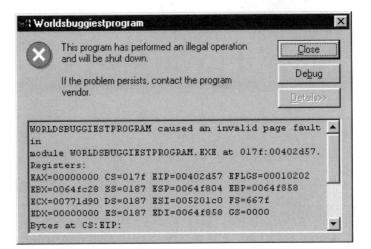

Figure 6.1 Windows 98 crash dialog box

This chapter looks at debugging from the point of view of Windows itself, largely independent of Visual C++ or any other programming tools. I present the basic information about Windows API error codes, Windows exceptions, the portable executable (PE) file format, some assembly language basics, the Windows stack, and how to read MAP files. I show you how to use Windows 98 crash dialog boxes and Dr. Watson log files for both Windows 2000 and Windows 98 to track down bugs. These techniques are often referred to as postmortem debugging because the debugging occurs after the program is quite dead. As you will soon see, these apparently useless hex dumps provide quite a lot of valuable information—once you know how to read them. Best of all, mastering these skills helps you get the most out of the Visual C++ debugger, even if you don't ever do any postmortem debugging.

As suggested by the introductory scenario, postmortem debugging is most useful when a nonprogrammer discovers a bug. Assuming Visual C++ is installed and Just-in-time (JIT) debugging is enabled, when a Windows crash dialog box appears, you should click the **Debug** button and immediately debug the program while it is still alive. Clearly, when a customer, manager, or tester produces the crash, this isn't going to happen. For tips on debugging live programs, see Chapter 7, Debugging with the Visual C++ Debugger, and Chapter 8, Basic Debugging Techniques.

Postmortem Debugging

Postmortem debugging has two fairly modest goals: (1) to determine where the program crashed, and (2) to determine what led to the crash. To oversimplify a bit, determining where a program crashed requires the address of the program instruction that crashed. Given the program's MAP files, you can then determine the offending source code file name and line number. To determine what led to the crash, you can use the thread's stack trace to determine where the function was called and the registers and stack contents to show the values of relevant variables.

Postmortem debugging can be a lot of work, and for many types of bugs there is no guarantee that you can obtain all the information you need to track down the problem. Here are debugging techniques in their typical order of preference.

- Local debugging using the debug build
- Local debugging using the release build with debugging symbols
- Remote debugging using the debug build
- Remote debugging using the release build with debugging symbols
- Postmortem debugging using a Dr. Watson log file
- Postmortem debugging using Windows 98 crash dialog box information

Given a choice, postmortem debugging is probably the last thing you want to do. But sometimes you don't have a choice: You can't reproduce the problem, you don't have the right source code, you don't have matching debugging symbols, the user won't let you perform remote debugging, and so on. In these circumstances, debugging with a Dr. Watson log file starts to look pretty good because it can bring you directly to the problem with the least amount of fooling around. Having some information is always better than having none, so you want to be able to take advantage of whatever information you can get.

Windows API Error Codes

The most basic information you need to know when debugging Windows programs is how Windows handles errors. Nearly all Windows error handling is done through function return values because Windows API functions do not intentionally throw exceptions. (A few Windows API functions such as *HeapCreate, HeapAlloc,* and *HeapReAlloc,* allow you to choose to have them throw exceptions by passing the appropriate flag. *InitializeCriticalSection* also throws exceptions.) Windows API error handling is a two-step process: First, the API function returns a special value to indicate an error, and then you can obtain the specific error code by calling the *GetLastError* API function.

The special return value used to indicate error depends on the specific API function, so always consult the documentation if you are not sure. In general, BOOL API functions return zero if they fail or nonzero if they succeed. As I pointed out in Chapter 2, Writing C++ Code for Debugging, since BOOL Windows API functions return values other than 0 or 1, comparing return values to TRUE is very risky and should not be done. Windows API functions that return a HANDLE generally return a null handle or INVALID_HANDLE_VALUE, which is −1 to signal failure. Windows API functions that return a LONG or DWORD generally return either 0 or −1. Finally, if an API function cannot fail (and there are only a few that can't), it returns VOID.

Once you have detected an error, you can determine the specific cause by calling *GetLastError*. The last error is set on a per-thread basis using thread local storage so that threads don't stomp on each other's error values. You should assume that just about any Windows API function can change the last error value (even some functions that succeed do this), so if you want the last error value, you should save it as soon as you can. Unfortunately, Windows 98 is based on Windows 3.1 code and therefore has limited support for *GetLastError*. This means that Windows 98 API functions that fail always return the right error code, but *GetLastError* may not indicate the specific cause.

> **TIP**
>
> Windows 98 has limited support for *GetLastError*.

The bits within the error code have fixed mapping (see Table 6.1), which is documented in *Winerror.h*. This error-code mapping should look familiar because Windows exception codes use the same mapping and COM HRESULT codes use a similar approach (this is also documented in *Winerror.h*).

By the way, if you like, you can add *GetLastError* support to your own functions by setting the error code with the *SetLastError* API function and returning a special value to indicate an error. Either use existing error codes or make up your own codes. If you make up your own, be sure the customer code is set

Table 6.1 Error code mapping

Bits	Meaning
Bits 30–31	Severity code: 0 = success, 1 = info, 2 = warning, 3 = error
Bit 29	Customer code: 0 = Microsoft defined, 1 = customer defined
Bit 28	Reserved: must be 0
Bits 16–27	Facility: Microsoft defined (in *Winerror.h*)
Bits 0–15	Status code for facility: Microsoft or customer defined

to one so that your error codes don't conflict with any error codes defined by Windows.

Once you get the last error code, the next problem is figuring out what to do with it. You can look up the value manually in *Winerror.h*, but there are better ways to use the error code. One approach is to use the Visual C++ Error Lookup utility shown in Figure 6.2. Note that you can use the **Modules** command to look up errors defined in any module that has a message table resource, such as *NetMsg.dll*.

To monitor the *GetLastError* value in the Visual C++ debugger, enter "@ERR" in the Watch window. This value is a debugger pseudo-register that displays the last error code. You can then translate the error code to text using the ",hr" formatting symbol, as shown in Figure 6.3.

TIP

You can monitor the *GetLastError* value in the Visual C++ debugger by entering "@ERR,hr" in the Watch window.

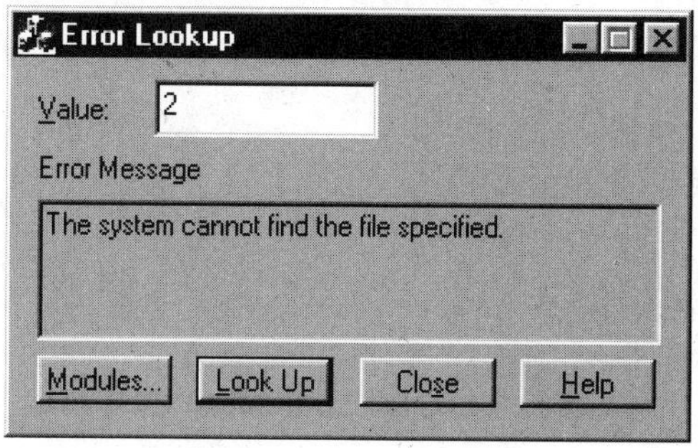

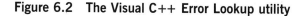

Figure 6.2 The Visual C++ Error Lookup utility

Figure 6.3 Debugging with the @ERR pseudo-register in the Watch window

Finally, if you want to display the error code in an error message, you can convert it to text using the *FormatMessage* API function. This function can translate using the user's default locale or the specific locale you specify. The following code shows *FormatMessage* in action.

```
int APIENTRY WinMain (HINSTANCE hInstance, HINSTANCE
     hPrevInstance, LPSTR lpCmdLine, int nCmdShow) {
  HANDLE hFile;
  WIN32_FIND_DATA findFileData;
  if ((hFile = FindFirstFile(_T("c:\\debug.win"),
      &findFileData)) == INVALID_HANDLE_VALUE)
    LastErrorMessageBox(0);
  ...
}


void LastErrorMessageBox (HWND hWnd) {
  DWORD  error = GetLastError();
  LPTSTR pText;

  if (FormatMessage(FORMAT_MESSAGE_FROM_SYSTEM |
      FORMAT_MESSAGE_ALLOCATE_BUFFER, 0, error, 0,
      (LPTSTR)&pText, 0, 0)) {
    MessageBox(hWnd, pText, _T("System Error Code"),
      MB_OK | MB_ICONERROR);
    LocalFree(pText);
  }
  else {
    TCHAR text[LARGE_SIZE];
    _stprintf(text,
      _T("Error code %#08x - Description not found."), error);
    MessageBox(hWnd, text, _T("System Error Code"),
      MB_OK | MB_ICONERROR);
  }
}
```

Windows Exception Basics

Windows programs crash as the result of an unhandled exception. In fact, you can do all sorts of horrible things within a Windows program as long as you handle the exception and you don't corrupt Windows, corrupt program memory, or throw an exception while an exception is being handled (during a stack unwind). Before you conclude that you can throw all caution to the wind, however, note that Windows 98 is fairly easy to corrupt. You'll find out why in Chapter 9, Debugging Memory.

The crash dialog box used to report an unhandled exception depends on the circumstances in which the program was run. If your program has an unhandled exception while running in Visual C++, you receive the message box shown in Figure 6.4. If you are not running from the debugger in Windows 98, you receive a variation of the Windows 98 crash dialog box shown in Figure 6.5. The variation used depends on whether or not Dr. Watson or JIT debugging is enabled. In this example, Dr. Watson was enabled. If you

Figure 6.4   The Visual C++ unhandled exception message box

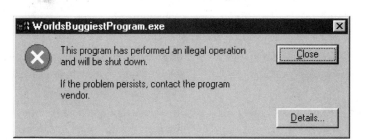

Figure 6.5   The Windows 98 crash dialog box with Dr. Watson enabled

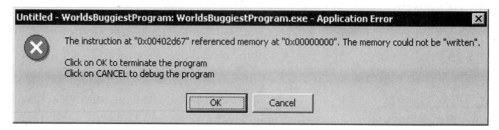

Figure 6.6   The Windows 2000 crash message box with JIT debugging enabled

are not running the debugger in Windows 2000 and JIT debugging is enabled, you receive the rather primitive Windows 2000 crash message box shown in Figure 6.6. Windows exception codes use the same bitmapping scheme as the Windows error codes. Since exceptions are errors and are defined by Microsoft, the highest four bits of an exception code are always 1100 in binary or 0xC in hex.

All Windows exceptions are listed in *Winnt.h,* but Table 6.2 shows the exceptions you are most likely to see.

Table 6.2   Commonly seen Windows exception codes

Exception	Meaning
STATUS_ACCESS_VIOLATION	A thread tried to read or write to memory that it cannot access.
STATUS_STACK_OVERFLOW	A thread has used its entire reserved stack space.
STATUS_FLOAT_DIVIDE_BY_ZERO	A thread tried to divide a floating-point value by 0.
STATUS_FLOAT_OVERFLOW	The exponent of a floating-point operation is greater than the maximum allowed by the type.
STATUS_FLOAT_UNDERFLOW	The exponent of a floating-point operation is less than the minimum allowed by the type.
STATUS_INTEGER_DIVIDE_BY_ZERO	A thread tried to divide an integer value by 0.

Floating-point exceptions are not enabled by default. You can have floating-point errors result in exceptions with the following code.

```
#include <float.h>
int cw = _controlfp(0, 0);
cw &= ~(EM_OVERFLOW | EM_UNDERFLOW | EM_INEXACT | EM_ZERODIVIDE |
        EM_DENORMAL | _EM_INVALID);
_controlfp(cw, MCW_EM);
```

A floating-point exception handler must call `_clearfp` as its first instruction to clear the floating-point exception.

Portable Executable Basics

To find your way around during postmortem debugging, you must understand some of the basics behind the PE file format, which is used by all 32-bit Windows executables and is based on the Common Object File Format (COFF). I will explain just enough to get you going here, but for more information see Matt Pietrek's "Peering Inside the PE: A Tour of the Win32 Portable Executable File Format."

The most important concept behind the PE file format is that it takes full advantage of memory-mapped files. Instead of building the executable image at load time, the code and data sections in the PE file are largely organized the way they will exist in virtual memory. Pietrek likens a PE file to a prefabricated home: Just plop it down in the virtual address space, wire it up (by connecting the DLLs), and go. By working through memory mapping, some portions of the executable image don't have to be loaded into physical memory until they are needed. Furthermore, swapping out such pages doesn't require any swap space because the image is already stored in the PE executable file on disk. Pretty cool, don't you think?

Of course, anything this good has to have a catch, and the catch here is that each executable file used by a program has a preferred base virtual address. As the next section shows, the loading process is significantly more complicated if a module can't be loaded at its preferred base. Windows processes (and therefore EXE files) have a preferred base address of 0x00400000. Although you can choose to load a Windows 2000 process at a lower base address (using the linker **Base address** option), 0x00400000 is the lowest base address that can be used by all versions of Windows. Since EXE files are the first to load, they always load at their preferred base address.

By contrast, DLL files may not be able to load at their preferred base address and may have to be relocated. To facilitate relocation, the internal code addresses are stored in terms of relative virtual addresses (RVAs), which are the actual virtual addresses minus the base address. However, pointers to global and static variables are stored by their preferred virtual addresses, so they must be fixed up if the DLL is relocated. To facilitate linking to DLLs, external virtual addresses (that is, addresses to imported DLL functions) are not accessed directly but indirectly through import thunks. Interestingly, if a DLL must be relocated, the resulting program requires more swap space because the fixed up code is no longer the same as what is stored in the PE file, thus partially defeating one advantage of using memory-mapped files.

If you look inside a PE file (shown in Figure 6.7), the first thing you see is an MS-DOS header and stub. Consequently, if you run a PE file from a version of MS-DOS that doesn't support Win32 programs, you get a "This program cannot be run in DOS mode" message from the stub instead of crashing. Next comes the image file header, which contains general information about the executable, such as its target platform and various sizes and offsets. The next item to appear is the image optional header, which contains various sizes, offsets, and version numbers. Then there is the section table, which is a directory of the program code and data in the executable. Next, there are the sections themselves, constituting the actual program code and data. Finally, there may be COFF and CodeView debugging information at the end of the file. The size of the information between the beginning of the file and the actual code (which consists of the MS-DOS stub, the image file header and image optional header, and the section table) is always 4,096 bytes (0x1000 bytes in hex), as indicated by the "Base of Code" record in the image optional header.

The specific code and data sections depend on the particular executable and the compiler used to build it. The sections shown in Table 6.3 (see page 222) appear in a typical executable created using Visual C++.

There are two common techniques for looking at a PE file's internals. The first is to use the Visual C++ DumpBin utility (in *Vc\bin*) with the appropriate command-line switches. A more convenient approach is to use the Windows 98

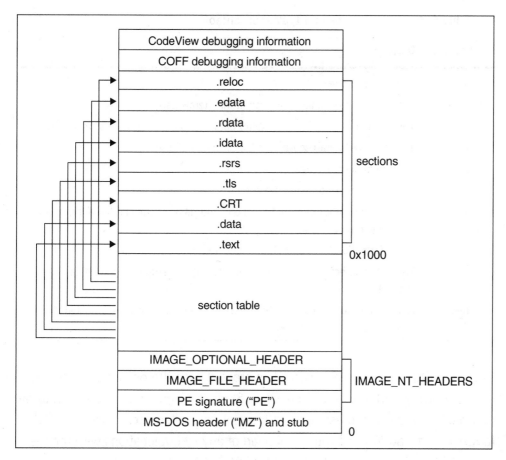

| CodeView debugging information |
| COFF debugging information |

| .reloc |
| .edata |
| .rdata |
| .idata |
| .rsrs |
| .tls |
| .CRT |
| .data |
| .text |

sections

0x1000

section table

| IMAGE_OPTIONAL_HEADER |
| IMAGE_FILE_HEADER |
| PE signature ("PE") |

IMAGE_NT_HEADERS

| MS-DOS header ("MZ") and stub |

0

Figure 6.7   The Portable Executable file format

Quick View utility, which dumps the PE file information when viewing an executable file. The **Quick View** command in Windows Explorer opens the Quick View utility.

TIP

Use the Windows 98 Quick View utility to dump PE file information.

Rebasing DLLs

Whereas EXEs always load at their preferred base address, DLLs cannot load at their preferred base address if that address space is already used by another module. For example, the default DLL base address given by Visual C++ is

Table 6.3 Data sections in a typical executable

Section	Usage
.text	The module code
.data	The initialized (global, static, and string literal) data
.bss	The uninitialized (global and static) data; bss stands for *block storage space*
.CRT	The initialized data used by the C Run-time Library
.tls	The thread local storage
.rsrc	The resources used by the module
.idata	The information for imported functions and data, containing the addresses used by import thunks
.edata	The information for exported functions and data
.rdata	The debug directory and the program description string, if any, defined in the DEF file
.reloc	A list of all the addresses in the image that would have to be adjusted if the module were relocated

0x10000000, so if you have two DLLs created with the default base address, you will have an address space collision. Such collisions require the DLL to be relocated to another address, and all internal data references must be updated to use the new addresses. You are notified of any DLL relocations with the message "LDR: DLL example.dll base 0x10000000 relocated due to collisions with c:\projects\bogus.dll," which you may have seen in the **Debug** tab of the Output window. (Windows NT 4.0 and Windows 98 show this message, but Windows 2000 does not.) See Ruediger Asche's MSDN article "Rebasing Win32 DLLs: The Whole Story" for a study of the effect of DLL relocation on performance.

> **TIP**
>
> Address space collisions make it difficult to identify modules by their addresses.

Not only do these DLL relocations increase program loading time, they also make it difficult to identify modules by their addresses. Windows selects the new base address used to relocate a DLL at load time. This makes the resulting base address system dependent because different versions of Windows and different system configurations could result in different base addresses. In general there is no simple way to determine the base addresses used by relocated DLLs.

Two approaches can ensure that your DLLs use unique address space ranges. The first approach is to use the Visual C++ Rebase utility (in *Vc\Bin*) as a post-build step. For example, suppose your program consists of *MyApp.exe*, *MyDll1.dll*, *MyDll2.dll*, and *MyDll3.dll*. First, create a text file in your project folder named *Rebase.txt* with the following contents.

```
MyApp.exe
MyDll1.dll
MyDll2.dll
MyDll3.dll
```

Now use the following Rebase command to rebase the DLLs for the debug build.

```
Rebase -b 400000 -R C:\Projects\ProjectRoot\Debug -G Rebase.txt
```

You can make this setting in the Projects Settings dialog box by setting the **Post-build command** in the **Post-build Step** tab. If you are using Windows 2000 (and therefore not receiving the DLL relocation messages), you might want to assume you have collisions and always use the Rebase utility to prevent base address relocations.

The other approach is to explicitly set a unique base address for each of your DLLs. You can change this value in the Project Settings dialog box by setting the **Base address** in the **Output** category of the **Link** tab. To avoid collisions, note that using the default DLL base address of 0x10000000 is probably a bad idea.

The approach to choose depends on your circumstances. Although using the Rebase utility is the better bet for more complex programs that use many DLLs, I find it isn't all that difficult to choose unique base addresses for simple programs. The virtual address space between 0x20000000 and 0x50000000 is usually wide open; so if you have a handful of DLLs, you can assign a series of base addresses, such as 0x20000000, 0x21000000, and 0x22000000. If your handpicked base addresses still result in collisions, you are probably better off using the Rebase utility.

You should definitely feel free to rebase your own DLLs; but in general don't rebase third-party DLLs, and never rebase Windows system DLLs. Others may disagree, but I think you can rebase third-party DLLs as long as you can guarantee that those DLLs will not be used by other programs. Rebasing DLLs used by other programs is definitely not cool! As long as you install these third-party DLLs in your program's folder and not in the Windows or System folders (in accordance with the Designed for Microsoft Windows logo requirements), you shouldn't have any problems. You can also *temporarily* rebase a third-party DLL if it is absolutely necessary to track down a bug.

Never rebase a third-party DLL that can be used by another program.

Once you have correctly rebased all your program's DLLs, you might as well take one more step and run your program through the Visual C++ Bind utility (in *Common\Tools*). The Bind utility resolves references to imported functions at build time. There is never a downside to using the Bind utility because any DLL that is incorrectly bound (either because it is a different version than the bound DLL or it is relocated at load) is loaded as if it weren't bound. Although it won't help your debugging efforts any, by performing both Rebase and Bind you can make your program load significantly faster. For more information on this subject, see Matt Pietrek's "Remove Fatty Deposits from Your Applications Using Our 32-bit Liposuction Tools."

If you Rebase, you should Bind as well.

Assembly Language Basics

To perform postmortem debugging using Dr. Watson and the Windows 98 crash dialog box, you need to know some assembly language basics. The goal here is not to turn you into an assembly language programmer but to provide enough understanding of Intel x86 assembly code to be able to dig through a Dr. Watson log file with confidence. Two of Matt Pietrek's "Under the Hood" columns (February 1998; June 1998) do an excellent job of presenting the essentials of assembly language for debugging, but I will try to get you going with even less to find simple bugs. With more advanced assembly language skills than I present here, you can debug more difficult problems, such as incorrect code generation by the compiler.

To keep things simple, the examples are in assembly code that hasn't been optimized. Although optimized code is functionally equivalent to unoptimized code, optimized code can be different enough to make it look like it has been run through a blender. That is, all the fundamental activities are still there, but they may be arranged in a completely different order from what you might expect from the source code. Keep this in mind when debugging release builds.

TIP

Optimized assembly code is much harder to debug than unoptimized assembly code.

Assembly Instructions and Addressing Conventions

To introduce you to assembly language, here is an overview of the various assembly language components and how they fit together. The first component is the assembly code instructions, which are the instruction set of the CPU. The assembly instructions used by x86 processors have the following format:

```
instruction [operand1], [operand2]
```

where *operand1* and *operand2* are the data used by the instruction, *operand1* being the destination of the instruction. As a result, if an operand is modified by the instruction, it is always *operand1*. Operand data can be constants, CPU registers, and memory, in which the specific usage of the data is determined by the addressing conventions. Here are the commonly used addressing conventions, with the move instruction as an example (using the general purpose EAX and EBX registers).

```
mov    eax,42                    ; move 0x42 to EAX
mov    eax,dword ptr [00420000]  ; move dword pointed to by
                                 ; 0x00420000 to EAX
mov    eax,ebx                   ; move contents of EBX to EAX
mov    eax,dword ptr [ebx]       ; move dword pointed to by EBX to
                                 ; EAX
```

```
mov     eax,dword ptr [ebx+42] ; move dword pointed to by EBX
                               ;  0x42 to EAX
mov     dword ptr [eax],ebx    ; move contents of EBX to dword
                               ; pointed to by EAX
mov     dword ptr [eax+42],ebx ; move contents of EBX to dword
                               ; pointed to by EAX + 0x42
```

In these examples, `dword ptr` means pointer to a double word and is equivalent to `*(DWORD *)` in C++. One notable addressing convention that isn't allowed in x86 CPUs is moving directly from one memory location to another. You always have to move using a register as either a source or destination. Also note that all numeric values are in hexadecimal, even if they lack a "Ox" prefix or an "h" suffix.

Common Instructions and CPU Registers

Table 6.4 lists the most commonly used assembly instructions and their meanings. Table 6.5 shows the most commonly used CPU registers and a brief description of how they are used.

Table 6.4 Commonly used assembly instructions

Instruction	Meaning
mov	Copy right operand to left operand.
lea	Load effective address. Used to obtain pointers to local variables and function parameters.
push	Push operand onto top of stack.
pop	Pop top of stack into operand.
pushad	Push all general purpose registers onto stack.
popad	Pop top of stack into general purpose registers.
call	Call a function. A function called using an offset from a register (such as call [eax + 32]) is most likely a call to a C++ virtual function.
ret	Return from a function. If there is an operand, pop that number of bytes from the stack, as required by the __stdcall calling convention.
leave	Shorthand for mov ESP,EBP / pop EBP, used to exit functions.

Table 6.4 *Continued*

Instruction	Meaning
add	Arithmetic addition.
sub	Arithmetic subtraction.
inc	Increment operand.
dec	Decrement operand.
mul	Unsigned integer multiplication. Operands must be registers or memory.
imul	Signed integer multiplication.
div	Unsigned integer division. Operands must be registers or memory.
idiv	Signed integer division. Operands must be registers or memory.
and	Logical AND.
or	Logical OR.
not	Logical NOT, using one's complement negation. Same as flipping all the individual bits.
neg	Negate, using two's complement negation. Same as multiplying value by −1.
xor	Exclusive OR. XORing a register with itself is often used to set the register to zero.
cmp	Compare the operands (using subtraction) and set the flags accordingly. The operands are not modified.
test	Compare the bits of the operands (using a logical AND) and set the flags accordingly. The operands are not modified.
jmp	Unconditional jump.
je	Jump if equal.
jne	Jump if not equal.
loop	Return to the beginning of a loop, depending on the conditions.
nop	No operation. Used for padding.
int	Trigger interrupt. `int 3` invokes the debugger, which is often used for padding instructions that should never be called, thus making it a paranoid `nop`.

Table 6.5 Commonly used CPU registers

Register	Usage
EAX	General purpose, used for function return values
EBX	General purpose
ECX	General purpose, used for the `this` pointer for objects
EDX	General purpose, used for high word of 64-bit return values
ESI	Source for memory move and compare operations
EDI	Destination for memory move and compare operations
EIP	Instruction pointer (current location of code)
ESP	Stack pointer (current location of stack)
EBP	Stack base pointer (bottom of current stack frame)
EFLAGS	Flag bits for comparisons and math operations; sometimes abbreviated EFL or EFLGS

In addition to these registers, there are also CS (code segment), SS (stack segment), DS (data segment), ES (extra segment), FS (another extra segment), and GS (yet another extra segment); but except for the FS register, these segment registers typically are not useful in 32-bit Windows debugging. The FS register is used to point to the Thread Information Block (TIB), which is discussed later.

The Thread Stack

You may have noticed that there are surprisingly few CPU registers to work with. The stack is used to temporarily store data that isn't currently being processed and to store function return addresses, stack base addresses, function parameters, and automatic (local) variables. A stack works using a last-in, first-out method, so all the activity is always at the top of the stack. Stacks are unusual in that they grow down in memory, so the top of the stack has a lower address than the bottom of the stack. Each thread in a process is given its own stack.

The ESP and EBP registers are dedicated to the stack. The stack base pointer (EBP) register establishes the start of the stack frame, whereas the stack

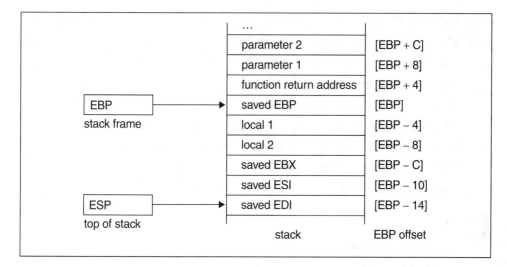

Figure 6.8 The thread stack frame

pointer (ESP) register points to the current top of the stack. Before a function is called, the function parameters and the function return address (the current EIP) are pushed on the stack. All parameters are widened to 32 bits when they are passed, but the return value of a function is passed not on the stack but through the EAX register. On function entry, the current stack base pointer is pushed on the stack and the current stack pointer becomes the new stack base pointer or stack frame. Also on function entry, room is made for local variables, and the various registers used by the function are saved on the stack. Consequently, Figure 6.8 shows how the typical stack frame looks after function entry.

The Stack Base Pointer and Frame Pointer Omission

The value of the stack base pointer is constant throughout the function, so it is used for finding the stack contents. Since the stack grows down in memory, function parameters are a positive offset from the stack base and local variables are a negative offset from the stack base.

To complicate matters, while what I just described is always true for debug builds, it may not be true for release builds because the stack base pointer may be optimized away. This type of optimization is called frame pointer omission (FPO). I say it *may* happen because it requires using the /Oy, /Ox, /O1, or /O2 compiler options and it is supported only by the Professional and Enterprise versions of Visual C++. Optimizers perform FPO to use the stack base register as another multipurpose register and eliminate the need to push and pop the EBP register for every function call. Using this optimization means that you won't find the EBP register pushed on the stack. This optimization also means that all parameters and local variables are a positive offset from the stack pointer and that the offset to a specific parameter or local variable in the stack changes as the top of the stack changes. Yuck! In assembly code optimization, performance is all that matters; readability doesn't score any points.

Optimized builds often do not use the EBP for a stack base pointer. This type of optimization is called frame pointer omission (FPO).

FPO optimization leads to an interesting bug in which the debug build works fine but the release build crashes. This bug occurs when there is a mismatch of function prototypes between the caller of a function and the function itself. For example, suppose the caller pushes four parameters on the stack but the function itself pops only three. This wouldn't cause a problem in a debug build because the stack base pointer contains the correct value for the stack frame, thereby allowing the function to find the correct return address to return to its caller. In a release build with FPO, the stack pointer doesn't point to the stack frame on function return so the program uses the wrong value for the function return address. To prevent this type of problem, be sure to declare all function prototypes in header files instead of in .cpp files. If you are using MFC, note that the signature for user-defined message handlers assigned using the ON_MESSAGE macro is

```
afx_msg LRESULT OnMyMessage (WPARAM wParam, LPARAM lParam);
```

If you use an incorrect signature, your program will crash with release builds but you will not receive any compiler or linker warnings. If you suspect an FPO optimization bug, the first thing you should do is double-check all your function prototypes. For debug builds, you can use the /GZ compiler option, which checks the stack pointer at the end of the function to make sure it hasn't been changed.

For release builds, you can explicitly disable FPO with the /Oy-compiler option and see if the problem goes away.

Function Calling Conventions

The manner in which parameters are pushed and popped off the stack is determined by the function's calling convention. Table 6.6 lists the calling conventions common in Windows programs.

Because using the wrong calling convention can lead to problems that are difficult to debug, it is worth spending some time to understand how to recognize the different calling conventions in action. Type-safe linking prevents most function prototype mismatches, but mismatches are always possible when

Table 6.6   Common calling conventions

Calling Convention	Description
__cdecl	The default calling convention for C/C++ programs. Arguments are passed from right to left, and the calling function removes the arguments from the stack. It is good for passing a variable number of parameters.
__stdcall	The calling convention used by the Windows API functions. Arguments are passed from right to left, and the called function removes the arguments from the stack. It results in smaller code than __cdecl, but it uses __cdecl if the function has a variable number of parameters. The WINAPI, CALLBACK, and APIENTRY macros are all defined as __stdcall.
thiscall (not a keyword)	The default calling convention used by C++ member functions that do not use variable arguments. It is the same as __stdcall except that the this pointer is stored in the ECX register instead of on the stack. Note that COM member functions use __stdcall.

function casting, generic function pointers (such as PVOID, FARPROC, or the *GetProcAddress* API), or functions declared using `extern "C"` are involved. At the source code level, you need to look for the calling convention keywords or equivalent macros.

For some examples, consider the following class.

```
class CMangledNames {
public:
    CMangledNames ()                    { m_Value = 0; }
    int Normal (int param)              { m_Value += param;
                                          return m_Value; }
    int __cdecl Cdecl (int param)       { m_Value += param;
                                          return m_Value; }
    int __stdcall Stdcall (int param) { m_Value += param;
                                          return m_Value; }
private:
    int m_Value;
};
```

In this class, the *Normal* function uses the *thiscall* calling convention, whereas the other functions use the specified calling convention.

You can also determine the calling convention by looking at the mangled symbols:

```
?Normal@CMangledNames@@QAEHH@Z
?Cdecl@CMangledNames@@QAAHH@Z
?Stdcall@CMangledNames@@QAGHH@Z
```

Here the third character in the mangled suffix is 'E' for *thiscall*, 'A' for `__cdecl`, and 'G' for `__stdcall`. If you are familiar with C++ name mangling, you know that `__stdcall` mangling for Windows API functions usually looks like _GetMessageA@16. You might then expect the `__stdcall` symbol to look like _Stdcall@CMangledNames@4, but this expectation is incorrect. This symbol format is used only for undecorated C symbols, such as functions declared using `extern "C"`.

At the assembly code level, *thiscall* sets the ECX register to the `this` pointer and the called function pops the parameters off the stack on function return. Here is the assembly code for calling the *Normal* function.

```
// example.Normal(0x42);
push          42                        ; push parameter
```

```
lea         ecx,[ebp-14h]    ; set ECX to this pointer
call        CMangledNames::Normal (004032b0)
```

Here is the assembly code that returns from *Normal*.

```
ret         4                        ; pop one parameter off stack
```

Although *Normal* has two parameters (*param* and `this`), only one parameter is passed on the stack.

The __cdecl calling convention requires the caller to push the `this` pointer and the other parameters on the stack and pop the parameters and the `this` pointer off the stack when the function returns. Here is the assembly code for calling the *Cdecl* function.

```
// example.Cdecl(0x42);
push        42               ; push parameter
lea         eax,[ebp-14h]    ; obtain this pointer
push        eax              ; push this pointer
call        CMangledNames::Cdecl (004032f0)
add         esp,8            ; pop two parameters off stack
```

Note that the parameters are popped off the stack by adding the size of the parameters to the ESP register immediately after the `call` instruction. Here is the assembly code that returns from *Cdecl*.

```
ret                          ; just return
```

The __stdcall calling convention pushes the `this` pointer and the other parameters on the stack, and the called function pops the parameters and the `this` pointer off the stack on function return. Here is the assembly code for calling the *Stdcall* function.

```
// example.Stdcall(0x42);
push        42               ; push parameter
lea         ecx,[ebp-14h]    ; obtain this pointer
push        ecx              ; push this pointer
call        CMangledNames::Stdcall (00403330)
```

Here is the assembly code that returns from *Stdcall*.

```
ret         8                        ; pop two parameters off stack
```

Variable Access

Variables are accessed in different ways, depending on their scope. Here are some examples.

```
add    dword ptr [0040c842],42   ; add 0x42 to a global or static
                                  ; variable
add    dword ptr [ebp-10],42     ; add 0x42 to a local variable
add    dword ptr [ebp+10],42     ; add 0x42 to a parameter
```

In these examples (which assume no FPO), a global or static variable is accessed directly from its virtual address, a local variable is accessed by a negative offset from the stack frame, and a parameter is accessed by a positive offset from the stack frame.

To access a data member in a structure, a pointer to the structure is moved to a register and the data member is accessed. For example, the following code initializes both the *x* and *y* members of a pointer to a POINT structure stored as a local variable.

```
mov    esi,dword ptr [ebp-8]     ; move POINT structure pointer to
                                 ; ESI
mov    dword ptr [esi],0         ; set x member to 0
mov    dword ptr [esi+4],0       ; set y member to 0
```

Reading Hex Dumps

There are two ways to store bytes in memory. The first way, known as Big Endian, is to store the high byte first, so 0x12345678 is stored as 0x12 0x34 0x56 0x78. The other way, known as Little Endian, is to store the low byte first, so 0x12345678 is stored 0x78 0x56 0x34 0x12. Intel CPUs use Little Endian. Whenever you see hexadecimal values in disassembled code, the disassembler always arranges the bytes in the correct order, so you will always see 0x12345678 in disassembled code. However, whenever you are reading a byte stream, such as a hex dump displayed in bytes, you must rearrange the bytes to obtain the correct values.

Using the Disassembly Window

At this point, you have enough assembly language knowledge to get you going. I used to know assembly language quite well, but that was so long ago it seems like another lifetime. Although I'm not exactly an assembly wiz, I find it fairly easy to figure out what is going on by looking in the debugger Disassembly window because it allows me to see how the source code translates into assembly code. Note that you can use the Disassembly window even if you are doing postmortem debugging. It's usually pretty straightforward, at least as long as it isn't optimized code.

> TIP
>
> Use the debugger Disassembly window to see how your source code translates into assembly code.

Debugging with MAP Files

To find your way around during postmortem debugging, you need a map. Specifically, you need a MAP file for all the modules that you created in your program. A MAP file contains the module's preferred load address, its section table, the addresses of exported symbols, the addresses of static symbols, and most importantly, the mapping between program code addresses and source code line numbers.

> TIP
>
> MAP files are your road map to postmortem debugging.

MAP files are somewhat primitive and require some effort to read, but they have two important advantages over other types of debugging files (such as PDB files): They are human readable text files, and they do not depend on any particular version of Visual C++.

Creating and Archiving MAP Files

To create MAP files for your program, you must make the appropriate settings for each of its Visual C++ projects. The first step is to enable MAP file generation. You do this from the Project Settings dialog box by selecting the **Generate mapfile** option in the **Debug** category of the **Link** tab. For some strange reason, Visual C++ does not output the mapping between program code addresses and source code line numbers by default. To get this information, type "/MAPINFO:LINES" at the end of the **Project Options** box. Having the export ordinals may also prove useful, so type "/MAPINFO:EXPORTS" at the end of the **Project Options** box as well.

> **TIP**
>
> To create the most useful MAP files, always use the /MAPINFO:LINES and /MAPINFO:EXPORTS project options.

You are most likely to perform postmortem debugging on programs you give to other people. This means that you should get into the habit of creating and archiving the MAP files for all the modules of programs you distribute. I suppose it is possible to recreate a MAP file for a previous version of a program, but that would require you to rebuild the program using exactly the same source code, exactly the same version of the compiler, and exactly the same project settings. It's much easier simply to archive the MAP files.

> **TIP**
>
> Archive the MAP files for all the modules of programs you distribute.

Reading MAP Files

Reading a MAP file is actually fairly simple. The first step, of course, is to find the MAP file that matches the module you are interested in and view that file in a text editor. At the top is the module name and the module's creation time. If the listed creation time doesn't match the module's file creation time, there's a chance the MAP file doesn't match the module. Next, check the preferred load base address, which is the virtual address at which the MAP file assumes the module was loaded. If you didn't rebase your program and there was a virtual address space collision for this module, all the virtual addresses (specifically, the Rva+Base values) must be adjusted to use the actual base address.

The next step is to find the closest matching function for the crash address. Public functions are listed before static functions, so you need to check both lists to find the matching function. In both function lists, the third column contains the Rva+Base value (for example, 0x00401044), which is the relative virtual address (for example, 0x00000044), plus the assumed base address (for example, 0x00400000), plus the PE file header size (0x00001000). The closest matching function is at the crash address or lower.

The final step is to find the closest matching source code line number. The MAP file lists line numbers in terms of the relative virtual addresses, so you have to work backward. That is, start with the crash address (for example, 0x00401044), subtract the actual base address (for example, 0x00400000) and the PE file header (0x00001000), and use the remainder (for example, 0x00000044). Now scan the line number RVAs until you find the closest match, which is the exact RVA or lower.

An Example

Let's work through a specific example. To illustrate postmortem debugging, I created a KillerApp program, which has a DLL that crashes with a variety of common bugs. The KillerApp main executable, which immediately follows, calls the *RandomCrash* function, a static function, with some easily recognizable parameters. In turn, *RandomCrash* then calls *RandomException* with a random first parameter and some other easily recognizable parameters. The *RandomException* function is in *KillerDLL.cpp*. Depending on its first paramter, *RandomException* crashes with either an access violation, stack overflow, or integer divide by zero exception. The fourth case in the switch statement is notable in that the crash occurs within Windows itself.

```
#include "stdafx.h"
#include <stdlib.h>
#include <time.h>
#include "..\KillerDLL\KillerDLL.h"

static void WINAPI RandomCrash (int arg1, int arg2, int arg3,
        int arg4) {
   int i = rand();
   RandomException(i, 0xDEADBEEF, 0xBADBAD00, 0xDECAF000);
}

int APIENTRY WinMain(HINSTANCE hInstance, HINSTANCE hPrevInstance,
                   LPSTR lpCmdLine, int nCmdShow) {
   srand(time(0));    // seed random number generator with current
                      // time
   RandomCrash(0xAAAAAAAA, 0xBBBBBBBB, 0xCCCCCCCC, 0xDDDDDDDD);
   return 0;
}
```

The *RandomException* function, in *KillerDLL.cpp,* follows.

```cpp
#include "stdafx.h"
#include <Limits.h>
#include "KillerDLL.h"

BOOL APIENTRY DllMain (HANDLE hModule, DWORD reason,
        LPVOID lpReserved) {
    return TRUE;
}

void WINAPI StackGlutton (int arg1, int arg2, int arg3, int arg4) {
    char bigArray[10000000];
}

void KILLERAPI WINAPI RandomException (int arg1, int arg2,
        int arg3, int arg4) {
    int i = 15, j = 0xEEEEEEEE;
    switch (arg1 % 6) {
        case 0:    // STATUS_ACCESS_VIOLATION
            j = *(int *)i;
            break;
        case 1: { // STATUS_STACK_OVERFLOW
            StackGlutton(arg1, arg2, arg3, arg4);
            break;
        }
        case 2:    // STATUS_INTEGER_DIVIDE_BY_ZERO
            j = 0;
            i /= j;
            break;
        case 3: { // crash in Windows
            CHOOSECOLOR cc;
            ZeroMemory(&cc, sizeof(cc));  // will crash Win98 if you
                                          // don't zero

            cc.lStructSize = sizeof(cc);
            ChooseColor(&cc);             // crashes since
                                          // lpCustColors isn't set
        }
        case 4: { // crash in structure access
            CHOOSECOLOR cc, *pcc = &cc;
            COLORREF rgb;
            ZeroMemory(&cc, sizeof(cc));
            rgb = pcc->lpCustColors[0];   // crashes since
                                          // lpCustColors is invalid
```

```
        }
        case 5: { // crash in structure access
            CHOOSECOLOR cc, *pcc = 0;
            COLORREF rgb;
            ZeroMemory(&cc, sizeof(cc));
            rgb = pcc->lpCustColors[0];    // crashes since pcc is
                                           // invalid
        }
    }
}
```

Here is the MAP file for *KillerApp.exe.*

```
KillerApp
 Timestamp is 384855c7 (Sat Jan 01 12:00:00 2000)
 Preferred load address is 00400000

 Start           Length      Name              Class
 0001:00000000 0000c2acH .text              CODE
 0002:00000000 000000e8H .idata$5           DATA
 0002:000000e8 00001047H .rdata             DATA
 0002:00001130 00000028H .idata$2           DATA
 0002:00001158 00000014H .idata$3           DATA
 0002:0000116c 000000e8H .idata$4           DATA
 0002:00001254 00000412H .idata$6           DATA
 0002:00001666 00000000H .edata             DATA
 0003:00000030 000009f0H .data              DATA
 0003:00000a20 00001640H .bss               DATA

  Address           Publics by Value          Rva+Base
      Lib:Object
 0001:00000000        _WinMain@16              00401000 f
      KillerApp.obj
 0001:000000b6        ?RandomException@@YGXHHHH@Z 004010b6 f
      KillerDll:KillerDLL.dll

 entry point at       0001:000002d0

 Static symbols
 0001:00000060        ?RandomCrash@@YGXHHHH@Z    00401060 f
      KillerApp.obj

Line numbers for .\Debug\KillerApp.obj
(C:\PROJECTS\KillerApp\KillerApp.cpp) segment .text
```

```
     12 0001:00000000      13 0001:00000018      14 0001:0000002b
     15 0001:00000044      16 0001:00000046       6 0001:00000060
      7 0001:00000078       8 0001:00000080       9 0001:000000a2
```

Here is the MAP file for *KillerDLL.dll*.

```
KillerDLL
 Timestamp is 38484c3d (Sat Jan 01 12:00:00 2000)
 Preferred load address is 10000000

 Start           Length      Name               Class
 0001:00000000  00011c5cH  .text               CODE
 0002:00000000  0000012cH  .idata$5            DATA
 0002:00000130  000018d9H  .rdata              DATA
 0002:00001a0c  00000028H  .idata$2            DATA
 0002:00001a34  00000014H  .idata$3            DATA
 0002:00001a48  0000012cH  .idata$4            DATA
 0002:00001b74  0000053aH  .idata$6            DATA
 0002:000020b0  0000005cH  .edata              DATA
 0003:00000030  00001480H  .data               DATA
 0003:000014b0  00001734H  .bss                DATA

  Address             Publics by Value            Rva+Base
     Lib:Object
 0001:00000000        _DllMain@12                 10001000 f
     KillerDLL.obj
 0001:00000030        ?StackGlutton@@YGXHHHH@Z    10001030 f
     KillerDLL.obj
 0001:00000060        ?RandomException@@YGXHHHH@Z 10001060 f
     KillerDLL.obj
 0001:00000182        _ChooseColorA@4             10001182 f
     comdlg32:comdlg32.dll

 Line numbers for .\Debug\KillerDLL.obj
 (C:\PROJECTS\KillerDLL\KillerDLL.cpp) segment .text

      5 0001:00000000       6 0001:00000018       7 0001:0000001d
      9 0001:00000030      11 0001:00000052      13 0001:00000060
     14 0001:0000007e      15 0001:0000008c      17 0001:000000b7
     18 0001:000000bf      20 0001:000000c4      21 0001:000000d9
     24 0001:000000db      25 0001:000000e2      26 0001:000000ec
     29 0001:000000ee      30 0001:000000fe      31 0001:00000105
     34 0001:0000010e      36 0001:00000114      37 0001:00000124
```

```
40 0001:0000012f      42 0001:00000136      43 0001:00000146
46 0001:00000154

    Exports
    ordinal      name
        1        ?RandomException@@YGXHHHH@Z (void __stdcall
                 RandomException(int,int,int,int))
```

To save space, I stripped the sections, symbols, and line number information for the C Run-time Library functions. The run-time library line number information isn't helpful unless you have the source code, but this information does allow you to determine which run-time library function crashed and perhaps dig through the disassembled code to figure out exactly why.

Now let's assume that *KillerDLL.dll* crashed at virtual address 0x100010BF. Checking *KillerDLL.map*, you can see that the preferred load base address is 0x10000000. Because KillerApp uses only a single DLL, you don't have to worry about virtual address space collisions; the preferred load base address confirms this. This means that you can use the MAP file virtual addresses without any adjustment. To find the closest matching function, take the crash address and find the public or static function with that Rva+base address or lower. This gives us the *RandomException* function. To find the closest matching source code line number, take the crash address (0x100010BF), subtract the base address (0x10000000) and the PE header size (0x00001000). This gives an RVA of 0x000000BF. Looking up that address in the line number section gives us line 18.

When looking up line numbers, keep in mind that the compiled code may be arranged in a completely different order from the source code. In the line number listings, the RVAs advance sequentially, but the source code line numbers may bounce around quite a bit. In this example, the line numbers for *KillerDLL.cpp* are sequential, but the line numbers for *KillerApp.cpp* are not.

Debugging with PDB Files

For a comparison, let's do some postmortem debugging with Visual C++ by finding the crash address in your source code using the debugger. This approach requires that you have the matching source code and PDB files for the program that crashed. In addition, you must use a version of Visual C++ that is compatible with that version of the PDB file format, which you cannot always take for granted. This technique may not work if the crash address is in a module that had to be relocated in virtual memory.

You can perform the following steps to find the source code file name and line number for a crash address.

1. Load your program's project in Visual C++.
2. Step into your program with the debugger using either the **Step Into** command in the **Debug** menu or the F11 key.
3. Display the Disassembly window.
4. Give the **Go To** command in the **Edit** menu. In the **Go To** dialog box, select **Address** in the **Go to what** box.
5. Enter the crash address in the **Enter address expression** box. This box is unavailable if the Disassembly window wasn't the active window. Be sure that the address starts with 0x.
6. To find the crash address in the Disassembly window, click the **Go To** button.
7. To find the source code location from the Disassembly window, give the **Go To Source** command in the context menu.

Clearly, as Visual C++ makes finding a crash location easier than using Map files, use it whenever you can.

> **TIP**
>
> You can also use PDB files for postmortem debugging directly from Visual C++.

Debugging Using a Windows 98 Crash Dialog Box

With the preliminaries out of the way, let's get down to business. Debugging using a Windows 98 crash dialog box simply requires you to combine all the information presented so far in this chapter. Let's continue with the KillerApp example by analyzing the following crash dump information obtained from a Windows 98 crash dialog box.

```
KILLERAPP caused an invalid page fault in module KILLERDLL.DLL at
    017f:10001189.
Registers:
```

```
EAX=0065fc60  CS=017f  EIP=10001189  EFLGS=00010212
EBX=00550000  SS=0187  ESP=0065fc08  EBP=0065fcdc
ECX=00000000  DS=0187  ESI=0065fcf4  FS=4cc7
EDX=00000000  ES=0187  EDI=0065fcdc  GS=0000
Bytes at CS:EIP:
8b 42 10 8b 08 89 8d 7c ff ff ff 5f 5e 5b 81 c4
Stack dump:
0065fd44 0065fcf4 00550000 cccccccc cccccccc cccccccc cccccccc
cccccccc cccccccc cccccccc cccccccc cccccccc cccccccc cccccccc
cccccccc cccccccc
```

Look first for the name of the program, the module that crashed, and the type of exception. Be sure that you are debugging your program and not something else. For example, a bug in your program might cause Windows Explorer to crash, but you won't get very far debugging Windows Explorer. The module that crashed tells you which MAP file to check the crash address in, so in this case you should check *KillerDLL.map* for that address. The exception type tells you the type of problem to look for.

Next, determine the source code file name and line number of the code that crashed. Using the previous procedure for reading MAP files, you can determine that the address 0x10001189 is line 43 of *KillerDLL.cpp*. Here is the offending code:

```
rgb = pcc->lpCustColors[0];
```

Now you can determine the exact problem. Given that an access violation exception occurred, you can conclude that either *pcc* or *lpCustColors* points to invalid memory. So which is it? You have plenty of information to make this determination. Let's set a breakpoint on *KillerDLL.cpp*, line 43 in the Visual C++ debugger, start the program, and then view the disassembled code in the Disassembly window using the **Code Annotation** and **Code Bytes** options.

```
43:                rgb = pcc->lpCustColors[0];
10001186 8B 55 80              mov       edx,dword ptr [pcc]
10001189 8B 42 10              mov       eax,dword ptr [edx+10h]
1000118C 8B 08                 mov       ecx,dword ptr [eax]
1000118E 89 8D 7C FF FF FF     mov       dword ptr [rgb],ecx
```

Working through the assembly code, the instruction at 0x10001186 moves *pcc* to the EDX register. However, the crash dump shows that EDX is 0. The instruction at 0x10001189 then dereferences EDX by 0x10 bytes and moves that to the EAX register. Crash bang! Address 0x00000010 is not accessible memory. Clearly, *pcc* is invalid because it is a null pointer. The specific crash address (0x10001189), the contents of EDX, and dump of the bytes at CS:EIP (which shows the specific code that crashed) all confirm this conclusion. Now all you have to do is figure out why *pcc* isn't valid, and you're done debugging this problem.

> **TIP**
>
> Use the specific crash address, the register values, and the disassembled code to determine the specific cause of a crash.

Although the other crash dump information is not needed in this example, let's quickly review how this information might be useful in other situations. The multipurpose EAX through EDX, ESI, and EDI registers are where most of the program action takes place, so the crashing instruction is likely to be manipulating one of these registers. Again, EAX is used for function return values and ECX is often used for C++ `this` pointers. It is sometimes useful to check the EFLGS values to determine results of math operations. You can safely ignore the CS, SS, DS, and ES segment registers because they aren't significant in 32-bit Windows.

The ESP register is the top of the stack, and the EBP is the stack base pointer for this function (assuming no FPO). These address values can help you interpret the meaning of the stack dump. Functions immediately push the EBP register on entry, so looking for these stack base pointers in the stack dump will help you identify the stack frames and function return addresses. Recall the order in which data is pushed on the stack for a function call: the function parameters, the return address, the EBP register, the local variables, and any saved registers. In this particular crash, the stack dump isn't very interesting. This stack dump displays only the saved values of the EDI, ESI, and EBX registers, as well as a lot of uninitialized local variables. Note that the uninitialized local variables are initialized to 0xCCCCCCCC since this is a debug build built with the /GZ compiler option. Were the /GZ compiler option not used, these values would contain garbage. Also note that having uninitialized local variables on the stack isn't necessarily a sign of a problem. In this case, the uninitialized stack data is one of the CHOOSECOLOR structures declared in the unexecuted `switch` statement cases.

TIP

Use the EBP register value to determine the stack frames in the stack dump.

Now let's make things interesting. Suppose your program crashes somewhere outside your code. If the program crashed in MFC, you are in luck because Visual C++ supplies the MAP files for all the MFC DLLs (found on the Visual C++ CD-ROM in the *\Vc\Debug* folder). If the program crashes in a C Run-time Library function, you are also in luck because the MAP file contains all the public function addresses. For KillerApp, a crash address of 0x00404030 would indicate that the program crashed in *strcpy*. But which *strcpy* function call? What if the program crashed within Windows? Your only hope for getting back to your program is to look at the stack trace. Since the return address is pushed on the stack before a function call, there may be a return address to your code on the stack. For KillerApp, the main executable has an address range of 0x00400000–0x00429FFF, whereas the KillerDLL has an address range of 0x10000000–0x10031FFFF. If you find a value within these ranges on the stack after something that looks like an EBP (actually, it is preceded by an EBP if you are reading from left to right) that is likely to be a return address to your code. You can then look up the source code information of the calling function in the MAP file. For more information on interpreting virtual address values, see Reading Windows Memory Addresses in Chapter 9.

TIP

If the crash didn't occur in your code, use the stack dump to determine the return address to your code.

What if the program crashed trying to execute code at some random address? For example, suppose the program crashed at a very low address, such as 0x00000008, or an unusual address, such as 0x73677562, and there clearly isn't any valid code there. The following are the leading causes for attempting to execute invalid code.

- The code is attempting to call a function using an invalid function pointer.
- There is a prototype mismatch between the caller and the actual function.
- The stack has been corrupted, often by having a local variable overflow into the function return address.

In the first two cases, since the function call wasn't successful, the called function never had the opportunity to push the stack base pointer, local variables, or saved register on the stack. This means the function return address is likely to be at the very top of the stack, which makes it easy to get back to your code. In the last case, the return address itself contains some of the overwritten data, possibly giving you a clue to the cause of the problem. For example, if the pointer address looks like four ANSI characters (such as the address 0x73677562, which is ANSI for "bugs"), it's likely that a local string was overwritten, as in the following code.

```
void StackAttack () {
    TCHAR bugsText[16], *bugs = _T("This function has bugs!");
    _tcscpy(bugsText, bugs);
}
```

In this case, the *bugs* string is eight bytes (if using ANSI text) too long for *bugsText*, so the string copy overwrites the return address with text.

It is important to understand that if the crash address is in Windows, this is almost certainly a bug in your program and not a bug in Windows. Most likely you passed a bad parameter or corrupted data to a Windows API. By contrast, if the crash address is in a device driver, there is a very good chance that the driver itself has a bug or the hardware is incorrectly set up. The reason is that Windows programs rarely communicate directly with device drivers; rather, they communicate with drivers indirectly through Windows. If you pass bad data to Windows that results in a crash, Windows itself should do the crashing, not the device driver.

TIP

Crashing in Windows is almost certainly the result of a bug in your code, whereas crashing in a device driver is most likely a bug in the driver itself.

To really perform postmortem debugging in these situations, however, what you need is a Dr. Watson log file.

Debugging Using Dr. Watson

When it comes to postmortem debugging, Dr. Watson is the real star. As long as there's an uncorrupted stack, a Dr. Watson log file (and a *User.dmp* file for Windows 2000) should provide everything you need to trace a crash back to the offending source code in your program. It gives a detailed stack trace, the assembly code that was running at each stack frame, and a summary of the system state. As discussed in Chapter 1, The Debugging Process, you need to give your testers instructions on setting up Dr. Watson and attaching the log files to bug reports to ensure that you get all the information you need to debug crashes.

Debugging Symbols

To get the most from a Dr. Watson log file, make sure that you (and your testers) have installed the system debugging symbols (DBG files) if you are running Windows 2000 or Windows NT. Having the debugging symbols allows Dr. Watson to provide the system function names in the stack trace. Note that Windows 98 doesn't have system debugging symbols, but Visual C++ supplies symbols for MFC and the C Run-time Library DLLs. To install the debugging symbols for Windows 2000, use the Customer Support Diagnostics CD-ROM, which starts the installation program automatically when you insert the CD. To install the debugging symbols for Windows NT 4.0, go to the Visual C++ program group and run the Windows NT Symbols Setup program. Both setup programs copy the system DBG files from the CD-ROM to the *WinNT*\\ *Symbols**Dlls* folder.

> **TIP**
>
> Be sure to install the system debugging symbols for Windows 2000 and Windows NT.

The only trick is that Dr. Watson uses the symbol files only if they exactly match the installed executable files. It is highly likely that a mismatch will occur after you install a service pack. Consequently, whenever you install a service pack, you should update the system symbols by copying them from the *Support**Debug* folder on the service pack CD-ROM. If you are unsure about the status of the symbols, run your program from the Visual C++ debugger. A message saying "Loaded 'EXAMPLE.DLL', no matching symbolic information found" appears in the **Debug** tab of the Output window whenever matching symbols aren't found.

Dr. Watson in Windows 98 versus Windows 2000

Dr. Watson is implemented differently in Windows 98 and Windows 2000. Although the information in the Dr. Watson log files is fundamentally the same, the presentation of the information is significantly different. I will first show you how to use the Windows 98 version of Dr. Watson by working through an example, then I'll explain how the Windows 2000 version differs.

Using Dr. Watson in Windows 98

To obtain log files, Dr. Watson must be running, which isn't the case by default in Windows 98. To have Dr. Watson launch automatically at startup in Windows 98, create a shortcut to the Dr. Watson executable (in *\Windows\DrWatson.exe*) in your Startup group.

To view a Dr. Watson log file, first you must double-click on the WLG file (found in *\Windows\Drwatson*) in the Windows Explorer to load the file into Dr. Watson. Dr. Watson log files in Windows 98 are now binary, unlike in the past, so you can't view them in a text editor. By default, Dr. Watson displays only the **Diagnosis** tab, which isn't especially useful. To see the good stuff, as shown in Figure 6.9, select the **Advanced View** option in the **View** menu. Whereas most of the tabs show information about the system when it crashed, the **Modules** tab shows the program's executable files along with their version numbers, descriptions, paths, file dates, and virtual address ranges. To debug a crash, the most useful information is in the **Details** tab, which gives the register values, the exception record, and the full stack trace. Unfortunately, you cannot copy any of this text directly to the clipboard, so if you want to extract text, you must save the log file as a text document using the **Save As** command in the **File** menu. Then you can view the text log file in a text editor.

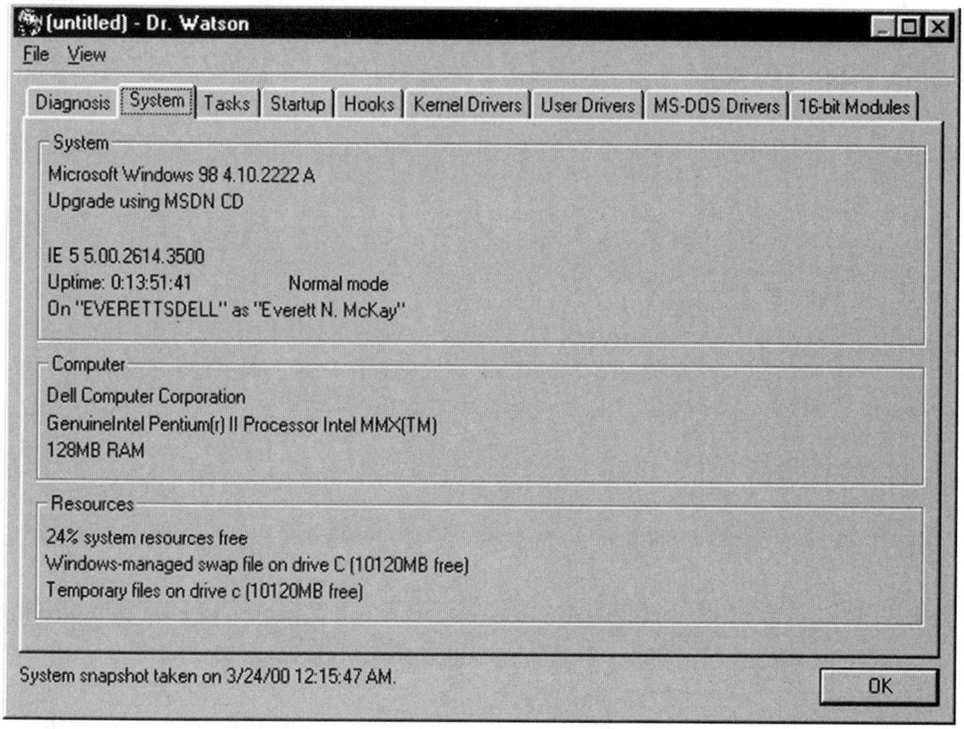

Figure 6.9 The Windows 98 Dr. Watson user interface

Let's debug the KillerApp crash within Windows that we weren't able to debug before by walking through a Windows 98 Dr. Watson log file and interpreting its information. Here is the KillerApp Dr. Watson log file, which I have edited severely to remove extraneous information.

```
System snapshot taken on 12/1/99 12:00:00 PM.
*—> Summary/Overview <—*
        Common Dialogs DLL attempted to use a null data pointer
            variable.
        Module Name: COMDLG32.DLL
        Description: Common Dialogs DLL
        Version: 4.72.3510.2300
        Product: Microsoft(R) Windows NT(R) Operating System
        Manufacturer: Microsoft Corporation
        Application Name: Killerapp.exe
        User's Remarks: This program sucks. It always crashes.
*—> System Information <—*
        Microsoft Windows 98 4.10.2222 A
```

```
           Upgrade using MSDN CD
           /SrcDir=F:\WIN98_SE\SETUP\WIN98 /IQ /U:xxxxxxxxxxxxxxxxx
           IE 5 5.00.2614.3500
           Uptime: 0:00:05:01
           Normal mode
           On "EVERETTSDELL" as "Everett N. McKay"
           Dell Computer Corporation
           GenuineIntel Pentium(r) II Processor Intel MMX(TM)
              Technology
           128MB RAM
           73% system resources free
           Windows-managed swap file on drive C (10483MB free)
           Temporary files on drive c (10483MB free)
*—> Details <—*
Command line: "C:\Projects\KillerApp\Debug\KillerApp.exe"
Trap 0e 0000 - Invalid page fault
eax=00000000 ebx=bff520a4 ecx=0064fbbc edx=00000016 esi=0064fa58
edi=bff54efc
eip=7fe14530 esp=0064f684 ebp=00000598
— — — nv up EI pl ZR na PE nc
cs=017f ss=0187 ds=0187 es=0187 fs=488f gs=0000
COMDLG32.DLL:.text+0x3530:
>017f:7fe14530 8b10                    mov       edx,dword ptr [eax]
    sel  type base      lim/bot
    —— —— ———— ————
cs 017f r-x- 00000000 ffffffff
ss 0187 rw-e 00000000 000087a0
ds 0187 rw-e 00000000 000087a0
es 0187 rw-e 00000000 000087a0
fs 488f rw— 817ab468 00000037
gs 0000 —
stack base:    00550000
TIB limits:    0064d000 - 00650000
— exception record —
   Exception Code: c0000005 (access violation)
Exception Address: 7fe14530 (COMDLG32.DLL:.text+0x3530)
   Exception Info: 00000000
                   ffffffff
COMDLG32.DLL:.text+0x3530:
>017f:7fe14530 8b10                    mov       edx,dword ptr [eax]
...
— stack summary —
0187:00000598 017f:7fe14530 COMDLG32.DLL:.text+0x3530
                             (f000ff59,00000000,f000fe6e,f000ff53,
                             f000ff53,f000f0a4,00000522,c00051bf)
```

```
0187:f00085dc 017f:f000efd2 017f:f000efd2
- stack trace -
0187:00000598 017f:7fe14530 COMDLG32.DLL:.text+0x3530
                              (f000ff59,00000000,f000fe6e,f000ff53,
                              f000ff53,f000f0a4,00000522,c00051bf)
  017f:7fe14509 ff74243c            push    dword ptr [esp+3c]
  017f:7fe1450d 55                  push    ebp
  017f:7fe1450e ff150c13e17f        call    dword ptr [7fe1130c] ->
     USER32.DLL!MoveWindow
  017f:7fe14514 56                  push    esi
  017f:7fe14515 55                  push    ebp
  017f:7fe14516 e82bfbffff          call    7fe14046 =
     COMDLG32.DLL:.text+0x3046
  017f:7fe1451b 8d8e64010000        lea     ecx,[esi+00000164]
  017f:7fe14521 8b442434            mov     eax,dword ptr [esp+34]
  017f:7fe14525 c744242c10000000    mov     dword ptr
     [esp+2c],00000010
  017f:7fe1452d 8b4010              mov     eax,dword ptr [eax+10]
     COMDLG32.DLL:.text+0x3530:
*017f:7fe14530 8b10                 mov     edx,dword ptr [eax]
  017f:7fe14532 83c004              add     eax,+04
  017f:7fe14535 8911                mov     dword ptr [ecx],edx
  017f:7fe14537 83c104              add     ecx,+04
  017f:7fe1453a ff4c242c            dec     dword ptr [esp+2c]
  017f:7fe1453e 75f0                jnz     7fe14530 =
     COMDLG32.DLL:.text+0x3530
  017f:7fe14540 ff7614              push    dword ptr [esi+14]
  017f:7fe14543 6683662600          and     word ptr [esi+26],+00
  017f:7fe14548 6683662800          and     word ptr [esi+28],+00
  017f:7fe1454d 66c746243000        mov     word ptr [esi+24],0030
  017f:7fe14553 56                  push    esi
  _____

0187:f00085dc 017f:f000efd2 017f:f000efd2
- stack dump -
0064f684 0064fa58 -> 01 00 00 00 b0 fc 64 00 00 00 00 00 98 05 00 00
0064f688 00000000
0064f68c 0064f734 -> 54 f7 64 00 3b 36 f7 bf 98 05 00 00 10 01 00 00
0064f690 00000598
0064f694 000005c8
0064f698 000000de
0064f69c 000000ea
0064f6a0 0000001d
0064f6a4 0000019b
0064f6a8 000000da
```

```
0064f6ac 7fe130cb = COMDLG32.DLL:.text+0x20cb
```

```
017f:100010ee 6a24                      push      +24
017f:100010f0 6a00                      push      +00
017f:100010f2 8d45d4                    lea       eax,[ebp-2c]
017f:100010f5 50                        push      eax
017f:100010f6 e8c5000000                call      100011c0 =
      KILLERDLL.DLL:.text+0x1c0
017f:100010fb 83c40c                    add       esp,+0c
017f:100010fe c745d424000000            mov       dword ptr [ebp-
      2c],00000024
017f:10001105 8d4dd4                    lea       ecx,[ebp-2c]
017f:10001108 51                        push      ecx
017f:10001109 e874000000                call      10001182 =
      COMDLG32.DLL!ChooseColorA
KILLERDLL.DLL:.text+0x10e:
*017f:1000110e 8d55b0                   lea       edx,[ebp-50]
 017f:10001111 8955ac                   mov       dword ptr [ebp-54],edx
 017f:10001114 6a24                     push      +24
 017f:10001116 6a00                     push      +00
 017f:10001118 8d45b0                   lea       eax,[ebp-50]
 017f:1000111b 50                       push      eax
 017f:1000111c e89f000000               call      100011c0 =
      KILLERDLL.DLL:.text+0x1c0
 017f:10001121 83c40c                   add       esp,+0c
 017f:10001124 8b4dac                   mov       ecx,dword ptr [ebp-54]
 017f:10001127 8b5110                   mov       edx,dword ptr [ecx+10]
 017f:1000112a 8b02                     mov       eax,dword ptr [edx]
```

```
0064fc04 0064fcb0 -> 24 00 00 00 00 00 00 00 00 00 00 00 00 00 00 00
0064fc08 0064fd44 -> a8 fd 64 00 44 10 40 00 aa aa aa aa bb bb bb bb
0064fc0c 0064fcf4 -> a8 fd 64 00 38 b2 7a 81 00 00 54 00 cc cc cc cc
0064fc10 00540000
0064fc14 cccccccc -> 90 98 a8 00 90 98 a8 00 90 98 a8 00 90 98 a8 00
0064fc54 00000003
0064fc58 cccccccc -> 90 98 a8 00 90 98 a8 00 90 98 a8 00 90 98 a8 00
0064fcb0 00000024
0064fcb4 00000000
0064fcd4 eeeeeeee
0064fcd8 0000000f
0064fcdc 0064fd44 -> a8 fd 64 00 44 10 40 00 aa aa aa aa bb bb bb bb
0064fce0 00401099 = KILLERAPP.EXE:.text+0x99
```

The Summary/Overview section describes the reason for the crash, the module that crashed and its version and description, the program that crashed, and the user remarks. The System Information section gives the Windows and Internet Explorer version numbers and a summary of the hardware and free resources. The Details section first gives the command line, the hardware exception number (which is defined by the CPU, not Windows), the register values, the program instruction that raised the exception, the stack base and the Thread Information Block address range. The TIB contains potentially useful information, such as the exception record, Structured Exception Handler (SEH) chain, the top and base of the stack, and the Tread Local Storage (TLS) array. For more information on the TIB, check Matt Pietrek's "Under the Hood" (May, 1996). The next information is the exception record, which gives the Windows exception code, the code address where the exception occurred, and the assembly code of the crash address. It also gives the RVA of the crash address, which in this case is 0x00003530.

Now for the interesting part. The remainder of the Details section gives a stack summary and then a detailed stack trace. Note that the specific number of stack frames in the stack trace is determined by the **Number of stack frames** setting in the Dr. Watson Options dialog box. The first stack frame shows where the crash occurred, and the crash location is labeled with an asterisk. Each of the following stack frames is also labeled with an asterisk to show the crash location, but you must be careful with these. These asterisks identify the return address on the stack, so the instruction that led to the crash actually precedes the labeled instruction.

TIP

The first stack frame labels the crash location with an asterisk, but the following stack frames label the instruction after the instruction that led to the crash.

To perform postmortem debugging, the first step is to review the Summary Overview information in the log file to understand what is going on and look for anything out of the ordinary. For example, you should check all the version information to make sure you are debugging what you think you are. As with the

Windows 98 crash dialog box, check the program name to make sure that you are debugging your program and not something else.

The next step is to review the stack trace. Assuming, as in this case, that the crash didn't occur in your code, trace back until you find the first stack frame for your program. Because I edited the Dr. Watson log file down significantly, this is quite easy to do here; but in the actual log file the crash occurs 14 frames back. Here is the specific program code that crashed.

```
017f:100010fe c745d424000000          mov      dword ptr [ebp-   2c],
     00000024
017f:10001105 8d4dd4                   lea      ecx,[ebp-2c]
017f:10001108 51                       push     ecx
017f:10001109 e874000000               call     10001182 =
     COMDLG32.DLL!ChooseColorA
KILLERDLL.DLL:.text+0x10e:
*017f:1000110e 8d55b0                   lea      edx,[ebp-50]
```

Again, note that the asterisk labels the return address instruction, so the instruction that led to the crash called the *ChooseColor* API function in *Comdlg32.dll*. Looking up the source code line number in the MAP file, you can determine that the source code line number is *KillerDLL.dll*, line 31, which is the last line in the following code.

```
CHOOSECOLOR cc;
ZeroMemory(&cc, sizeof(cc));   // crashes Win98 if you don't zero
cc.lStructSize = sizeof(cc);
ChooseColor(&cc);              // crashes since lpCustColors isn't
                              // set
```

(Now don't get ahead of me—you have to pretend you don't know why the program crashed yet.) As I noted earlier, crashing in Windows suggests that the program passed a bad parameter to an API function. Since there is only one parameter to *ChooseColor*, the next step is to look at the top of the stack for this stack frame and check the actual value passed.

```
0064fc04 0064fcb0 -> 24 00 00 00 00 00 00 00 00 00 00 00 00 00 00 00
```

The top of the stack dump for this frame shows that the top of the stack address is 0x0064FC04 and it contains the value 0x0064FCB0. Since 0x0064FCB0 is a valid address for this process, Dr. Watson is kind enough to assume that this value is a pointer, and it dumps the first 16 bytes pointed to by that address. From this dump, you see that the first byte is 0x24 and the remaining bytes are 0, which suggests an uninitialized parameter.

At this point, the bug is pretty much solved. Were the problem less obvious, however, the next step would be to go back to the top of the stack and try to determine specifically what was wrong with the parameter. Here is the code at the top of the stack.

```
017f:7fe1452d 8b4010                 mov       eax,dword ptr [eax+10]
   COMDLG32.DLL:.text+0x3530:
*017f:7fe14530 8b10                   mov       edx,dword ptr [eax]
```

Walking through the code, the address in the EAX register is offset by 16 (0x10) bytes and the pointer is then moved to the EAX register. The code then attempts to dereference the value in the EAX register and move it to EDX, but that instruction crashes. From the register values given in the log file, you can see that EAX has a value of 0, so the program crashed trying to deference a null pointer. Note that this diagnosis matches the problem identified at the top of the log file. Since this code is deep within Windows, you can't be too sure what is really going on. However, if you assume the program crashed directly using the bad parameter passed to *ChooseColor*, it makes sense to look at CHOOSECOLOR structure.

```
typedef struct tagCHOOSECOLORA {
    DWORD           lStructSize;
    HWND            hwndOwner;
    HWND            hInstance;
    COLORREF        rgbResult;
    COLORREF*       lpCustColors;
    DWORD           Flags;
    LPARAM          lCustData;
    LPCCHOOKPROC    lpfnHook;
    LPCSTR          lpTemplateName;
} CHOOSECOLORA, *LPCHOOSECOLORA;
```

Significantly, the *lpCustColors* data member is offset 16 bytes into this structure, and having a null pointer there is in fact the problem. Of course, the other members of this structure aren't initialized either, but a null pointer in *lpCustColors* is the one that led to this particular crash.

That wasn't so bad, was it?

Using Dr. Watson in Windows 2000

Dr. Watson is running by default in Windows 2000, but you have to make sure that JIT debugging is disabled to use it. (This isn't something you would normally want to do, because it is better to debug a live program with Visual C++ than a dead one with Dr. Watson.) You can disable JIT debugging by using the **Options** command in the Visual C++ **Tools** menu, selecting the **Debug** tab, and clearing the **Just-in-time debugging** option. Once this is done, if your program crashes, you will receive the Windows 2000 crash message box as shown in Figure 6.10. The Windows 2000 Dr. Watson has several options you can configure by running Dr. Watson from the Windows Explorer (in *\WinNT\System32\Drwtsn32.exe*). Most likely you will want to select the options shown in Figure 6.11. Clearing the **Dump Symbol Table** and **Append To Existing Log File** options helps prevent the log files from becoming too large. Selecting the **Visual Notification** option presents the previously shown crash message box when a program crashes. Selecting the **Create Crash Dump File** option creates a *User.dmp* file, which is discussed later in this chapter.

To view a Dr. Watson log file, double-click on the *Drwtsn32.log* file (found in *\Documents and Settings\All Users\Documents\DrWatson*) to view the log file using Notepad. The Windows 2000 Dr. Watson log file for the KillerApp crash within Windows is listed here (ending on page 260).

```
Microsoft (R) Windows 2000 (TM) Version 5.00 DrWtsn32
Copyright (C) 1985-1999 Microsoft Corp. All rights reserved.

Application exception occurred:
        App: Debug/KillerApp.exe (pid=452)
        When: 01/1/2000 @ 12:00:00.000
        Exception number: c0000005 (access violation)

*——> System Information <—*
        Computer Name: EVERETTSDELL
        User Name: Everett N. McKay
        Number of Processors: 1
        Processor Type: x86 Family 6 Model 5 Stepping 1
```

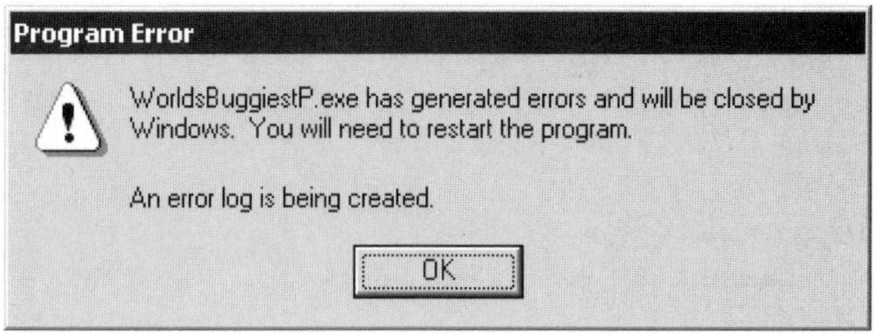

Figure 6.10   The Windows 2000 crash message box with Dr. Watson enabled

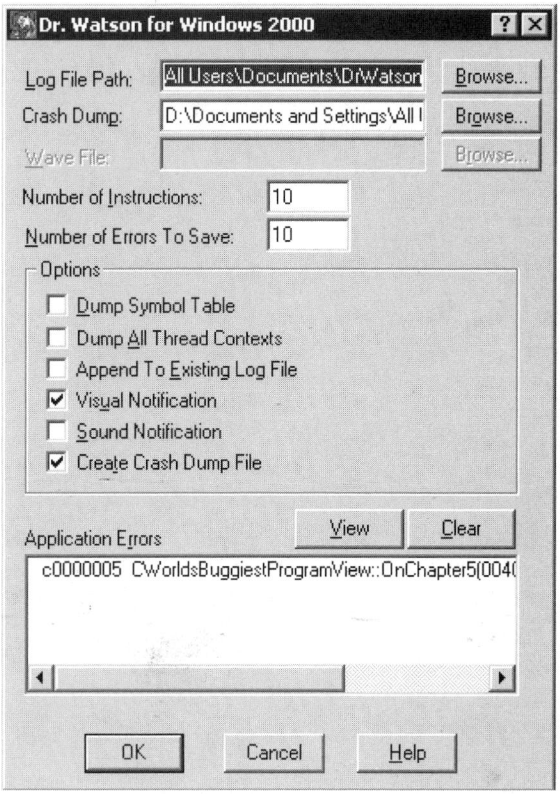

Figure 6.11   The Windows 2000 Dr. Watson options dialog box

```
Windows 2000 Version: 5.0
Current Build: 2128
Service Pack: None
Current Type: Uniprocessor Free
Registered Organization: Windmill Point Software
Registered Owner: Everett N. McKay
```

```
        *—> Task List <—*
      0 Idle.exe
      8 System.exe
    136 smss.exe
    164 csrss.exe
    160 winlogon.exe
    212 services.exe
    224 lsass.exe
    388 svchost.exe
    416 spoolsv.exe
    448 svchost.exe
    488 regsvc.exe
    504 MSTask.exe
    684 Explorer.exe
    656 findfast.exe
    516 Winword.exe
    724 NOTEPAD.exe
    312 ntvdm.exe
    480 NOTEPAD.exe
    908 drwtsn32.exe
    912 mspaint.exe
    740 MSDEV.exe
    668 KillerApp.exe
    452 KillerApp.exe
    208 drwtsn32.exe
      0 _Total.exe

(00400000 - 00413000) .\KillerApp.pdb
(77F80000 - 77FF9000)
(77E10000 - 77E74000)
(77E80000 - 77F35000)
(77F40000 - 77F7C000)
(10000000 - 10022000)
(76B20000 - 76B5E000)
(77C50000 - 77C9A000)
(77DB0000 - 77E07000)
(77D30000 - 77DA2000)
(77B30000 - 77BBA000)
(775A0000 - 777DE000)
(78000000 - 78046000)

State Dump for Thread Id 0x350

eax=00000000 ebx=77e17896 ecx=0012fd40 edx=00000016 esi=0012fbdc
edi=001b01ec eip=76b2c245 esp=0012f8fc ebp=77e27326 iopl=0
```

```
nv up ei pl zr na po nc
cs=001b  ss=0023  ds=0023  es=0023  fs=0038  gs=0000
efl=00000246

function: ChooseColorW
        76b2c221 56                  push     esi
        76b2c222 6a00                push     0x0
        76b2c224 e8d70b0000          call     WantArrows+0x939
           (76b2ce00)
        76b2c229 56                  push     esi
        76b2c22a 57                  push     edi
        76b2c22b e810fcffff          call     ChooseColorW+0x144e
           (76b2be40)
        76b2c230 8d8e64010000        lea      ecx,[esi+0x164]
           ds:0012fd40=00000000
        76b2c236 8b442434            mov      eax,[esp+0x34]
           ss:00b4ced3=????????
        76b2c23a c744242c10000000 mov      dword ptr [esp+0x2c],0x10
           ss:00b4ced3=????????
        76b2c242 8b4010              mov      eax,[eax+0x10]
           ds:00a1d5d6=????????
FAULT ->76b2c245 8b10                mov      edx,[eax]
           ds:00000000=????????
        76b2c247 83c004              add      eax,0x4
        76b2c24a 8911                mov      [ecx],edx
           ds:0012fd40=00000000
        76b2c24c 83c104              add      ecx,0x4
        76b2c24f ff4c242c            dec      dword ptr [esp+0x2c]
           ss:00b4ced3=????????
        76b2c253 75f0                jnz      PageSetupDlgW+0x2cbd
           (76b3c245)
        76b2c255 ff7614              push     dword ptr [esi+0x14]
           ds:00b4d1b2=????????
        76b2c258 6683662600          and      word ptr [esi+0x26],0x0
           ds:00b4d1b3=????
        76b2c25d 6683662800          and      word ptr [esi+0x28],0x0
           ds:00b4d1b3=????
        76b2c262 66c746243000        mov      word ptr
           [esi+0x24],0x30   ds:00b4d1b3=????
        76b2c268 56                  push     esi
        76b2c269 e814f8ffff          call     ChooseColorW+0x1090
           (76b2ba82)

*──> Stack Back Trace <──*
```

```
FramePtr ReturnAd Param#1  Param#2  Param#3  Param#4  Function Name
77E27326 FEBD45E8 74C085FF 74FF5618 E8500C24 FFFFFFB5
    comdlg32!ChooseColorW
04244C8B 00000000 00000000 00000000 00000000 00000000 <nosymbols>

*——> Raw Stack Dump <——*
0012f8fc  dc fb 12 00 00 00 00 00 - b8 f9 12 00 ec 01 1b 00
          ...............
0012f90c  18 03 02 00 00 00 00 00 - e4 00 00 00 07 00 00 00
          ...............
0012f91c  95 01 00 00 c4 00 00 00 - fa ad b2 76 10 00 00 00
          ...........v....
0012f92c  3c 02 0a 00 68 2f 13 00 - 10 01 00 00 dc fb 12 00
          <...h/..........
0012f93c  30 1a 48 00 00 00 00 00 - 00 00 00 00 c8 f9 12 00
          0.H............
0012f94c  6c f9 12 00 f8 35 e1 77 - f8 02 02 00 81 00 00 00
          l....5.w........
0012f95c  00 00 00 00 f0 f9 12 00 - c8 f9 12 00 cd ab ba dc
          ...............
0012f96c  88 f9 12 00 e8 5f e1 77 - 3c c1 e2 77 f8 02 02 00
          ....._.w<..w....
0012f97c  81 00 00 00 80 45 13 00 - 51 b0 e2 77 80 45 13 00
          .....E..Q..w.E..
0012f98c  18 04 0a a8 20 00 00 00 - 98 40 49 00 87 00 00 00   ....
          ....@I.....
0012f99c  28 ec 4b 00 00 00 00 00 - c8 02 00 00 00 00 00 00
          (.K............
0012f9ac  00 00 00 00 00 00 00 00 - 00 00 00 00 d8 f9 12 00
          ...............
0012f9bc  f8 35 e1 77 ec 01 1b 00 - 10 01 00 00 3c 02 0a 00
          .5.w........<...
0012f9cc  dc fb 12 00 dc fb 12 00 - cd ab ba dc 14 fa 12 00
          ...............
0012f9dc  be 88 e2 77 bf ab b2 76 - ec 01 1b 00 10 01 00 00
          ...w...v........
0012f9ec  3c 02 0a 00 dc fb 12 00 - 90 ce 47 00 10 01 00 00
          <.........G.....
0012f9fc  30 1a 48 00 f8 02 02 00 - 87 00 00 00 00 00 00 00
          0.H............
0012fa0c  00 00 00 00 00 00 00 00 - 44 fa 12 00 70 58 e1 77
          ........D...pX.w
0012fa1c  ec 01 1b 00 10 01 00 00 - 3c 02 0a 00 dc fb 12 00
          ........<.......
0012fa2c  00 00 00 00 00 00 00 00 - 30 1a 48 00 3c 02 0a 00
          ........0.H.<...
```

As you can see, the Windows 2000 Dr. Watson log file is something of a cross between the Windows 98 Dr. Watson log file and the Windows 98 crash dialog box. This means that you can analyze the log file using a combination of the previously presented techniques. The log gives the program that crashed and the exception number, some general system information, the task list, the virtual address ranges for the program modules (which would be annotated if I had installed the system debugging symbols), the register values, the disassembled code where the crash occurred, the stack trace, and a dump of the stack contents.

What is most notable about the Windows 2000 Dr. Watson log file is what is not provided. Specifically, the log file gives only the name of the program that crashed, not the specific module name, which makes it very difficult to determine the specific module that crashed if any program modules had to be relocated. Worse yet, the log file gives only the disassembled code at the top of the stack trace, which makes it impossible in this case to trace back to the offending program source code.

The Windows 2000 Dr. Watson makes up for the weakness of the log file by also creating a *User.dmp* file, which contains a dump of the committed virtual address space and the state of the threads and registers when a crash occurred. You can perform postmortem debugging with a *User.dmp* file using the WinDbg system debugger and check things such as the stack trace, register values, and memory contents.

Miscellaneous Tips

The following sections discuss a few miscellaneous tips that will help you get the most out of debugging with Windows.

Using Windows 98 Dr. Watson Log Files in the Microsoft System Information Utility

You can load Windows 98 Dr. Watson log files in the Microsoft System Information utility. Just run System Info, give the **Open** command in the **File** menu, select the "Dr. Watson Log File (*.WLG)" file type, and then select the file. Note that Windows 98 Dr. Watson log files are binary, so you can't view them with a text editor.

Although I tend to prefer the Windows 98 Dr. Watson user interface, there are some things you can do with System Info that you can't do with Dr. Watson. For example, you can use System Info to select specific entries or a range of entries and copy them to the clipboard, whereas you cannot copy from the Dr. Watson user interface. Both utilities allow you to export to a text file. Whereas the text file exported by Dr. Watson has all the crash-specific information, the text file exported by System Info does a better job at presenting the module information by giving all the information in a tab-delimited format. By contrast, the Dr. Watson export gives only selected module fields (module name, version, manufacturer, and description), each on a single line.

Converting Mangled Symbols

All the public symbols listed in a MAP file use their mangled or decorated names. You can use the Visual C++ Undname utility (in *Common\Tools\ Undname.exe*) to convert mangled names to unmangled names. For example, given the command line

```
Undname ?RandomException@@YGXHHHH@Z
```

the output is

```
>> ?RandomException@@YGXHHHH@Z == RandomException
```

This result is hardly surprising, but you can use the –f option to display the entire function prototype. For example, given the command line

```
Undname -f ?RandomException@@YGXHHHH@Z
```

the output is

```
>> ?RandomException@@YGXHHHH@Z == void __stdcall RandomException
   (int, int, int, int)
```

This makes the Undname utility useful when reading MAP files that have overloaded functions.

Using Dependency Walker

When debugging Windows programs, it is often useful to dig around inside a PE file to determine things such as the DLLs an executable depends on, the exported functions and data, mangled function names, exported function ordinals, file paths, file versions, and base addresses. The Visual C++ Dependency Walker utility (in *Common\Tools\Depends.exe*) does all this and more.

Microsoft has released version 2.0 of Dependency Walker—see *www. dependencywalker.com*. This version has many advanced features, including a system information dialog box, an option to display either mangled function names or function prototypes, and the ability to detect dynamically loaded modules and dynamically called functions. The module list view displays new useful information, such as the actual virtual base address used (in case you forgot to rebase your program), the virtual size of the module, the debug symbol type (PDB, COFF, DBG, or none), and the module load order.

Using the MFC and ATL DEF Files

Speaking of exported function ordinals, you should know that the DEF files for all versions of MFC and ATL are located in the *Vc\Mfc\Src\Intel* and *Vc\Atl\Src* folders. The DEF files provide the mapping between function names and ordinals. For example, if a user receives the error message "The ordinal 6880 could not be located in the dynamic link library MFC42.DLL" when running your program, you can look up the 6880 ordinal in *Mfc42.def* and see that it is used by the *CWnd::ScreenToClient* function. Because many MFC functions are overloaded, you can then use the Visual C++ Undname utility to translate the mangled name to the function prototype.

Debugging the Windows 2000 Blue Screen of Death

If you have used Windows 2000 at all, you may have seen the infamous Blue Screen of Death (BSOD). When the BSOD occurs, the screen switches to text mode with a blue background and a very unfriendly hex dump. At this point, the only thing you can do is restart Windows and hope it doesn't crash again. You should understand what causes this screen to happen and what, if anything, you can do with it.

Windows 2000 programs run in two distinct modes: kernel mode (or Ring 0 for Intel processors), which is used by drivers and some parts of the operating system, and user mode (or Ring 3 for Intel processors), which is used by applications and other parts of the operating system. Exceptions are handled largely the same way in both modes. First, the exception is thrown, then it should be handled. If it is not handled, the process that threw it must be terminated. In user mode, unhandled exceptions are dealt with as you have seen throughout this chapter. Unfortunately, with kernel-mode exceptions, the terminated process is in the operating system itself, so the operating system must stop itself to prevent further corruption. The system must display the information in a way that doesn't require any system services, so using a dialog box is out of the question. This makes a text mode screen the best alternative. Microsoft chose to use a blue background because it is a very soothing color (just kidding).

Unless your program communicates directly with a driver or your program includes a driver, it is unlikely that a BSOD is your program's fault. If the crash is your program's fault, you can debug the Blue Screen of Death pretty much the same way as a Windows 98 crash dialog box. The blue screen contains the name of the module that crashed, the crash address, the unhandled exception, a list of running drivers, and a stack dump. See the *Microsoft Windows 2000 Server Operations Guide* for more information on how to resolve blue screen problems.

If you are receiving blue screens and want to save the information, you don't have to write it down. Rather, you can enable saving the blue screen information to *Minidump* or *Memory.dmp* by running the System Control Panel, clicking the **Advanced** tab, clicking **Startup and Recovery**, and selecting either **Small Memory Dump (64 KB)** or **Complete Memory Dump**. You can then obtain a dump file when you restart after a BSOD. Generally, you should choose the small memory dump option; the complete memory dump files tend to be huge because they are literally a memory dump (although they compress well). Alternatively, you can save only the information on the blue screen using the BlueSave utility from Systems Internals (*www.sysinternals.com*).

Recommended Reading

Asche, Ruediger. "Rebasing Win32 DLLs: The Whole Story." MSDN, September 18, 1995. Gives a detailed analysis of the performance benefits of rebasing DLLs at build time instead of load time, as well as other tips to iimprove DLL loading performance.

Microsoft Corporation. *Microsoft Windows 2000 Server Operations Guide.* Redmond, WA: Microsoft Press, 2000. Chapter 16, "Windows 2000 Stop Messages," gives a detailed description of the Stop message that results in the blue screen of death and advice on how to resolve the problem. This book is part of The Resource Kit.

Pietrek, Matt. "Peering Inside the PE: A Tour of the Win32 Portable Executable File Format." *Microsoft Systems Journal,* March 1994. Describes everything you will ever need to know about the PE and COFF file formats. Also gives the PEDump utility, which dumps PE files in an easier to understand format than DumpBin.

Pietrek, Matt. "Remove Fatty Deposits from Your Applications Using Our 32-bit Liposuction Tools." *Microsoft Systems Journal,* October 1996. Describes how to use Visual C++ Rebase utility to avoid address space collisions and Visual C++ Bind utility to resolve references to imported functions. Adding both of these steps to your build process can greatly reduce executable loading time, but using Rebase helps you debug DLLs as well.

Pietrek, Matt. "Under the Hood." *Microsoft Systems Journal,* June 1998. Presents "Matt's Just Enough Assembly to Get By, Part II." Focuses on the details of several assembly instructions and gives some excellent advice on how to debug when a program crashes on an invalid instruction pointer address. It gives particularly good advice for debugging stack overflows.

Pietrek, Matt. "Under the Hood." *Microsoft Systems Journal,* February 1998. Presents "Matt's Just Enough Assembly to Get By," which provides assembly language basics to help you debug.

Pietrek, Matt. "Under the Hood." *Microsoft Systems Journal,* October 1997. Gives a detailed description of Windows exception handling and how hardware exception codes are translated to Windows exception codes. It also presents a simple program that generates each type of exception.

Pietrek, Matt. "Under the Hood." *Microsoft Systems Journal,* May 1996. Gives a detailed description of the Thread Information Block contents for Windows NT and Windows 95.

Richter, Jeffrey. *Programming Applications for Microsoft Windows: Master the Critical Building Blocks of 32-Bit and 64-Bit Windows-based Applications.* Redmond, WA: Microsoft Press, 1999. Chapter 1 describes the error-handling system used by Windows. Chapter 20 has a good description of rebasing and binding DLLs. Chapter 24 presents Windows exceptions and how to handle them using SEH.

Robbins, John. "Bugslayer." *Microsoft Systems Journal,* December 1999. Gives a brief overview of the WinDbg system debugger, including its most useful commands and options.

Robbins, John. "Bugslayer." *Microsoft Systems Journal,* October 1999. Presents useful information for using MAP files to convert crash addresses to source code file and line numbers.

Robbins, John. "Bugslayer." *Microsoft Systems Journal,* June 1998. Presents several ways to use the information presented in this chapter to take full advantage of the Visual C++ debugger.

Robbins, John. "Bugslayer." *Microsoft Systems Journal,* April 1998. Gives some important rules to help you maximize the chance of finding a crash location. It also presents the CrashFinder utility, which, when given a crash address, finds the module, function, source code file, and line number using Imagehlp.dll. If you have a matching PDB file, however, you can find the crash location almost as easily using Visual C++, as described here in this chapter.

Chapter 7

Debugging with the Visual C++ Debugger

When it comes to finding and removing bugs, the Visual C++ debugger is your best friend. There are several notable features that make it efficient and easy to use. Here are some of my favorites:

- The Visual C++ debugger is fully integrated into the Visual C++ development environment, allowing you to manipulate the debugger directly from the source code windows to set breakpoints and control program execution.
- While debugging, the source code windows display variable values using datatips, allowing you to obtain a tremendous amount of information simply by moving the mouse pointer around the source code and largely eliminating the need to use dialog boxes to view variables.
- It has a powerful Watch window that not only displays variables and structures but also allows you to evaluate expressions, execute functions, and specify display formats.
- The Visual C++ debugger has a useful Variables window that conveniently displays the variables for the current and previous statements. It also displays the return values when you step over or out of a function; the local variables for the current function; or the object pointed to by the `this` pointer. The variables window often eliminates the need to enter variables into the Watch window.
- It supports a variety of advanced breakpoints, such as conditional code location breakpoints, data breakpoints, and message breakpoints.
- It allows you to debug DLLs usually without any extra effort.

- It supports remote debugging for situations in which you must debug remotely or you can't install Visual C++.
- It supports Just-in-time (JIT) debugging to facilitate postmortem debugging.
- It supports attaching the debugger to running processes.
- It supports Edit and Continue to minimize the time and effort needed to perform a debug cycle.

This chapter presents some of the more advanced and less obvious features to help you get the most out of the Visual C++ debugger. I am assuming that you have basic debugging skills: You know how to create a debug build, how to set breakpoints in the code, how to step over and into code, how to check variable values with datatips and the Watch window, and how to use the Call Stack window. Instead of these subjects, my goal for this chapter is to explain pretty much everything else. By the way, if you do need help with these basic skills, see the Debugger section of the Visual C++ User's Guide on MSDN.

Compiler and Linker Options

The first step in using the Visual C++ debugger is to select the appropriate compiler and linker options. Table 7.1 lists the most useful compiler options for tracking down bugs, whereas Table 7.2 lists the most useful linker options

As discussed in Chapter 2, Writing C++ Code for Debugging, the Visual C++ compiler can detect the use of uninitialized local variables, but it does a much better job at this detection with release builds than with debug builds because this situation is checked for during optimization. You can get these important warnings by creating a release build using the /W4 compiler option and either the /O1, /O2, /Os, or /Ot optimization options.

Debug versus Release Builds

Programmers are often confused by the differences between debug builds and release builds, especially when the debug build works and the release build doesn't. Let's start by looking at the different compiler options used in debug builds and release builds and discovering what these differences really mean.

Table 7.1 Compiler options for finding bugs

Compiler Options	Meaning
/W4	Compiles using the maximum warning level. (Use for all builds.)
/D "_DEBUG"	Enables conditionally compiled debug code, such as assertions and trace statements. (Use for debug builds only.)
/GZ	Helps you catch bugs typically found in release builds with debug builds, including uninitialized automatic (local) variables, stack problems, and incorrect function prototypes. (Use for debug builds only.)
/Od	Disables optimization, making the code easier to walk through with the debugger. (Use for debug builds only.)
/GF	Eliminates duplicate strings and places strings in read-only memory, thus protecting them from accidental writes. Automatically enabled with the /ZI (program database for Edit and Continue) compiler option. (Use explicitly for release builds.)
/ZI	Creates a program database with debugging symbols and Edit and Continue information to minimize the time and effort needed to perform a debug cycle. (Use for debug builds only.)
/Zi	Creates a program database with debugging symbols. (Use for release builds.)

Table 7.2 Linker options for finding bugs

Linker Options	Meaning
/MAP:"Debug/ProgramName.map"	Creates a MAP file
/MAPINFO:LINES	Adds line number information to a MAP file.

Table 7.3 lists the compiler options specific to a typical debug build. Table 7.4 lists the compiler options specific to a typical release build. In addition to these options, various other compiler options are used (specifically, /Fd, /Fo, and /Fp) to direct output to the Debug and Release folders.

What I find most interesting about these compiler options is what is missing. Specifically, there is no /Debug option to specify a debug build or a /Release option to specify a release build. Rather, the debug build uses a set of options

Table 7.3   Compiler options for a debug build

Linker Options	Meaning
/MDd, /MLd, or /MTd	Uses a debug run-time library
/Od	Disables optimization
/D "_DEBUG"	Enables conditionally compiled debug code
/ZI	Creates a program database for Edit and Continue
/GZ	Catches release-build errors in debug builds
/Gm	Enables minimum rebuild to reduce build times

Table 7.4   Compiler options for a release build

Compiler Options	Meaning
/MD, /ML, or /MT	Uses a release run-time library
/O1 or /O2	Enables optimization to minimize size or maximize speed.
/D "NDEBUG"	Disables conditionally compiled debug code (typically the ANSI C `assert` function)
/GF	Eliminates duplicate strings and places strings in read-only memory, thus protecting them from accidental writes

that help you debug, whereas the release build uses a set of options to generate efficient code. In either build, you can select any set of compiler options you want (the only restriction being that some options are incompatible with others), so you can have a release build with debugging symbols, trace statements, and assertions if you so choose. The compiler doesn't care because it is completely unaware of the distinction between the two types of builds.

TIP

The compiler is unaware of the differences between debug builds and release builds.

This begs the question: What really is the difference between a debug build and a release build? To some degree, the different builds are a state of mind. After all, a release build with debugging symbols and without optimization is pretty much a debug build. The different builds are used to achieve different objectives, and you can select whatever compiler options you want to accomplish those objectives. If I had to choose one compiler option that best characterizes the difference between the builds, however, it would be optimization. A release build generally implies some type of optimization, whereas a debug build implies no optimization. For example, earlier in this chapter I said that the Visual C++ compiler can detect the use of uninitialized local variables, but it does a much better job at this detection with release builds than with debug builds. The difference is due to optimization, but you could safely make that conclusion on your own.

> **TIP**
>
> A release build generally implies some type of optimization, whereas a debug build implies no optimization.

Let's look at each debug build compiler option in more detail and compare it to the release build.

Using a Debug Run-time Library

Debug builds link with the debug version of the C Run-time Library, which is built to help you debug. Aside from having debugging symbols, the most notable difference in the debug run-time library is that it uses a debug heap. The debug heap is discussed in detail in Chapter 9, Debugging Memory, but here is a brief summary of its most important features.

- The debug run-time library keeps track of memory allocations and allows you to check for memory leaks.
- It writes byte patterns (0xCD) to newly allocated memory to help detect when you are using uninitialized data.
- It writes byte patterns (0xDD) to freed memory to detect when you are using freed data.
- It allocates four bytes of guard data on each side of a buffer and initializes it with a byte pattern (0xFD) to detect memory overwrites and underwrites.
- It keeps track of the source code file name and line number for each allocation to help you locate the memory allocation in the source code.

Given these features, one obvious difference between the builds is that a debug build detects many types of memory bugs, whereas a release build does not. Another important difference is that a debug build tolerates (and reports) a memory overwrite or underwrite of up to four bytes without harm, whereas the same bug results in memory corruption in a release build.

Disabling Optimization

Unoptimized code is easier to debug than optimized code because the resulting assembly language code directly corresponds to the source code. As a result, the debugger behaves as you expect when you trace through the code, whereas optimized code tends to jump around unexpectedly and variables are often optimized away. Furthermore, unoptimized code compiles and links much more quickly, resulting in faster debugging cycles.

Ideally, the debug build would always be less forgiving than the release build, so that once you debugged the debug build, you could be confident that the release build would work at least as well. Unfortunately, this ideal breaks down with respect to optimization. (It also does not apply to small memory overwrites in the debug heap guard bytes, as previously noted.) Optimized code requires the compiler to make some assumptions and remove redundancy; but sometimes those assumptions are wrong, and the redundancy masks bugs. The following is a discussion of some optimization-related problems.

Frame Pointer Omission

In debug builds, the value of the stack base pointer (the EBP register) is constant throughout a function, so it can be used for finding the stack contents, particularly the function return address. For release builds, however, the stack base pointer may be optimized away. This type of optimization is called frame pointer omission (FPO), and it is done to use the stack base register as a multipurpose register and eliminate the need to push and pop the EBP register for every function call. See Chapter 6, Debugging with Windows, and Chapter 9, Debugging Memory, for more information on frame pointer omission.

TIP

Frame pointer omission reveals mismatches of function prototypes that result in crashes on function return in debug builds only.

Exception Optimization

As I pointed out in Chapter 5, Using Exceptions and Return Values, exception handlers may be optimized away if your program is compiled using the synchronous exception model, which is set using the /GX or /EHs compiler options and is the default model. When using this exception model, Visual C++ assumes that a C++ exception can be caused only by code that has a `throw` statement or that calls a function (which might have a `throw` statement). Any other code can't receive a C++ exception, so the compiler optimizes away the unnecessary exception-handling code in release builds, but not in debug builds. Consequently, the synchronous exception model prevents you from reliably catching structured exceptions (which result from access violations, division by zero, stack overflow, and such) using C++ exception handling. To catch structured exceptions, you must use the asynchronous exception model, which is set using the /EHa compiler option. Any programmer who doesn't completely understand this behavior is in for a big surprise when some exception handlers disappear in the release build.

The `volatile` Keyword

The `volatile` keyword tells the compiler that a specific variable may be changed in a way unknown by the compiler, such as by the operating system, by hardware, or by a concurrently executing thread, so the compiler must not use the variable in any optimizations. Consequently, a `volatile` variable is always read from and written to where it is stored instead of being kept in a register for optimization. Because debug builds aren't optimized, this effectively makes all variables `volatile` in a debug build. By contrast, a release build will have an optimization-related bug if a variable is incorrectly not made `volatile`. There is a significant chance of your program having such a bug if it is multithreaded, as described in Chapter 10, Debugging Multithreaded Programs.

TIP

In effect, all variables are `volatile` in a debug build.

Variable Optimization

Optimization eliminates unnecessary variables and reuses variables, which in turn may reveal bugs. Consider the following code.

```
void StackAttack () {
    int optimizedOut1, optimizedOut2;
    TCHAR bugsText[16], *bugs = _T("This function has bugs!");
    _tcscpy(bugsText, bugs);
}
```

In this function, the *bugsText* buffer is eight bytes too short (if using ANSI text) to receive the *bugs* string. The unnecessary variables *optimizedOut1* and *optimizedOut2* protect the stack contents from damage in the debug build, but these variables would be eliminated in a release build. Consequently, the buffer overwrite would destroy the function return address on the stack, leading to an access violation exception in the release build but not the debug build.

Ordinarily, variables that are optimized away aren't usually this obvious. The *GetInitializedPoint* function I describe later in the chapter is a more realistic example.

Optimization Bugs

A release build may have a genuine optimization bug, caused either by an overly aggressive optimization or even a bug in the optimizer (which has been known to happen, especially with earlier versions of Visual C++). As the previous optimization problems suggest, however, if your program is well behaved without optimization but crashes with optimization, this is not necessarily the result of a bug in the optimizer. Rather, the optimizer could be revealing a latent bug in your code that is masked by the rather brutish debug build.

You can determine if a bug is related to optimization in the following ways.

- Turn optimization off completely.
- Use a safer form of optimization, such as optimizing for size instead of speed. Avoid custom optimizations (such as **Assume No Aliasing** and **Assume Aliasing Across Function Calls**) because they may be too aggressive.
- Turn optimization off or use safer optimization for selected files.
- Turn optimization off for selected code using `#pragma optimize`.

If the bug disappears as the result of any of these measures, the bug is optimization related. Keep in mind that most likely the bug is in your code, not in the optimizer itself. The only real way to verify an optimizer bug is to rebuild your program completely (checking possibly out-of-date code doesn't count) and check the disassembled code for translation errors. Short of this proof, assigning blame to the optimizer is merely a hypothesis.

TIP The only way to verify an optimizer bug is to rebuild your program completely and check the disassembled code for errors.

Enabling Conditionally Compiled Debug Code

The Visual C++ C Run-time Library and Microsoft Foundation Class (MFC) debug code is compiled if the _DEBUG symbol is defined. When _DEBUG is defined, the run-time library includes the _ASSERT, _ASSERTE, _RPTn, _RPTFn, and debug heap statements. MFC includes the ASSERT, VERIFY, ASSERT_VALID, ASSERT_KINDOF, TRACE, and DEBUG_ONLY statements. MFC also includes the *Dump* and *AssertValid* functions for *CObject*-derived classes and makes *GetDocument* functions inline for *CView*-derived classes. ANSI C assertions are compiled when the NDEBUG symbol is *not* defined.

Regarding inline functions, it is interesting to note that many programs conditionally compile inline functions as normal functions for debug builds to facilitate stepping into the functions with the debugger. This technique isn't necessary, however, because Visual C++ disables inlining by default for debug builds. (Specifically, inlining is disabled by the /Ob0 compiler option, which is enabled by default.) Inlining is enabled for release builds by the /O1 (minimize size), /O2 (maximize speed), or /Ox (full optimization) compiler options.

TIP Inlining is disabled by default for debug builds.

Whereas the version of the C Run-time Library is determined by compiler options, MFC uses the _DEBUG symbol to help determine which version of the library to link with. It does this using the `comment` pragmas, as shown in the following code (from *Afx.h*).

```
#ifdef _AFXDLL
    #ifndef _UNICODE
        #ifdef _DEBUG
            #pragma comment(lib, "mfc42d.lib")
            #pragma comment(lib, "mfcs42d.lib")
        #else
            #pragma comment(lib, "mfc42.lib")
            #pragma comment(lib, "mfcs42.lib")
        #endif
    #else
        #ifdef _DEBUG
            #pragma comment(lib, "mfc42ud.lib")
            #pragma comment(lib, "mfcs42ud.lib")
        #else
            #pragma comment(lib, "mfc42u.lib")
            #pragma comment(lib, "mfcs42u.lib")
        #endif
    #endif
#endif
```

Here the `lib` comment is used to supply a library for the linker to search. Note how this technique gives you far more control over libraries than what is possible from the project settings.

If correctly done, conditionally compiled debug code should not result in a difference in program behavior between the debug build and the release build. Consequently, the primary concern is to make sure that there is no nondebug program code in any of the conditionally compiled code and that the debug code has no side effects. The sole exception is the MFC VERIFY macro, which is specifically intended to allow you to put program code in its Boolean expression. Also, assertions and trace statements can change program behavior in multithreaded code because assertions that take a long time to evaluate can change relative timing of threads and trace statements have the effect of serializing threads.

Using a Program Database for Edit and Continue

Enabling Edit and Continue has the side effect of enabling the /GF compiler option, which eliminates duplicate strings and places strings in read-only memory. The debug build and the release build should have the same behavior as long as the release build uses the /GF compiler option.

Catching Release-Build Errors in Debug Builds

The /GZ compiler option does the following:

1. Initializes all automatic variables with a 0xCC byte pattern, causing the use of uninitialized pointers to result in access violation exceptions (at least in Windows 2000)
2. Validates the stack pointer to check for function-calling convention mismatches when functions are called through function pointers
3. Checks the stack pointer at the end of a function to make sure it hasn't been changed

Features 2 and 3 help debug builds reveal function prototype mismatches, resulting in roughly the same outcome as FPO optimization in release builds.

Many programmers believe that Visual C++ initializes automatic variables to zero in debug builds but not in release builds. This belief is best described as an urban legend because it has never been true. In fact, automatically initializing variables to zero only in debug builds would be one of the worst things a compiler could do. As I pointed out earlier, the compiler isn't aware that a build is a debug build, so the compiler has no way of knowing to perform such an initialization. However, with the /GZ compiler option (which is incompatible with optimized builds), the compiler initializes all automatic variables with a 0xCC byte pattern.

Enabling Minimum Rebuild

Assuming the code successfully compiles, enabling minimum rebuild should not affect debug build program behavior.

Debugging Release Builds

Suppose you have a bug in your program that shows up only in the release build. Unless you are an assembly language expert, you need the debugging symbols to have a clue what is going on. As you know now, this problem isn't as bleak as it first appears because you can create a release build with symbols and debug it directly from the debugger. Although the Visual C++ AppWizard doesn't create debugging symbols for release builds by default, you can create debugging symbols by making a few changes in the project settings. Doing so makes the release executable slightly, but not significantly, larger (usually less than 100 bytes) because debugging symbols are stored in a program database (PDB) file rather than in the executable itself. You could create debugging symbols for release builds on an as-needed basis or even create a new build configuration, but the fact that you can create debugging symbols without a significant penalty leads to the **Golden Rule of Visual C++ Debugging**: *Always create debugging symbols for your program's executables, even for release builds, and archive the resulting PDB files*. It's unfortunate that Visual C++ doesn't create debugging symbols by default because this misleads programmers into believing that release builds can't have debugging symbols.

TIP

Always create debugging symbols for your program's executables, even for release builds, and archive the resulting PDB files.

To create debugging symbols for a build, perform the following steps for each of the Visual C++ projects used by your program.

1. Display the Project Settings dialog box and select the desired build (such as "Win32 Release") from the **Settings for** box.

2. In the project tree control, select the entire project by clicking the top node.

3. Select the **General** category on the **C/C++** tab. For **Debug info,** select **Program Database** for release builds or **Program Database for Edit and Continue** for debug builds. (Note that Edit and Continue cannot be used with optimized builds and it makes executable sizes larger, making it unsuitable for release builds.)

4. Select the **Debug** category on the **Link** tab. Then select the **Debug info** and **Microsoft format** options. Also make sure that the **Separate types** option is not selected so that all the debug information is consolidated into a single PDB file. While you're at it, make sure the **Generate mapfile** option is selected because you need MAP files for postmortem debugging.

5. For release builds, go to the end of the **Project Options** box on the **Link** tab and enter "/OPT:REF". The option prevents unreferenced functions and data from being included in the executable file, which would unnecessarily bloat the file size. Don't use this option for debug builds because it disables incremental linking.

6. Recompile the project with the **Rebuild All** command.

If you find that your executable size is much larger with debugging symbols than without, most likely you forgot to include the /OPT:REF linker option.

Now you're ready to roll. Once you start debugging a release build, however, you will quickly realize the advantages of debugging unoptimized code. First, breakpoints are harder to set because the source code lines are rearranged, thus making it hard to find valid breakpoint lines. The problem is that the debugger can't always determine the source code that corresponds to a set of optimized instructions. In fact, you will probably find it easier to give the **Go To Disassembly** command from the source code context menu and set breakpoints using the Disassembly window with the **Source Annotation** option set. You should be able to trace into functions, but note that inlining is enabled in release builds for both inline functions and intrinsic library functions. Also, most likely you won't have debugging symbols for release builds of libraries (including the C Run-time Library and MFC), so tracing into library functions isn't likely to be helpful. Again, you might find it easier in some cases to trace through code using the Disassembly window for greater control.

Use the Disassembly window when tracing through release builds for greater control.

Happily, the most important debugging tool—the call stack—still works as usual, which actually requires special effort from the debugger. Specifically, FPO optimization eliminates the stack frame pointer normally used for walking the stack, but the debugger can still construct the call stack and find function return addresses using special FPO debugging information stored in the PDB file.

The biggest challenge in release builds is debugging variables—or more accurately, debugging what used to be variables. Some assembly language knowledge really pays off when debugging release builds (see Chapter 6 for assembly language basics). Let's take a look at a simple example to see the problem. The following function returns an initialized POINT object.

```
POINT GetInitializedPoint () {
    POINT pt;
    pt.x = 13;    // 0x0D in hex
    pt.y = 42;    // 0x2A in hex
    return pt;
}
```

Here is the unoptimized assembly code version of this function, which is pretty much a direct translation of the source code, along with the standard function entry and cleanup code.

```
push        ebp               ; save the stack base pointer
mov         ebp,esp           ; copy the stack pointer to
                              ; the stack base
sub         esp,48h           ; make room for local
                              ; variables on stack
push        ebx               ; save the EBX, ESI, and EDI
                              ; registers
push        esi
push        edi
lea         edi,[ebp-48h]     ; initialize the local variables
                              ; with 0xCC
mov         ecx,12h
mov         eax,0CCCCCCCCh
rep stos    dword ptr [edi]
mov         dword ptr [ebp-8],0Dh   ; set x to 13
mov         dword ptr [ebp-4],2Ah   ; set y to 42
mov         eax,dword ptr [ebp-8]   ; copy x to EAX
mov         edx,dword ptr [ebp-4]   ; copy y to EDX
pop         edi               ; restore the EBX, ESI, and
                              ; EDI registers
pop         esi
pop         ebx
mov         esp,ebp           ; copy the stack base to the
                              ; stack pointer
pop         ebp               ; restore the stack base pointer
ret
```

Walking through the code, we see that the function entry code sets up the stack by saving the stack frame pointer and current stack pointer, making room for the POINT automatic variable, and saving the EBX, ESI, and EDI registers. Because this code was compiled with the /GZ option, it initializes the automatic variables with the 0xCC byte pattern. It then sets the x data member to 13 and the y data member to 42. Finally, it sets the function return value, restores everything from the stack, and returns. By convention, if the return value is 64 bits, the lower 32 bits are stored in the EAX register and the upper 32 bits are stored in the EDX register. Note how this assembly code directly corresponds with the source code, including the use of the automatic variable.

Now let's look at the optimized version of the assembly code.

```
mov         eax,0Dh                 ; set EAX to 13
mov         edx,2Ah                 ; set EDX to 42
ret
```

This version is indeed optimized. All it does is set the EAX register to 13, the EDX register to 42, and return, which is the absolute minimum this function needs to do. (OK, you could eliminate the return by making the function inline.) Note how this assembly code has no correspondence to the original source code and that the POINT variable is nowhere to be found. Attempting to display *pt* results in "CXX0017: Error: symbol 'POINT' not found." As simple as this example is, the only way to really know what is going on in this function is to debug the assembly code.

The Test Build

Now is a good time to address an important testing issue: If you can't depend on the debug and release builds having the same behavior, which build should QA use for testing? Keep in mind that the debug and release builds are effectively different programs that happen to be generated from the same source code. You should never assume that the builds behave exactly the same unless you have verified that they do through careful testing.

Some people believe it is better to test only with the release build since that is what the customer will actually use. After all, you must test the code you ship, so the release build is the only build that really matters. There is some logic to this opinion, but it clearly misses the point of the debug build. A debug build, by definition, is intended to help reveal, locate, and remove bugs. For QA never to test with the debug build would be a serious mistake because it undermines the value of many of the debugging strategies presented in this book. For example, the whole point behind using assertions is to detect automatically many types of run-time errors. Not testing with the debug build would require testers to find such problems manually. Furthermore, once a bug has been detected, tracking down its cause is much easier with the debug build than with the release build.

Clearly, the best solution is to test both builds, using the debug build almost exclusively in the beginning of the development process and gradually shifting over to the release build as the program nears completion. Just as clearly, testing the release build for the first time right before the program ships is living very dangerously.

> **TIP**
>
> You need to test both the debug and release builds. Never assume that the builds behave exactly the same unless you have verified that they do through careful testing.

Debugging Symbols

Unless you are an assembly language expert (and who is these days?), debugging symbols are essential to productive debugging. There are several types of debugging symbols and options and, as a result, several types of debugging symbol problems. The goal of this section is to review the different types of debugging symbols, the debugging symbol options, and how to deal with debugging symbol problems.

PDB Files

Program database files contain the debugging and program information required by the Visual C++ debugger. This debugging information includes the names and types of variables, function prototypes, source code line numbers, class and structure layouts, FPO debugging information (to reconstruct stack frames), and information required to perform incremental linking. Additionally, for programs built with the **Program Database for Edit and Continue** option, the program database also contains the information required to perform Edit and Continue. That's a lot of stuff, so you will find that PDB files are typically much larger than their corresponding executables.

Given that PDB files are separate from the executable files, there is never a good reason not to create a PDB file, even for release builds; however, having separate files does create an extra responsibility for you. Specifically, if you want to debug your program with symbols, you must archive the PDB files along with your source code and executable files for any versions of your program that you release. If you don't, the debugging symbols are worthless. And as you will soon see, most debugging symbol problems relate to missing or out-of-synch program database files.

Vcx0.PDB Files

If you have ever looked carefully at your program's Debug folder, you might have noticed that there are actually two PDB files. If your executable is named *MyProject.exe*, you will find both a *MyProject.pdb* and a *Vcx0.pdb* file, where *x* is the Visual C++ version number. The reason there are two files is that the Visual C++ compiler uses the generically named *Vcx0.pdb* file while it compiles the individual source code files to store all data type information. The compiler uses *Vcx0.pdb* because it doesn't know the name of the executable when it is compiling an individual source file (well, that's the official story anyway), so this file is shared by all the object files in a project. When the linker creates the executable, it creates a single project PDB with all the debugging information from the *Vcx0.pbd* as well as other information merged in.

This means the *Vcx0.pdb* file is temporary and can be completely ignored, right? Well, maybe. The problem is that Visual C++ has an innocuous-looking linker option called **Separate types** (which is enabled by default and found in the Project Settings dialog box, in the **Debug** category of the **Link** tab). This option shows up in your project options as /pdbtype:sept. If you select this option, the linker will not merge the *Vcx0.pdb* information into the project PDB file, thus requiring you to have both PDB files to fully debug your program. Using separate PDB files is especially undesirable in projects with many executable files because you may be required to have multiple *Vcx0.pdb* files copied to the same folder (which is impossible). If the Visual C++ debugger ever prompts you for a *Vcx0.pdb* file with a Find Symbols dialog box, you know you have selected the **Separate types** option. In this case, you can debug the program by dismissing the dialog box with the **Cancel** button, but you won't be able to see any of your data types with the debugger.

There is an advantage to using the **Separate types** option, which is that the linker has much less work to build the project, and the resulting files require less hard disk space. Unless you are building a very large project on a very slow computer, however, this option is pure evil and should not be used.

> **TIP**
>
> Unless you are building a very large project on a very slow computer, do not use the **Separate types** linker option.

DBG Files

To get the most out of the debugger, make sure that you have installed the system debugging symbols if you are running Windows 2000 or Windows NT. Having the debugging symbols allows the debugger to provide the system function names in the call stack. Note that Windows 98 doesn't have system debugging symbols, but Visual C++ supplies symbols for MFC and the C Run-time Library DLLs. To install the debugging symbols for Windows 2000, use the Customer Support Diagnostics CD-ROM, which starts the installation program automatically when you insert the CD. To install the debugging symbols for Windows NT 4.0, go to the Visual C++ program group and run the Windows NT Symbols Setup program. Both setup programs copy the system DBG files from the CD-ROM to the *\WinNT\Symbols\Dlls* folder.

> Be sure to install the system debugging symbols for Windows 2000 and Windows NT.

The only trick is that the debugger uses the symbol files only if they exactly match the installed executable files. It is highly likely that a mismatch will occur after you install a service pack. Consequently, whenever you install a service pack, you should update the system symbols by copying them from the *\Support\Debug* folder on the service pack CD-ROM. If you are unsure about the status of the symbols, run your program from the Visual C++ debugger. A message saying "Loaded 'EXAMPLE.DLL', no matching symbolic information found" appears in the **Debug** tab of the Output window whenever matching symbols aren't found.

> Always update the system symbols whenever you install a service pack.

These DBG files contain debugging information primarily intended for Windows system debuggers, but they can be used by the Visual C++ debugger as well. This debugging information includes the names of global variables and functions as well as FPO debugging information. DBG files use both COFF and

---

CodeView formats, but the Visual C++ debugger uses only the CodeView format information.

You may wonder why the system debugging symbols don't use the PDB file format. The reason is that the Windows system developers at Microsoft use different debugging tools (specifically, the WinDbg, NTSD/CDB, and KD debuggers) from the ones we normal folks use, so they use different debugging formats that are designed for these tools. System-level debugging is quite different from application-level debugging, so the Visual C++ debugger isn't quite ideal for system-level debugging. One significant advantage of DBG files over PDB files is that the DBG format doesn't change often. The PDB format tends to change with every new version of Visual C++, thereby making the files incompatible with other versions. Having to supply different system debugging files for every recent version of Visual C++ just wouldn't do.

Other Debugging Symbol Options

If you are using the Visual C++ debugger, almost certainly you will use the **Program Database for Edit and Continue** option for debug builds and the **Program Database** option for release builds. However, there are two more debugging options you may need to use in unusual circumstances. The first is the **C7 Compatible** option, which appends the debugging information to the executable file instead of putting it in a separate PDB file. This option may make sense if you absolutely don't want to have a separate debugging file. The second is the **Line Numbers Only** option, which appends only the global symbol and line number information to the executable file. This option may make sense if you don't want to have a separate debugging file and you want to keep the size of the executable file small. Both options turn off incremental linking, which can significantly increase link times. Offhand, I can't think of any compelling reasons to use either of these options in practice.

Debugging Symbols Problems

Debugging symbols are yet another example of Murphy's law in action because everything that can go wrong will go wrong. The following are the types of debugging symbol problems you may encounter.

- Debugging symbols not found.
- Debugging symbols found, but they don't match the executable.
- Debugging symbols found, but the executable wasn't found in the expected folder.
- Matching debugging symbols found, but they are incompatible with the version of Visual C++ you are using.

In short, for successful debugging you need to make sure that the executable files, the source code files, the debugging symbol files, and the version of Visual C++ you are using all match and can be found in their expected locations. Note that a debugging symbols file is considered to match an executable when it has the same internal time stamp, so you can't necessarily determine if the files match by looking at file dates.

To ensure everything matches, you need to archive all your project's executables, source code, and PDB files. If you are maintaining code generated by different versions of the Visual C++ compiler, you also need to keep all those compiler versions installed so that you can use the version that matches the program you are debugging. In this case, you may also want to archive the critical compiler version-dependent library files, such as *Msvcrtd.dll* and *Mfc42d.dll*, including both the release and debug versions as well as their debugging symbols. All these steps serve to keep everything synchronized.

You can determine if the debugging symbols were loaded successfully by checking the **Debug** tab of the Output window. If the debugging symbols were successfully loaded, you will receive a message saying "Loaded symbols for 'C:\SOMEPATH\SOMEEXE.DLL'." If the symbols couldn't be loaded, you will receive a message saying "Loaded 'C:\SOMEPATH\SOMEEXE.DLL', no matching symbolic information found." In this case, either the debugging symbols file wasn't found or it didn't match the executable. Unfortunately, the error message doesn't give you a clue to the specific problem. Since the error message gives the full path and the debugging symbols file should be located in the same folder as the executable, you can easily determine the problem by checking the contents of the folder. (Technically, the debugger checks for the symbol file by first checking a path stored in the executable. It then looks for the file using the Windows file search sequence, which is documented with the *LoadLibrary* API function. Your life will be much easier if you always keep the files together.) If necessary, you can compare the executable and DBG file timestamps using the Dumpbin utility (in *Vc\Bin*) with the "/headers" command line option and checking the "time date stamp" records.

The debugger loads DLL debugging symbols automatically when the main executable loads if those DLLs were linked at build time. Symbols are not automatically loaded for DLLs that are linked at run time, such as DLLs loaded using the *LoadLibrary* API or using COM. As a result, you will not be able to set breakpoints in these modules. You can solve this problem by preloading the debugging symbols using the **Additional DLLs** category of the **Debug** tab in the Project Settings dialog box and adding all the DLLs that are linked at run time. However, note that Windows itself determines the rules for loading DLLs and the registry determines the components loaded by COM, so it is possible that the program may load a DLL from a folder other than the one you specified, resulting in a "Preloaded symbols may not match" error. In this case, you should either correct the path given in **Additional DLLs** (if the right DLL is being loaded), remove the DLL being loaded (if the wrong DLL is being loaded), or fix the registry (if the wrong COM component is loaded.)

TIP Use the **Additional DLLs** feature to preload the debugging symbols for modules loaded at run time. This step allows you to set breakpoints in these modules.

The Debug Windows

In this section, I review the Visual C++ debug windows and give you some tips to help you get the most out of them. The following features are shared among the debug windows.

- For all windows that display data, as you step through your program, data entries may appear in red to indicate that they have just changed value. Once you continue to step through the program, the data entry changes back to black until its value changes again.
- Editable text fields support the standard cut, copy, paste, and undo editing commands, whereas read-only text supports the copy command.

- All windows that have columns allow you to size the first column to fit its contents automatically by double-clicking on the vertical divider at the column edge.
- The Watch, Variables, and Call Stack windows have a **Hexadecimal Display** option in their context menu, which affects input as well as how data is displayed. Changing this option from one window changes it for all debug windows.

The Watch Window

You use the Watch window to monitor variables and expressions while you debug your program. I present the Watch window expressions and formatting symbols in more detail later. You can enter expressions directly into the Watch window, or you can drag expressions from your source code and the Variables, Registers, Memory, and Call Stack windows.

If you are watching a single variable, you can edit the **Value** column to change the variable's value while debugging. This technique can be very help- ful in performing debugging experiments or temporarily fixing bugs.

Contrary to what is described in the Visual C++ documentation, there is no **Type** column in the Watch window. You can determine the base type of a vari- able by selecting the variable, giving the **Properties** command in the context menu, and checking the **Type** field.

The QuickWatch Dialog Box

Much of what I describe in this chapter about the Watch window also applies to the QuickWatch dialog box. For example, QuickWatch supports the ability to change values and the autosize feature, whereas it doesn't support drag and drop, drawing recently changed text in red, or the **Properties** command.

I personally don't use the QuickWatch dialog box much. Since it is modal, there is nothing quick about it.

The Variables Window

The Variables window contains three tabs: The **Auto** tab displays the variables used in the current statement and the previous statement, the **Locals** tab dis- plays the variables local to the current function, and the **this** tab displays the object pointed to by the this pointer. The **Auto** tab also displays function return values, but it works only for return values of 32 bits or less. If you are simply tracing through the code, the Variables window allows you to see what is going on without constantly having to enter variables into the Watch window.

The most interesting feature of the Variables window is the **Context** box, which allows you to display the variables and their values at any point in the call stack that has debugging symbols. You can also display these variables using the Watch window and the context operator, but that approach usually requires much more effort. If you don't see the **Context** box, select the **Toolbar** option in the context menu.

You can edit the **Value** column to change a variable's value while debugging. This technique can be very helpful in performing debugging experiments or temporarily fixing bugs. You can determine the base type of a variable by selecting the variable, giving the **Properties** command in the context menu, and checking the **Type** field. (Contrary to the documentation, the Variables window doesn't have a **Type** column.)

The Registers Window

Use the Registers window to monitor the CPU register and flag values as well as the floating-point stack. You can edit a register's value using the Registers window, either by clicking on the value with the mouse or using the Tab key and then entering the value you want.

Obviously, you shouldn't change a register's value unless you really know what you are doing. Even if you do know what you are doing, you should rarely need to change register values with this window because there is usually a simpler, less risky way to accomplish the same task using another debugger feature. For example, you could change the current instruction by changing the EIP register, but a better way to accomplish this task is to use the **Set Next Statement** command, which has the benefit of warning you if you attempt to do something really stupid.

The Memory Window

Use the Memory window to display the virtual memory contents starting at a specified address. You can edit the memory contents using the Memory window, either by clicking on the value with the mouse or using the Tab key and then entering the value you want. You can determine how the memory contents are displayed using the **Byte Format**, **Short Hex Format**, and **Long Hex Format** options in the context menu.

The most interesting feature of the Memory window is the **Address** box, which allows you to indicate the starting virtual memory address to display. The **Address** box accepts virtual memory address locations (such as 0x00400000), variables (such as *rect*, **pRect*, or **this*), and registers (such as ESP). Note that for variables you need to give an object, not a pointer to an object. For example, if you have a pointer to a rectangle, you need to input the dereferenced pointer (such as **pRect*) to obtain the right address. If you give a register, the register value is immediately replaced with its virtual memory address, so don't expect contents of the Memory window to change as the register changes. If you don't see the **Address** box, select the **Toolbar** option in the context menu. Also, instead of using the **Address** box, you can instead use the **Go To** command in the **Edit** menu.

You can enter addresses directly into the Memory window, but you can also drag addresses and variables from your source code and the Watch, Variables, Registers, and Call Stack windows. However, note that the memory data list, not the **Address** box, is the drop target, which I find a bit confusing. Also, for some reason the address you enter isn't always at the very top of the memory data list but may be a few lines down. Consequently, it's always a good idea to double-check the address you entered and see where it really starts before panicking.

The Call Stack Window

Use the Call Stack window to display the function calls that led to the current source code statement, which is displayed at the top of the stack. You can determine how the call stack is displayed using the **Parameter Types** and **Parameter Values** options in the context menu. The **Parameter Types** option displays the data types for the function parameters, whereas the **Parameter Values** option displays the values for the function parameters. Both options are enabled by default.

Double-clicking on a function call places you in a source code window if source code is available or the Disassembly window if it is not. The **Go To Code** command has the same effect. The code window displays a yellow arrow to indicate the current statement or a green arrow for code in inactive stack frames. You can also give the **Insert/Remove Breakpoint** and **Run to Cursor** commands from the Call Stack window. All these commands are in the context menu.

The Disassembly Window

Use the Disassembly window to view the assembly instructions that the compiler generates for the source code. You can display the assembly code for a specific code location using the **Go To** command in the **Edit** menu.

Use the Disassembly window much as you would use a read-only source code window, only with more control. Specifically, you can set breakpoints using the **Insert/Remove Breakpoint** command, change program execution using the **Set Next Statement** command, and determine the current program statement using the **Show Next Statement** command. Choose how the assembly code is displayed using the **Source Annotation** and **Code Bytes** options. You can also display the associated source code using the **Go To Source** command. All these commands and options are in the context menu.

Watch Expressions

The Watch window has far more functionality than meets the eye. (Actually, none of its functionality meets the eye because it's a blank window by default and the documentation isn't very good.) In addition to entering variables in the **Name** column, you can enter simple C++ expressions and even call functions. This capability makes the Watch window very cool!

In this section, I provide an overview of how to use Watch window expressions. When using the Watch window, if you're not sure what to do or what will work, just give it a try. Most likely you will be pleasantly surprised by the fact that it actually works.

Evaluation Rules

Here are the Watch window evaluation rules.

- Only the expressions on the active tab are evaluated.
- The expressions are evaluated each time the debugger breaks (from a breakpoint, single step, or exception) or when the active tab is changed.
- The expressions are evaluated from top to bottom.

These evaluation rules allow you to use the tabs strategically. You can group expressions you want to watch together on the same tab. Alternatively, you can group expressions you need to perform specific debugging tasks on the same tab, so you can use one tab to debug memory, another tab to debug variables, another to debug registers, and so on. You can also use different tabs to toggle between variable assignments. For example, suppose you have a global *Debug* variable. You can enter "Debug=1" on one tab and "Debug=0" on another, then toggle between the tabs to change the variable value.

Expression Syntax

A Watch window expression may consist of the following operands:

- Constants (decimal, hexadecimal, octal, character, and floating point, but not program constants)
- Program variables
- Registers and pseudo-registers (see next section for details)

It also has the following operators:

- Arithmetic (+, - , *, /, %, ++, —)
- Assignment (=, +=, -=, *=, /=, %=, >>=, <<=, &=, ^=, |=)
- Relational (==, !=, <, <=, >, >=)
- Boolean (!, ||, &&)
- Bitwise (~, >>, <<, &, |, ^)
- Address (&, *)
- Array ([])
- Class/structure/union (., ->)
- Sizeof
- C casts (but with only one level of indirection)
- Function calls

You can also use parentheses, which aren't considered operators. Note that the Watch window doesn't support the conditional operator (?:) or the comma operator.

You can use assignment expressions to set variable values. For example, suppose you want to change the value of *x* to 100. You could enter "x" as an expression and change its value from the **Value** column. Alternatively, you could enter "x=100" as an expression, and then the value of *x* will be set every time this expression is evaluated. This approach may be more convenient if you have to make this assignment often. However, you should probably delete the assignment expression afterward or change the active Watch window tab because the expression will continue to be evaluated, potentially leading to confusing results later.

TIP

Use assignment expressions with caution because they continue to be evaluated and can lead to confusing results.

For constants, one oddity you must be aware of is that if you have enabled the **Hexadecimal Display** option (from any of the debugger window context menus), constants used in expressions are always interpreted as hexadecimal. For example, if you enter the expression "myVar+16", you are adding 0x16, not 16 decimal. To use decimal, you must use the "0n" prefix, as with "myVar+0n16". This applies to the Variables window as well.

TIP

If you have enabled the **Hexadecimal Display** option, constants used in expressions are always interpreted as hexadecimal. To use decimal, you must use the "0n" prefix.

The Context Operator

The Watch window uses the context operator to give scope to expressions and resolve ambiguity. The context operator has the following syntax.

```
{[function name],[source code file],[executable file]}
```

You supply a function name, source code file, executable file, or any combination of these. Both commas are required unless you omit both the source code file and the executable file. Also, if the source code file or executable file names include a comma, space, or brace, you must enclose the name in quotation marks. You can use "{*}" to indicate the current context.

For Watch window expressions, typically you need to supply only a single item in a context operator. Most often you give an executable file with function calls to indicate the module that defines the function. For example, you would call the _CrtCheckMemory function in the Visual C++ C Run-time Library as follows:

```
{,,msvcrtd.dll}_CrtCheckMemory()
```

Give the source code file name to resolve ambiguous global variables. For example, if you have a static global variable *ErrorStatus* defined in several different source code files, you would display a specific variable as follows:

```
{,MyFile.cpp,}ErrorStatus
```

Give the function name to resolve ambiguous automatic variables and function parameters. For example, suppose you have a *Function1* with a local variable *count* that calls *Function2* that also has a local variable *count*. You can display either variable as follows:

```
{Function1}count
{Function2}count
```

Without the context operator, the current context always hides any previous contexts, thus making the *count* variable in *Function1* inaccessible from *Function2*.

Finally, you can apply the context operator to variables, functions, types, and breakpoints. Using the context operator on types allows you to cast using data types defined in other modules. For example, if you need to cast a pointer variable *pSomeObject* in the current context to a *CSomeType* type defined in *MyDll.dll*, you can display the variable as follows:

```
{,,MyDll.dll}(CSomeType *){*}pSomeObject
```

Calling Functions

My favorite Watch window feature is the ability to call program functions, although this feature does have some restrictions. While you are debugging, it is useful to call a function from the Watch window to display its return value or see its side effect. For example, you can call a debugging function that dumps an object or writes trace information to the **Debug** tab of the Output window.

You can use this feature to call regular functions and member functions, including even private member functions. However, you can call only one function per expression, and you can't call inline functions, constructors, or destructors. Oddly, you can't call Windows API functions either; but you can call them if you wrap them in your own program function. All breakpoints are ignored, and a function won't evaluate if it takes longer than 20 seconds or throws an uncaught exception. Functions are restricted to run in the current thread and should not create or use other threads; but other threads in the process are allowed to execute, and a context switch may occur as a result.

Since Watch window expressions are evaluated each time the debugger breaks, functions in Watch window expressions are called quite often. If you want to call a function only once, enter the expression in the QuickWatch dialog box instead.

TIP

Enter expressions in the QuickWatch dialog box if you want them to be evaluated once.

If you receive an "CXX0017: Error: symbol "functionName" not found" message, be sure to enter the function using the context operator. You shouldn't have any trouble calling functions without parameters or functions with constant or register parameters, but calling functions with variable parameters can be very confusing. For example, you can try to enter the *AfxDump* MFC function to dump a `this` pointer to the **Debug** tab of the Output window.

```
{,,mfc42d.dll}AfxDump(this)
```

This results in an "Error: Symbol 'this' not found" message. The problem is that the context operator applies to the entire expression (more accurately, the remainder of the expression), so the debugger is trying to find the `this` pointer in *mfc42d.dll*, which of course won't work. The solution is to use the "{*}" context operator, which uses the current context. Of course, the following expression doesn't work either (that would be too easy).

```
{,,mfc42d.dll}AfxDump({*}this)
```

This results in an "Error: argument list does not match a function" message. To solve this problem, you need to cast the `this` pointer, so the following expression works as expected.

```
{,,mfc42d.dll}AfxDump((const CObject*){*}this)
```

OK—it's a pain in the neck to figure out, but once you do, it's really worth it.

TIP

If you can't pass variables to Watch window functions, most likely you need to use the "{*}" context operator to use the current context.

One problem with function calls in Watch window expressions is that they can take a fair amount of time to evaluate. If you find the debugger is taking forever to step through code, there's a good chance you have functions in the Watch window. Just close the Watch window and check the performance. If it is back to normal, you have Watch window expressions that take too much time to evaluate.

TIP

If you find that the debugger is taking forever to step through code, close the Watch window and check the performance.

Finally, entering a function name without parameters (and also omitting the parentheses) displays the function's base virtual memory address and its prototype, which can be handy at times.

Datatip Expressions

The Visual C++ debugger datatip feature also supports expressions similar to Watch window expressions, except that the following features are not supported.

- Register and pseudo-register operands
- Assignment operators
- Function calls
- Context operators

Consequently, if an expression you want to see is on the screen and within the current scope, you don't need to type it into the Watch window. Just select a valid expression, move the mouse pointer over the selection, and you will see the expression and its results in the datatip. For example, if your program has the following code:

DEBUGGING TOOLS

```
int fred, wilma, barney, betty;
...
fred = (wilma + barney + 4) / (betty + 8);
```

you can select any valid expression, such as "wilma + barney", "barney + 4", "wilma + barney + 4", "betty + 8", and see the results of the expression in the datatip.

> **TIP**
>
> You can use datatips to display expressions in the source code within the current scope.

By the way, if a source code expression you want to see has a function call or assignment operators, the easiest approach to evaluate the expression is either to drag and drop the selected expression on the Watch window or to use the **QuickWatch** command.

Registers and Pseudo-registers

As I just mentioned, you can enter registers and pseudo-registers in Watch window expressions, as well as in the Memory window **Address** box. You can also view the registers using the Registers window, but the Watch window is more versatile since you can use registers in expressions. Furthermore, using the Watch window eliminates the need to display an additional debug window, thereby reducing the clutter of windows a bit.

The Watch and Memory windows support the registers listed in Table 7.5. These names are the "official" register names, but you can often use variations of these names. For example, for the EAX register you can also use @eax, EAX, eax, or even Eax. However, using the @ prefix eliminates the possibility of variable name clashes, so you can use @eax even if you have a variable named *eax*.

The Watch window also supports the pseudo-registers listed in Table 7.6. The Memory window also recognizes these pseudo-registers, but they have no meaning in that context. The @ERR pseudo-register is useful for monitoring the *GetLastError* value in the Watch window. You can enter "@ERR,hr" to see the text for Win32 error codes. (Similarly, you can enter "@EAX,hr" to monitor COM HRESULTs.) The @CLK pseudo-register can be used to perform simple

Table 7.5 Registers that Watch and Memory windows support

Register	Usage
@EAX	General purpose, used for function return values
@EBX	General purpose
@ECX	General purpose, used for the `this` pointer for objects
@EDX	General purpose, used for high word of 64-bit return values
@ESI	Source for memory move and compare operations
@EDI	Destination for memory move and compare operations
@EIP	Instruction pointer (current location of code)
@ESP	Stack pointer (current location of stack)
@EBP	Stack base pointer (bottom of current stack frame)
@EFL	Flag bits for comparisons and math operations
@CS	Code segment
@SS	Stack segment
@DS	Data segment
@ES	Extra segment
@FS	Another extra segment, used to point to the TIB
@GS	Yet another extra segment

Table 7.6 Pseudo-registers that the Watch window supports

Pseudo-register	Meaning
@ERR	Displays the last error code returned by the *GetLastError* API function for the current thread
@CLK	Displays the accumulated time in microseconds
@TIB	Displays the address of the TIB

profiling. (See Chapter 8, Basic Debugging Techniques, for more information on profiling from the debugger.) The @TIB pseudo-register displays the TIB address. The TIB contains potentially useful information, such as the exception record, Structured Exception Handler (SEH) chain, the top and base of the stack, and the Thread Local Storage (TLS) array. The structure of the TIB and its usefulness in debugging is described in Matt Pietrek's "Under the Hood" (May, 1996).

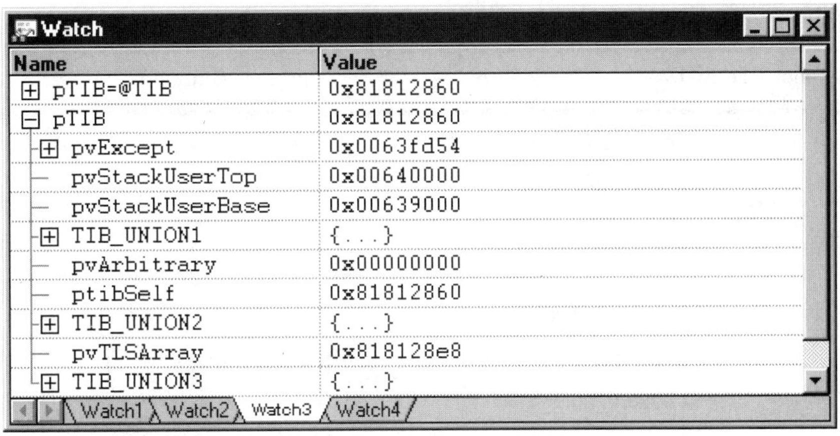

Figure 7.1   The Watch window with TIB

To display the TIB structure in the Watch window, first add the following code to your program.

```
#ifdef _DEBUG
#include "tib.h"
PTIB pTIB;
#endif
```

The *Tib.h* header and the PTIB structure are from Pietrek's article. Now by assigning pTIB to @TIB and displaying *pTIB* in the Watch window, you can explore the TIB, as shown in Figure 7.1.

Watch Window Formatting Symbols

The Watch window always displays pointers in hexadecimal format, but you can choose to display all other expressions using either decimal or hexadecimal formats using the **Hexadecimal Display** option in the context menus. This display option also affects the format used in the Variables and Call Stack windows, the QuickWatch dialog box, and the source code datatips. In many situations, however, the global setting is insufficient, such as when you want to display variables in decimal and hexadecimal formats simultaneously. You may also choose to display expressions using other formats, such as strings, characters, or even as raw memory. You can control the display format for individual expressions in the Watch window using the formatting symbols shown in Table 7.7.

Table 7.7 Watch window formatting symbols

Symbol	Format	Example	Output
d or i	Signed decimal integer	−42,d	−42
u	Unsigned decimal integer	42,u	42
o	Unsigned octal integer	42,o	052
x	Hexadecimal integer	42,x	0x0000002a
X	Hexadecimal integer	42,X	0x0000002A
h	Short prefix for d, i, u, o, x	42,hx	0x002a
f	Signed floating point	1.5,f	1.500000
e	Signed scientific notation	1.5,e	1.500000e+000
g	Compact signed floating point	1.5,g	1.5
c	Character	42,c	'*'
s	ANSI string	"bugs",s	"bugs"
su	Unicode string	"bugs",su	"bugs"
st	Default string type (ANSI or Unicode)	"bugs",st	"bugs"
hr	HRESULT and Win32 error code	0x06,hr	The handle is invalid.
wm	Windows message number	0x01,wm	WM_CREATE
[digits]	Display array items	s,5	Displays first 5 items

To use a formatting symbol, enter the expression you want to see, then a comma followed by the formatting symbol. The result of the "st" formatting symbol is determined by the **Display unicode strings** setting on the **Debug** tab of the Options dialog box. If you are debugging a Unicode program, you definitely want to enable this option.

TIP

> When debugging a Unicode program, be sure to enable the **Display unicode string** option and use the "st" formatting symbol for strings.

You may have noticed that the Watch window expands pointers to one level only, so if a pointer points to an array of several items, you can see only the first item. You may also have noticed that being able to access only the first item isn't especially useful. On the other hand, you can expand arrays to view all their items, although this expansion may take a long time if there are many items. (Note that although pointers and arrays are similar, they are not the same. An array is a pointer to a fixed number of objects, whereas a pointer points to an unknown number of objects.) This problem makes the ability to format array items very useful. For example, consider the following declarations:

```
char *s1 = _T("This program has bugs!");
CString s2 = _T("This program has bugs!");
```

You can display the first five characters of the char string by entering "s1,5" in the Watch window. Similarly, you can display the first five characters of the CString by entering "s2.m_pchData,5". You can also display substrings by using pointer arithmetic expressions. For example, to display the "bugs!" substrings, enter "(s1+17),5" and "(s2.m_pchData+17),5". However, the index displayed in the Watch window always starts with zero, regardless of the offset specified in the expression, so you must do some arithmetic to get the actual array index.

 TIP

If a pointer points to an array of items, you can use array items formatting to display the first items in an array. You can also use pointer expressions to display subarrays.

You can format the display of raw memory in the Watch window using the formatting symbols listed in Table 7.8. These formatting symbols allow you to display raw memory in the Watch window instead of the Memory window.

Table 7.8   Watch windows raw memory formatting symbols

Symbol	Format
ma	64 ANSI characters
m or mb	16 bytes in hexadecimal followed by 16 ANSI characters
mu	8 words in hexadecimal followed by 8 Unicode characters
mw	8 words
md	4 double words
mq	4 quad words

Table 7.9   Value operators

Operator	Output
BY(exp)	Displays the contents of the byte pointed to by *exp*
WO(exp)	Displays the contents of the word pointed to by *exp*
DW(exp)	Displays the contents of the double word pointed to by *exp*

You can display the contents of a value pointed to by a register, variable, or virtual memory address using the operators shown in Table 7.9. For example, to display the double word pointed to by the ESP register, use the expression "DW(ESP)". You can also combine these operators with formatting symbols, so you can display a double word pointed to by the ESP register as an unsigned decimal integer using "DW(ESP),u". You can use lower case for the operators and omit the parentheses, so "dw esp,u" is also acceptable.

Using *Autoexp.dat*

The Watch window formatting symbols are powerful and convenient, but sometimes they aren't powerful and convenient enough. Specifically, they don't recognize data types, so you must always enter the formatting symbols manually; they don't work for classes and data structures; and they work only with the Watch window and not the Variables window or the source code datatips.

TIP   Use *Autoexp.dat* to control the display of class objects and data structures and to control the **Step Into** command.

Fortunately, the rules for displaying Windows API, MFC, and ATL class objects and data structures aren't hard-wired into Visual C++ but are defined in *Autoexp.dat* (in *Common\Msdev\Bin*). Consequently, you can add new rules or change existing rules by following the documentation in the file header. These rules are then used by the Watch and Variables windows as well as source code datatips. The *Autoexp.dat* file is reloaded with debugger **Go** command, making it easy to experiment with. Also as a bonus, you can use the *Autoexp.dat* file to control the **Step Into** command to prevent stepping into specific functions, either because you don't have the source code or because stepping into the code is a waste of time.

One small warning: Technically the *Autoexp.dat* file is an "undocumented" feature, so you can't rely on continued support. However, this may be the most widely documented undocumented feature I have ever seen, so I doubt it is going away anytime soon.

Using *AutoExpand*

The class and data structure display rules are defined in the *AutoExpand* section of the *Autoexp.dat* file. The rules use the following format:

```
type=[text]<member[,format]>...
```

In this format, *type* is the name of the type, *text* is the description of the data member to display, *member* is the name of the class or structure data member, and *format* is an optional Watch window formatting symbol. Note that the equals sign (=), angle brackets (<>), and comma are taken literally, whereas square brackets ([]) indicate optional items. You can also use the <,t> format to display the name of the most-derived type of the object. If there is no rule for a class, the base classes are checked for a matching rule. Here are some examples.

```
[AutoExpand]
CPoint =x=<x> y=<y>
CRect =top=<top> bottom=<bottom> left=<left> right=<right>
CWnd =<,t> hWnd=<m_hWnd>
```

Figure 7.2 shows how those types appear in the Watch window.

If a variable isn't expanding the way you expect, first double-check the rule for typos. Then double-check the variable type to make sure the variable is what you think it is. You can check variable types in the Watch window by giving the **Properties** command in the context menu and checking the **Type** field. Note that the debugger doesn't know anything about `typedefs`, so the debugger considers an LPCTSTR a `const char *`, whereas it considers a BSTR an `unsigned short *`.

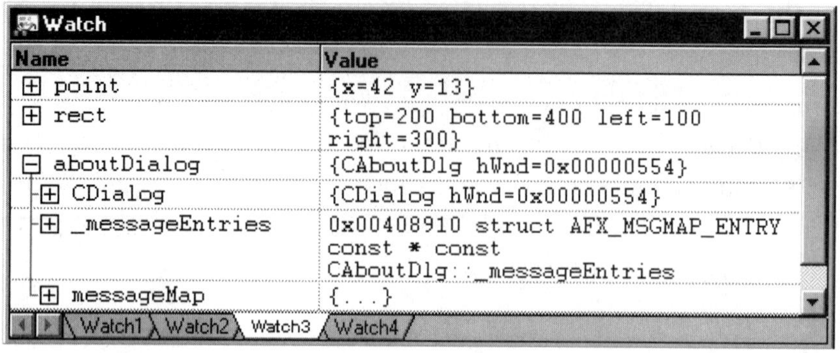

Figure 7.2 The Watch window with classes and data structure defined
in *AutoExpand.dat*

Using *ExecutionControl*

The Visual C++ debugger uses the following rules when you trace through functions using the **Step Into** command.

- If the function is in the program database and the debugger can find source code, the debugger steps into the source code.
- If the function is in the program database and the debugger can't find source code, the debugger prompts you for the source code path with the Find Source dialog box. If you give a valid path, the debugger steps into the source code. Otherwise, the debugger steps into assembly code.
- If the function is not in the program database, the debugger performs a **Step Over** instead.

Most of the time, this is exactly the behavior you want. In some situations, however, this approach becomes tedious, often because you don't have the source code or because stepping into the code is a waste of time. Here is a typical example.

```
int TraceFunction (const CString &s);

int APIENTRY WinMain (HINSTANCE hInstance, HINSTANCE
    hPrevInstance, LPSTR lpCmdLine, int nCmdShow) {
  TraceFunction(_T("This is a case for execution control."));
  ...
}
```

In this example, if you were to **Step Into** *TraceFunction*, you would first step into the *CString* constructor that converts the string literal into a *CString* object. If you did this a few times, the easiest solution would be to **Step Out** of the constructor. If you traced into *TraceFunction* hundreds of times, however, constantly having to **Step Out** of the *CString* constructor would become very tedious. You can eliminate this problem by adding the following statements to *Autoexp.dat* and restarting Visual C++ (unlike the *AutoExpand* rules, the *ExecutionControl* rules require Visual C++ to restart to take effect).

```
[ExecutionControl]
CString::CString=NoStepInto
```

Here are examples of the various forms of execution control.

```
[ExecutionControl]
RandomFunction=NoStepInfo        ; Don't step into this function
CRandom::RandomMethod=NoStepInto ; Don't step into this member
                                 ; function
CRandom::*=NoStepInfo            ; Don't step into any functions
                                 ; of this class
ATL::*=NoStepInfo                ; Don't step into any ATL
                                 ; functions
```

An *Autoexp.dat* Example

Let's put everything together by working through an example. Suppose you have created a bug database with the following classes:

```
enum BugType { CrashBug, MajorBug, MinorBug, UsabilityBug,
               SetupBug, DocBug };

class CBug {
public:
   BugType    m_Type;
   CString    m_Description;
};

class CProgramBug : public CBug {
public:
   CString    m_File;
   int        m_LineNumber;
};
```

Figure 7.3 A datatip for a class defined in *AutoExpand.dat*

If you view a *CBug* or *CProgramBug* variable with the Watch window, Variables window, or source code datatips, you will find the variable displayed as "{...}"—which isn't useful. Now add the following statements to the *AutoExpand* section of *Autoexp.dat*.

```
CBug =<,t> BugType=<m_Type>
    Description=<m_Description.m_pchData,st>
CProgramBug =<,t> BugType=<m_Type>
    Description=<m_Description.m_pchData,st>
    File=<m_File.m_pchData,st> Line=<m_LineNumber>
```

Note that displaying *CString*s correctly requires you to display the *m_pchData* member. Also, I have used the "st" formatting symbol instead of "s" to display Unicode strings correctly. Now save the file and give the **Go** command. Figure 7.3 shows how such a variable is now displayed.

Debugging with Breakpoints

Using breakpoints effectively is crucial to debugging productivity. Think about it—without breakpoints, the only way to use a debugger would be to single-step through a program until you found the problem or let the program run until it crashes. Breakpoints in effect allow you to describe the circumstances of the problem to the debugger and have the debugger set up the program state for you. Ideally, at that point all you would have to do is check the call stack, step through a few lines of code, check a few variables, and solve the problem.

Of course, you are familiar with the **Insert/Remove Breakpoint** command, which allows you to set a breakpoint on a specific line of source code (in a source code window) or assembly instruction (in the Disassembly window). You are also probably familiar with the **Run to Cursor** command, which sets a temporary breakpoint that is automatically removed when the code is reached. The **Step Over**, **Step Into**, **Step Out**, and **Break Execution** commands also work by setting temporary breakpoints. In addition, Visual C++ provides rich functionality for setting advanced breakpoints with the Breakpoints dialog box, which is accessed with the **Breakpoints** command in the **Edit** menu. You can set the following types of breakpoints.

- **Code location breakpoints** You can make code location breakpoints unconditional, or conditional on an expression changing or the code being reached a specific number of times.
- **Data breakpoints** You can make data breakpoints conditional on an expression changing. For arrays and structures, you can also give the number of array items or structure elements to watch.
- **Message breakpoints** You can make message breakpoints for when a specific window procedure receives a specific message.

Pretty powerful stuff. Remember that the alternative to breakpoints is to single-step through your code, so these features are definitely worth knowing and using.

All three types of breakpoints are easier to set when the program is running from the debugger because Visual C++ can verify the breakpoint immediately after you enter it. By contrast, when the program isn't running, Visual C++ will allow you to enter any advanced breakpoint that is syntactically correct. Consequently, if your program isn't running, start it with the **Step Over** command, and then set the advanced breakpoints.

Advanced breakpoints are easier to set when the program is running.

Breakpoint Expressions

Two types of expressions are used in the Breakpoints dialog box: breakpoint condition expressions and advanced breakpoint expressions.

Breakpoint Condition Expressions

Breakpoint condition expressions are used to determine if the debugger stops at the breakpoint. An expression can be a Boolean expression, which causes the debugger to break if the expression is true, or it can be a non-Boolean expression, which causes a break if the expression has changed since the last time the breakpoint was reached.

Breakpoint conditional expressions may consist of the following operands:

- Constants (decimal, hexadecimal, octal, character, floating point, but not program constants)
- Program variables
- Registers and pseudo-registers

and the following operators:

- Arithmetic (+, - , *, /, %)
- Relational (==, !=, <, <=, >, >=)
- Boolean (!, ||, &&)
- Bitwise (~, >>, <<, &, |, ^)
- Address (&, *)
- Array ([])
- Class/structure/union (., ->)
- Sizeof
- C casts (but with only one level of indirection)
- Memory contents (DW(), WO(), BY())

You can also use parentheses, which aren't considered operators. Unlike Watch window expressions, breakpoint conditional expressions do not support assignment operators or function calls. Also, for structures or arrays you must compare one item at a time. For example, to break when the string *s* contains "bugs", you would use the following expression:

```
s[0]=='b' && 's[1]=='u' && s[2]=='g' && s[3]=='s'
```

Advanced Breakpoint Expressions

The Visual C++ debugger uses advanced breakpoint expressions to represent breakpoints internally. You can see these expressions in the **Breakpoints** list at the bottom of the Breakpoints dialog box. You can also enter these expressions yourself on the **Break at** box on the **Location** tab and the **Enter the expression to be evaluated** box on the **Data** tab.

These expressions use the same context operator used by Watch window expressions, together with a source code line number, variable name, function call name, virtual memory address, or statement label. Here are some examples.

```
a line number:
{[function],[source],[executable]}.100
a variable name:
{[function],[source],[executable]}MyVariable
a function name:
{[function],[source],[executable]}MyFunction
a function name:
{[function],[source],[executable]}CMyClass::MyFunction
a memory address:
{[function],[source],[executable]}0x00401234
a statement label:
{[function],[source],[executable]}Barney
```

If you enter an expression in either the **Break at** box or the **Enter the expression to be evaluated** box that uses a variable in the current program scope, the debugger will add the correct context operator automatically. Otherwise, you must add the context operator yourself.

Code Location Breakpoints

Code location breakpoints are the most commonly used breakpoints. You can set the following types of code breakpoints.

- Source code line number breakpoints
- Code virtual memory address breakpoints
- Function name breakpoints
- Statement label breakpoints

The context operator allows you to set a breakpoint on a function name, but that may not be enough information because C++ function overloading allows several functions to have the same name. For overloaded functions, Visual C++ displays the Resolve Ambiguity dialog box to let you choose the desired function, as shown in Figure 7.4.

You can make a code location breakpoint conditional on a Boolean expression becoming true or a non-Boolean expression changing value. For example, suppose your program leaks memory that has a size of 123 bytes and you want to see the call stack when this memory is allocated. Because this memory block has an unusual size, you can easily track it down using a conditional breakpoint. Start by setting an unconditional code location breakpoint on the first line of the _malloc_dbg function in *Dbgheap.c*. Next, make it conditional

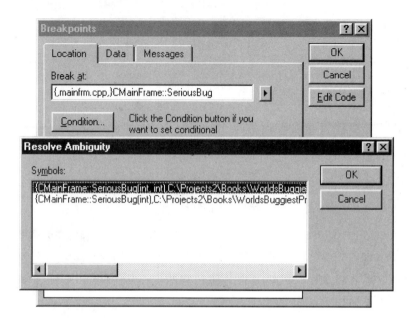

Figure 7.4 The Visual C++ Resolve Ambiguity dialog box

by selecting the **Location** tab of the Breakpoints dialog box, selecting the *Dbgheap.c* breakpoint in the **Breakpoints** list, and clicking the **Condition** button. In the **Enter the expression to be evaluated** box in the Breakpoint Condition dialog box, enter "nSize==123", where *nSize* is the parameter to *_malloc_dbg* that determines the size of the allocation (Figure 7.5).

You can also make a code location breakpoint conditional on the code being reached a specific number of times. For example, if you have a bug that occurs at the 100th iteration in a loop, set a breakpoint in the loop and have it skip the first 99 times. One interesting trick is if you don't know the number of times a breakpoint is hit before a bug occurs, you can specify a large number of times to skip (such as 10,000), and then run the program. When the bug occurs, you can check the Breakpoints dialog box to see the remaining number of times to skip the breakpoint (such as 8,765), as shown in Figure 7.6. You can then change the conditional breakpoint to skip the original number minus the remaining number minus 1 (such as 10,000 –8,765 –1 = 1,234.)

Unfortunately, two quirks in Visual C++ conspire to make this technique difficult. First, the remaining number of times to skip the breakpoint is at the end of the text, but you can't scroll the text horizontally, thereby making it

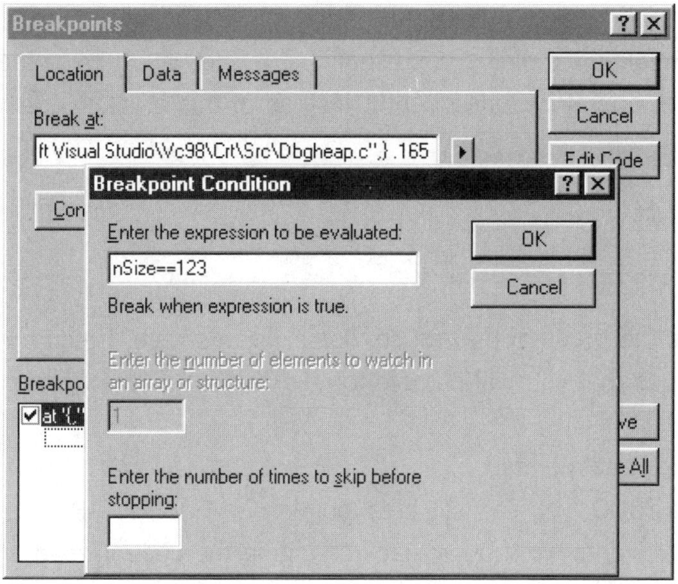

Figure 7.5   The Breakpoint Condition dialog box for a code location breakpoint

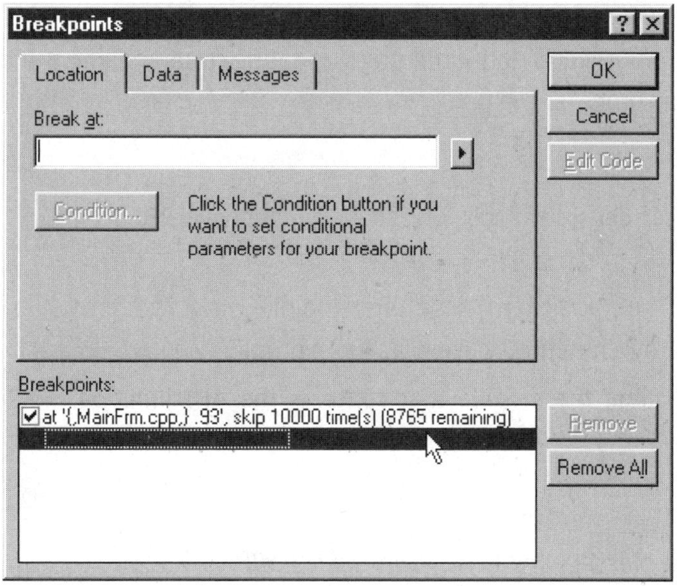

Figure 7.6   The Breakpoints dialog box showing the number of times remaining to skip the breakpoint

difficult (if not impossible) to see the number. Second, when you edit a break-point, the Breakpoints dialog box usually adds the full paths to the arguments in the context operator. Consequently, instead of this breakpoint expression

```
{,MyProgram.cpp,}.888
```

you end up with

```
{,C:\Projects\MyProgram\MyProgram.cpp,}.888
```

thus making the problem that much worse. In this case, I recommend removing the path so that you will be able to read the text in the **Breakpoints** list.

System Code Breakpoints

In Windows 2000, you can set breakpoints on Windows API functions. Code location breakpoints work by actually changing the code in memory, replacing the first byte of the instruction with a breakpoint with an `int 3` instruction to break into the debugger. If you attempt to set a breakpoint on a Windows API using Windows 98, you will actually change (that is, screw up) the operating system. However, you can set a system call breakpoint in Windows 2000 because it supports copy-on-write page updating, thus making the change local to the current process.

> **TIP**
>
> You can set system code breakpoints in Windows 2000.

You can set a system code breakpoint using the following steps. The *MessageBox* API function is used as an example.

1. **Determine the module that contains the API function.** You can use the *Win32api.csv* file (in *Vc\Lib*) as a roadmap for all the Windows API functions. For example, the following command line

```
findstr MessageBox win32api.csv
```

indicates that *MessageBox* is found in *User32.dll.*

2. **Determine if the debugging symbols for that module are loaded.** Run the program and check the contents of the **Debug** tab of the Output window. If the debugging symbols were successfully loaded, you see a "Loaded symbols for 'C:\WINNT\SYSTEM32\USER32.DLL'." message. Otherwise, you receive a message

saying "Loaded 'C:\WINNT\SYSTEM32\USER32.DLL ', no matching symbolic information found."

3. **Determine the actual function name.** If debugging symbols were loaded, use this command line

```
dumpbin -symbols user32.dbg | findstr MessageBox
```

which returns the fully mangled name "_MessageBoxA@16". If debugging symbols weren't loaded, use this command line

```
dumpbin -exports user32.dll | findstr MessageBox
```

which returns "MessageBoxA." Note that the name "MessageBox" is seen only by the preprocessor, which converts it to either "MessageBoxA" or "MessageBoxW", where "A" stands for ANSI and "W" stands for wide or Unicode characters.

4. **Set the breakpoint in the Breakpoints dialog box.** If debugging symbols were loaded, enter

```
{,,user32.dll}_MessageBoxA@16
```

If debugging symbols weren't loaded, enter

```
{,,user32.dll}MessageBoxA
```

If debugging symbols weren't loaded, you also need to enable the **Load COFF & Exports** option on the **Debug** tab of the Options dialog box. This option allows you to set breakpoints on exported functions without debugging symbols.

If you don't have the *findstr.exe* utility, you can get it from the Windows Resource Kit. Alternatively, you can use the Visual C++ **Find in Files** command instead.

Data Breakpoints

Most bugs are best isolated by tracing through specific code, but some are best isolated by tracking changes in data. For example, it is usually easiest to debug memory corruption by tracking the memory being corrupted. In these situations, data breakpoints are incredibly useful.

TIP

Data breakpoints are awesome. Use them!

You make a data breakpoint conditional on a Boolean expression becoming true or a non-Boolean expression changing value. For arrays and structures, you can also give the number of array items or structure elements to watch. If you specify a dereferenced pointer, you can enter the length in bytes of the memory addressed by the pointer.

Unlike code location breakpoints, you need to use data breakpoints carefully because under certain circumstances they can require a significant amount of processing power to monitor. Consequently, they can make your program run very slowly from the debugger—even on a fast computer. Here are some tips to make data breakpoints as efficient as possible.

• Try to use as few data breakpoints at a time as possible. Intel CPUs have four debugging registers that can be used for data breakpoints. The key to efficient data breakpoints is to take advantage of these debugging registers, so try to limit your data breakpoints to what can be evaluated in four 32-bit registers. Try to watch a single element in arrays and structures.

• Close the Watch window or remove all unnecessary Watch window expressions, especially those that make function calls.

• Disable data breakpoints until you really need them. For example, before you start the program, use the Breakpoints dialog box to disable all data breakpoints. Set a code location breakpoint where you know you will need the data breakpoints. Run the program until you break at that code, and then enable the data breakpoints. Although this is extra work for you, the program will run much faster. Note that you can disable breakpoints while the program is running (in case you forget).

• Data breakpoints on variables are slow, but data breakpoints on data members are even slower. Data breakpoints on virtual memory addresses are much more efficient because they use a single debug register, so you can improve performance by setting the breakpoint using the variable address. Virtual memory addresses within a process are also context independent, so the breakpoint will apply in all scopes. For example, suppose you want to break when *count* is 0 and the address of *count* is 0x00631234 (which you can easily determine by entering "&count" in the Watch window). Instead of using the expression "count==0", use "*(int *)0x00631234==0". Note that using the equivalent expression "DW(0x00631234)==0" is much slower. Also, variable addresses aren't usually random (especially at the beginning of a program); so if a stack or heap variable has a certain address in one run, there's a good chance it will have the same address later. However, stack addresses are constantly reused, so stack address breakpoints should be used only within a single function.

- Avoid data breakpoints in code that uses debug heap diagnostic functions such as _CrtCheckMemory and _CrtDumpMemoryLeaks. Combining these features will really bring your program to a crawl. If necessary, temporarily remove these diagnostics.

> **TIP**
>
> To improve data breakpoint performance, take advantage of the debugging registers. Write breakpoint expressions in terms of a variable's virtual memory address.

One more significant problem with data breakpoints is that they sometimes don't go away. That is, if you set a data breakpoint and then disable or remove it, the breakpoint may still be in effect. The only way around this problem is to restart Visual C++ or even Windows.

Message Breakpoints

Message breakpoints allow you to have the debugger break when a specific window procedure receives a specific message. To monitor multiple messages for a window, just use multiple message breakpoints.

This feature *sounds* useful, but most likely you will use code location breakpoints instead. For Windows API-based programs, it is easier to simply set a breakpoint on the code that handles the specific message. Similarly, for MFC-based programs, it is easier to set a breakpoint on the appropriate message handler function. Note that you can't use message breakpoints directly in MFC programs because these breakpoints require you to supply a C-based window procedure. Consequently, you must set message breakpoints on the global MFC window procedures, as shown in Figure 7.7. However, using a message breakpoint on a global window procedure such as *AfxWndProc* isn't very practical because it is used by most of the windows in an MFC program.

Breakpoint Problems

Breakpoints don't always work, and their error messages aren't exactly self-explanatory. Here is some guidance on how to solve the most common breakpoint problems.

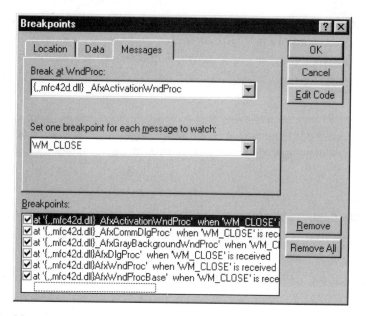

Figure 7.7   Message breakpoints set on global MFC window procedures

For starters, to set symbolic breakpoints you need to have debugging symbols that match both the executable and the source code, as described earlier in this chapter. Without matching symbols, the debugger doesn't know where the line numbers, functions, variables, and statement labels are in the executable; so the only breakpoints you can set without symbols are for virtual memory addresses and for exported functions if you enabled the **Load COFF & Exports** option.

If you have matching symbols but aren't able to enter a breakpoint expression in the Breakpoints dialog box, check the breakpoint expression for the following problems:

- Expression typos or incorrect operands
- Expressions that need context operators
- Wrong information in the context operators, including function, source code, and executable names in the wrong order or with misplaced commas

The most common breakpoint problems result in the dreaded message shown in Figure 7.8.

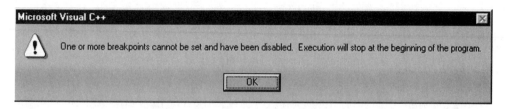

Figure 7.8 The dreaded "One or more breakpoints cannot be set" message box

To understand this message fully, it helps to know how Visual C++ sets breakpoints. Internally, Visual C++ stores the breakpoint information as shown in the **Breakpoints** list at the bottom of the Breakpoints dialog box. After a program is loaded, the debugger then walks through the list, looks up the necessary information in the program database, and sets the breakpoints. If any of the breakpoints cannot be set, Visual C++ then displays this message box. The only exception is with breakpoints set in modules listed in the **Additional DLLs** category of the **Debug** tab in the Project Settings dialog box. Any breakpoints in these modules are considered virtual, and the debugger sets physical breakpoints after the DLL is dynamically loaded.

Given this procedure, Visual C++ can fail to set a breakpoint for the following reasons:

- Matching debugging symbols weren't found. Make sure debugging symbols are loaded for all modules with breakpoints.
- A module, file, or function specified in the context operator wasn't found in the program database or the **Additional DLLs** list. Be sure to add modules loaded using the *LoadLibrary* API function and COM to the **Additional DLLs** list to preserve the breakpoints.
- A breakpoint that requires a context operator didn't use one, so the breakpoint couldn't be found.
- A code location breakpoint using a source code line number doesn't refer to valid code, which suggests that the source code doesn't match the executable. If you edit the code outside Visual C++ in a way that changes the line numbers, line number breakpoints may become invalid. In this case, you need to rebuild your program and reset the breakpoints. Another cause of this problem is debugging optimized code because the source code doesn't directly map to the executable. One way around this problem is to set breakpoints by function name instead of by line number.

- A virtual memory address breakpoint doesn't refer to valid code. Most likely you need to update or remove the breakpoint.

On receiving the message shown in Figure 7.8, the best thing to do is display the Breakpoints dialog box, determine which breakpoints in the **Breakpoints** list were disabled (they won't be checked), and fix them. You can use the **Edit Code** button to help you locate the relevant source code for code location breakpoint problems.

Just-in-time Debugging

There are three fundamentally different ways to debug a program using the Visual C++ debugger.

- Run the program directly from the debugger.
- Run the program as a standalone program, and use JIT debugging if the program crashes with an unhandled exception.
- Run the program as a standalone program, and attach the debugger to the processes.

Ordinarily when you are developing a program, the simplest approach is always to run the program directly from the debugger. That way, if you ever need to check what is going on in the program, you can just break into the debugger. Because debugged programs ordinarily load quickly from Visual C++, there is no real benefit to running outside the debugger during development. (However, I have seen a situation where a debugged program seemed to take forever to load. In this case, the Visual C++ workspace—a DSW file—contained dozens of large projects; the delay resulted from Visual C++ determining if any of the program files needed to be rebuilt. Debugging the program using the main executable's project a—DSP file—immediately solved that problem.)

Generally, it is preferable to run programs directly from the debugger. In some situations, however, a program runs fine from within the debugger but crashes when run as a standalone program. Furthermore, testers are unlikely to run programs from the debugger. In these cases, the best approach to tracking down bugs is to use JIT debugging. (Of course, to run JIT debugging on a tester's computer, you must make sure Visual C++ is installed.) To enable JIT debugging, select the **Options** command in the **Tools** menu. From the Options dialog box, select the **Debug** tab and then the **Just-in-time debugging** option. Now if the program crashes with an unhandled exception, you can load the program into the debugger by clicking the **Debug** button in the Windows 98 crash dialog box or the **Cancel** button in the Windows 2000 crash message box.

Although JIT debugging can be extremely helpful, it has one significant problem—it doesn't always work. The problem is that the JIT debugging code is in the crashed process. Consequently, for really bad crashes, clicking the **Debug** or **Cancel** button may fail to launch the debugger or even result in a Blue Screen of Death. In such situations, the best alternative is to attach the debugger to an already running program using the **Start Debug | Attach to Process** command in the **Build** menu. After giving this command, you then select the desired process from the **Attach to Process** dialog box. You can attach the debugger to a process before it crashes (which is preferable), and if you disable JIT debugging, you can also attach to a crashed process. If this technique fails to work, you can also attach the debugger from the command prompt using the following command line.

```
Msdev.exe -p <processID>
```

You can easily obtain the process ID from the **Process** tab of the Windows 2000 Task Manager. In fact, you can attach to the process directly from the Task Manager by selecting the task from the list and choosing the **Debug** command from the context menu.

JIT debugging allows a crashed program to be attached by any debugger, not just the Visual C++ debugger. You can see which debugger is being used by checking the *Debugger* value in *HKEY_LOCAL_MACHINE\SOFTWARE\ Microsoft\WindowsNT\CurrentVersion\AeDebug* in Windows 2000. In Windows 98, the JIT debugger information is stored in the *Win.ini* file using the *Debugger* key in the *AeDebug* section. In either case, to perform JIT debugging with Visual C++, the value should be set to the equivalent of the following:

```
"c:\Program Files\Visual Studio\Common\MSDev\Bin\Msdev.exe" -p %ld -e %ld
```

You may find this value is set to use Dr. Watson, which is probably not what you want in most cases. To restore this value, simply display the **Options** dialog box, select the **Debug** tab, and then select the **Just-in-time debugging** check box. Postmortem debugging with Dr. Watson has its place, but it's probably the last thing you want to do. It's always better to debug a live program than a dead one.

Remote Debugging

Visual C++ supports remote debugging, which can be extraordinarily valuable in certain circumstances. Remote debugging allows you to run your program and a small debug monitor on one computer (the remote computer) and the debugger on another (the host computer), communicating over a network using TCP/IP. This feature is surprisingly easy to overlook because the only clue that it exists is the **Debugger Remote Connection** command in the **Build** menu. My primary goal in this section is to make sure you know that the feature exists.

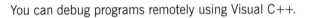

TIP

You can debug programs remotely using Visual C++.

Here are some of the situations where remote debugging is most valuable.

- Debugging problems related to the Heisenberg Uncertainty Principle, in which the presence of the debugger disturbs the behavior you are trying to debug, such as window drawing, window activation, and input focus
- Debugging full-screen programs, such as games or screen savers
- Debugging client/server programs, such as with DCOM, MTS/COM+, and SQL Server
- Debugging a problem on a customer's or tester's computer that you can't reproduce on your computer
- Debugging in environments that cannot run Visual C++
- Debugging on test computers that are intended to represent a typical user's system or computers that have a system configuration problem and therefore shouldn't have a development environment installed since that would disturb the system configuration

Remote debugging is surprisingly easy to set up and use. It requires only about seven files, so it has minimal impact on the remote computer. The steps to perform remote debugging using Visual C++ are fully documented in the MSDN Visual C++ Programmer's Guide, under Debugging Remote Applications. Here are a few more tips to help you get going.

- If you are debugging on a local area network and are not connected to the Internet, the debugger will present you with a Dial-up Connection dialog box. Just click **Cancel**—you don't have to be on line to perform remote debugging.

- The debugger will ask you for a remote executable path and file name, which is the executable path as seen by the remote computer. Although you can copy the executable files from the host to the remote computer for complex projects, you are likely to have trouble keeping all the files synchronized. Any debugging effort made with out-of-synch files is pretty much a frustrating waste of time. To eliminate this problem, you can make your development drive fully sharable and supply a universal naming convention (UNC) file name to the executable on the host computer. Alternatively, you can assign the development drive a drive letter on the remote computer (such as X:) using the Windows Explorer **Map Network Drive** command, and then use that drive letter for the executable path. This technique should save you a lot of effort, but there is a performance penalty because the remote computer must access the program on the host across the network. If the performance penalty is too high, instead add a script to copy the executable files to the remote computer as a **Post-build step** in the Project Settings dialog box.

- The **Remote Debugger Connection** setting is a global setting, not a project setting. You must switch back to local debugging manually when you are finished with remote debugging. Consequently, don't be alarmed if you unexpectedly see a **Remote Executable Path and File Name** dialog box after a remote debugging session.

Debugging with Edit and Continue

Perhaps the biggest downside to writing a program using a compiled programming language is that you must compile it. If you have ever developed using an interpreted language, you know what I mean. For example, in Visual Basic you can make changes to the program while it is running in the debugger and they immediately take effect, which greatly simplifies the debugging process. With the Visual C++ Edit and Continue feature (introduced with Visual C++ 6.0), you can get the best of both worlds. With Edit and Continue, you can change your source code while debugging your program and apply the changes by breaking into the debugger or even while the program is running (with some limitations in both cases). You can then continue to debug, thereby eliminating the standard debugging cycle of having to stop the program, recompile and link, and then return the program to the state it was originally running in. Edit and

Continue accomplishes this feat by changing the program image in memory rather than modifying files. Using Edit and Continue can significantly improve your debugging productivity.

The only real disadvantage of Edit and Continue occurs when you accidentally type something into the source code while debugging and have the change applied before you even realize what has happened. In such situations, Edit and Continue can be a bit too easy to use. In this respect, Edit and Continue does take some time to get used to.

Setting Up Edit and Continue

Edit and Continue is enabled by default for debug builds created with Visual C++ 6.0 or later. To enable Edit and Continue, perform the following steps.

1. Display the Project Settings dialog box and select the debug build (such as "Win32 Debug") from the **Settings for** box. As previously noted, Edit and Continue isn't compatible with release builds.
2. In the project tree control, select the entire project by clicking the top node.
3. Select the **General** category on the C/C++ tab. For **Debug info,** select **Program Database for Edit and Continue.** Also, verify that all optimizations are disabled.
4. Select the **Customize** category on the **Link** tab. Select the **Link incrementally** option.
5. Recompile the project with the **Rebuild All** command.
6. Optionally, display the Options dialog box and select the **Debug** tab. Then select the **Debug commands invoke Edit and Continue** option. This option eliminates the need to give the **Apply Code Changes** command in the **Debug** menu.

Edit and Continue requires special information that is stored in the PDB file to apply code changes from the debugger. If this information is not in the PDB for the modified file, Edit and Continue is disabled and any code changes made during debugging result in the message box shown in Figure 7.9.

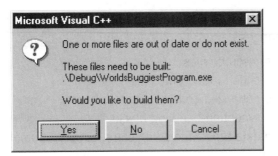

Figure 7.9   The Visual C++ "One or more files out of date" message box

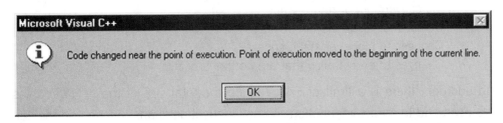

Figure 7.10   The Visual C++ "point of execution changed" message box

Using Edit and Continue

Using Edit and Continue is very simple. Just make the change to the source code and give the **Apply Code Changes** command. If you have selected the **Debug commands invoke Edit and Continue** option, you don't even need to give the **Apply Code Changes** command because it is performed automatically the next time you give the **Go, Run, Run to Cursor, Step Into, Step Over, Step Out**, or **Step Into Specific Function** commands in the **Debug** menu.

The only trick is that some code changes cause the currently executed statement to be changed. Edit and Continue tries to set the point of execution correctly, but the results may not always be right. You will be informed of any such execution changes with the message box shown in Figure 7.10. You should then verify that the point of execution is correct and, if necessary, change it using the **Set Next Statement** command.

Edit and Continue Limitations

Edit and Continue has some limitations with respect to the types of code changes you can make. Happily, if you make a change that Edit and Continue doesn't support, you are notified with an error message in the Output window. The following changes cannot be applied while debugging.

- Changes to resource files
- Changes to code in read-only files
- Changes to optimized code
- Changes to exception-handling blocks
- Changes to data types, including class, structure, union, or enumeration definitions
- Adding new data types
- Changes to function prototypes, including function name, arguments, calling convention, or return value
- Removal of functions
- Changes to global or static code
- Changes to executables that are not built locally

In addition, there is a limit of 64 bytes on the total size of the new variables you can add to an active function. An active function is any function on the call stack—the current function or one of its callers. There is no limit for functions not currently on the call stack.

Tips for Using Edit and Continue

These tips will help you get the most out of Edit and Continue.

- Using Edit and Continue and the **Set Next Statement** command together make a powerful combination. If you find a bug while tracing through your code, fix the code, apply the change, and use **Set Next Statement** to continue program execution at code located before the change. This way, you can immediately fix the problem, verify the change, and continue execution, usually as if the bug never happened.

- You can apply code changes while a program is running. Instead of breaking into the debugger, making changes, applying the changes, and resuming the program, you can just make the changes and give the **Apply Code Changes** command. What could be easier?

- Edit and Continue is not restricted to changes to files of the currently loaded project. You may apply code changes to any executing code that was originally built for Edit and Continue. Generally, if you can debug the code, you can perform Edit and Continue on it. This applies to EXEs, DLLs, and COM components that were built with Edit and Continue enabled. Again, just make the changes and give the **Apply Code Changes** command.

- Edit and Continue presents a significant problem to projects that have pre-link and post-build steps, which are set in the Project Settings dialog box. Typical post-build steps include copying executable files as well as rebasing and binding. The problem is that when you stop debugging, the modified executables are automatically relinked without performing these steps, typically resulting in an invalid build. In this situation, giving the **Build** command has no effect because Visual C++ believes the project is up to date. The best solution to this problem is to prevent Edit and Continue from performing the automatic relink after you stop debugging, thus requiring you to rebuild the program directly from Visual C++. You can disable Edit and Continue relinking by running the Registry Editor and setting the following registry key to zero.

```
HKEY_CURRENT_USER\Software\Microsoft\DevStudio\X.0\Debug\ENCRelink
```

Don't make this change while Visual C++ is running because it won't take effect.

Recommended Reading

Pietrek, Matt. "Under the Hood." *Microsoft Systems Journal,* May 1996.   Gives a detailed description of the Thread Information Block contents for Windows NT and Windows 95.

Richter, Jeffrey. *Programming Applications for Microsoft Windows: Master the Critical Building Blocks of 32-Bit and 64-Bit Windows-based Applications.* Redmond, WA: Microsoft Press, 1999.   Chapter 25, Unhandled Exception and C++ Exceptions explains how unhandled exceptions and just-in-time debugging work.

Robbins, John. "Bugslayer." *Microsoft Systems Journal,* August 1999.   Presents information on setting and using breakpoints and remote debugging.

Robbins, John. "Bugslayer." *Microsoft Systems Journal,* June 1998.   Presents information on system debugging symbols, setting breakpoints in a system DLL, and other tips on using the Visual C++ debugger.

PART III

Debugging Techniques

Chapter 8

Basic Debugging Techniques

This chapter answers many common Windows debugging questions, primarily focusing on basic debugging techniques. It is something of a Windows debugging FAQ, loosely based on questions I have found in debugging newsgroups.

General Debugging Techniques

What steps should I take to maximize my ability to debug code that I ship?

Take the following steps.

- Rebase your program's executables to prevent virtual address space collisions. Virtual address space collisions and rebasing are discussed in Chapter 6, Debugging with Windows.
- Create MAP files for your program's executables and archive them. Creating and using MAP files is discussed in Chapter 6.
- Create debugging symbols for your program's executables (even for release builds) and archive the resulting PDB files. Be sure not to use the **Separate types** linker option. Creating and using PDB files is discussed in Chapter 7, Debugging with the Visual C++ Debugger.
- Archive your program's project, source code, and executables.
- Create a mechanism for users to submit bug reports, including a bug report form and instructions. The instructions should recommend installing system debugging symbols, copying whatever is on the screen, and submitting Dr. Watson log files for crashes. Bug report forms and instructions are discussed in Chapter 1, The Debugging Process.

I want to include some debugging code in the release build, but I don't want it to affect run-time performance. What should I do?

You can key the release build debug code off the *IsDebuggerPresent* API function (note that this function isn't supported by Windows 95). For example, the following code affects performance only if the program is run from a debugger.

```
if (IsDebuggerPresent())
    PerformTimeConsumingDebugCheck();
```

Users, however, aren't likely to have a debugger present, so a better approach is to key the release-build debug code off an INI file or registry setting, such as shown in the following code.

```
BOOL ReleaseDebug = GetPrivateProfileInt(_T("My App"),
    _T("Debug"), FALSE, _T("MyApp.ini"));
...
if (ReleaseDebug)
    PerformTimeConsumingDebugCheck();
```

I can't debug a problem because there is too much data to isolate the problem in the debugger. What should I do?

Consider using one of the following techniques.

- **Create debug data.** Create special debug data that eliminates all the extraneous data not needed to isolate the problem.

- **Temporarily filter data from the program.** If it isn't practical to create debug data, you can temporarily filter out all the extraneous data to isolate the problem from within the program itself. For example, if your program displays a large list of data points but the problem occurs only for data with an x-axis offset of 42, you can use the following approach.

```
#ifdef DEBUG_FILTER_DATA
    // filter data only when DEBUG_FILTER_DATA is defined
    if (data[i].x != 42)
        continue;
#endif
```

- **Enable debugging code dynamically using a global variable.** Typically, debugging code is an all-or-nothing deal because its inclusion is determined at compile time by the preprocessor. Sometimes it's better to enable debugging code dynamically once the program state is set to reproduce a bug. For example, you can define a *Debug* global variable and control its value with code, an INI file or registry setting, or the debugger by changing its value using the Watch window.

```
#ifdef _DEBUG
BOOL Debug = FALSE;    // define global debug variable
#endif
...
#ifdef _DEBUG
    // filter data using a global variable, change Debug value
    // from Watch window
    if (Debug && data[i].x != 42)
        continue;
#endif
```

* **Enable debugging code dynamically using the keyboard.** Sometimes it's better to enable the debugging code dynamically by pressing a key combination. For example, you can enable the debugging code only when the Control key is pressed by checking its state with the *GetAsyncKeyState* API function.

```
#ifdef _DEBUG
    // filter data only when the Control key is pressed
    if (GetAsyncKeyState(VK_CONTROL) < 0 && data[i].x != 42)
        continue;
#endif
```

I believe the C preprocessor isn't outputting the code I expect. How can I debug this problem?

The C preprocessor is a wonderful thing, but its behavior is completely invisible from both the source code and the debugger. For example, suppose you have several overloaded `operator new` functions and then you have redefined `new` using the preprocessor to help you debug dynamically allocated memory. Suppose also that your program isn't using the version of `operator new` that you expect or perhaps it doesn't even compile. It can be very difficult to debug such a problem using the source code alone because it is difficult to know for sure what the preprocessor is doing.

You can examine the preprocessor output using the following technique: In the Project Settings dialog box, select the entire project and then click the **C/C++** tab. In the **Project Options** box, add the /P compiler option to the end of the settings. Now rebuild the files you are having problems with, such as *bogus.cpp*. You will now find *bogus.i* in the project folder (not in the *Debug* or *Release* folders). You can then view this file in a text editor. The preprocessor file is likely to be huge because the beginning of the file is filled with preprocessor muck, so you should immediately go to the end of the file because that is the location of your program code. You can now see exactly what the preprocessor has output. You can then search up through the file to find how all the relevant preprocessor symbols are really defined.

When done, be sure to remove the /P compiler option from your project settings. With this option, the compiler outputs the preprocessor output in lieu of object files, so you can't build your project until this option has been removed.

I am optimizing my program for speed, but there seems to be an optimization bug I can't get around. What should I do?

You don't want to ship unoptimized code because it tends to *very* unoptimized. Try optimizing the program for size instead, which is much safer and almost as effective as optimizing for speed because small code is fast code. If the bug goes away and the performance is acceptable, you're done. Otherwise, optimize selected files for speed. Alternatively, if you know the specific functions that fail when optimized, optimize the program the way you want, then fine-tune the optimization of the problem functions using `#pragma optimize`. For more information on optimization, see Matt Pietrek's "Remove Fatty Deposits from Your Applications Using Our 32-bit Liposuction Tools."

Keep in mind that, although there may be a bug in the Visual C++ optimizer, most likely the bug is in your code and it is revealed by optimization. If you can't track down the cause of an optimization-related bug in code you have to ship, however, using the techniques above is entirely appropriate.

All of a sudden, nothing makes sense anymore. What should I do?

Restart Windows, delete your project's *Debug* and *Release* folders, and completely rebuild your program. If that doesn't solve the problem, see Chapter 12, Desperate Measures, for more ideas.

Visual C++ Debugger Techniques

How can I debug an infinite loop?

Use the **Break** command in the **Debug** menu. For Windows 2000, you can break using the F12 key if the program has input focus. Then check the Call Stack window or step through the code to find the infinite loop.

TIP

Use the **Break** command to debug infinite loops.

How can I determine where a message box came from?

When the message box is displayed in a single-threaded program, use the **Break** command in the **Debug** menu or the F12 key in Windows 2000 and check the Call Stack window to find the cause of the message box.

My program uses the F12 key for an important function, but the debugger breaks every time I press it. What should I do?

Obviously, there is a downside to having Windows 2000 use the F12 for a debug break if your program uses that key as well. One solution to this problem is to reassign the function to use Alt+F12, Shift+F12, or some other key when the _DEBUG symbol is defined. For Windows 2000 (but not Windows NT 4.0), you can also change the debug break keyboard assignment in the registry. For example, to change the debug break to use the Scroll Lock key, set *UserDebuggerHotKey* value in *HKEY_LOCAL_MACHINE\SOFTWARE\Microsoft\ WindowsNT\CurrentVersion\AeDebug* to 145, which is the virtual key code for Scroll Lock. You must then restart Windows for the change to take effect.

Part of my program seems very slow. How can I determine the problem?

You could instrument your program to perform profiling (and you should if you really need to), but often you can determine the cause of poor performance simply by running your program from the debugger. Use the **Break** command a few times when the performance is bad, and check the Call Stack window for patterns. If the performance problem is limited to a fairly narrow set of code, chances are that randomly breaking into the debugger will land you in that code most of the time.

TIP

You can perform simple profiling using the debugger.

If you want to monitor how much time specific code takes to execute, you can enter "@CLK" in the Watch window. This value is a debugger pseudo-register that displays the time in microseconds. Alternatively, you can enter "@CLK / 1000" in the Watch window to monitor time in milliseconds, which is sometimes a bit easier to work with. You can also add the ",d" Watch window formatting symbol to ensure that the output is in decimal. To see the elapsed time for each step in the debugger instead of the accumulated time, enter "@CLK=0" in the Watch window immediately after (but not before) the "@CLK,d" statement, as shown in Figure 8.1.

When stepping through code, I tend to overshoot the code I want to debug. What should I do?

It's common to overshoot the code you're interested in while debugging. Fortunately, you rarely have to restart a program to reexecute a specific set of code, even if that code is normally executed once during the program. The Visual C++ debugger doesn't have a **Step Back** command to undo the **Step Into** and **Step Over** commands, but it does have a **Set Next Statement** command that allows you to set the next statement to be executed to the selected statement in a source code window. You can also use the **Set Next Statement** command to set the next "statement" to the selected instruction in the Disassembly window.

Figure 8.1 Profiting code using the @CLK pseudo-register in the Watch window

DEBUGGING TECHNIQUES

Let's explore the capabilities of the **Set Next Statement** command by looking at some sample code.

```
int ReallyBadNews () {
    int value = 0;
    POINT *pPoint = 0;
    pPoint->x = 4;    // will crash here with an access violation
    pPoint->y = 5;    // will crash here with an access violation
    value = pPoint->x * pPoint->y;
    return value;
}

int BadNews () {
    int value;
    {
        int value2 = 40, value3;
        value3 = ReallyBadNews();
        value = value2 / value3; // will crash here with integer
                                 // divide by zero
    }
    return value;
}
```

If you walk through the *BadNews* function using the **Step Over** command,
you find that the program crashes with an unhandled access violation exception
in the *ReallyBadNews* function. The bug, of course, is that *pPoint* is not initialized to point to a valid POINT structure. From within *ReallyBadNews*, you can
use the **Set Next Statement** command to continue execution on any other statement within that function, even though the program has crashed with an
unhandled exception. Once you return to *BadNews*, you can then use the **Set
Next Statement** command to continue execution on any of its statements as
well. In both functions, you can reexecute any code that doesn't crash as much
as you like, which is true in general as long as the code doesn't have any significant side effects that prevent the program from running. About the only thing
you can't do is use the **Set Next Statement** command to move execution from
one function scope to another. Attempting to do so results in the message box
shown in Figure 8.2. Always respond to this message box by clicking **Cancel**
because continuing will effectively corrupt the stack.

You might be surprised by the fact that you can continue to run the program
after an unhandled exception. Visual C++ itself handles the exception when

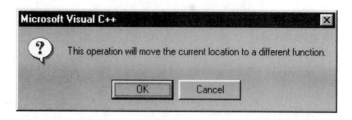

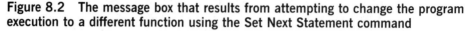

Figure 8.2 **The message box that results from attempting to change the program execution to a different function using the Set Next Statement command**

running from the debugger, so you can continue to execute as long as you use the **Set Next Statement** command to bypass any code that crashes. You can do this in *ReallyBadNews* by making `return` the next statement. Typically, this means that you can continue to run the program if the unhandled exception occurs within your source code, so that you can recover by setting the next statement within the function that crashed. If the unhandled exception occurs within a Windows API function or library function, it is unlikely that you can continue execution from within the same function, so most likely the program is doomed.

You might also be surprised by the fact that you can jump into or out of the block scope defined by the curly braces in *BadNews*. To understand how this is possible, you need to know exactly what the **Set Next Statement** command does. Quite simply, it does exactly what its name suggests: It sets the next statement to be executed by changing the value of the instruction pointer (EIP) register. It doesn't change the stack, execute any code, create or destroy any variables, or do anything else. For automatic (local) variables, note that the compiler makes space for all automatic variables defined within a function on function entry, not on block scope entry. So, although the variables *value2* and *value3* appear to exist only within the block, their allocated stack space exists for the entire duration of the function. The only thing that happens in the block scope entry is that the automatic variables are initialized. In this case, *value2* is initialized to 40.

The situation becomes more complex when objects are involved. If the variables *value2* and *value3* were objects, their constructors would be called on block entry and their destructors would be called on block exit, which would be apparent by checking the code in the Disassembly window. Obviously, having a mismatch between constructors and destructors is bad news indeed, so you must use caution when using **Set Next Statement** in the presence of object creation and destruction.

Once you become more familiar the **Set Next Statement** command, you will find that it is quite powerful and it can make your debugging sessions much more productive. If you are not using **Set Next Statement** often, you're not using it right. However, keep in mind that whenever you use **Set Next Statement**, you are effectively executing a different program from the actual program; such program execution is best regarded as an experiment. This means that you should not become overly concerned if the program crashes, leaks resources, or does anything else wrong because the actual program may behave differently when executing on its own. Also, keep in mind that debug builds are a direct translation of the source code, but release builds are not. Therefore you will have better success using **Set Next Statement** in release builds by using it in the Disassembly window.

TIP

Use the **Set Next Statement** command to make your debugging sessions more productive.

I need to debug or test specific error-handling code, but I can't cause the error to happen. What should I do?

Use the **Set Next Statement** command and perhaps change the values of relevant variables in the Watch window to create specific error conditions to test and debug your error-handling code. For example, consider the following code.

```
BOOL CMyApp::InitInstance () {
    try {
        m_pMainWnd = new CMainWindow;
        m_pMainWnd->ShowWindow(m_nCmdShow);
        m_pMainWnd->UpdateWindow();
        return TRUE;
    }
    catch (CMemoryException *e) {
        e->ReportError();
        e->Delete();
        return FALSE;
    }
}
```

It is highly unlikely that `operator new` will fail due to lack of memory, which makes the error handling difficult to test and debug. Although the out-of-memory error handling within this function is rather simple, you may need to debug the error handling outside the function by verifying that the program handles a FALSE return value correctly. Interestingly, you can't test this exception handling code just by using **Set Next Statement** to set the next statement within the exception handler (even if you skip over the *ReportError* and *Delete* functions) because you can't jump into an exception handler the way you can jump into a block scope. Consequently, the easiest way to debug the exception handling is to **Step Into** the `operator new` function, which in this case is the MFC version.

```cpp
void* __cdecl operator new (size_t nSize, int nType, LPCSTR
                            lpszFileName, int nLine) {
    void* pResult;
    _PNH pfnNewHandler = _pfnUninitialized;
    for (;;) {
        pResult = _malloc_dbg(nSize, nType, lpszFileName, nLine);
        if (pResult != NULL)
            return pResult;
        if (pfnNewHandler == _pfnUninitialized) {
            AFX_MODULE_THREAD_STATE* pState =
                AfxGetModuleThreadState();
            pfnNewHandler = pState->m_pfnNewHandler;
        }
        if (pfnNewHandler == NULL || (*pfnNewHandler)(nSize) == 0)
            break;
    }
    return pResult;
}
```

Now you can cause an out-of-memory exception either by setting *pResult* to 0 after *_malloc_dbg* (which would leak memory, but that's not likely a problem for this test) or by using **Set Next Statement** to skip over *_malloc_dbg* and the two statements following it.

> **TIP**
>
> Use the **Set Next Statement** command and change variable values in the Watch window to debug code that is unlikely to execute.

The principle presented here applies in general: By combining the **Set Next Statement** with changing variable values in the Watch window, you can easily test and debug code that otherwise is unlikely to execute.

How can I check a function return value if I didn't assign it to a variable?

You can check function return values directly from the debugger, so you don't have to add a temporary variable to your code and recompile to view a return value. If a return value is 32 bits or less, it is stored in the EAX register, which you can view in the Registers window or by entering "@EAX" in the Watch window. If the return value is 64 bits, the lower 32 bits are stored in the EAX register and the upper 32 bits are stored in the EDX register. If the return value is greater than 64 bits, a pointer to the return value is stored in the EAX register, which you can view by casting in the Watch window (for example, if a function returns a *CRect*, you could display the results by entering "(CRect *)@EAX") or by entering "EAX" in the **Address** box of the Memory window. You can also check function return values in the Variables window, but this technique works only for return values of 32 bits or less.

Similarly, if a Windows API function fails, you can check the *GetLastError* value directly from the debugger by entering "@ERR" in the Watch window. This value is a debugger pseudo-register that displays the last error code. You can then translate the error code to text using the ",hr" formatting symbol, as with "@ERR,hr".

TIP

You can view function return values by checking the EAX register and *GetLastError* values by checking the ERR pseudo-register in the Watch window.

How can I debug a "The thread 0xFF0BC5CF has exited with code −1 (0xFFFFFFFF)" message?

Having a thread exit with code of −1 isn't a bug, so this is nothing to worry about. Windows itself creates threads that exit with a code of −1, such as when your program displays one of the Windows common dialogs.

My program crashes without a trace. What should I do?

Make sure Just-in-time (JIT) debugging is enabled to give you an opportunity to check the problem with the debugger. To enable JIT debugging, choose the **Options** command in the **Tools** menu. From the Options dialog box, select the **Debug** tab and then the **Just-in-time debugging** option.

I want to see all the data on the stack, not just the function calls as displayed by the Call Stack window. What should I do?

You can view the stack contents using the Memory window. Display the Memory window, then enter either "ESP" in the **Address** box to display the stack pointer or "EBP" to display the stack base pointer. Then select the **Long Hex Format** display option from the Memory window context menu to make the stack contents easier to read.

Windows Debugging Techniques

How can I debug drawing code?

As I mentioned in Chapter 1, window drawing code is an excellent example of the Heisenberg Uncertainty Principle in debugging, where the presence of the debugger disturbs what you are trying to debug. Specifically, if the window being drawn is overlapped by the debugger when it activates, the window being drawn will be constantly invalidated. The debugger activation changes the way the window is drawn—if it can be drawn at all.

The solution to this problem is to prevent the window overlap. You can do this by laying out the program and debugger windows side by side on the screen. Using the highest screen resolution supported by your system will help. If there isn't enough room to prevent all overlap, at least make sure that the window being debugged isn't overlapped by the debugger. You may have to rearrange the Visual C++ toolbars a bit to make the debugger usable. If your program runs only as a maximized window (games and screen savers are good examples), you should allow the program to run as a restored (that is, not maximized) window for debug builds. Similarly, if the window being debugged has a WS_EX_TOPMOST attribute, that attribute should be removed for debug builds.

Another alternative is to use remote debugging, in which the program being debugged and the debugger run on different computers on a network. The steps to perform remote debugging using Visual C++ are fully documented in MSDN Visual C++ Programmer's Guide, under Debugging Remote Applications.

If you debug a lot of drawing code, perhaps the best alternative is to invest in a second video card and monitor so that you can display the program code in one monitor and the debugger in another. This approach can be more expensive than the others, but it is the most flexible and ultimately requires the least effort.

Finally, note that the GDI accumulates GDI function calls into batches and processes a batch at a time instead of a call at a time on a per-thread basis. This technique can significantly improve drawing performance, but it can also make drawing code difficult to debug because you don't always see the results of each line of code. You can disable the batch processing for debug builds by putting the following code in your thread initialization.

```
#ifdef _DEBUG
    GdiSetBatchLimit(1);    // disable thread GDI batch processing
#endif
```

TIP

Disable GDI batch processing to make drawing code easier to debug.

How can I debug drawing code that flashes?

Unnecessary flashing is one aspect of windows drawing that is especially difficult to debug. Unnecessary flashing is caused by a window's background being erased when it doesn't need to be. This problem is difficult to debug because the message-based nature of Windows makes it difficult to determine the specific code that sent the unnecessary erase background message.

Instead of using the debugger, I find it easier to analyze the source code for the following problems.

- **Inappropriately calling *UpdateWindow*** Windows assigns a low priority to paint messages to prevent a window from being redrawn unnecessarily. However, a program can force a window to be drawn immediately using the *UpdateWindow* API function. Inappropriately calling *UpdateWindow* can result in unnecessary redrawing.

- **Calling *InvalidateRect* without an update rectangle** The *InvalidateRect* API function allows you to pass an update rectangle to limit the redrawing to the area that must be redrawn. It is easier to pass a null pointer to *InvalidateRect* to invalidate the entire window, but this approach takes much longer to draw and can result in unnecessary flashing and slow drawing.

- **Calling *InvalidateRect* with the erase background parameter inappropriately set to true** If a background doesn't need to be repainted, you can eliminate unnecessary flashing by making sure the erase background parameter is set to false. Note that the erase background parameter is true by default in MFC.

- **Inappropriately using the CS_HREDRAW and CS_VREDRAW window styles** These window styles are necessary only if changing the size of the client area requires a complete redraw. This is true when something in the window is centered; but most windows don't center anything, so they don't need these class styles. If you are using MFC, note that MFC uses these styles by default, so you must register your own class in the window's constructor to remove these styles.

How can I debug mouse handling code?

Mouse handling code is another excellent example of the Heisenberg Uncertainty Principle in debugging. It can be difficult to debug mouse handling code because the debugger disturbs the sequence of mouse messages when it activates.

Debugging WM_MOUSEMOVE messages is particularly difficult because once you set a breakpoint for a mouse move message, the debugger breaks the instant the mouse moves into the window. Most likely you want the debugger to break at a particular location on the screen or under particular circumstances. I find the *GetAsyncKeyState* debugging technique presented earlier in this chapter works quite well for debugging mouse move messages, as shown here.

```
void CMyWnd::OnMouseMove (UINT nFlags, CPoint point) {
#ifdef _DEBUG
    if (GetAsyncKeyState(VK_CONTROL) < 0) {
        int bogus = 0;    // set breakpoint here to break when
                          // control key is down

    }
#endif
    ...
}
```

If you then set a breakpoint on the code that assigns *bogus*, the mouse move message handler will break only when you press the Control key.

Debugging the WM_LBUTTONDOWN and WM_LBUTTONUP messages can be a challenge as well because setting a breakpoint in the WM_LBUTTON DOWN handler will most likely result in the debugger eating the WM_LBUTTON UP message. One way around this problem is to keep the mouse button depressed while in the debugger and operate the debugger using the keyboard alone. Once the program has regained focus, you can release the mouse button.

How can I debug message problems?

Message problems are difficult to analyze with the debugger because the debugger gives you very little information. By placing breakpoints on the various message handlers, you can determine that a message has been received and its parameter values. With the debugger, you don't know where the message came from or if the message was sent with the *SendMessage* or *PostMessage* API functions because the message-passing mechanism prevents this information from showing up on the call stack. The debugger also makes it very difficult to visualize the overall picture of the messages being received as well as their order.

The best way to debug message problems is with the Visual C++ Spy++ utility. Spy++ has features for checking windows, messages, processes, and threads. To monitor and debug messages, start by choosing the **Messages** command in the **Spy** menu. This command displays the Message Options dialog box. From the **Windows** tab, you can select the window you want to spy on with the **Window Finder Tool**, as well as options to spy on related windows. You can then select the specific messages you want to view on the **Messages** tab, which is very important because Windows blasts hundreds of different messages through the typical window. You can also choose how you want the message information displayed with the **Output** tab. Note that you can choose to decode the message parameters and return values, thereby making it easy to interpret the results. You can also choose to redirect the output to a log file. This way you can run Spy++ minimized so that it doesn't interfere with the program you are debugging, thus avoiding any Heisenberg Uncertainty Principle problems.

Figure 8.3 shows the typical Spy++ message output. Assuming the default output options, the first column shows the Spy++ output line number and the second column indicates the handle of the window that received the message. The third column shows "S" for messages sent with *SendMessage*, "P" for messages posted with *PostMessage*, and "R" for the value returned by the message handler. The fourth column gives the decoded message name, and the remaining information is the decoded message parameters or return value.

You can use Spy++ to watch the messages sent to your program as well as the messages sent to other programs to check for differences in behavior. You should focus on message behavior and use the message order only as a guide. Generally, avoid making assumptions about message order in your code be-

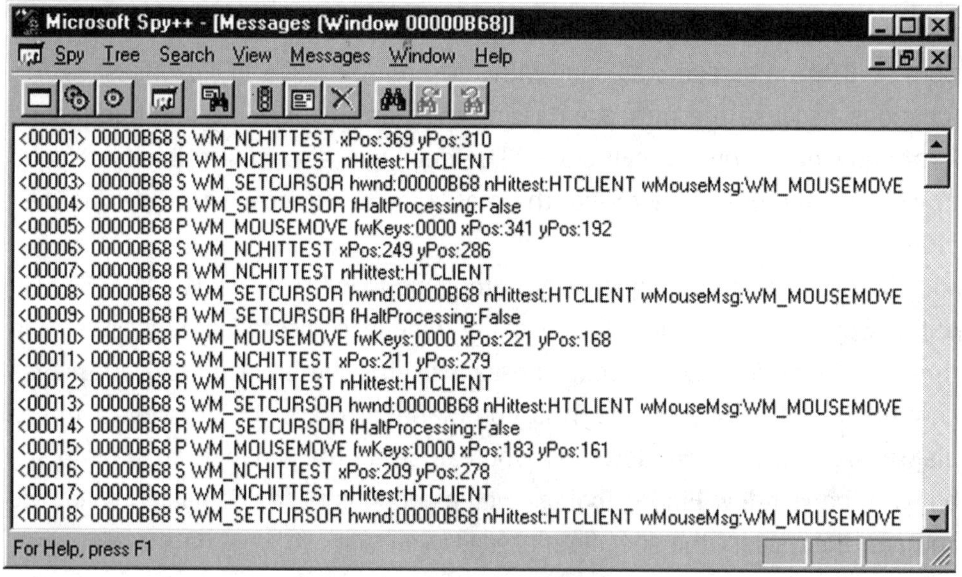

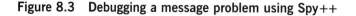

Figure 8.3 Debugging a message problem using Spy++

cause the message order may be different in different versions of Windows. Message order also may be affected by calling the *PeekMessage* API function in your program, which can remove messages from the message queue in a different order than their received order. However, you can take advantage of a specific message order if that order is defined in the Windows documentation. For example, Windows API documentation states that WM_NCDESTROY is the last message sent before a window is destroyed, and the design of MFC takes advantage of this fact.

TIP

Use Spy++ to debug message problems.

How can I debug tooltip code?

The problem with debugging tooltip code is that once you set up everything, Windows itself is responsible for displaying the tooltips. If the tooltips are displayed incorrectly or not displayed at all, you have no information to work with because all the relevant code is within Windows. The trick to debugging tooltips is to make sure you use a callback to obtain tooltip text by specifying LPSTR_TEXTCALLBACK for the text—even if the tooltip text is static and doesn't require a callback. This way, you can then set a breakpoint in the callback code to make sure that tooltips are being handled the way you expect them to be. For example, you can verify that the tooltip rectangles are in the right locations by moving the mouse to the expected locations and making sure the callback function is called with the right parameters.

This principle applies in general. Callbacks are easier to debug than the alternative because they allow you to hook into Windows to see what it is doing.

TIP

Use callbacks to help you debug Windows code: Callbacks allow you to hook into Windows to see what it is doing.

How can I debug an executable that crashes on load?

To debug this problem, it's important to understand that the program's startup code isn't necessarily the first code in the program to run. Consequently, if you place a breakpoint at the first line of the program's startup code (in *WinMain* for Windows API programs or in *CWinApp::InitInstance* for MFC programs), your program may crash before that code is ever reached.

To debug such crashes, it helps to know the steps in the Windows executable loading process, which go roughly as follows:

- Windows creates the default heap, the stack, and thread local storage for the primary thread.
- Windows loads the main executable and all its DLLs into virtual memory. The DLLs are rebased as needed.
- Windows resolves all imported symbols for functions and data.
- Windows calls the *DllMain* function for all DLLs that have it with the DLL_PROCESS_ATTACH notification.
- Windows calls the C Run-time Library *WinMainCRTStartup* startup code.
- The run-time library parses the command line and sets the environment variables.
- The run-time library initializes itself.
- The run-time library creates the global and static variables for the main executable and all the DLLs.
- The run-time library calls the program's *WinMain* function. For MFC programs, WinMain immediately calls *AfxWinMain,* which initializes MFC itself by calling *AfxWinInit* and then initializes the application by calling *CWinApp::InitInstance.*

Of these steps, constructing the global and static objects is the one vulnerable to crashing because there may be a bug in an object's constructor. The code in the *DllMain* functions is also vulnerable, especially since these functions are called before the program is completely loaded. You should be able to locate such problems from the debugger by checking the Call Stack window after the crash. Any problems resulting from finding the executable files and loading them into virtual memory are reported by Windows itself. See Matt Pietrek's "Under the Hood" for more detailed information on the Windows 2000 program loading process.

How can I debug an executable that crashes on exit?

The program shutdown process is the mirror image of the startup processes, so the program's shutdown code is not necessarily the last code in the program to run. Consequently, if you place a breakpoint at the last line of the program's shutdown code (in *WinMain* for Windows API programs or in *CWinApp::ExitInstance* for MFC programs), the program may crash after that code is executed. Of the shutdown steps, destructing global and static objects and calling *DllMain* with the DLL_PROCESS_DETACH notification are the most vulnerable to crashing. You should be able to locate such problems from the debugger by checking the Call Stack window after the crash.

How can I debug a function that crashes on return?

A function crashes on return if the function return address on the stack has been corrupted. Here are the leading causes for corrupting the return address.

- **Automatic variable overwrite** The return address will be corrupted if an automatic variable array is written beyond its bounds. Since a stack grows down in memory, overwriting an automatic variable clobbers the data last pushed on the stack, such as the function return address. This problem happens in both debug and release builds.
- **Function prototype mismatch** The stack will be corrupted if there is a mismatch in the function parameters or the calling convention between the called function and the caller, possibly resulting in a corrupted function return address. This problem does not happen in debug builds because the debug build uses the stack base pointer (the EBP register) to find the function return address, but it does happen in release builds that use FPO optimization.

Both of these stack corruption problems are discussed in detail in Chapter 9, Debugging Memory.

MFC Debugging Techniques

What bugs common to MFC programs should I be aware of?

The following are the most common MFC-specific bugs.

- **Using the wrong function prototypes for user-defined messages** Using the wrong function prototype to handle user-defined messages is by far the most common bug specific to MFC programs. This problem occurs in MFC because the ON_MESSAGE and related macros cast the input function and therefore the compiler doesn't warn you if there is a mismatch. In general, the simplest way to debug this type of problem is to compile your debug builds with the /GZ compiler option, but unfortunately the debug build of MFC currently does not use this option. Note that the correct function prototype is as follows:

```
afx_msg LRESULT OnMyMessage (WPARAM wParam, LPARAM lParam);
```

This problem is discussed in detail in Chapter 9.

- **Saving pointers to temporary MFC objects** MFC tries to maintain the illusion that Windows is a C++ object-oriented operating system by conveniently wrapping handles returned by Windows API functions in MFC objects. Each MFC thread contains two maps of objects: a list of permanent objects, in which objects exist until they are destroyed by the program, and a list of temporary objects, in which objects exist until they are destroyed by MFC when the program's message loop has idle time. Each of these maps allows MFC to translate from Windows handles to C++ object pointers.

For example, if you call *CWnd::GetParent* to get the parent of an MFC window object, chances are that parent window doesn't already exist as a permanent MFC object, so MFC has to create a temporary object. The *GetParent* function is implemented as follows.

```
_AFXWIN_INLINE CWnd* CWnd::GetParent() const {
    ASSERT(::IsWindow(m_hWnd));
    return CWnd::FromHandle(::GetParent(m_hWnd));
}
```

The *CWnd::FromHandle* function looks for the handle in the permanent list, then in the temporary list. If the handle isn't found in either list, MFC then creates a *CWnd* object, adds it to the temporary list, and returns a pointer to the object. This mechanism works quite well—unless you attempt to save the *CWnd* object. A temporary object becomes invalid possibly as soon as when the next message is processed, which leads to a bug that is very difficult to track down.

The bottom line is that you need to be very careful when saving pointers to MFC objects that you didn't explicitly create. Any object obtained from a function that calls *FromHandle* cannot be saved across messages, such as objects returned by the *CWnd* functions *GetDlgItem*, *GetFocus*, *GetWindow*, *GetActiveWindow*, *Find Window*, *GetOwner*, *GetFont*, *GetMenu*, and *GetDC*. To make an object returned by one of these functions into a permanent object, allocate the MFC object and attach the Windows handle for the object using the *Attach* function, as shown in this example.

```
CWnd * GetPermanentParent (CWnd *pWnd) {
    ASSERT_VALID(pWnd);
    HWND hParent = ::GetParent(pWnd->GetSafeHwnd());
    CWnd *pParent = new CWnd;
```

```
    pParent->Attach(hParent);
    return pParent;
}
```

 TIP

Any object obtained from a function that calls *FromHandle* cannot be saved across messages.

When passing objects using messages or between threads, be sure to pass the underlying Windows handle and not the MFC object. See the MSDN Technical Note TN003, Mapping of Window Handles to Objects, for more information.

• **Forgetting to put a message handler in the message map** MFC uses message maps instead of virtual functions to handle most Windows messages to prevent objects from having huge vtables. Beginning MFC programmers tend to use the MFC ClassWizard to set up the message handling code, but more experienced programmers often enter the code unaided. If you define a message handling function but forget to add an entry to the message map, however, the message handler will not be called and the compiler and linker won't complain. If you have defined message handling code that is mysteriously never executed, be sure to check the message maps.

• **Incorrectly creating or destroying *CFrameWnd-* and *CView-derived* objects** Both the *CFrameWnd* and *CView* objects are designed for auto-cleanup, which is revealed by their implementation of *PostNcDestroy.*

```
void CFrameWnd::PostNcDestroy()
{
    // default for frame windows is to allocate them on the heap
    // the default post-cleanup is to 'delete this'.
    // never explicitly call 'delete' on a CFrameWnd, use
    // DestroyWindow instead
    delete this;
}
```

These auto-cleanup objects delete themselves on receiving the WM_NCDE-STROY message, which is the last message a window receives. There are two implications to this design. The first is that these objects must be created on the heap because you never want to delete an object on the stack. The other is that these window objects must be destroyed by calling the *DestroyWindow* API function because explicitly calling `delete` results in an attempt to delete the object twice. See the MSDN Technical Note TN017, Destroying Window Objects, for more information.

I don't seem to be getting MFC trace statements. What should I do?

The output of the MFC TRACE macro can be turned on or off by changing the *TraceEnabled* setting in the *Diagnostics* section of the *Afx.ini* file. MFC tracing output is enabled by default. Instead of editing this file directly, the standard way to change this value is to run the Visual C++ Tracer utility and make sure that the **Enable tracing** option is turned on.

> **TIP**
>
> If you are not seeing TRACE macro output, most likely tracing has been disabled. Run the Tracer utility and verify that tracing is enabled.

Recommended Reading

DiLascia, Paul. "Meandering Through the Maze of MFC Message and Command Routing." *Microsoft Systems Journal*, July 1995.   Presents a detailed description of MFC message routing. Essential reading if you have to debug a message problem in an MFC program.

Pietrek, Matt. "Remove Fatty Deposits from Your Applications Using Our 32-bit Liposuction Tools." *Microsoft Systems Journal,* October 1996.   Explains how compiler optimization is often wrongly accused as a source of bugs, then compares optimizing for speed to optimizing by size.

Pietrek, Matt. "Under the Hood." *Microsoft Systems Journal*, September 1999.   Presents a detailed description of the Windows 2000 program loading process, including debugging techniques and the Global Flags utility (*GFlags.exe*, in \Support\Tools on the Windows 200 CD-ROM), which has a **Show Loader Snaps** setting that allows you to get much more detailed trace information during program loading.

Chapter 9

Debugging Memory

The ability to dynamically allocate memory easily and efficiently is one of the greatest strengths of the C++ programming language. When it comes to debugging, the ease of incorrectly using dynamically allocated memory is one of its greatest weaknesses. Windows programs also can have memory problems related to system resource leaks and the stack. Memory problems are a common source of bugs in Windows programs and without the right tools, they can be one of the hardest to track down.

There are two fundamental types of dynamically allocated memory bugs: memory corruption and memory leaking. *Memory corruption* occurs when a pointer or the memory it points to becomes invalid or when internal memory allocation data structures become corrupted. Pointers can be invalid by not being initialized, by being initialized to an invalid address, by being changed incorrectly or inadvertently, or by being used after the associated memory has been freed (referred to as a *dangling pointer*). Memory itself can be corrupted by writing through a corrupted or dangling pointer, by casting a pointer to an incompatible data structure, or by writing beyond its bounds. The memory allocation system can become corrupted by deleting an uninitialized pointer, deleting a nonheap pointer, deleting a pointer more than once, or overwriting a pointer's internal data structures. Memory corruption in C++ provides endless opportunities.

Memory leaks occur when memory that has been dynamically allocated is not freed. There are many ways to cause memory leaks, such as not freeing memory in all execution paths (particularly in functions with multiple `return` statements or when an exception is thrown), not freeing memory in constructors that fail, not freeing all memory in destructors, forgetting to make a base class destructor virtual, or just plain forgetting to free the memory.

The bad news is that memory problems can be extremely difficult to debug manually without aid. They can be difficult to detect because the symptoms are often subtle or even unnoticeable. For example, a memory leak may not have any symptoms at all—except for crashing the program after it has been running for a while. Once a memory problem is detected, the cause may be difficult to track down because a great distance in both code and time can come between the cause of a memory problem and its noticeable effect. It can be difficult to determine that memory corruption has occurred just by walking through the code with the debugger, although the debugger can help you find memory corruption at specific addresses using memory breakpoints, as described in Chapter 7, Debugging with the Visual C++ Debugger. It simply isn't practical to find memory leaks by manually keeping track of the allocations and deallocations. The only practical technique for finding these bugs is to instrument the dynamic memory allocation process so that a program can detect its own memory problems automatically.

The good news is that the Visual C++ C Run-time Library does an excellent job of instrumenting the dynamic memory allocation process and provides extensive support for detecting and analyzing dynamic memory errors. I refer to this instrumented heap as the *debug heap*. The Visual C++ compiler itself provides options to help detect uninitialized pointer variables and some types of stack corruption. You can also use C++ destructors and smart pointers to help prevent memory leaks by providing for automatic destruction when an object goes out of scope. By taking full advantage of these features, you can detect and eliminate most memory bugs with a minimum of pain and suffering.

Why Memory Leaks Aren't Acceptable

Memory corruption is obviously a serious problem, but the significance of memory leaks is far less obvious. After all, Windows reclaims leaked memory once a program terminates, so memory leaks are only a temporary problem. Why should you care about memory leaks as long as your program otherwise runs correctly?

Beyond the need to reclaim memory, memory leaks must be eliminated for three reasons. First, memory leaks often result in system resource leaks, which can have an immediate effect on system performance. Second, although leaked memory is reclaimed once a program terminates, quality software in general and server software in specific must be able to run indefinitely. Do not assume that it is acceptable for users to have to periodically restart your program. Third, memory leaks are often a symptom of other bugs or bad programming practices, so by tracking down memory leaks you often find other problems. Let's look at the first two reasons in more detail.

TIP

Memory leaks are often a symptom of other bugs or bad programming practices.

Resource Leaks

In Windows programs, dynamically allocated memory often represents more than just a chunk of storage. Often, this memory represents some type of system resource, such as a file, process, thread, semaphore, timer, window, device context, font, brush, pen, or database connection. These system resources are often scarce, making the consequences of such a memory leak far more significant than just a leak in memory. Leaking scarce system resources can quickly result in reduced system performance or even cause Windows to crash well before the available memory is exhausted. These memory leaks are referred to as *resource leaks* to emphasize this problem.

TIP

Leaking scarce system resources can quickly result in reduced system performance or even cause Windows to crash.

Graphics device interface (GDI) resource leaks in Windows 98 are an excellent example of this problem. Windows 98 uses a fixed, systemwide 64 KB heap to allocate brushes, pens, and other GDI data structures. If a program fails to delete a brush or a pen properly, this 64 KB heap can become exhausted quickly, bringing Windows 98 down and all running programs with it. Even if you have hundreds of megabytes of free physical memory, you will receive the dreaded Low Resources message box shown in Figure 9.1.

On receiving this message box, often the best thing to do is save your work, exit all running programs, and restart Windows. Definitely not cool. With GDI resources, you don't dynamically allocate these resources directly. Rather, Windows allocates them in the GDI heap on your program's behalf whenever you call API functions such as *CreatePen* or *CreateSolidBrush*. Windows 2000 doesn't use a systemwide 64 KB heap, but a GDI leak still impairs performance—only not nearly as quickly.

Quality Software Should Run Indefinitely

There was a time when resource leaks were acceptable in Windows programs. For example, a simple utility that users typically ran for a few minutes and then quit could have a small resource leak without any noticeable effect. Windows itself wasn't very stable and had to be restarted at least daily, so some Windows programs never had the opportunity for small resource leaks to become a serious problem. Furthermore, computers didn't have much memory, so users had to economize their memory usage by constantly quitting programs that weren't being used at the moment. This periodic program restarting gave Windows ample opportunity to reclaim any leaked resources.

Times have changed. Windows is now quite stable, so users are able to keep Windows programs and Windows itself running for extended periods. Computers now have much more memory, so users can now run dozens of programs simultaneously without problems. As a result, users' expectations have changed: They now expect Windows programs to be able to run indefi-

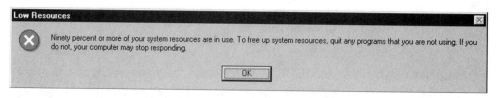

Figure 9.1 The Windows 98 Low Resources message box

DEBUGGING TECHNIQUES

nitely. Constantly having to restart Windows or Windows programs is no longer acceptable.

> Users expect programs to be able to run indefinitely. Constantly having to re-start programs is no longer acceptable.

Of course, there are many ways to make a program crash, and leaking resources is just one of them. The longer a program is able to run before crashing, the more likely the cause of any crash is related to a resource leak. The reason is that resource leak bugs are time dependent (since it takes a while for the resources to become exhausted), whereas other types of bugs are generally not time dependent. For example, although a logic error in rarely executed code can make a program crash occasionally, such a crash is just as likely to happen immediately after the program starts as it is to happen after the program has been running for several days. By contrast, a program that slowly leaks resources could take weeks to grind to a halt. A crash that happens only after a program has been running for an extended period is likely the result of a resource leak. Making your programs leak-free is essential to their long-term stability.

> A crash that happens only after a program has been running for an extended period is likely the result of a resource leak.

Types of Memory Debugging

Windows provides the fundamental dynamic memory allocation functions through its *VirtualAlloc/VirtualFree*, *HeapAlloc/HeapFree*, and *GlobalAlloc/GlobalFree* API functions. The Visual C++ C Run-time Library then implements the `new/delete` and `malloc/free` functions on top of the *HeapAlloc* and *HeapFree* memory management functions. The MFC and ATL application frameworks then add their own pieces to the memory management puzzle. For most new Windows programs, the C Run-time Library has everything you need for memory management and debugging; but for completeness I will review memory debugging in all these environments.

Windows Memory Debugging

The fundamental method of dynamic memory allocation in Windows is the *VirtualAlloc* and *VirtualFree* API functions. Windows provides all processes with a 4 GB virtual address space (and, of course, all Windows programs are processes). That may seem like a lot of address space, but remember that this is virtual memory, so it is nothing but a range of addresses. You can't do anything useful with virtual memory until physical memory has been committed to a page of virtual memory. (Note that x86 CPUs use a 4 KB page size.) All memory used by a program (specifically, the main executable, DLLs, stack, heap, memory mapped files, and operating system) is mapped to virtual memory, but it is unlikely that a Windows program would need to deal with the virtual memory API functions directly unless it has to manage a large amount of data (such as a 3-D graphics program) or it performs system functions (such as Windows itself).

Rather than dealing with virtual memory directly, most C++ programs use the `new` and `delete` functions provided by the C Run-time Library. The `new` and `delete` functions work by allocating a chunk of virtual memory (Windows allocates 1 MB by default, but you can change this value using the /HEAP linker option) and subdividing (called *suballocating*) that memory into pieces as required by the program. This suballocation is implemented by the C Run-time Library's use of the *HeapAlloc* and *HeapFree* API functions. When a process loads, Windows creates a heap in the process's virtual address space by default, which is known as the *default* heap. For most programs, one heap is enough; but you can sometimes optimize memory management performance by creating additional heaps. Each instance of the C Run-time Library in a process has its own heap. One situation in which your program may have multiple heaps (perhaps without you knowing it) is when the program uses a DLL that has its own instance of the run-time library. The heap managed by a specific instance of the C Run-time Library is known as the *local* heap. Consequently, the behavior of all C Run-time Library memory debugging functions is defined in terms of the local heap.

The *GlobalAlloc* and *GlobalFree* functions are holdovers from 16-bit Windows. They are basically backward-compatible wrappers for the *HeapAlloc* and *HeapFree* functions because they do little more than suballocate memory from the default heap. The only reason to use these functions in new programs is to transfer data to Windows, as when copying data to the clipboard. You should use these memory functions only if the Windows API documentation specifically recommends them.

The memory debugging support provided by Windows is very primitive. Windows provides the *IsBadCodePtr*, *IsBadReadPtr*, *IsBadStringPtr*, and *IsBad WritePtr* API functions to help you determine if various types of pointers are valid. A *HeapWalk* API function allows you to examine the contents of a heap if you really get desperate. Beyond these functions, you are pretty much on your own when it comes to debugging memory obtained directly from Windows.

Windows Protected Memory

While Windows doesn't have many API functions to help you debug memory, Windows and the CPU together provide protected memory, which is enormously helpful in tracking down bad pointers and corrupted memory. It is worth taking a quick look at what protected memory can and cannot do to help debug memory problems.

First, the good news. Since 32-bit Windows provides a 4 GB address space, the chance of a random address pointing to valid memory is quite small for a typical program. Because Windows 2000 protects the first 64 KB of address space and Windows 98 protects the first 4 KB, attempting to access memory with a null pointer or even a small offset from a null pointer results in an access violation exception. In Windows 2000, all operating system address space (the upper 2 GB of address space) is completely protected as well. For all versions of Windows, memory that belongs to other processes is completely inaccessible. Windows also protects the stack against both overflow and underflow using guard pages, so a stack written beyond its bounds results in an access violation exception (and it won't smack into the heap, as it did in 16-bit Windows). Additionally, memory pages that are fully accessible to a process can have a read-only attribute, thereby protecting memory contents such as program code and read-only data.

Now the bad news. Since memory is allocated in 4 KB pages, protected memory provides no protection at all within a writable page. A common memory corruption problem is writing memory beyond its bounds within the heap.

Since heap memory is suballocated from memory that is fully accessible by the process, Windows provides no protection against memory corruption that occurs entirely within the heap. Fortunately, the Visual C++ C Run-time Library does an excellent job of detecting heap corruption, as you shall soon see.

Visual C++ C Run-time Library Memory Debugging

The Visual C++ C Run-time Library provides extensive functionality to help you detect both memory corruption and memory leaks for dynamically allocated memory. This functionality is provided only in debug builds, so it has no effect in release builds and consequently no impact on performance. Most of this debugging support was originally part of MFC, but it moved to the C Run-time Library starting with Visual C++ 4.0 so that all programs built using Visual C++ could take advantage of these features.

Of course, dynamic memory is allocated in C++ using `new` and freed using `delete`. By default, `new` returns a null pointer on failure; but you can have `new` throw an exception instead by installing a handler using `_set_new_handler`. Unless you are maintaining existing code that assumes `new` returns null, you should always have `new` throw an exception on failure because this makes it easier to write robust code. After all, it is easy to overlook null pointers, but exceptions are impossible to ignore. (See Chapter 5 for example code.)

> **TIP**
>
> Unless you are maintaining existing code that assumes `new` returns null, always have `new` throw an exception on failure.

The Visual C++ C Run-time Library helps you debug memory corruption in a number of ways. One major help is that it writes fixed byte patterns into allocated and freed memory to help reveal bugs. Table 9.1 lists the patterns it uses.

Table 9.1   Visual C++ C Run-time Library patterns

Byte Pattern	Meaning
0xCD	Allocated data (mnemonic: "alloCated Data")
0xDD	Freed data (mnemonic: "Deleted Data")
0xFD	Guard data (mnemonic: "Fence Data")

The 0xCD pattern is used to fill in memory that has been newly allocated, whereas 0xDD is used to fill memory that has been freed. The guard bytes are written in the four bytes just before and after the memory buffer to help detect overflow and underflow. For example, after the following code executes

```
float *pData = new float;
int fence1 = *(((int *)pData) - 1);
int fence2 = *(int *)(((char *)pData) + sizeof(float));
```

pData is set to an address in the heap, **pData* is set to 0xCDCDCDCD, and *fence1* and *fence2* are set to 0xFDFDFDFD. When the following code executes

```
delete pData;
```

*pData is then set to 0xDDDDDDDD. If you did not select the _CRTDBG _DELAY_FREE_MEM_DF debug heap option (described later in this chapter) and you were to recalculate *fence1* and *fence2*, you would find that they were also set to 0xDDDDDDDD because the freed data byte pattern is applied to the internal data structures as well.

As documented in the run-time library source code (in *Crt\Src\Dbgheap.c*), these pattern values were carefully chosen to reveal as many bugs as possible. Specifically, the patterns were chosen to be nonzero (to contrast with initialized data), constant (to make bugs reproducible), odd (since dereferencing an odd address traps on the Macintosh—why not?), large (to be outside a process's usable address space, resulting in access violation exceptions), and atypical (since the patterns are not often found in real data). By contrast, initializing to zero would hide bugs and initializing to a random value would produce random bugs.

These byte patterns are also easily recognizable, which may be their most important attribute. If you see that a program is trying to dereference a pointer address of 0xCDCDCDCD or 0xDDDDDDDD (or similar pattern, like 0xCDCDCDF0, which would result from taking an offset from a bad pointer), then you definitely have a bug. I also like the fact that the names have reasonably good mnemonics, although Microsoft's mnemonic for 0xCD is "clear" and for 0xDD is "dead," which don't work as well for me. They could have chosen patterns that are even more obvious. For example, Brian Kernighan and Rob Pike, in *The Practice of Programming* (Addison-Wesley, 1999), recommend using the pattern 0xDEADBEEF.

Table 9.2   Visual C++ C Run-time Library memory block type identifiers

Block Type	Meaning
_NORMAL_BLOCK	Memory allocated directly by a program
_CLIENT_BLOCK	Memory allocated directly by a program that is to be given special handling by the memory debugging functions (You can also create subtypes of client blocks for greater control.)
_CRT_BLOCK	Memory allocated internally by the run-time library
_FREE_BLOCK	Memory that has been freed but is still being kept track of, which happens if you select the _CRTDBG_DELAY_FREE _MEM_DF debug heap option
_IGNORE_BLOCK	Memory that was allocated while the memory debugging operations were turned off using the _CrtSetDbgFlag function (These memory blocks are not checked by the memory debugging functions and are assumed not to have problems.)

Another aid to debugging memory corruption is that the run-time library divides memory into five types of blocks using the memory block type identifiers shown in Table 9.2, which determine how the memory is tracked and reported. The byte patterns are helpful, but they aren't regularly checked; so you need ways to detect memory corruption at any point. The Visual C++ C Run-time Library provides several useful functions to help debug memory corruption, as shown in Table 9.3.

Again, note that all these functions are defined only in debug builds, so don't expect a function like _CrtIsValidPointer to work in release builds. For release builds, use the IsBadReadPtr and IsBadWritePtr API functions instead. Similarly, instead of _CrtCheckMemory, use _heapchk for release builds. Table 9.4 on page 362 lists several useful run-time library functions to help debug memory leaks. Finally, the run-time library provides several useful functions for general memory debugging (see Table 9.5 on page 363). Most of these memory debugging functions are discussed in more detail later in the chapter.

Table 9.3 Visual C++ C Run-time Library functions to help debug memory corruption

Function	Usage
_CrtCheckMemory	Checks the heap for integrity by checking the internal data structures and the guard bytes for each memory block. Useful for debugging memory corruption, but can slow a program significantly if called often.
_CrtIsValidHeapPointer	Verifies that the given pointer is within the local heap.
_CrtIsValidPointer	Verifies that the given memory range is valid for reading or writing.
_CrtIsMemoryBlock	Verifies that the given memory range is within the local heap and has a valid memory block type identifier, such as _NORMAL_BLOCK. (It can also be used to obtain the allocation number and source code file name and line number where the memory was allocated.)

MFC Memory Debugging

As I mentioned earlier, the memory debugging support in the Visual C++ C Run-time Library was originally part of MFC. The original MFC memory debugging support was preserved, but it is now mostly a thin wrapper around the run-time library functions.

One difference in memory handling with MFC is that new is set to throw an exception on failure by default. In MFC you must change the behavior of allocation failures using the *AfxSetNewHandler* function instead of with the _set_new_handler function. The default exception hander is *AfxNew Handler*, which throws exceptions of the type *CMemoryException.* If absolutely necessary (and hopefully it never is), you can have new return a null pointer on failure by calling AfxSetNewHandler(0). Also, in MFC you can throw a memory exception directly by calling the *AfxThrowMemoryException* function. You might want to see the source code in *Afxmem.cpp* for more details.

Another difference in memory handling is that MFC overloads *CObject:: operator new* and *CObject::operator delete* to give all *CObject*-derived objects a _CLIENT_BLOCK memory block type identifier. Primarily, this allows

Table 9.4 Visual C++ C Run-time Library functions to help debug memory leaks

Function	Usage
_CrtSetBreakAlloc	Sets a breakpoint on the given allocation number, where each block of allocated memory is assigned a sequential allocation number. Useful for finding a specific memory leak.
_CrtDumpMemoryLeaks	Determines if a memory leak has occurred. If so, it dumps all the currently allocated memory in the local heap in a user-readable form. Useful for detecting memory leaks at program termination.
_CrtMemCheckpoint	Creates a snapshot of the current state of the local heap in a _CrtMemState structure.
_CrtMemDifference	Compares two heap checkpoints and saves their differences in a _CrtMemState structure. Returns TRUE if the two checkpoints are different. Useful for detecting memory leaks for a specific region of code.
_CrtMemDumpAllObjectsSince	Dumps information about all memory allocated since the given heap checkpoint or the beginning of the program in a user-readable form.
_CrtMemDumpStatistics	Dumps the information in a _CrtMemState structure in a user-readable form. The structure may contain a heap checkpoint or a difference in checkpoints. For a heap checkpoint, it is useful for getting an over-all view of how the dynamic memory is being used. For a difference in checkpoints, it is useful for detecting memory leaks.

MFC to call _CrtSetDumpClient to install the _AfxCrtDumpClient function (in *Dumpinit.cpp*) so that valid *CObject*-derived objects are dumped using their *CObject::Dump* virtual function. By implementing the dump virtual functions for your *CObject*-derived classes, you can obtain more useful memory diagnostics. (Tips for implementing this function are presented in Chapter 4, Using Trace Statements.)

Table 9.5 Visual C++ C Run-time Library functions for general memory debugging

Function	Usage
_CrtSetDbgFlag	Controls the behavior of the memory debugging functions
_CrtSetAllocHook	Installs a function that hooks in the memory allocation process. Useful for monitoring memory usage or simulating insufficient memory conditions
_CrtSetReportHook	Installs a function that performs custom report handling. Useful for filtering report data or sending it to different destinations, such as sending data corruption reports to a message box
_CrtSetDumpClient	Installs a function to dump client blocks. Useful for displaying data in a more readable format
_CrtDoForAllClientObjects	Calls the given function for all the data allocated as client blocks

TIP

Implement the dump virtual function for *CObject*-derived classes to obtain more useful memory diagnostics.

However, the *_AfxCrtDumpClient* function does not call the *CObject::Dump* virtual functions by default; rather, it dumps an object's class name, pointer value, and size. I assume this default is used because some objects, such as arrays, lists, and maps, can have rather large dumps. To use the dump virtual functions, you must add the following code to your program, preferably at initialization.

```
#ifdef _DEBUG
    afxDump.SetDepth(1);    // dump CObjects using a deep dump
#endif
```

TIP

To use the dump virtual function for *CObject*-derived classes in memory diagnostics, you must call `afxDump.SetDepth(1)`.

Many dump functions also use the depth value to determine if they should do a shallow dump or a deep dump. For example, the *CObList* class implements its dump function as follows:

```
void CObList::Dump(CDumpContext& dc) const {
    CObject::Dump(dc);
    dc << "with " << m_nCount << " elements";
    if (dc.GetDepth() > 0) {
        POSITION pos = GetHeadPosition();
        while (pos != NULL)
            dc << "\n\t" << GetNext(pos);
    }
    dc << "\n";
}
```

Why Microsoft chose to make this an all-or-nothing deal escapes me. It seems like you should be able to choose a shallow dump that also uses the dump virtual functions.

Finally, the *_AfxCrtDumpClient* function dumps everything to *afxDump*, MFC's predefined global *CDumpContext*. This means that the MFC debug heap output is controlled by the Visual C++ Tracer utility. If you are not getting the memory dump information you expect, run Tracer and make sure that the **Enable tracing** option is enabled.

▶ TIP

If you are not getting MFC memory dump output, most likely tracing has been disabled. Run the Tracer utility and verify that tracing is enabled.

Because the MFC memory support is mostly a thin wrapper around the C Run-time Library functions, there is no reason to repeat the same function descriptions I presented earlier. Instead, Table 9.6 shows a handy MFC/C Run-time Library memory debugging function translation dictionary.

So, which set of memory debugging functions should you use in MFC programs? If you are maintaining an existing MFC program that already uses the MFC functions, continue to use those functions. If you are developing a new program, however, I recommend using the C Run-time Library functions. Although using the MFC functions may be slightly more convenient, your code will

Table 9.6   MFC/C Run-time Library memory debugging function translation dictionary

MFC Function	C Run-time Library Function
AfxCheckMemory	_CrtCheckMemory
AfxDoForAllObjects	_CrtDoForAllClientObjects
AfxDumpMemoryLeaks	_CrtDumpMemoryLeaks
AfxIsMemoryBlock	_CrtIsMemoryBlock
CMemoryState::Checkpoint	_CrtMemCheckpoint
CMemoryState::Difference	_CrtMemDifference
CMemoryState::DumpAllObjectsSince	_CrtMemDumpAllObjectsSince
CMemoryState::DumpStatistics	_CrtMemDumpStatistics
AfxSetAllocStop	_CrtSetBreakAlloc
AfxEnableMemoryTracking	_CrtSetDbgFlag
afxMemDF	_CrtSetDbgFlag
AfxSetNewHandler	_set_new_handler

be more portable (at least to non-MFC programs) if you use the C Run-time Library functions. The library functions also give you a bit more control.

TIP

Prefer the C Run-time Library memory debugging functions to the MFC version.

ATL Memory Debugging

ATL's contribution to memory debugging is that it maintains a list of all the COM interface pointers created using *QueryInterface* and can monitor their lifetime by tracing the *AddRef* and *Release* calls. Any interface that hasn't been released when a COM server shuts down is a resource leak. You can trace for interface leaks by defining the _ATL_DEBUG_INTERFACES preprocessor constant at the top of *StdAfx.h* (before `#include <atlcom.h>`). This setting traces all the *AddRef* and *Release* calls by displaying the current reference count, the class name, and the name of the interface being referenced.

Here's how to debug COM interface leaks. At program termination, check the trace statement output for text labeled with "INTERFACE LEAK:", such as

```
INTERFACE LEAK: RefCount = 7, MaxRefCount = 10, {Allocation = 42}
    CMyComClass - ILeak
```

Then use the allocation number to help you find the leak by setting the *m_nIndexBreakAt* member of the *CComModule* object when the server is initialized. For example

```
#define _ATL_DEBUG_INTERFACES   // define in StdAfx.h
BOOL WINAPI DllMain (HINSTANCE hInstance, DWORD dwReason, LPVOID) {
    if (dwReason == DLL_PROCESS_ATTACH) {
        . . .
        _Module.m_nIndexBreakAt = 42; // set breakpoint to find
                                      // interface leak
    }
    return TRUE;
}
```

The debugger then breaks when that allocation number occurs the next time you run the program. Of course, this technique requires the allocation number to remain constant between instances of the program, which does not always happen.

Using the Debug Heap

So far, so good, but how do you use the debug heap in your program? To use the debug heap, you must make sure that you are using the debug build, which links with the debug version of the C Run-time Library and defines the _DEBUG symbol to use the instrumented versions of `new` and `delete`. With these settings, your program is now capable of detecting memory corruption and memory leaks. Unfortunately, you're not quite done yet: You must take some extra steps to select the exact instrumentation options you want, display memory leaks at program termination, have the source code file names and line numbers reported correctly, and display the data in a readable format.

Debug Heap Options

Before I explain how to make your program display memory leaks, I must present the available debug heap options. You control how the debug heap performs its checking using the *_CrtSetDbgFlag* function. Here are the options, which can be ORed together.

- **_CRTDBG_ALLOC_MEM_DF** turns on the heap allocation checking. When turned off, memory allocation is handled largely the same way, but the _IGNORE_BLOCK memory block type is used. This option is best used to turn off heap checking altogether or to ignore specific memory allocations that you know are correct and want to have ignored. (It is on by default.)

- **_CRTDBG_DELAY_FREE_MEM_DF** prevents memory from actually being freed. It is best used to check for bugs that access freed memory or to simulate low-memory conditions. Note that freed memory is always filled with the 0xDD byte pattern even without this option; but without it freed memory may be immediately reused, thus making freed pointer access much harder to detect. Also, *_CrtCheck Memory* doesn't check freed memory without this option. (It is off by default.)

- **_CRTDBG_CHECK_ALWAYS_DF** causes *_CrtCheckMemory* to be called at every allocation and deallocation. It is good for finding memory corruption, but it can slow a program down significantly if a lot of memory has been allocated. (It is off by default.)

- **_CRTDBG_CHECK_CRT_DF** causes blocks marked with the _CRT_BLOCK memory block type to be included in the leak detection and state difference functions. This option isn't normally used because it identifies some run-time library memory as being leaked because it is allocated until the end of the program. It is best used when you suspect a leak in memory allocated by the run-time library, which is unlikely in normal circumstances. (It is off by default.)

- **_CRTDBG_LEAK_CHECK_DF** causes *_CrtDumpMemoryLeaks* to be called at program termination. (It is off by default.)

I recommend always using the _CRTDBG_ALLOC_MEM_DF and _CRTDBG _LEAK_CHECK_DF debug heap options but using the _CRTDBG_CHECK _ALWAYS_DF and _CRTDBG_DELAY_FREE_MEM_DF options only when needed to help debug memory corruption. Most likely you will use _CRTDBG _CHECK_CRT_DF only when you think you have memory leaks but *_CrtDump MemoryLeaks* doesn't report any.

Displaying Memory Leaks

By using the debug build, your program is capable of dumping memory leaks; but this doesn't happen by default. You can dump the memory leaks by explicitly calling *_CrtDumpMemoryLeaks* at program termination; but the problem with this approach is that your program may terminate in several different ways, thus requiring you to make this call in several different places. Consequently, the easiest approach is to use the _CRTDBG_LEAK_CHECK_DF debug heap option. For example, if you add the following code to your program

```
#include <crtdbg.h>      // include to call _Crt functions
int APIENTRY WinMain (HINSTANCE hInstance, HINSTANCE
    hPrevInstance, LPSTR lpCmdLine, int nCmdShow) {
  _CrtSetDbgFlag(_CRTDBG_ALLOC_MEM_DF | _CRTDBG_LEAK_CHECK_DF);
  ...
}
```

then memory leaks will be reported as shown here

```
Detected memory leaks!
Dumping objects ->
{21} normal block at 0x00780DA0, 8 bytes long.
 Data: <J  M ! @> 4A D8 12 4D FB 21 09 40
{20} normal block at 0x00780E50, 4 bytes long.
 Data: <*   > 2A 00 00 00
{19} normal block at 0x00780E80, 16 bytes long.
 Data: <A memory leak!! > 41 20 6D 65 6D 6F 72 79 20 6C 65 61 6B
                          21 21 00
{18} normal block at 0x00780EC0, 1 bytes long.
 Data: <E> 45
Object dump complete.
```

If you are unsure if leaks are being reported, a simple test is to leak some memory intentionally (for example, by adding `int *pLeak = new int;` to your code without a corresponded `delete`) and see if the leak is reported at program termination.

That's a good start, but these memory leaks would be much easier to debug if they displayed the source code file names and line numbers. You can get the source code information displayed by adding the following lines at the top of *StdAfx.h*.

```
#define _CRTDBG_MAP_ALLOC  // define to get line numbers
#include <stdlib.h>        // define the memory allocation
                          // functions
```

```
#include <crtdbg.h>          // redefine the memory allocation
                             // functions
#define DEBUG_NEW new(_NORMAL_BLOCK, THIS_FILE, __LINE__)
```

Be sure to place this code before the inclusion of any other header files. If you don't get source code information, you positioned it too late. The _CRTDBG _MAP_ALLOC symbol causes the memory allocation functions to be redefined in *Crtdbg.h*, as shown here.

```
#ifdef  _CRTDBG_MAP_ALLOC
inline void* __cdecl operator new(unsigned int s)
        { return ::operator new(s, _NORMAL_BLOCK, __FILE__,
            __LINE__); }
#define   malloc(s)            _malloc_dbg(s, _NORMAL_BLOCK,
              __FILE__, __LINE__)
#define   free(p)              _free_dbg(p, _NORMAL_BLOCK)
...
#endif
```

Memory leaks will now be reported like this:

```
Detected memory leaks!
c:\program files\microsoft visual
    studio\vc98\include\crtdbg.h(552) : {21} normal block at
    0x00780DA0, 8 bytes long.
 Data: <J  M ! @> 4A D8 12 4D FB 21 09 40
c:\program files\microsoft visual
    studio\vc98\include\crtdbg.h(552) : {20} normal block at
    0x00780E50, 4 bytes long.
 Data: <*   > 2A 00 00 00
C:\Projects\WorldsBuggiestProgram\WorldsBuggiestProgram.cpp(78) :
    {19} normal block at 0x00780E80, 16 bytes long.
 Data: <A memory leak!! > 41 20 6D 65 6D 6F 72 79 20 6C 65 61 6B
    21 21 00
C:\Projects\WorldsBuggiestProgram\WorldsBuggiestProgram.cpp(77) :
    {18} normal block at 0x00780EC0, 1 bytes long.
 Data: <E> 45
Object dump complete.
```

Unfortunately, you're not quite done yet. If you look closely at this source code information, you will see that many of the leaks are coming from the redefined `operator new` in *Crtdbg.h*, which clearly isn't useful. The correct source code information is given for `malloc`, however. To get the right source code information for `new`, you must define the following code at the top of each .cpp file.

```
#ifdef _DEBUG
#define new DEBUG_NEW
#undef THIS_FILE
static char THIS_FILE[] = __FILE__;
#endif
```

Now memory leaks are reported with the correct source code information.

```
Detected memory leaks!
C:\Projects\WorldsBuggiestProgram\WorldsBuggiestProgram.cpp(80) :
    {21} normal block at 0x00780DA0, 8 bytes long.
 Data: <J  M ! @> 4A D8 12 4D FB 21 09 40
C:\Projects\WorldsBuggiestProgram\WorldsBuggiestProgram.cpp(79) :
    {20} normal block at 0x00780E50, 4 bytes long.
 Data: <*   > 2A 00 00 00
C:\Projects\WorldsBuggiestProgram\WorldsBuggiestProgram.cpp(78) :
    {19} normal block at 0x00780E80, 16 bytes long.
 Data: <A memory leak!! > 41 20 6D 65 6D 6F 72 79 20 6C 65 61 6B
    21 21 00
C:\Projects\WorldsBuggiestProgram\WorldsBuggiestProgram.cpp(77) :
    {18} normal block at 0x00780EC0, 1 bytes long.
 Data: <E> 45
Object dump complete.
```

For MFC programs, displaying memory leaks is much simpler because everything is already set up. All you have to do is define the previous code at the top of each .cpp file, which is added automatically by the Visual C++ AppWizard. If the memory leaks don't have source code information, you forgot to add this code to the source file with the leak.

Displaying Meaningful Source Code File Names and Line Numbers
In some situations, having the source code file name and line number for an allocation isn't very useful. For example, suppose you have an employee database and all the employee records are allocated using the following function.

```
CEmployee * CreateEmployeeRecord (const CString &name,
                const CString &department) {
   return new CEmployee(name, department);
}
```

Suppose further that the program creates thousands of employee records by calling *CreateEmployeeRecord* from several different locations in the code. In this case, if there is a memory leak involving employee records, knowing that the leak occurred in this function tells you nothing. What you really want is the source code information for the function that called *CreateEmployeeRecord*.

You can get the calling function's source code information using the following technique. In the header file that declares *CreateEmployeeRecord*, create the following macro.

```
#ifdef _DEBUG
#define CreateEmployeeRecord(name, dept) \
        CreateEmployeeRecord(name, dept, \
        __FILE__, __LINE__)
#endif
```

Now change the *CreateEmployeeRecord* function to pass the file name and line number of the calling function to `new` for the debug build.

```
CEmployee * CreateEmployeeRecord (const CString &name,
            const CString &department
#ifdef _DEBUG
            , const char *file, int line
#endif
            ) {
#ifdef _DEBUG
    #undef new              // temporarily remove the new macro
    return new(file, line) CEmployee(name, department);
    #define new DEBUG_NEW  // restore the new macro
#else
    return new CEmployee(name, department);
#endif
}
```

Although this code is a little ungainly, it helps reveal the cause of the memory leak with a minimum of fooling around.

TIP

When the source code file name and line number tell you nothing about the cause of a leak, consider reporting the file name and line number of the calling function instead.

By the way, you can pass parameters to `new` as you can with any other function, just as long as there is a matching overload of `operator new` defined. Unlike other functions, however, the first parameter is always the size of the allocation in bytes, which is passed implicitly by the compiler.

Displaying Data in a Readable Format

Sometimes you need to know the contents of the memory block being corrupted or leaked to help you find the bug, but the standard memory output isn't very helpful. For example, if a *CEmployee* object had a leak, the standard output might look as shown in the following code.

```
Detected memory leaks!
Dumping objects ->
C:\Projects\WorldsBuggiestProgram\WorldsBuggiestProgram.cpp(1075)
   : {29} normal block at 0x00760BD0, 8 bytes long.
 Data: <  v   v > 8C 04 76 00 DC 04 76 00
strcore.cpp(118) : {28} normal block at 0x00760480, 28 bytes long.
 Data: <          Fred> 01 00 00 00 0F 00 00 00 0F 00 00 00 46
   72 65 64
strcore.cpp(118) : {27} normal block at 0x007604D0, 23 bytes long.
 Data: <          Acco> 01 00 00 00 0A 00 00 00 0A 00 00 00 41
   63 63 6F
Object dump complete.
```

In this case, only the last four characters are intelligible, so the memory contents dump isn't very helpful. To obtain more useful information, you need to make these objects client blocks and install a client dump function using *_CrtSetDumpClient*. One way to make *CEmployee* objects use a client block is simply to pass _CLIENT_BLOCK to `new`, as shown here.

```
CEmployee * CreateEmployeeRecord (const CString &name,
            const CString &department
#ifdef _DEBUG
            , const char *file, int line
#endif
            ) {
#ifdef _DEBUG
   #undef new                // temporarily remove the new macro
   return new(_CLIENT_BLOCK, file, line)
      CEmployee(name, department);
   #define new DEBUG_NEW  // restore the new macro
```

```
#else
    return new CEmployee(name, department);
#endif
}
```

If for some reason you are using `malloc` instead of `new`, you could obtain the same result with the following code.

```
#ifdef _DEBUG
    return _malloc_dbg(bufferSize, _CLIENT_BLOCK, file, line);
#else
    return malloc(bufferSize);
#endif
```

This technique works well in general, but for class objects the best approach is to overload `operator new` and `operator delete` for that class to ensure that all heap objects are created consistently.

```
class CEmployee
{
public:
#ifdef _DEBUG
    void * operator new(size_t size, LPCSTR filename, int line);
    void   operator delete(void *p, LPCSTR filename, int line);
#endif

    ...
};

#ifdef _DEBUG
void * CEmployee::operator new (size_t size, LPCSTR filename,
        int line) {
    return ::operator new(size, _CLIENT_BLOCK, filename, line);
}

void CEmployee::operator delete (void *pObject, LPCSTR filename,
        int line) {
    _free_dbg(pObject, _CLIENT_BLOCK);
}
#endif
```

For a final touch, you might want to use a memory block subtype to differentiate easily between different types of client blocks. This technique is especially useful in MFC because MFC already uses client blocks. You can use a subtype as shown in the following code.

```
#define SET_BLOCK_TYPE(subtype)    (_CLIENT_BLOCK | (subtype << 16))
#define EMPLOYEE_SUBTYPE   1

#ifdef _DEBUG
void * CEmployee::operator new (size_t size, LPCSTR filename,
      int line) {
   return ::operator new(size, SET_BLOCK_TYPE(EMPLOYEE_SUBTYPE),
      filename, line);
}

void CEmployee::operator delete (void *pObject, LPCSTR filename,
      int line) {
   _free_dbg(pObject, SET_BLOCK_TYPE(EMPLOYEE_SUBTYPE));
}
#endif
```

To display the data any way you want, you can create a dump function that handles the employee subtype specially and register it using _CrtSet DumpClient.

```
#define GET_BLOCK_SUBTYPE(typeID) ((typeID >> 16) & 0xFFFF)
#define EMPLOYEE_SUBTYPE       1
#ifdef _DEBUG
void __cdecl DumpClientData (void *pData, size_t bytes) {
   _CrtMemBlockHeader *pHead = pHdr(pData);
   if (GET_BLOCK_SUBTYPE(pHead->nBlockUse) == EMPLOYEE_SUBTYPE) {
      CEmployee *pEmployee = static_cast<CEmployee *>(pData);
      _RPT2(_CRT_WARN, " Employee Name: %s  Department: %s\n",
         pEmployee->GetName(), pEmployee->GetDepartment());
   }
   else
      _printMemBlockData(pHead); // do standard dump, from
                                 // Dbgheap.c
}
#endif

int APIENTRY WinMain (HINSTANCE hInstance, HINSTANCE
      hPrevInstance, LPSTR lpCmdLine, int nCmdShow) {
   _CrtSetDumpClient(DumpClientData);
   ...
}
```

Note that *_CrtMemBlockHeader* and *pHdr* are discussed in the next section, and the *_printMemBlockData* function is documented in *Dbgheap.c*.

TIP

Use memory block subtypes to differentiate easily between different types of client blocks.

At last, the *CEmployee* data memory leaks are presented with useful source code file names and line numbers and in a user-readable format. Sure, this is a bit of work, but it makes finding memory bugs a snap.

```
Detected memory leaks!
Dumping objects ->
C:\Projects\WorldsBuggiestProgram\WorldsBuggiestProgram.cpp(1076)
    : {29} client block at 0x00760BD0, subtype 1, 8 bytes long.
  Employee Name: Fred Flintstone  Department: Accounting
strcore.cpp(118)  : {28} normal block at 0x00760480, 28 bytes long.
  Data: <            Fred> 01 00 00 00 0F 00 00 00 0F 00 00 00 46
    72 65 64
strcore.cpp(118)  : {27} normal block at 0x007604D0, 23 bytes long.
  Data: <            Acco> 01 00 00 00 0A 00 00 00 0A 00 00 00 41
    63 63 6F
Object dump complete.
```

How the Debug Heap Works

To take full advantage of the C Run-time Library debug heap, it pays to understand how it is implemented. When you allocate memory using the debug version of either `new` or `malloc`, both functions end up calling *_malloc_dbg*, which calls *_heap_alloc_dbg* to do the actual allocation (both functions can be found in *Dbgheap.c*). In fact, the only significant difference between `new` and `malloc` in their underlying implementation is that `new` calls the object's constructor after the memory is allocated, which cannot be done using `malloc`.

The goal of the debug heap is to detect both memory corruption and memory leaks and to report where in the source code a problem occurred. It accomplishes this goal by allocating additional memory for a memory block header as well as guard bytes before and after the actual data. The following code shows the structure that is used (it is defined in *Dbgint.h*, a file that is not included with Visual C++), and Figure 9.2 shows the structure graphically.

```
#define NoMansLandSize 4
#define pHdr(pData) (((_CrtMemBlockHeader *)pData) - 1)

typedef struct _CrtMemBlockHeader
{
    struct _CrtMemBlockHeader *pBlockHeaderNext;
    struct _CrtMemBlockHeader *pBlockHeaderPrev;
    char            *szFileName;      // source code file name
    int             nLine;            // source code line number
    size_t          nDataSize;        // size of allocation
    int             nBlockUse;        // memory block type
    long            lRequest;         // allocation number
    unsigned char   gap1[NoMansLandSize]; // 0xFDFDFDFD
    // unsigned char data[DataSize];     // the actual data buffer
    // unsigned char gap2[NoMansLandSize]; // 0xFDFDFDFD
} _CrtMemBlockHeader;
```

Given this structure, the way in which the debug heap works is hardly mysterious. The *_heap_alloc_dbg* function first checks to see if the _CRTDBG _CHECK_ALWAYS_DF debug heap option is set. If it is set, the function calls *_CrtCheckMemory* to check the heap for integrity. It then checks to see if *_CrtSetBreakAlloc* has been called and causes a debug break if it is currently allocating that allocation number. It then calls the allocation hook set by *_CrtSetAllocHook*, if any. Next, it determines if the memory block will use

memory block header (w/gap1) [sizeof(_CrtMemBlockHeader)]		data [nDataSize]	gap2 [4 bytes]
_CrtMemBlockHeader fields	0xFDFDFDFD	the actual data buffer 0xCD when newly allocate 0xDD when freed	0xFDFDFDFD

Figure 9.2   Debug heap memory block layout

the _IGNORE_BLOCK memory block type, which is true if the _CRTDBG _ALLOC_MEM_DF debug heap option is turned off or if the block is of the _CRT_BLOCK type and the _CRTDBG_CHECK_CRT_DF option is not turned on.

With the preliminaries out of the way, the _heap_alloc_dbg function is now ready to roll. It allocates a block of memory from the heap of the requested size plus room for the memory block header and guard bytes, which results in a total overhead of 36 bytes per allocation. It then saves the source code file name pointer, the source code line number, the size of the actual allocation request, the memory block type, and the allocation number. The function fills the data region with the 0xCD byte pattern and the guard bytes with the 0xFD byte pattern. To keep track of all the memory blocks that aren't ignored, the block is then inserted into a doubly linked list of all the allocated blocks that don't use the _IGNORE_BLOCK memory block type. Finally, it updates its internal book-keeping for the total memory allocated, the memory currently allocated, and the largest amount of memory allocated at once and returns a pointer to the start of the actual data buffer.

Compared with allocation, deallocation is fairly simple. Both the delete and free functions end up calling _free_dbg, which first checks to see if the _CRTDBG_CHECK_ALWAYS_DF debug heap option is set. If so, it then calls _CrtCheckMemory to check the heap for integrity. Next, it calls the allocation hook set by _CrtSetAllocHook, if any. The function checks the validity of the pointer being freed by calling _CrtIsValidHeapPointer, then it checks the integrity of the block itself by making sure it has a valid memory block type. If the _CRTDBG_CHECK_ALWAYS_DF debug heap option is not set (so that the entire heap wasn't checked), the function checks the integrity of the memory block being deleted by checking its guard bytes. Next, it updates its internal book-keeping by subtracting the memory block size from the memory currently allocated. If the _CRTDBG_DELAY_FREE_MEM_DF debug heap option is not set, it removes the block from the doubly linked list, fills the entire block (including the memory block header and guard bytes) with the 0xDD byte pattern, and frees the block. If the _CRTDBG_DELAY_FREE_MEM_DF option is set, it sets its block type to _FREE_BLOCK and fills the actual data region with the 0xDD byte pattern.

It is useful to know when the various byte patterns and memory leaks are checked and how you are notified of problems. The allocated data byte pattern (0xCD) is never checked by the debug heap, but this pattern is useful in helping you recognize uninitialized data and causing access violation exceptions when an uninitialized pointer is dereferenced. The freed data byte pattern (0xDD) is checked by _CrtCheckMemory_ when the _CRTDBG_DELAY_FREE _MEM_DF debug heap option is set and by the allocation and deallocation functions when the _CRTDBG_CHECK_ALWAYS_DF debug heap option is set. If a problem is found with writing to a freed _NORMAL_BLOCK or _CLIENT _BLOCK, the following trace messages appear.

```
memory check error at 0x00772170 = 0x78, should be 0xDD.
memory check error at 0x00772171 = 0x56, should be 0xDD.
memory check error at 0x00772172 = 0x34, should be 0xDD.
memory check error at 0x00772173 = 0x12, should be 0xDD.
DAMAGE: on top of Free block at 0x00772170.
DAMAGED allocated at file c:\PROJECTS\WorldsBuggiestProgram\
    WorldsBuggiestProgramView.cpp(191).
DAMAGED located at 0x00772170 is 4 bytes long.
```

The guard byte pattern (0xFD) is checked by _CrtCheckMemory_ and by _free_dbg_ for all memory when the _CRTDBG_CHECK_ALWAYS_DF debug heap option is set and for the block being freed when that option is not set. If a problem is found with a _NORMAL_BLOCK, you receive these trace messages for an overwrite

```
memory check error at 0x00772144 = 0x78, should be 0xFD.
memory check error at 0x00772145 = 0x56, should be 0xFD.
memory check error at 0x00772146 = 0x34, should be 0xFD.
memory check error at 0x00772147 = 0x12, should be 0xFD.
DAMAGE: after Normal block (#109) at 0x00772140.
Normal allocated at file c:\PROJECTS\WorldsBuggiestProgram\
    WorldsBuggiestProgramView.cpp(196).
Normal located at 0x00772140 is 4 bytes long.
```

and these trace messages for an underwrite

```
memory check error at 0x0077210C = 0x78, should be 0xFD.
memory check error at 0x0077210D = 0x56, should be 0xFD.
memory check error at 0x0077210E = 0x34, should be 0xFD.
memory check error at 0x0077210F = 0x12, should be 0xFD.
DAMAGE: before Normal block (#110) at 0x00772110.
```

```
Normal allocated at file c:\PROJECTS\WorldsBuggiestProgram\
    WorldsBuggiestProgramView.cpp(200).
Normal located at 0x00772110 is 4 bytes long.
```

Memory leaks are checked by the _CrtDumpMemoryLeaks_ function and at program termination if the _CRTDBG_LEAK_CHECK_DF debug heap option is set. If memory leaks are found, you will receive the trace messages shown earlier in the chapter.

Finally, you may find that memory corruption errors reported using trace statements are too easy to ignore. After all, memory corruption is definitely a bug, so using message boxes might be more appropriate. You can have _Crt CheckMemory_ report memory errors with message boxes by using _CrtSet ReportMode_, as shown here.

```
int oldMode = _CrtSetReportMode(_CRT_WARN, _CRTDBG_MODE_WNDW);
_CrtCheckMemory();
_CrtSetReportMode(_CRT_WARN, oldMode);
```

Now if your program overwrites a _CLIENT_BLOCK, you will receive the message box shown in Figure 9.3. The disadvantage to this approach is that you will receive one message box for every trace statement, so you will receive many such message boxes if you have a lot of memory errors.

TIP

Use _CrtSetReportMode_ to make memory errors reported by _CrtCheck Memory_ more obvious.

Microsoft Visual C++ Debug Library ☒

Debug Warning!

Program: ...ROJECTS\WORLDSBUGGIESTPROGRAM\DEBUG\WORLDSBUGGIESTPROGRAM.EXE

DAMAGE: after Client block (#217) at 0x00773AA0.

(Press Retry to debug the application)

| Abort | Retry | Ignore |

Figure 9.3 The result of having _CrtCheckMemory_ report memory errors with message boxes

Given the implementation of the debug heap, one implication should be fairly clear: Mixing release and debug build modules that use the heap is a very bad idea. The _free_dbg_ and _CrtCheckMemory_ functions assume that all memory in the debug heap was allocated with the memory block header and guard bytes, and bad things will happen (specifically, failed assertions and access violation exceptions) if that isn't the case.

TIP

Don't mix release and debug build modules that use the heap.

Reading Windows Memory Addresses

Debugging memory typically involves looking at many variables and data structures that contain pointers. You can improve your ability to find memory problems if you can determine whether a pointer is reasonable or unreasonable just by looking at its value. Because Windows partitions a process's 4 GB virtual address space using a fixed set of ranges, you can easily determine if an address is reasonable once you know these ranges. You can also use a couple different techniques to determine more specifically how your program's address space is laid out. The only trick is that the partition ranges are different for Windows 2000 than for Windows 98, so a reasonable memory address in one version of Windows may not be reasonable in another.

TIP

You can debug memory problems more efficiently if you learn how to read pointer values. You can easily determine the reasonableness of a pointer value if you know how Windows partitions the virtual address space.

Windows 2000 and Windows 98 partition a process's virtual address space as shown in Table 9.7. For all versions of Windows, the addresses listed in Table 9.8 have special meanings.

As described in Chapter 6, Debugging with Windows, Windows processes are usually loaded at address 0x00400000. Although you can choose to load a Windows 2000 process at a lower base address (using the linker **Base address** option), 0x00400000 is the lowest base address that can be used by

Table 9.7   Windows virtual address space partitioning

Address Range	Usage
Windows 2000	
0–0xFFFF (64 KB)	Inaccessible to detect null pointer assignments (access violation)
0x10000 (64 KB)– 0x7FFEFFFF (2 GB–64 KB)	Private to Win32 processes—unreserved, usable for program code and data
0x7FFF0000 (2 GB–64 KB)– 0x7FFFFFFF (2 GB)	Inaccessible to prevent overwrites into OS partition (access violation)
0x80000000 (2 GB)– 0xFFFFFFFF (4 GB)	Reserved for operating system—inaccessible (access violation)
Windows 98	
0–0x0FFF (4 KB)	MS-DOS—inaccessible (access violation)
0x1000 (4 KB)– 0x3FFFFF (4 MB)	MS-DOS and 16-bit Windows—read/writable but should do neither from Win32 processes
0x400000 (4 MB)– 0x7FFFFFFF (2 GB)	Private to Win32 processes—unreserved, usable for program code and data
0x80000000 (2 GB)– 0xBFFFFFFF (3 GB)	Shared Win32 DLLs, memory-mapped files, shared by all Win32 processes—usable, read/writable
0xC0000000 (3 GB)– 0xFFFFFFFF (4 GB)	Virtual device drivers, system code, shared by all Win32 processes—read/writable, but writing may corrupt the system

Table 9.8   Special meanings of Windows addresses

Address Value	Meaning
0	Null pointer—always invalid
0x00400000	Program base address
0xCCCCCCCC	Uninitialized automatic (local) variable pointer

all versions of Windows. Not coincidentally, a process's instance handle value is always the same as its base address.

The special meaning of the 0xCCCCCCCC address was introduced by Visual C++ 6.0, and it is used only when a program is compiled with the /GZ compiler option. Contrary to popular belief, uninitialized automatic variables are normally not initialized in debug builds, but they are initialized to 0xCCCCCCCC when compiled with the /GZ option to help identify uninitialized pointers. Note that all uninitialized automatic variables are given this value, not just pointer variables. (OK—uninitialized `char` variables are initialized to 0xCC and uninitialized `short` variables are initialized to 0xCCCC, but you get the idea.) This compiler option is automatically used in new programs created with the Visual C++ AppWizard, but you must add this option manually to the debug builds for projects created with earlier versions of Visual C++.

Table 9.9 shows more detail about how the typical Windows 2000 and Windows 98 programs use virtual address space for the executable, DLLs,

Table 9.9 Use of Windows 2000 and Windows 98 virtual address space

Address Range	Usage
Windows 2000	
0x00030000–0x0012FFFF	Thread stack
0x00130000–0x003FFFFF	Heap (sometimes the heap is here)
0x00400000–0x005FFFFF	Executable
0x00600000–0x0FFFFFFF	Heap (sometimes the heap is here)
0x10000000–0x5FFFFFFF	App DLLs, Msvcrt.dll, Mfc42.dll
0x77000000–0xFFFFFFFF	Advapi32.dll, Comctl32.dll, Gdi32.dll, Kernel32.dll, Ntdll.dll, Rpcrt4.dll, Shell32.dll, User32.dll
Windows 98	
0x00400000–0x005FFFFF	Executable
0x00600000–0x0FFFFFFF	Thread stack, then heap
0x10000000–0x7FFFFFFF	App DLL's, Msvcrt.dll, Mfc42.dll, Shell32.dll, Shlwapi.dll
0x80000000–0xFFFFFFFF	Advapi32.dll, Comctl32.dll, Gdi32.dll, Kernel32.dll, User32.dll, Version.dll

stack, and heap. (Each item listed within a range may be found within that range but doesn't take up the whole range.)

These values are typical; any specific program may use different DLLs and different-sized stacks and heaps and as a result may have somewhat different address values. You can determine the exact module addresses used by a program in Visual C++ using the **Modules** command in the **Debug** menu. If you want to know the exact location of the stack and heap and you have Jeffrey Richter's *Programming Applications for Microsoft Windows* handy, you can obtain a detailed virtual memory map for a program using the VMMap utility. Unfortunately, VMMap doesn't label the heap, but it is typically the read/writable block with a default size of 1,048,576 bytes somewhere in the partitions noted above.

You can also use the x86 memory alignment rules to determine if a pointer is reasonable. Heap and stack pointers are double-word aligned, so they should end with a 0, 4, 8, or C hex digit. Whereas x86 instructions can be any size and instruction addresses can end with any digit, functions are 16-byte aligned; so function pointers should always end with a zero.

In most debugging situations, you don't need to know the exact address space layout to determine if pointer values are reasonable. For example, if you are debugging a program in Windows 2000, you know that 0x0046004C is a reasonable address for dynamically allocated memory, whereas 0x5F4CCB14 is not. Note that global variables are stored within the address space of the module that defined them, so pointers to global variables don't have addresses within the heap or stack. This might seem obvious, but don't panic if you see an unexpected address for a pointer you didn't assign. For example, an empty MFC *CString* will have its internal *m_pchData* member pointing to an address such as 0x5F4CCB14 because all empty *CString*s point to a global variable within MFC itself (specifically, *_afxDataNil*).

Handles are not pointers, nor are they pointers to pointers. In fact, their interpretation depends on the type of handle; often they are indices into a table of handles. It can be difficult to determine if a handle value is reasonable by inspection in Windows 2000, but it is very easy to determine in Windows 98. In Windows 98, handle values are small because they are indices, typically less than 0x00010000.

Dealing with Unprotected System Memory in Windows 98

There is a bit of bad news that I have let slip by until now. As discussed, reading or writing to the addresses 0xCDCDCDCD, 0xCCCCCCCC, and 0xDDDDDDDD results in an access violation exception in Windows 2000 but not in Windows 98. To make matters worse, assertions written using the *IsBadReadPtr* and *IsBadWritePtr* API functions as well as the MFC *AfxIsValidAddress* will not fail with these addresses in Windows 98. This means that it won't be obvious when you are using uninitialized pointers in Windows 98, which makes Windows 2000 the preferred Windows version for tracking down memory corruption.

> Reading or writing to the addresses 0xCDCDCDCD, 0xCCCCCCCC, and 0xDDDDDDDD doesn't result in an access violation exception in Windows 98, which makes Windows 2000 the preferred Windows version for tracking down memory corruption.

Unfortunately, the fact that operating system memory isn't protected means that Windows 98 is fairly easy to corrupt. For example, executing the following code causes Windows 98 to crash with a blue screen with a debug build.

```
#include <commdlg.h>
int APIENTRY WinMain (HINSTANCE hInstance, HINSTANCE
      hPrevInstance, LPSTR lpCmdLine, int nCmdShow) {
   CHOOSECOLOR cc;
   cc.lStructSize = sizeof(cc);
   ChooseColor(&cc);
   . . .
}
```

Apparently, Windows 98 assumes that any common dialog structure that has the *lStructSize* field properly filled out is valid. In this case, all the remaining fields are set to 0xCCCCCCCC, which is unprotected system memory. Accessing this memory then causes *Krnl386.exe* to crash.

All is not lost, however. Although having unprotected system memory in Windows 98 is far from ideal, you can have the debugger notify you when the 0xCDCDCDCD, 0xCCCCCCCC, and 0xDDDDDDDD addresses are changed by setting data breakpoints on these addresses, as shown in Figure 9.4.

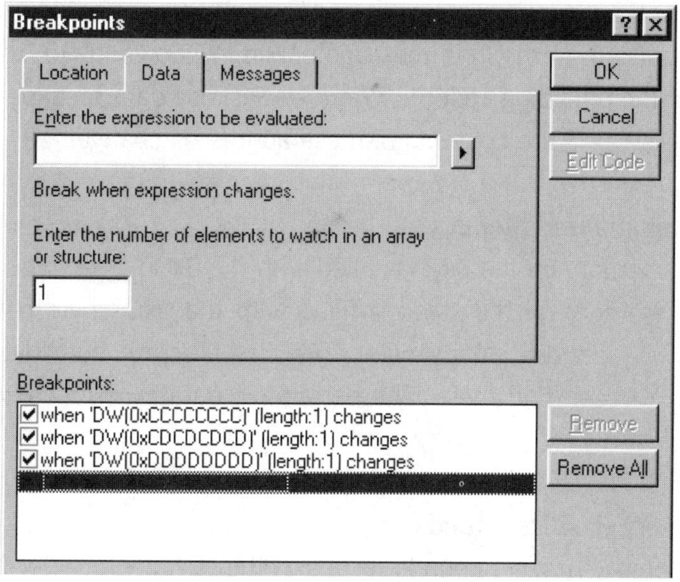

Figure 9.4 Using data breakpoints to detect writing to byte pattern addresses in Windows 98

TIP

> You can have the debugger notify you when the 0xCDCDCDCD, 0xCCCCCCCC, or 0xDDDDDDDD addresses are changed by setting data breakpoints.

Debugging Memory Corruption

Now that your program is properly instrumented to find memory corruption and you understand how it all works, let's look at how to debug some typical memory corruption problems.

Accessing a Null Pointer

Reading and writing to a null pointer results in an access violation exception in all versions of Windows for both debug and release builds. After you dismiss the exception message box, the debugger points you to the offending code.

Accessing an Uninitialized Pointer

Reading and writing to an uninitialized pointer on the heap (address 0xCDCDCDCD) and on the stack (address 0xCCCCCCCC) results in an access violation exception for debug builds in Windows 2000, but not in Windows 98. After you dismiss the exception message box in Windows 2000, the debugger points you to the offending code. In Windows 98, use data breakpoints to have the debugger break if the contents of these addresses change.

Accessing Uninitialized Memory

Uninitialized memory on the heap is filled with the 0xCD byte pattern, whereas uninitialized memory on the stack is filled with the 0xCC byte pattern in debug builds. Uninitialized global memory is zero filled for both debug and release builds. You can find these byte patterns in data by inspection within the debugger.

Writing Memory Past Its Bounds

Writing to memory past its bounds results in the "DAMAGE: after block" trace message for overwrites and "DAMAGE: before block" trace message for underwrites in debug builds. However, this occurs only if the damage happens to the four bytes immediately before or after the data. Writing to memory past its bounds may not be detected if the writing skips over the guard bytes.

Because detection of the corruption may occur well after the damage is done, you can track down the code that caused the corruption using a data breakpoint. Determine the address of the memory being corrupted (in this case, the guard byte address) from the trace message, run the program again, and set a data breakpoint at that address using the Breakpoints dialog box (obtained with the **Breakpoints** command in the **Edit** menu).

Use data breakpoints to determine the cause of memory corruption.

Accessing Memory after Being Freed

Freed memory on the heap is filled with the 0xDD byte pattern in debug builds. However, you can read or write to freed memory without receiving an access violation in all versions of Windows because the address points to valid memory. To detect memory access easily after the memory has been freed, be sure to always set freed pointers to null. (The same goes for handles.) Also, since freed memory can be reused immediately by the next memory allocation, you cannot depend on freed memory having the 0xDD byte pattern unless you have set the _CRTDBG_DELAY_FREE_MEM_DF debug heap option.

 TIP

> To detect memory access easily after the memory has been freed, be sure to always set freed pointers to null.

Deleting an Uninitialized Pointer, Deleting a Nonheap Pointer, and Deleting a Pointer More Than Once

Attempting to delete a pointer to an address that hasn't been allocated from the debug heap results in the failed assertion shown in Figure 9.5 in debug builds. Similarly, attempting to delete a pointer more than once results in the failed assertion shown in Figure 9.6 in debug builds. Click **Retry** and check the stack to find the offending line of code. Depending on the value of the pointer being freed, clicking **Ignore** may result in an access violation exception.

In most of these cases memory corruption problems are fairly easy to detect. If you know you have some sort of memory corruption but are having trouble finding the problem, try using the _CRTDBG_CHECK_ALWAYS_DF and _CRTDBG_DELAY_FREE_MEM_DF debug heap options to help find the problem. Again, consider debugging memory corruption with Windows 2000, if you aren't already.

Microsoft Visual C++ Debug Library ☒

Debug Assertion Failed!

Program: ...ROJECTS\WORLDSBUGGIESTPROGRAM\DEBUG\WORLDSBUGGIESTPROGRAM.EXE
File: dbgheap.c
Line: 1044

Expression: _CrtIsValidHeapPointer(pUserData)

For information on how your program can cause an assertion failure, see the Visual C++ documentation on asserts.

(Press Retry to debug the application)

[Abort] [Retry] [Ignore]

Figure 9.5 The message box that results from deleting unallocated memory

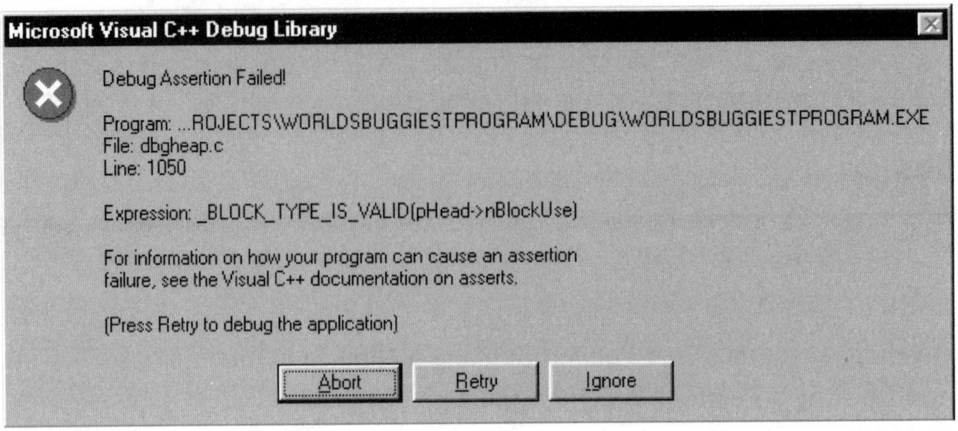

Figure 9.6 The message box that results from deleting allocated memory more than once

> **TIP**
>
> To debug difficult memory corruption problems, try using the _CRTDBG _CHECK_ALWAYS_DF and _CRTDBG_DELAY_FREE_MEM_DF debug heap options.

Debugging Memory Leaks

Now that your program is properly instrumented to find any memory leaks in the heap at program termination and you understand how it all works, let's look at the most common causes of memory leaks and some ways to debug them.

Common Memory Leak Causes

We'll start by rounding up the usual suspects, which are variations of not deallocating the memory at all or having code that can bypass the deallocation. Being aware of the common causes of memory leaks can help you find the leaks just by looking at your code or, better yet, can help you prevent creating the leak in the first place.

Forgetting to Delete

One of the most common causes of memory leaks is allocating memory and simply forgetting to deallocate it. For example, an object that is particularly easy to forget to delete is the MFC *CException* object. In the following code it is necessary to delete the *CFileExeception* object to prevent a memory leak.

```
try {
   // do something that throws a file exception
}
catch (CFileException *e) {
   if (e->m_cause == CFileException::fileNotFound)
      TRACE(_T("File not found\n"));
   e->Delete();   // required to prevent a memory leak
}
```

You must delete MFC exceptions with the *Delete* member function instead of `delete` because some MFC exceptions are created as static objects.

Constructors That Fail

When writing a constructor that allocates memory, it is important to remember that destructors are called only when an object is successfully constructed; so you cannot expect a destructor to clean up an object whose constructor throws an exception. Techniques for handling constructors that can fail are discussed in detail in Chapter 2, Writing C++ Code for Debugging. See also Item 10 in Scott Meyers' *More Effective C++*, which examines several different approaches.

Leaky Destructors

You can leak memory in a destructor by forgetting to deallocate all memory allocated by an object or even by forgetting to write the destructor at all. When writing a destructor, it is a good idea to review all data members that allocate resources and make sure they are properly cleaned up. Note that making sure the destructor cleans up all memory allocated by the constructor isn't sufficient because memory might be allocated by other member functions as well. Consequently, it isn't a good idea to regard the destructor as simply the inverse of a constructor. If a destructor calls code that can throw an exception, it is necessary to handle the exception within the destructor because not doing so can lead to memory leaks or even result in program termination. Also make sure that base class destructors are virtual (but don't routinely make all destructors virtual because nonbase classes won't benefit). Doing so guarantees that the derived class's constructor is called, even if the object exists as a pointer to a base class. Techniques for handling destructors that can fail are also discussed in Chapter 2. See also Item 11 in Scott Meyers' *More Effective C++*.

When writing destructors, you need to be aware of the Law of the Big Three: If a class needs a destructor or a copy constructor or an assignment operator, it needs all three of them. Failing to do so can result in memory corruption and memory leaks. For additional information on this subject, see Chapter 30, The Big Three, in *C++ FAQs, Second Edition,* by Marshall Cline, Greg Lomow, and Mike Girou.

Leaky Exception Handlers

Exception handlers must perform the same cleanup as the normal execution path does, otherwise you have a memory leak. Consider the following code.

```
BOOL LeakyExceptionHandler (int arg) {
   try {
      CMyObject *pObject = new CMyObject(arg);
      ...   // do something that throws an exception
      pObject->MemberFunction();
      delete pObject;
   }
   catch (...) {
      return FALSE;
   }
   return TRUE;
}
```

In this example, if the function does something that throws an exception, the exception handler fails to delete *pObject*, resulting in a leak. The standard way to combat this type of problem is to use the C++ `auto_ptr` smart pointer template class, which relies on the C++ language to clean up resources instead of programmer discipline. Here is the preceding code rewritten to use an `auto_ptr`.

```
BOOL LeakProofExceptionHandler (int arg) {
   try {
      auto_ptr<CMyObject> pObject(new CMyObject(arg));
      ...   // do something that throws an exception
      pObject->MemberFunction();   // can still call member
                                   // functions as normal
      // no need to delete pObject
   }
```

```
   catch (...) {
      return FALSE;
   }
   return TRUE;
}
```

In this case, you are now creating a local object *pObject* that is responsible for destroying the underlying *CMyObject* object. The C++ language guarantees that the underlying object will be destroyed once *pObject* goes out of scope, thus making a leak impossible. This approach has the additional benefit of eliminating the need for redundant cleanup code. Also, note that the syntax for calling member functions is unchanged.

TIP

Consider using the C++ `auto_ptr` to make memory leaks impossible.

In *The C++ Programming Language, Third Edition,* Bjarne Stroustrup describes the technique for managing resources using local objects as "resource acquisition is initialization." Note that `auto_ptr`s solve the resource leak problem in constructors and destructors as well. For additional information on this subject, see Chapter 14, Exception Handling, in *The C++ Programming Language, Third Edition.* Also check Scott Meyers' *More Effective C++*, Item 9; Stanley Lippman and Josée Lajoie's *C++ Primer, Third Edition,* Section 8.4, Dynamically Allocated Objects; and Marshall Cline, Greg Lomow, and Mike Girou's *C++ FAQs, Second Edition,* Chapter 31, Using Objects to Prevent Memory Leaks.

Multiple Return Statements

Having multiple return statements in a function that frees memory can lead to memory leaks. Consider the following code.

```
BOOL MultipleReturnStatments (int arg) {
   CMyObject *pObject = new CMyObject(arg);
   if (pObject->IsEmpty())
      return FALSE;
   ...
   delete pObject;
   return TRUE
}
```

In this example, if *pObject* is empty, the function returns FALSE without first deleting the object, resulting in a leak. Unfortunately, this type of leak is all too common. For this reason, some programmers go to the extreme of avoiding multiple `return` statements entirely, which might be a good idea for this specific example. I generally prefer to use multiple `return` statements because the alternative often leads to unnecessarily complex code. If you use multiple `return` statements, you must be especially careful in functions that free memory. Again, note that using C++ `auto_ptr`s completely solves this problem.

Using the Wrong Form of Delete

You must always use the same form of `delete` that you used for `new`. More specifically, if you allocate a single object using `new`, you must use the normal form of `delete`, whereas if you allocate an array using `new`, you must use the array form of `delete`. (Using placement `new` is an exception since it doesn't allocate memory. To destroy an object created with placement `new`, you call the destructor directly.) For example:

```
CMyObject *pMyObjectArray = new CMyObject [10];
delete [] pMyObjectArray;    // this form works
delete pMyObjectArray;       // this form doesn't work
```

Here, `new` allocates enough memory for ten *CMyObject* objects, then calls the default constructor for each. The array form of `delete` calls the destructor for each object, then deallocates the memory, whereas the normal form of `delete` calls the destructor only for the first object, resulting in a memory leak if the *CMyObject* destructor frees memory (although technically, the result is considered undefined). If you make this mistake with the debug build, you will receive the failed assertion shown in Figure 9.7.

For additional information on this subject, see Item 5 in Scott Meyers' *Effective C++, Second Edition,* and Item 8 in *More Effective C++.*

Plugging Memory Leaks

You can use several techniques to track down the cause of a memory leak. The following are the most common, in order of preference.

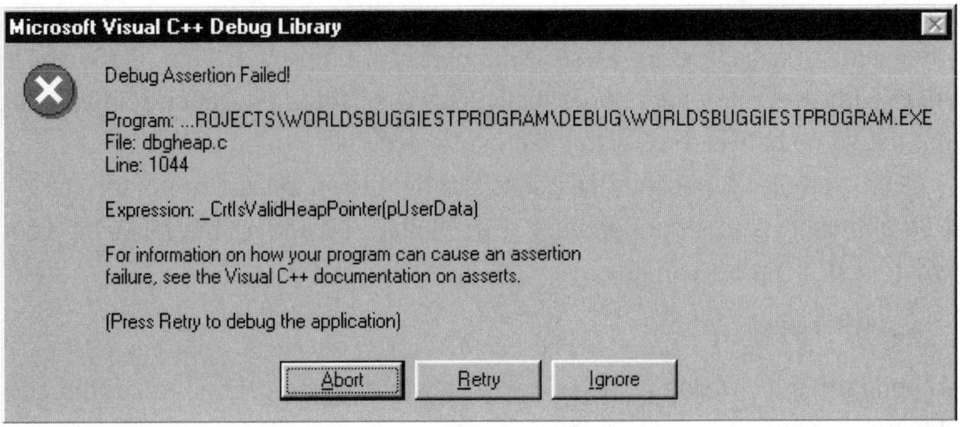

Figure 9.7 The message box that results from using the wrong form of `delete`

Using the Source File Name and Line Number

I have already discussed how to make sure your memory allocations have the correct source code file name and line number so that this information is reported by _CrtDumpMemoryLeaks. I have also discussed how to display the source code information of the calling function instead of the callee when that is more relevant. Using the source code information is usually the simplest approach to finding memory leaks—when it works.

Using the Dumped Data

Unfortunately, the source code information isn't always enough to find a leak. You can use the source code information to find a leak if that code always leaks, but the situation is more difficult when that code is called thousands of times but only leaks once. In this case, you can often find the leak by looking at the dumped data and recognizing the specific data that is leaking. If the standard memory leak output isn't helpful, you can install a client dump function using _CrtSetDumpClient, as previously discussed.

Using the Allocation Number

You can track down a specific leak by using its allocation number, which is the number in braces in the leak output. First, note the allocation numbers of the leaked memory and run the program again exactly the same way. Now recheck the allocation numbers of the leaked memory. If they are the same (and they often are), you can debug these leaks one at a time by calling _CrtSetBreak Alloc with these numbers sequentially. However, if the allocation numbers are not the same between runs, this technique isn't likely to be effective.

For example, suppose a leak consistently has an allocation number of 27. One approach is to set a conditional breakpoint by adding the following code where your program initializes.

```
_CrtSetBreakAlloc(27);
```

Although this technique works, a more convenient approach is to set the conditional breakpoint directly in the debugger by entering the following statement into the Watch window.

```
{,,msvcrtd.dll}_CrtSetBreakAlloc(27)
```

Alternatively, you can also set the equivalent C Run-time Library global variable in the Watch window for the same effect.

```
{,,msvcrtd.dll}_crtBreakAlloc = 27
```

The interactive approach is usually preferable because you don't have to change your code and you can track down several leaks in a single debugging session.

> **TIP**
>
> You can set memory allocation breakpoints interactively in the debugger using the Watch window.

By the way, if you receive a mysterious "User breakpoint called from code at . . ." message box, there's a chance you set an allocation breakpoint and forgot to remove it.

Reviewing the Source Code

As suggested earlier, if you understand the common causes of memory leaks, you can often quickly find memory leaks simply by reviewing your source code. This technique is especially effective if the previous approaches don't pan out. If you have a good idea where the problem is, you might want to try this technique first.

Using Memory Checkpoints

Memory checkpoints are an excellent way to determine if a section of code has a leak and to pinpoint a leak within a section of code. In most cases, using memory checkpoints requires more effort than the previous techniques, so it should probably be used as a last resort.

To find a memory leak using checkpoints, place checkpoints using _CrtMem Checkpoint at the beginning and end of the region you are interested in, then check for differences using _CrtMemDifference, which returns TRUE if differences are found. You can then dump a summary of the differences using _CrtMemDumpStatistics, dump all the memory allocated since the beginning of the region using _CrtMemDumpAllObjectsSince, or both. Despite its name, _CrtDumpMemoryLeaks is of no value here because it dumps all allocated memory, not just leaked memory. This function only works as advertised when it is run at program termination, when it is assumed that all remaining allocated memory has leaked.

TIP

Despite its name _CrtDumpMemoryLeaks dumps all allocated memory, not just leaked memory, so it only finds leaks at program termination.

For example, you can find a leak in a function using the following technique.

```
void LeakyFunction () {
    // the beginning checkpoint
    _CrtMemState oldState, newState, stateDiff;
    _CrtMemCheckpoint(&oldState);

    // the actual function
    CString notALeak = _T("Not a leak.");
    TCHAR *leakingString = new TCHAR[50];
    _tcscpy(leakingString, _T("Leaking string."));

    // the ending checkpoint
    _CrtMemCheckpoint(&newState);
    if (_CrtMemDifference(&stateDiff, &oldState, &newState)) {
        _CrtMemDumpStatistics(&stateDiff);
        _CrtMemDumpAllObjectsSince(&oldState);
    }
}
```

Executing this function results in the following output.

```
0 bytes in 0 Free Blocks.
74 bytes in 2 Normal Blocks.
0 bytes in 0 CRT Blocks.
0 bytes in 0 Ignore Blocks.
0 bytes in 0 Client Blocks.
Largest number used: 0 bytes.
Total allocations: 74 bytes.
Dumping objects ->
c:\PROJECTS\WorldsBuggiestProgram\WorldsBuggiestProgramView.cpp
   (192) : {118} normal block at 0x00772190, 50 bytes long.
 Data: <Leaking string. > 4C 65 61 6B 69 6E 67 20 73 74 72 69 6E
   67 2E 00
strcore.cpp(118) : {117} normal block at 0x007721F0, 24 bytes
   long.
 Data: <            Not > 01 00 00 00 0B 00 00 00 0B 00 00 00 4E
   6F 74 20
Object dump complete.
```

Interestingly, this output is wrong because it reports two leaks when in fact
there is only one. The problem is that the *notALeak* string allocates memory
from the heap that isn't freed until the variable goes out of scope at the end of
the function. The simplest solution is to enclose the original function in braces
to make sure all local variables are out of scope before calling *_CrtMem
Difference*, as the following code shows.

> **TIP**
>
> When using memory checkpoints to find leaks in a region of code, be sure to
> enclose the region in braces so that local variables go out of scope.

```
void LeakyFunction () {
    _CrtMemState oldState, newState, stateDiff;
    _CrtMemCheckpoint(&oldState);
    {

    CString notALeak = _T("Not a leak.");
    TCHAR *leakingString = new TCHAR[50];
    _tcscpy(leakingString, _T("Leaking string."));

    }
    _CrtMemCheckpoint(&newState);
```

```
    if (_CrtMemDifference(&stateDiff, &oldState, &newState)) {
        _CrtMemDumpStatistics(&stateDiff);
        _CrtMemDumpAllObjectsSince(&oldState);
    }
}
```

Of course, real code with memory leaks is much more complex than this example. Not a problem. Suppose you have a giant, complex function that you suspect has a memory leak. By placing the checkpoints at the beginning and end of the function, you can confirm that the function has a leak. You can then move the beginning and ending checkpoints in a binary search fashion to isolate the specific code that has the leak.

It's worth taking a look at the _CrtMemState_ structure so that you can understand its limitations.

```
typedef struct _CrtMemState
{
    struct _CrtMemBlockHeader *pBlockHeader;
    unsigned long lCounts[_MAX_BLOCKS];
    unsigned long lSizes[_MAX_BLOCKS];
    unsigned long lHighWaterCount;
    unsigned long lTotalCount;
} _CrtMemState;
```

TIP

Use the _CRTDBG_DELAY_FREE_MEM_DF debug heap option to prevent _CrtMemDumpAllObjectsSince_ from giving incorrect results.

This structure is indeed a snapshot of the memory state because the information it stores is at a very high level. The _pBlockHeader_ member is a pointer to the last block of memory allocated when the snapshot was taken, _lCounts_ and _lSizes_ store the number of allocations and their sizes for each type of memory block, _lHighWaterCount_ is the maximum amount of memory ever allocated at once, and _lTotalCount_ is the sum of all allocations. All these members except _pBlockHeader_ are used by _CrtMemDumpStatistics_, whereas _pBlockHeader_ is used by _CrtMemDumpAllObjectsSince_. It is worth noting that _CrtMemDump AllObjectsSince_ becomes very confused if the memory block that _pBlock Header_ points to has already been freed. In this case, it dumps all allocated memory because it doesn't know when to stop. If you see all your memory being reported as leaking, don't panic. Instead, use the _CRTDBG_DELAY_FREE _MEM_DF debug heap option to get the correct results.

Debugging Windows Resource Leaks

Windows resource leaks are a serious problem, especially GDI resource leaks. Windows allocates these resources itself on your program's behalf, so you can't detect Windows resource leaks using the previously described techniques because the C Run-time Library doesn't instrument memory allocated within Windows. Consequently, you must use different techniques to detect and remove Windows resource leaks.

To eliminate leaks, any resource that Windows creates for your program must be cleaned up using the appropriate API function. The typical Windows resource requires the following pattern.

```
HSOMEOBJECT hObject = CreateSomeObject(...);
... // use hObject
DestroyObject(hObject);
```

The Windows GDI further complicates the situation because GDI objects cannot be deleted while selected by a valid device context. There are two common approaches to this problem. The first approach is to keep a handle to the original GDI object and reselect it before deleting the new GDI object, as with

```
HPEN hPen, hOldPen;
hPen = CreatePen(PS_SOLID, 1, RGB(0, 0, 0xff));
hOldPen = (HPEN)SelectObject(hDC, hPen);
... // use hPen to do some drawing
SelectObject(hDC, hOldPen);   // reselect the original GDI object
DeleteObject(hPen);
```

The second approach is to deselect the new GDI object by restoring a stock object, as shown by this MFC example.

```
CPen pen(PS_SOLID, 1, RGB(0, 0, 0xff));
dc.SelectObject(&pen);
... // use pen to do some drawing
dc.SelectStockObject(BLACK_PEN);
```

The second approach is preferable when it is difficult to keep track of the original GDI object that was in the device context.

TIP

Be sure that GDI objects are not selected in a device context before deleting them.

As this last example shows, one significant advantage of using C++ classes to wrap Windows resources (as done in MFC) is that the resource objects are automatically destroyed when they go out of scope, thus entirely eliminating the need to explicitly call the object destruction API functions. Unfortunately, you still have to deselect GDI objects before you delete them, even when using C++ classes.

Windows Resource Cleanup

One significant problem with preventing Windows resource leaks is that there are so many different types of Windows resources and they are cleaned up in several different ways. It is often difficult to remember which function cleans up the various types of resources. Further complicating matters is the fact the some Windows resources don't need to be cleaned up at all, such as stock GDI objects and strings. Table 9.10 shows a sample of the various Windows API and C Run-time Library functions that allocate resources and their cleanup functions. Note that some, but not all, load functions don't require cleanup.

As the table suggests, it isn't a good idea to try to guess what the right cleanup function is for the various Windows resource construction functions. Whenever you are using a Windows resource that isn't wrapped in a C++ class, review the documentation to make sure you are using the correct cleanup function.

TIP

See the Windows documentation to make sure you are using the correct cleanup function.

Table 9.10   Windows API and C Run-time Library resource and cleanup functions

System Resource Function	Cleanup Function
CreateProcess	CloseHandle (call twice to close both process and thread handles)
CreateThread/_beginthreadex	CloseHandle/_endthreadex
CreateFile/fopen	CloseHandle/fclose
FindFirstFile/_findfirst	FindClose/_findclose
LoadLibrary	FreeLibrary

GDI Resource Function	Cleanup Function
CreateDC	DeleteDC
GetDC	ReleaseDC
BeginPaint	EndPaint
GetStockObject	No cleanup required
CreateSolidBrush	DeleteObject
CreatePen	DeleteObject
CreateRectRgn	DeleteObject
LoadImage	DeleteObject/DestroyCursor/DestroyIcon
CreateBitmap	DeleteObject
LoadBitmap	DeleteObject
CreatePalette	DeleteObject
CreateFont	DeleteObject

User Resource Function	Cleanup Function
CreateWindow	DestroyWindow
CreateDialog	DestroyWindow
CreateMenu	DestroyMenu
LoadMenu	DestroyMenu
LoadString	No cleanup required
CreateCursor	DestroyCursor
LoadCursor	No cleanup required
CreateIcon	DestroyIcon
LoadIcon	No cleanup required
SetTimer	KillTimer

DEBUGGING TECHNIQUES

How to Detect Windows Resource Leaks

The easiest way to detect resource leaks in Windows 98, especially GDI leaks, is to run the Resource Meter utility (named *Rsrcmtr.exe,* located in the Windows folder) that comes with Windows 98. This program monitors the Windows system, user, and GDI resources, as shown in Figure 9.8.

To find leaks, check the percentage of resources free, and then run your program. Once your program and data are loaded, these resources should maintain a fairly steady state. Monitor the resource usage pattern as you perform tasks with your program. A steady decline is a good sign of a resource leak. Enabling the **Show window contents while dragging** option on the **Effects** tab of the Display Properties control panel is especially effective in revealing GDI resource leaks. If you suspect a leak, perform the same task several times and watch for a continued decline. Once you quit the program, the free resource values should return to what they were before you started the program. If not, that again is a good sign of a resource leak. Although the granularity of this program isn't very fine (there are 655 bytes per percentage change), it is usually fairly obvious when you have a leak, so you don't have to worry about leaks being so small that they go undetected.

TIP

The Resource Meter utility is an effective way of detecting Windows resource leaks in Windows 98.

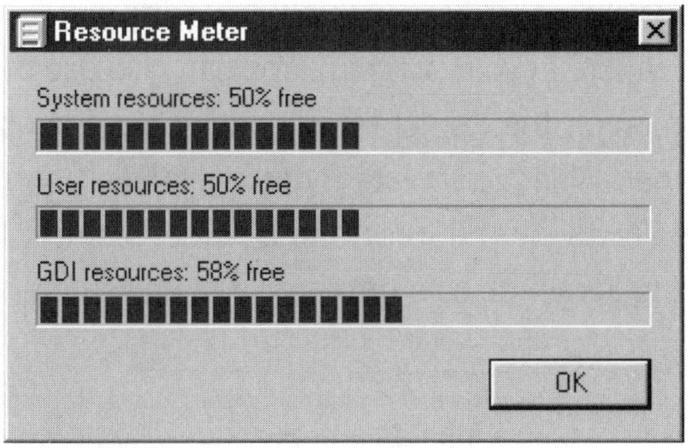

Figure 9.8   The Windows 98 Resource Meter utility

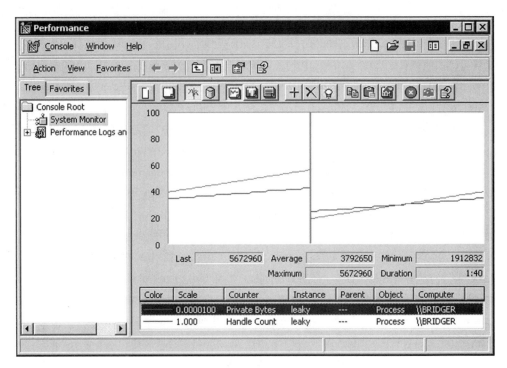

Figure 9.9   The Windows 2000 Performance Monitor utility

The easiest way to detect resource leaks in Windows 2000 is to run the Performance Monitor utility and monitor your program's Private Bytes and Handle Count over time as shown in Figure 9.9. The Private Bytes value is the amount of nonshared memory a process is using, whereas the Handle Count is the number of handles currently open by the process. If the Private Bytes or Handle Count values continue to increase over time without achieving a steady state, you have a memory leak somewhere in your program. You can also use the Windows 2000 Task Manager and monitor the Kernel Memory, which is the amount of memory allocated by the kernel. Where a Private Bytes or Handle Count leak indicates a resource leak made directly by your program, a Kernel Memory leak is a sign that the program is leaking kernel objects or other kernel resources.

TIP

The Performance Monitor utility is an effective way of detecting Windows resource leaks in Windows 2000.

DEBUGGING TECHNIQUES

For handling the problem of deleting selected GDI objects, unfortunately, there is no simple way to determine if a nonstock object is selected in a device context. According to the MSDN documentation, the *DeleteObject* API function is supposed to return zero when deleting a GDI object currently selected in a device context. This suggests that asserting the *DeleteObject* return value would be a simple way to locate GDI resource leaks caused by deleting selected objects. Unfortunately, my tests show that *DeleteObject* can return a nonzero value when called with a selected object, so this approach is not reliable.

Alternatively, you can determine if a specific GDI object is selected in a device context by selecting the object and comparing the handle of the old object to the object in question, as shown here.

```
BOOL IsGDIObjectSelected (HDC hDC, HGDIOBJ hObj) {
   HGDIOBJ hOldObj = SelectObject(hDC, hObj);  // select object
   SelectObject(hDC, hOldObj);   // restore the original object
   return hObj == hOldObj;       // compare handles
}
```

Although knowing that a specific object is selected might be useful in certain circumstances, such as when tracking down a specific bug, it simply isn't practical to rummage through all your GDI resources to see if any one of them is still selected.

How to Remove Windows Resource Leaks

Once you determine that you have a resource leak, usually the easiest way to remove the leak is to analyze the source code. By testing your program and watching Resource Meter or Performance Monitor, you can isolate the leak to a specific task and consequently to a specific set of code. You can then find the leak by looking for missing Windows resource cleanup statements in the task's code.

Although you can try to find Windows resource leaks using the debugger, this approach should be considered a last resort simply because the debugger doesn't really help much. That is, stepping through the code with the debugger isn't much better than simply reading the code and looking for leaks. For this type of problem, the debugger is best used to reveal paths through your code that have leaks that you might otherwise have overlooked, such as leaky exception handling. As a desperate measure, you can also track down leaks by temporarily removing suspicious code to see if the leak goes away, perhaps using a binary search to locate the problem.

How to Prevent Windows Resource Leaks

You can eliminate Windows resource leaks through detection and removal, but leak prevention is definitely the better way to go. If you are programming directly with the Windows API, a good solution is to wrap Windows resources in C++ classes to ensure cleanup on object destruction. This way resource cleanup is guaranteed by the C++ language instead of being the responsibility of the programmer. Furthermore, for dynamically allocated resources, this technique ensures that all resource leaks are memory leaks, for which good detection techniques already exist. Note that you cannot use C++ `auto_ptr`s for this purpose because they assume that objects are destroyed by calling `delete`. Of course, if you are using MFC, you are all set because nearly all Windows resources are already wrapped in C++ classes.

TIP

Leak prevention is much more effective than leak detection and removal. You can prevent leaks by wrapping Windows resources in C++ classes.

If you are programming using the Windows API or ATL, you can wrap a Windows resource (in this case a pen) using the following approach.

```
class CAutoPen {
public:
    CAutoPen (HPEN pen = 0) : m_hPen(pen) {}
    ~CAutoPen () { DeleteObject(); }
    CAutoPen & operator= (const HPEN hPen)
        { DeleteObject(); m_hPen = hPen; }
    BOOL DeleteObject ()
        { if (m_hPen == 0) return FALSE;
          BOOL retVal = ::DeleteObject(m_hPen);
          m_hPen = 0; return retVal; }
    operator HPEN() const { return m_hPen; }
```

```
private:
    HPEN m_hPen;
    // prevent the compiler from automatically writing the copy
    // constructor and assignment operator
    CAutoPen (const CAutoPen &pen);
    CAutoPen & operator= (const CAutoPen &hPen);
};
```

You can then use a pen as follows:

```
HPEN hOldPen;
CAutoPen pen(CreatePen(PS_SOLID, 1, RGB(0, 0, 0xff)));
hOldPen = (HPEN)SelectObject(hDC, pen);
... // use pen to do some drawing
SelectObject(hDC, hOldPen);    // reselect the original GDI object
```

By creating similar wrappers for all GDI objects and other selected Windows resources, you can easily prevent most Windows resource leaks.

The problem remains of making sure that GDI objects are deselected before deleting them. For this problem, I find the most effective solution is manual labor. Before I release new code that uses GDI objects, I quickly search all files for "SelectObject", which locates all relevant code. I do this because nothing of interest can be done with a GDI object without selecting it into a device context. (Similarly, you can quickly locate most non-GDI resource code by searching for "Create" and "Load".) I then make sure that each selected GDI object that the program creates is eventually deselected with either the original GDI object or a stock object. This requires carefully looking at all execution paths, paying particular attention to `return` and `break` statements and exception handlers for leaks. If I am not using MFC and didn't wrap the GDI objects with C++ classes, I also make sure that each GDI object is deleted in all execution paths as well. This work may seem tedious, but I find I can do it fairly quickly (in a few minutes). In fact, I find it much easier to detect GDI resource leaks by scanning the source code than any of the alternatives.

TIP

Scanning the source code is the most effective way to make sure that you have deselected GDI objects before deleting them.

Debugging Windows Thread Stacks

Windows protected memory does a good job of preventing stack overflow and underflow using guard pages. This protection prevents program corruption and makes stack problems relatively easy to debug. Let's look at how the Windows stack works, the types of stack bugs, and how to debug them.

Each thread in a process is given its own stack. By default, Windows reserves 1 MB of virtual address space and commits two pages (8 KB) of physical memory for a stack. A stack works using a last-in, first-out method, so all the activity is always at the top of the stack. Stacks are unusual in that they grow down in memory, so the top of the stack has a lower address than the bottom of the stack. A stack can grow until the entire reserved address space has been committed and the top of the stack has reached the stack's base address. Any attempt to grow the stack further results in a stack overflow exception. Note that the 1 MB default stack size is quite large, certainly much larger than the 8 KB and 16 KB stacks common to 16-bit Windows programs. The large size makes it easy to forget that the stack can overflow.

 TIP

A stack overflow exception is a one-shot exception, so you can receive only one stack overflow exception per thread.

It is important to understand that a stack overflow exception is a one-shot exception, so you can receive only one stack overflow exception per thread. This means that if you somehow handle a stack overflow exception and expect to receive another one later, you'll be disappointed. At best, you will receive an access violation exception; at worst, the process will terminate. The reason for this problem is that in Windows 2000 the top and the bottom of the stack are protected with memory blocks with PAGE_GUARD access. As the stack grows and runs out of committed memory, it tries to access a guard page and throw an exception. Windows handles this exception by converting the guard page to a normal page and then making a new guard page. Once the entire reserved stack space is committed, Windows still attempts to grow the stack by converting the guard page to a normal page and making a new guard page. The guard page conversion succeeds, but the new guard page allocation fails, re-

Table 9.11   Windows calling conventions

Calling Convention	Description
__cdecl	The default calling convention for C/C++ programs. Arguments are passed from right to left, and the calling function removes the arguments from the stack. Good for passing a variable number of parameters.
__stdcall	The calling convention used by Windows API functions. Arguments are passed from right to left, and the called function removes its arguments from the stack. It results in smaller code than __cdecl, but it uses __cdecl if the function has a variable number of parameters. The WINAPI, CALLBACK, and APIENTRY macros are all defined as __stdcall.
thiscall (not a keyword)	The default calling convention used by C++ member functions that do not use variable arguments. It is the same as __stdcall except the this pointer is stored in the ECX register instead of on the stack. Note that COM member functions use __stdcall.

sulting in a stack overflow exception. Since there is no longer a guard page, Windows will not generate another stack overflow exception for this thread. Windows 98 uses a similar technique (but it doesn't support the PAGE_GUARD memory attribute), so the outcome is the same.

The stack is used to store function return addresses, stack base addresses, function parameters, automatic variables, and saved register values. All parameters are widened to 32 bits when they are passed. The return value of a function isn't passed on the stack, but through the EAX register. The manner in which parameters are pushed and popped off the stack is determined by the function's calling convention. Table 9.11 shows the calling conventions that are common in Windows programs.

In terms of debugging, the stack is an excellent example of Murphy's law: Anything that can go wrong will go wrong. The things listed at the top of the next page can (and do) go wrong in stacks.

- The stack overflows if the automatic variables are too large to fit on the stack.
- The stack overflows if there is infinite or very deep recursion.
- The function return address on the stack is corrupted if a local variable array is written beyond its bounds.
- The stack is corrupted if there is a mismatch of function parameters or calling conventions between the called function and the caller.

We'll look at each of these problems in more detail.

Large Automatic Variables

The stack overflows if the automatic variables are too large to fit on the stack. Depending on the circumstances, either the stack size used is too small or large data is inappropriately stored on the stack instead of the heap or directly in Virtual Memory. Here is a typical example.

```
void StackGlutton () {
   char bigArray[10000000];
   ...
}
```

Calling *StackGlutton* causes a stack overflow exception on function entry. The stack is still intact, so you can debug this problem by displaying the Call Stack window, finding the offending function, and noticing that it crashed at function entry. In this example, the problem isn't that the stack is too small but that the automatic data is too large. Don't create a 10-million-byte array on the stack; create the array on the heap or with *VirtualAlloc* instead. If a larger stack is really necessary, you can change the stack size in the Project Settings dialog box by setting the **Stack Allocations Reserve** in the **Output** category of the **Link** tab.

Infinite Recursion

The stack overflows if there is infinite or overly deep recursion because each function call adds to the stack. Here is an example.

```
int InfiniteRecursion () {
   ...
   return InfiniteRecursion();
}
```

Calling *InfiniteRecursion* causes a stack overflow exception after many recursions. Displaying the Call Stack window shows the function that has the infinite recursion, but it can't show its original calling function because it is too far down in the call stack to be displayed. The problem is that the call stack can display a limited number of calls. A simple way to display the entire call stack is to reduce the size of the stack temporarily to force the overflow sooner.

TIP

To debug infinite recursion, reduce the size of your stack temporarily to force the overflow sooner.

Here's a slightly different example.

```
int BigInfiniteRecursion () {
    char midSizedArray[1000];
    ...
    return BigInfiniteRecursion();
}
```

In this case, each function call takes much more stack space than before, so fewer calls are required to blow out the stack. Consequently, displaying the Call Stack window in this situation is likely to display the entire stack.

In the real world, recursion problems aren't usually so obvious. A more realistic example of an infinite recursion looks like this.

```
int InfiniteRecursion1 () {
    ...
    return InfiniteRecursion2();
}
int InfiniteRecursion2 () {
    ...
    return InfiniteRecursion1();
}
```

This example is more realistic because you can't tell there is infinite recursion by looking at each function individually. Another way to obtain infinite recursion in Windows programs is to have two windows procedures send dependent messages to each other, as shown in the following code.

```
HWND hWindow1;    // has WndProc1 for windows procedure
HWND hWindow2;    // has WndProc2 for windows procedure

LRESULT CALLBACK WndProc1 (HWND hWnd, UINT msg, WPARAM wParam,
      LPARAM lParam) {
   if (msg == WM_USER)
      SendMessage(hWindow2, msg, wParam, lParam);
   return DefWindowProc(hWnd, msg, wParam, lParam);
}

LRESULT CALLBACK WndProc2 (HWND hWnd, UINT msg, WPARAM wParam,
      LPARAM lParam) {
   if (msg == WM_USER)
      SendMessage(hWindow1, msg, wParam, lParam);
   return DefWindowProc(hWnd, msg, wParam, lParam);
}
```

Although very deep recursion is not the same as infinite recursion, finite but unbounded recursion, such as traversing a tree that can be of any depth, is potentially just as bad as infinite recursion because you can never be sure you have a big enough stack. When using recursion, you must be able to prove that in all situations the function can be performed within the available stack space. If you can't prove this, use an iterative algorithm instead.

> **TIP**
>
> When using recursion, you must be able to prove that in all situations the function can be performed within the available stack space. If not, use an iterative algorithm instead.

Function Return Corruption

The function return address on the stack can be corrupted if an automatic variable array is written beyond its bounds. Since a stack grows down in memory, overwriting an automatic variable beyond its bounds clobbers the data last pushed on the stack, such as the function return address, the stack base pointer, or even automatic variables of the calling function. Here is a typical example.

```
void StackClobber () {
   char array[100];
   for (int i = 0; i < 110; i++)
      array[i] = 0;
}
```

Calling *StackClobber* causes an access violation exception on function return because the corrupted stack is trying to return the program to an invalid address (in this case using a null pointer). Since the stack has been severely damaged, displaying the Call Stack window won't show a stack. The inability to display the call stack is a sure sign that the function return address and stack base pointer have been clobbered. Perhaps the easiest way to debug this problem is to determine which functions are likely to have the problem and place a breakpoint on the final bracket of each function. The function that crashes on its return is the one with an automatic variable written beyond its bounds. Alternatively, if you have trace statements for function exit, you could check the trace messages to find the last function exited. You can then monitor the arrays within that function to determine which variable is overwritten and where the overwriting happens. Data breakpoints are ideal for this type of debugging.

TIP

Not being able to display the call stack is a sure sign that the function return address has been clobbered.

Function Prototype Mismatches

The stack will be corrupted if there is a mismatch of the function parameters or the calling convention between the called function and the caller, possibly resulting in a corrupted function return address. Type-safe linking prevents most function prototype mismatches, but mismatches are always possible in situations involving function casting, generic function pointers (such as PVOID, FARPROC, or the *GetProcAddress* API), or functions declared using `extern "C"`. For example, in MFC you can handle a user-defined message with the ON_MESSAGE, ON_REGISTERED_MESSAGE, ON_THREAD _MESSAGE, and ON_REGISTERED_THREAD_MESSAGE macros. The ON_ MESSAGE and ON_REGISTERED_MESSAGE macros expect to be given a callback function with the following prototype.

```
afx_msg LRESULT OnMyMessage (WPARAM wParam, LPARAM lParam);
```

Programmers sometimes make the mistake of using this prototype:

```
afx_msg LRESULT OnMyMessage ();
```

Unfortunately, these macros cast the input function, so the compiler won't warn you if there is a mismatch.

The problem is that the caller pushes two parameters on the stack, but the called function doesn't expect any parameters on the stack. This results in the function expecting to find the return address and the last stack base pointer in the wrong location, resulting in an access violation exception when the function returns. Further complicating matters is that such a program works fine with the debug build but crashes with the release build because the debug build uses the EBP register to find the function return address (and the EBP has the correct value), whereas the release build with FPO optimization uses the EBP register for other purposes. The EBP register and FPO are discussed in Chapter 6.

In general, the simplest way to debug this type of problem is to compile your debug builds with the /GZ compiler option. This option checks the stack pointer at the end of the function to make sure it hasn't been changed. If it has, your program receives the failed assertion shown in Figure 9.10.

> **TIP**
>
> Use the /GZ compiler option to detect function prototype mismatches that can lead to stack corruption.

Unfortunately, the debug build of MFC currently does not use the /GZ compiler option. Consequently, the best way to solve the ON_MESSAGE problem is to redefine the ON_MESSAGE macro (in *stdafx.h* after *afxwin.h*) to replace the C-style cast with a C++ `static_cast`, as the code on the next page shows.

```
Microsoft Visual C++ Debug Library                                          ☒

  ⊗   Debug Error!

        Program: ...ROJECTS\WORLDSBUGGIESTPROGRAM\DEBUG\WORLDSBUGGIESTPROGRAM.EXE
        Module:
        File: i386\chkesp.c
        Line: 42

        The value of ESP was not properly saved across a function call. This is usually a result of calling a function declared with one calling
        convention with a function pointer declared with a different calling convention.

        (Press Retry to debug the application)

                        ┌─────────┐   ┌─────────┐   ┌─────────┐
                        │  Abort  │   │  Retry  │   │ Ignore  │
                        └─────────┘   └─────────┘   └─────────┘
```

Figure 9.10   Stack corruption detected using the /GZ compiler option

```
#undef  ON_MESSAGE
#define ON_MESSAGE(message, memberFxn) \
{ message, 0, 0, 0, AfxSig_lwl, \
  (AFX_PMSG) (AFX_PMSGW) (static_cast< LRESULT (AFX_MSG_CALL \
  CWnd::*)(WPARAM, LPARAM) > (&memberFxn)) },
```

With this macro, a wrong function prototype results in a compile-time error, as expected.

Miscellaneous Tips

The following are a few miscellaneous tips that will help you get the most out of debugging memory.

Designing Object Ownership

Part of the process of designing objects should be determining how the objects are created and how they are destroyed. Designing an object's lifetime usually requires determining some kind of ownership, in which one object is made responsible for destroying another object when it is no longer needed. The simplest kind of ownership is an object being destroyed by the object that created it. You must be fully aware of how the objects you are using get destroyed; assuming that it just happens usually results in memory leaks.

Performing Interactive Debugging

As suggested earlier in this chapter and discussed in Chapter 7, you can execute many debug heap diagnostic functions directly from the Watch window. For example, to check the heap for integrity, type the following into the Watch window:

```
{,,msvcrtd.dll}_CrtCheckMemory()
```

This statement is evaluated as soon as you press the Enter key. It is then continuously reevaluated as you step through the program, so it is a simple way to check the memory integrity continuously as you debug your program. Of course, doing this also slows down your program significantly if it allocates thousands of memory blocks. To prevent this statement from being executed, either delete the statement from the Watch window or change the active tab because only the statements on the active tab are evaluated. You can use the same technique to perform other debugging functions as well, such as _CrtSetBreakAlloc, _Crt DumpMemoryLeaks, _CrtMemDumpAllObjectsSince, and _CrtSetDbgFlag.

You can also enter watch statements to monitor the guard bytes or any other diagnostic data interactively as you trace through your program. For example, you can enter the following statements to watch the guard bytes for a *pData* variable:

```
*(((int *)pData) - 1),x
*(int *)(((char *)pData) + sizeof(*pData)),x
```

If you have a debug statement you would like to execute, try to perform it interactively from the Watch window before you modify your code. If you enter any of these statements in the Watch window, however, remember that they continue to be executed as long as they are on the active tab. Don't be surprised if you see a bunch of unexpected output the next time you debug your program.

> **TIP**
>
> You can execute memory debugging statements interactively from the debugger Watch window.

Debugging Nonheap Variables

Although the debug heap does a remarkable job of finding bugs for dynamically allocated variables, it does nothing to help you debug global and automatic variables. For these variables, you are pretty much on your own. If you suspect a global or automatic variable is being corrupted or leaking, you can take advantage of the debug heap by temporarily replacing the variable with a dynamically allocated variable. For example, temporarily replace this global variable

```
CMyObject BuggyGlobal;    // a global variable you suspect has a
                          // problem
```

with the following

```
#define BuggyGlobal     (*pBuggyGlobal)
CMyObject *pBuggyGlobal;

int APIENTRY WinMain (HINSTANCE hInstance, HINSTANCE
     hPrevInstance, LPSTR lpCmdLine, int nCmdShow) {
```

```
    pBuggyGlobal = new CMyObject;
    ...
    delete pBuggyGlobal;
}
```

Consider Using _CrtSetReportMode, _CrtSetReportFile, and _CrtSetReportHook

The C Run-time Library debug heap output is displayed in the Output window, but this default behavior can be changed. You can use the _CrtSetReportMode function to have these trace messages output to message boxes, to the Output window, to a file, or to any combination of these. You can use the _CrtSet ReportFile function to indicate which file to output the report to. In certain circumstances, changing the output destination is useful; for example, you can choose to have trace messages both display in Output window and be written to a log file for testing. Having log files helps your testers provide accurate information in their bug reports.

You might want to have memory corruption be reported with message boxes, but have all other memory problems be reported with trace statements. To accomplish this, you can install the following custom report filter using _CrtSetReportHook.

```
#ifdef _DEBUG
_CRT_REPORT_HOOK pfnOldCrtReportHook = 0;
int CustomReportHook (int reportType, char *message,
        int *pRetVal) {
    if (reportType != _CRT_ASSERT &&
        strstr(message, "DAMAGE") != 0) {
        if (_CrtDbgReport(_CRT_ASSERT, __FILE__, __LINE__, NULL,
            message) == 1)
          _CrtDbgBreak();
    }
    // call the old report hook if there is one
    if (pfnOldCrtReportHook != 0 &&
        (*pfnOldCrtReportHook)(reportType, message, pRetVal))
      return TRUE;

    *pRetVal = 0;  // don't start the debugger
    return FALSE;
}
#endif
```

```
int APIENTRY WinMain (HINSTANCE hInstance, HINSTANCE
    hPrevInstance, LPSTR lpCmdLine, int nCmdShow) {
  DEBUG_ONLY(pfnOldCrtReportHook =
    _CrtSetReportHook(CustomReportHook));

  . . .

}
```

The *CustomReportHook* function checks for reports that aren't assertions (to prevent an infinite loop) and that have the word "DAMAGE" in the message. Any such reports are then displayed using an assertion instead of a trace statement.

Be Aware of Bogus MFC Memory Leaks

Despite its name, *_CrtDumpMemoryLeaks* dumps all allocated memory, so it only really dumps leaks when a program terminates. MFC automatically calls this function when it unloads to display the memory leaks. In some situations, however, a program can load more than one MFC DLL, such as when both the ANSI and Unicode versions of MFC are used. The problem is that memory leaks reported by the first MFC DLL to unload are bogus because the program hasn't terminated, whereas the memory leaks reported by the second MFC DLL to unload are correct. You can quickly determine the DLLs your program uses with the Visual C++ Dependency Viewer utility, and you should try to use only one version of MFC (or any other library) if you can. Check the MSDN problem report Q167929 for more information. By the way, this problem isn't specific to MFC—it can happen to any DLL that calls *_CrtDumpMemoryLeaks*.

Recommended Reading

Cline, Marshall, Greg Lomow, and Mike Girou. *C++ FAQs,* 2nd ed. Reading, MA: Addison-Wesley, 1999.   Chapter 30, The Big Three, presents the Law of the Big Three and its relationship to ownership, copy semantics, and `auto_ptr`s. Chapter 31, Using Objects to Prevent Memory Leaks, discusses why eliminating memory leaks is important, how to prevent them using local objects to manage pointers, the principles of resource management, and other important leak-related concepts.

DiLascia, Paul. "C++ Q & A." *Microsoft Systems Journal*, November 1998.   Presents a helpful description of how the memory-checking features of the Visual C++ C Run-time Library work, as well as other debugging tips.

Lippman, Stanley B., and Josée Lajoie. *C++ Primer,* 3rd ed. Reading, MA: Addison-Wesley, 1998.   Chapter 8, Scope and Lifetime, gives a comprehensive presentation of dynamically allocated objects and arrays as well as a very practical discussion on using `auto_ptr`s.

Meyers, Scott. *Effective C++: 50 Specific Ways to Improve Your Programs and Designs,* 2nd ed. Reading, MA: Addison-Wesley, 1998. Item 5 gives a detailed description of the difference between `delete` and `delete[]`.

Meyers, Scott. *More Effective C++: 35 New Ways to Improve Your Programs and Designs.* Reading, MA: Addison-Wesley, 1996. Item 8 provides a good explanation of the different forms of `new` and `delete`. Items 9, 10, and 11 give an excellent explanation of how to avoid memory leaks in the presence of exceptions.

Pietrek, Matt. "Under the Hood." *Microsoft Systems Journal*, November 1999. Presents the MemDiff utility, which allows you to track all types of memory used by a process, not just dynamically allocated memory. Because this utility is for Windows 2000 only and it can be difficult to interpret the results, you might want to reserve it for desperate situations.

Pietrek, Matt. "Under the Hood." *Microsoft Systems Journal*, June 1998. Presents "Matt's Just Enough Assembly to Get By, Part II" column. This column gives some excellent advice on how to debug when a program crashes on an invalid instruction pointer address. It gives particularly good advice for debugging stack overflows.

Richter, Jeffrey. *Programming Applications for Microsoft Windows: Master the Critical Building Blocks of 32-Bit and 64-Bit Windows-based Applications,* 4th ed. Redmond, WA: Microsoft Press, 1999. Chapter 13, Windows Memory Architecture, is the ultimate resource for understanding how the different versions of Windows partition the virtual memory space and how Windows manages heaps and thread stacks. The book's CD-ROM has the VMMap utility (with source code), which allows you to obtain a detailed virtual memory map for a program.

Robbins, John. "Introducing the Bugslayer: Annihilating Bugs in an Application Near You." *Microsoft Systems Journal*, October 1997. A good overview of using the debugging features of the Visual C++ C Run-time Library. It also presents Mem DumperValidator, which displays and validates memory blocks, and MemStressLib, which selectively fails memory allocations. These utilities fully exercise the run-time library customization hooks.

Stroustrup, Bjarne. *The C++ Programming Language,* 3rd ed. Reading, MA: Addison-Wesley, 1997. Section 14.4, Resource Management, gives an excellent overview of how to prevent resource leaks by taking full advantage of the C++ language. The techniques discussed include resource pointer classes and the `auto_ptr` smart pointer template class.

Chapter 10

Debugging Multithreaded Programs

Threads. It's amazing how such an elegant construct as threads can lead to such difficulties for the poor soul faced with reproducing and diagnosing a problem in a multithreaded program. No matter how simple or straightforward the design, the introduction of just one additional thread into a program can wreak a surprising amount of debugging havoc. The decision to use multiple threads in a program, *at all,* should not be taken lightly.

If you fail to take into account the impact multithreading can have on the correctness of a program and the additional time multithreading can add to the debugging adventures, you would be better off not multithreading in the first place. In this situation, you might consider using Windows timers as an alternative technique for performing background work. However, certain programs can benefits from multithreading. While one thread is performing an I/O-bound operation or doing other things that involve periods of waiting, another thread can use the processor to accomplish its work. If the program is executed on a multiple processor machine, multiple threads can perform their work simultaneously. By using multiple threads in a program you can also prioritize each thread according to your own design demands.

This chapter presents some techniques for safely and effectively navigating the debugging waters in a multithreaded world. As you read it, please keep in mind that the techniques presented here are meant to complement the techniques presented earlier in the book. Multithreaded programs have the same types of bugs that single-threaded programs do, such as the use of uninitialized pointers. Only after ruling out the typical bugs should you start to suspect that a bug is specifically related to multithreading.

What Is Multithreading?

Without trying to replicate a complete text on multithreading (of which there are many available), I present here the basics of threads. I assume that you already have some experience writing multithreaded programs and have read one or more texts on multithreading. You can refer to any of the texts listed in Recommended Reading at the end of the chapter for a full treatment of the topic. I've found that although many programmers have gone through the motions of using critical sections, mutexes, and the other synchronization primitives available to Windows programmers, they haven't fully internalized what's going on at the most fundamental level. To make sure we're all on the same page, I'll define a thread on the Windows platform and briefly explain how the operating system treats threads.

A *thread* represents an execution path through code and is the basic unit of scheduling inside Windows. Windows maintains a data structure for each thread called a *thread information block* (TIB) in which it keeps track of the thread-specific state. This state includes a copy of the processor registers, including the instruction and stack pointers, and information used to make scheduling decisions, such as thread priority and time quantum remaining. At some periodic interval (approximately every 20–40 milliseconds), Windows receives a timer interrupt and uses this opportunity to make scheduling decisions. If the scheduler decides to steal the processor away from the currently executing thread, it saves the current contents of the registers into the TIB, puts the thread back in the scheduling queue, and chooses a new thread to execute. The interrupted thread remains in stasis until it is serviced by the scheduler again.

This thread handling is preemptive, and the preemption is what makes certain multithreading bugs so difficult to reproduce. With different runs of a program, the timing of code execution and the thread context in which execution occurs is likely to change according to the whims of the scheduler. This is why I consider myself lucky to receive an unhandled exception message box. If I can diagnose and fix the problem, it's one less bug that's likely to be shipped to customers. What fills most people with fear is the realization that one is looking at just one of many timing-related bugs—you'll never know how many there actually are.

Issues in Multithreaded Programs

The moment your program goes from a single-threaded program to a multithreaded program, an entirely new class of bugs becomes possible. A *thread-safe* program works correctly in the presence of multiple threads. As with many 12-step programs, the first step a multithreaded programmer takes on the road to rehabilitation is admitting he has a problem, or more accurately, the potential for problems. The following four sections discuss some of the problems that multithreaded programmers must be aware of and deal with.

Race Conditions

A *race condition* is a situation in which the correct outcome of a given operation depends on timing. If all goes well, the outcome is correct. If the scheduler happens to catch you at an inopportune moment, however, the outcome is incorrect. Consider something as simple as incrementing an integer variable.

```
int g_x = 2;   // a global variable
DWORD WINAPI ThreadProc (void *) {
   g_x++;
   return 0;
}
```

If this thread procedure were thread safe, then assuming *g_x* is initialized to 2 and two threads were to execute this thread procedure, the final value of *g_x* must always be 4. If this assertion cannot be made, you haven't written the code correctly. It turns out that this particular function has a race condition and the outcome isn't always correct. The reason is that one C++ statement does not necessarily translate to one assembly instruction. In debug builds, the increment statement would probably compile like this:

```
; Assembly code for g_x++
mov eax, dword ptr [g_x]   ; read contents of g_x into eax register
add eax, 1                 ; increment contents of eax register
mov dword ptr [g_x], eax   ; store result in variable
```

When viewed from the assembly-code level, the race condition becomes more apparent. If Thread A were to execute all three assembly instructions before Thread B had a chance to execute the same sequence, the outcome would be correct. However, if Thread A were to be preempted by the scheduler after reading g_x into its own copy of the EAX register but before storing the incremented value back into memory, then you're in trouble. In this situation, it would be possible for Thread B to read g_x (whose value is still 2) from memory before Thread A could update the variable. If this were to happen, both threads would read g_x while its value was 2, increment its own private copy of the EAX register from 2 to 3, and store the result of 3 back into memory. Because the correctness of the outcome depends on timing, a race condition exists. As you'll soon see, race conditions are the root cause of most multithreading problems. Everything else is just a variation on this theme.

> **TIP**
>
> Race conditions are the root cause of most multithreading problems.

Deadlock

Anytime you write code in which it's possible for one thread to hold ownership of one resource while waiting to acquire ownership of another resource, you have the potential for deadlock. Consider a scenario in which multiple threads operate on bank accounts and a mutex is associated with each bank account that must be acquired before any operations can be performed on that particular account. If a thread wants to operate on just one account, it simply calls *WaitForSingleObject* to acquire the associated mutex, operates on the account as needed, and then calls *ReleaseMutex* to relinquish ownership of the mutex. But what if a thread wants to transfer funds from one account to another? In this situation, the thread must first acquire ownership of two mutexes, one for each account being operated on. Only after acquiring ownership of both mutexes can the transfer be performed safely. Here's what the code might look like.

```
void TransferFromCheckingToSavings () {
    WaitForSingleObject(g_hCheckingMutex, INFINITE);
    WaitForSingleObject(g_hSavingsMutex, INFINITE);
```

```
    // transfer funds...
    ReleaseMutex(g_hSavingsMutex);
    ReleaseMutex(g_hCheckingMutex);
}
```

By itself, this code looks fine. But what if another thread in the system were to call the following slightly different function to transfer funds in the other direction?

```
void TransferFromSavingsToChecking () {
    WaitForSingleObject(g_hSavingsMutex, INFINITE);
    WaitForSingleObject(g_hCheckingMutex, INFINITE);
    // transfer funds...
    ReleaseMutex(g_hCheckingMutex);
    ReleaseMutex(g_hSavingsMutex);
}
```

Given this code, it's possible for one thread to call *TransferFromCheckingTo Savings,* acquire ownership of *g_hCheckingMutex,* and then get preempted. If another thread happens to call *TransferFromSavingsToChecking* at this point, it might acquire ownership of *g_hSavingsMutex* and then become blocked waiting for ownership of *g_hCheckingMutex,* which is owned by the first thread. Eventually, the first thread will resume execution and try to acquire ownership of *g_hSavingsMutex,* which is now already owned by the second thread. At this point, neither thread can proceed. Each is holding a resource that the other thread needs and waiting for a second resource that the other thread already holds. This deadly embrace results in an impasse because there is no way for either thread to proceed. These two threads are deadlocked. And, because it's likely that other threads in the program will eventually reach a point where they need one or both of these mutexes, the program will soon grind to a halt.

▶ **TIP**

Deadlock occurs when two or more threads are holding a resource that another thread needs and are waiting for a second resource that another thread already holds.

Nonreproducibility of Bugs

When a program bug is reported, the first thing most programmers attempt is to reproduce the bug. If the bug happens to be related to timing, reproducing the behavior reported by someone else can be very difficult. Many things influence timing in a multithreaded program: the speed and number of processors in the system, the amount of memory, the amount of available hard disk space, whether a debug or release build of the program is used, whether or not a debugger is attached, and which other programs are running at the same time, no matter how unrelated they may be. Very often you find yourself unable to reproduce the faulty behavior, no matter how detailed the bug report is. Unfortunately, the only defense against this unpleasant experience is to not have any bugs in your program. Because most of us will have a bug at some point, knowing how to cope with bugs that are difficult to reproduce is a required skill.

Exception Handling

Once you add threads to your program, dealing with unhandled exceptions becomes much more difficult. The problem stems from the fact that exception handling is a per-thread activity: While one thread is dealing with an exception, the other threads in the process continue to operate. If an exception goes unhandled in a thread, the entire process shuts down. You can always use the *SetUnhandledExceptionFilter* API function to install a processwide hook that gets called in this situation, but you are still left with the issue of how to respond. Should you record the issue and silently terminate the thread that crashed? Should you regenerate a new thread to carry on for the dying thread? Should you notify the user? If the user of the program decides to terminate the program altogether, how do you perform cleanup procedures? You can't just start accessing data structures and freeing buffers because the other threads in the program are still executing and may be in the middle of operating on those data structures.

The only safe way to attempt shutdown is to somehow signal to all the threads that they need to go through shutdown procedures and then to wait until they've done so. But what if they get into trouble as a result of the original exception? What if one or more of the data structures are in an invalid state as a result of the exception? And how long should you wait for them to finish? These questions have no absolute answers, but you get an idea of just how much more complex multithreaded programming and debugging can be. It's the job of the multithreaded programmer to be aware of these issues and take steps to deal with them.

Writing Thread-safe Code

Windows provides several facilities that you can use to make your programs thread safe. Knowing when to use these tools is the difficult part. I don't want to repeat the material that you can find in any book on multithreaded programming, but I summarize the basic techniques.

Preventing Race Conditions

The first step in preventing race conditions is to identify resources that are shared by multiple threads. Having done this, you must evaluate exactly how the resources are being accessed to determine whether you have the potential for a problem. Consider our earlier example of an integer variable that was being incremented by multiple threads. The potential for problems exists not solely because multiple threads were involved but because multiple threads involved were reading, modifying, and updating the variable. Had multiple threads been merely reading the variable, no preventive measures need be taken.

When the data being shared is as simple as an integer, it's often sufficient to use the interlocked API functions, such as *InterlockedIncrement*. These functions provide atomic increment, decrement, exchange, and conditional exchanges of single 32-bit variables. In this example, the safe way to modify *g_x* would be to call

```
InterlockedIncrement(&g_x);
```

However, if the example thread procedure needed to update two integer variables by calling the following function, simply calling the Interlocked API functions two times is insufficient.

```
long g_cAvailableWidgets = MAX_WIDGETS;   // # free widgets
long g_cUsedWidgets = 0;                   // # used widgets
void TakeWidget () {
   if (g_cAvailableWidgets > 0) {
      // consume a widget...
```

```
        InterlockedDecrement(&g_cAvailableWidgets);
        InterlockedIncrement(&g_cUsedWidgets);
    }
    // else there are no widgets available
}
```

Although each integer variable is updated atomically, there is no guarantee that the test for a nonzero widget count and both subsequent updates will be done together as one uninterruptable operation. To solve this problem, something more sophisticated is necessary. This is where facilities such as critical sections and mutexes come into play.

 TIP

Use the interlocked API functions to perform thread-safe operations on single integer variables.

The critical section and mutex API functions both provide a facility for ensuring single-threaded access to shared resources. The usage model with both is the same: Call a function to acquire exclusive ownership of the lock (critical section or mutex), access the shared resource being protected by that lock, then release the lock. If the lock is already owned by another thread when you try to acquire it, Windows blocks the calling thread inside the function call. Only when the owning thread releases the lock is the blocked thread allowed to acquire the lock and continue execution. If we were to rewrite the *TakeWidget* function shown earlier using a mutex, the code might look something like this.

```
HANDLE g_hWidgetLock = CreateMutex(0, FALSE, 0);
long g_cAvailableWidgets = MAX_WIDGETS;   // # free widgets
long g_cUsedWidgets = 0;                  // # used widgets
void TakeWidget () {
  // before we do anything, acquire the widget lock
  if (WAIT_OBJECT_0 ==
         WaitForSingleObject(g_hWidgetLock, INFINITE))
  {
     if (g_cAvailableWidgets > 0) {
        // consume a widget...
        g_cAvailableWidgets--;
        g_cUsedWidgets++;
     }
```

```
            ReleaseMutex(g_hWidgetLock);    // release the lock
        }
    }
```

The difference between a critical section and a mutex is performance. To acquire ownership of a mutex, a thread calls the *WaitForSingleObject* API function. This is a system call into the kernel, and it requires a processor mode switch from user mode (where programs execute) to kernel mode (where Windows and device drivers execute). If the mutex is currently available, Windows notes that the calling thread is the owner and allows that thread to return immediately from the system call. If the lock is owned, the calling thread is blocked in the kernel. If it turns out that there is rarely any actual contention for a mutex at run time (the threads tend to get ownership without blocking), the overhead of transitioning into kernel mode and back is fairly costly without being strictly necessary.

This is where the critical section comes in. The critical section is like an optimistic mutex. When you call the *EnterCriticalSection* API function to acquire ownership of a critical section, the kernel simply performs an interlocked update on an integer variable inside the CRITICAL_SECTION data structure without transitioning into kernel mode. The purpose of this update is to attempt to claim ownership of the critical section. If it turns out that the critical section was not owned by another thread, the trip to kernel mode can be avoided and the function simply returns to the caller. When there is no contention for the critical section at run time, this optimism results in a significant performance improvement. If the critical section was already owned by another thread, however, the critical section falls back to using an internal event to block the calling thread until ownership can be acquired and a transition to kernel mode is necessary. One limitation of the critical section is that it can only be used to synchronize threads that are in the same process address space. The reason is that it's a normal C++ data structure that internally holds process-relative resources, such as the HANDLE to the event. There is also no way to specify a timeout while waiting for ownership of a critical section or request ownership of more than one critical section simultaneously. On the other hand, mutexes are kernel objects that can be shared by threads in different processes on the same system. Also, the synchronization API functions *WaitForSingleObject* and

WaitForMultipleObjects that are used to acquire ownership of mutexes allow you to specify a timeout or attempt to claim multiple locks at the same time with one function call. Both techniques are important for deadlock prevention.

> **TIP**
>
> Critical sections are more efficient than mutexes when there is no contention for the lock, but they work only within a single process, do not allow you to specify a timeout, and cannot be used to acquire multiple locks.

Preventing Deadlock

Generally, there are two ways to deal with deadlock: Take steps to prevent deadlock or detect and break deadlock. Detecting deadlock is possible, but it typically takes more effort than it's worth because deadlock tends to occur infrequently. Even if the cost of detection were relatively small, the question of what to do remains once a deadlock has been identified. Should Windows arbitrarily designate one thread as the winner and allow it to proceed while giving the other threads some kind of error code, such as a WAIT_DEADLOCK _DETECTED return value? Or should Windows notify all threads that they were involved in a deadlock? Even then, what should the thread do once they've all been notified? Combine these issues with the fact that you can prevent deadlock with little or no overhead and it is clear why prevention is the most frequently employed strategy. Like most operating systems, Windows does not proactively detect or break deadlock, but it does provide some facilities that allow you to prevent deadlock.

When dealing with multiple locks, as in our earlier bank account transfer example, there are three ways you can prevent deadlock from occurring.

- Not using INFINITE timeout periods with the *WaitForSingleObject* API function
- Creating rules to acquire locks in an established order
- Using the *WaitForMultipleObjects* API function

In the example, if a timeout period other than INFINITE were used in the calls to *WaitForSingleObject*, then even if a deadlock occurred, it wouldn't last forever. Once the timeout period elapsed, one or both of the threads would have seen a return value of WAIT_TIMEOUT from its call to *WaitForSingleObject*. Choosing a timeout period is simply a matter of deciding how long you can tolerate deadlock, should it occur. If the period is too small, such as 1 millisecond, the threads will not tolerate momentary contention for the lock. If the period is too large, such as a few minutes, the user may perceive the program as hung and terminate it. Clearly, the selection of an appropriate timeout period is key. Try to choose a value that basically represents "forever" in computer time but that is relatively small and unnoticeable to the user.

TIP

A simple way to prevent deadlocks is to use an appropriate timeout period with the *WaitForSingleObject* API function.

The second alternative is to establish a rule that governs the order in which multiple locks are acquired. This is known as hierarchical lock acquisition. In the example, the difficulty occurred because the *TransferFromCheckingToSavings* and *TransferFromSavingsToChecking* functions tried to acquire the two mutexes in the opposite order. Even with the INFINITE timeout periods, had both functions been written to acquire the checking account mutex followed by the savings account mutex, there would be no potential for deadlock. Although this approach is conceptually simple, it isn't practical in real-world programs. You can easily spot the potential for deadlock in this code because both functions are fairly small, related to one another, located next to each other, and all the locks are acquired together in the same function. But if more than two locks are involved or the acquisition of those locks is spread across several functions, it is much harder to realize that there is a problem.

For example, suppose your program has four shared resources, each protected by a lock (named A through D), in which the order of acquisition must be alphabetical. Consider the following example.

```
void UseAD(){
    Lock(A);
    Lock(D);
    // ... use resources A and D ...
    UseBCD();
    // ... use resources A and D some more ...
    Unlock(D);
    Unlock(A);
}
```

```
void UseBCD(){
    Lock(B);
    Lock(C);
    Lock(D);
    // ... use resources B, C, and D ...
    Unlock(D);
    Unlock(C);
    Unlock(B);
}
```

Both *UseAD* and *UseBCD* follow the protocol for acquiring the locks based on the alphabetical ordering of the lock names, but the potential for deadlock still exists. Suppose there are two threads in this program, and Thread 1 calls *UseAD* while Thread 2 calls *UseBCD*. Depending on timing, the following lock acquisition sequence is possible.

1. Thread 1 calls *UseAD*.
2. Thread 1 acquires lock A.
3. Thread 2 calls *UseBCD*.
4. Thread 2 acquires lock B.
5. Thread 2 acquires lock C.
6. Thread 1 acquires lock D.
7. Thread 1 calls *UseBCD*.
8. Thread 1 blocks trying to acquire lock B (which is owned by Thread 2).
9. Thread 2 blocks trying to acquire lock D (which is owned by Thread 1).

At step 8, Thread 1 is holding locks A and D while waiting to acquire lock B. At step 9, Thread 2 is holding locks B and C while waiting to acquire lock D. At this point, threads 1 and 2 are deadlocked. The bug is at step 8, where Thread 1 tries to acquire lock B out of order. One solution is to recode *UseAD* to release locks A and D before calling *UseBCD* and then reacquire the locks after returning from *UseBCD*. However, this means that the two phases of work being performed on resources A and D by *UseAD* before and after calling *UseBCD* are not done atomically with respect to one another, which may not be correct.

As the number of functions being called while locks are held increases, this type of situation becomes more difficult to prevent. The only way to really *prevent* this type of coding error when using hierarchical lock acquisition is to take the additional measure of mandating that if you want to acquire lock

A and D, you must acquire ownership of locks A, B, C, and D, in that order. Such a requirement reduces the parallelism that can be achieved through multithreading. Because people are not good at following such rules and because the safest solution reduces the benefit of threads, hierarchical lock acquisition isn't always appropriate.

TIP   Hierarchical lock acquisition can prevent deadlock, if used very carefully.

Hierarchical lock acquisition is best suited for platforms that offer no other alternative and for dealing with critical sections (the option I'm about to present works only with mutexes, not critical sections). Windows, however, offers programmers a third alternative to deadlock prevention: the *WaitForMultiple Objects* API function. This function takes as input an array of HANDLEs to kernel objects, a Boolean flag (*fWaitAll*) that tells Windows whether the calling thread wants to block until it acquires one or all of the specified resources, and a timeout period. If this function were used in the bank account transfer example, Windows would ensure that only one thread acquired both mutexes in a safe fashion, without the risk of hold-and-wait. Deadlock also would have been avoided with the use of *WaitForMultipleObjects* in *UseAD* and *UseBCD* because *WaitForMultipleObjects* does not hold any locks internally on your behalf until you can acquire all the requested locks. Perhaps the only downside to this function is that it operates only on kernel objects such as mutexes; there is no equivalent facility for critical sections. The critical section API functions don't include a function like *EnterMultipleCriticalSections*, nor is there a way to extract anything from within a CRITICAL_SECTION data structure that can be used with the *WaitForMultipleObjects* function because only an integer is being operated on in the no-contention scenario.

TIP   The *WaitForMultipleObjects* API function is the most practical and efficient way to prevent deadlocks when using mutexes.

Dealing with Nonreproducibility of Bugs

Unfortunately, there is very little you can do to guarantee that you'll always be able to reproduce any bug reported by a customer, aside from the ideal goal of having a bug-free program. If a program has no timing-related bugs, reproducing bugs is often fairly straightforward. If the user enters some invalid data into a dialog box in a single-threaded program and the program crashes as a result of that data, you should have little trouble reproducing the problem—simply reproduce the user's actions that led to the crash and investigate from there. In a multithreaded program, however, the user's description of what she did to precipitate a problem often is not the only mitigating factor. Timing plays a role. Even worse, the user's actions might be completely unrelated to the problem. Once, a user of a video-conferencing product I was working on logged a bug report with an elaborate and detailed description of the actions leading up to an unhandled exception that crashed the program. This user was very conscientious—and a developer's dream in preparing detailed bug reports. Unfortunately, the crash had nothing to do with the user's actions. The actual cause was that some invalid data came over the network that raised an exception deep within the communications subsystem.

Since you can't predict what timing-related problems your program will have, the best way to deal with nonreproducibility is to accelerate the time to failure for any latent bugs. This means that it's crucial to test your program early and often throughout the entire coding process under conditions that are likely to affect the timing of your program. Specifically, your testing environment should include the following scenarios.

- Test using single as well as multiprocessor systems. Running a program that you believe is thread safe on a multiprocessor system is a sure way to uncover latent synchronization issues. To a lesser extent, running your program on single-processor systems of varying speeds is also useful.

- Test using systems with varying amounts of memory and available hard disk space. The combined availability of physical memory and available hard disk space that can be used for a swap file affects the total amount of virtual memory a program can commit. The less physical memory a system has, the more work Windows must do to manage memory by handling page faults, which tends to slow things down. Large amounts of physical memory reduce page faults, which tends to speed things up.

- Test using varying loads of stress caused by other programs. This means running your program when no other programs are running, as well as when several programs are running. The other programs should vary in terms of the tasks they perform. Programs that require large amounts of memory help stress the virtual memory manager. Programs that are computationally intensive keep the processors busy and help stress the scheduler. Programs that are I/O intensive, such as disk defragmentation tools, or video intensive, such as movie players, help stress other areas of Windows. By testing your program in such circumstances, you more accurately simulate the varied environments that your program will operate in on users' machines.

- Test using both debug and release builds of your program. I've seen organizations spend 18 months developing and testing large products without ever performing a release build of their code until the final four-week "QA cycle" just before the release date. Typically, the first time they create a release build, they turn up numerous compiler errors to resolve before testing could even begin. Inevitably, the QA department then complained that the product was so unstable that they could get through only a small portion of their test suite. Failure to test release builds of a product are on the extreme end of the "asking for trouble" scale. Debug builds typically have all compiler optimizations disabled. Additionally, debug builds include assertions, trace statements, and other diagnostics in the program code as well as in third-party components, such as the C Run-time Library and MFC and ATL framework libraries. Although this debugging code is exceedingly useful, it does affect the timing of the program. It is critical to test release builds (that is, the code that you will ultimately ship to the customer) throughout the development cycle.

> **TIP**
>
> The best way to deal with timing-related problems is to accelerate the time to failure for any latent bugs.

Dealing with Compiler Optimizations

The last suggestion brings up a more general issue in multithreaded development: compiler code generation. Someone once remarked that if you look at the assembly code while you're in the debugger and it makes perfect sense, it wasn't optimized by the compiler. Either someone wrote the assembly code by hand or the compiler's optimizations were disabled. Programmers tend to write assembly code because they need to do something that the programming language doesn't support. But conscientious programmers still write the assembly code so that it makes sense to other people who may read the code later. Although this practice helps maintenance programmers, the code might not be fully optimized. However, the compiler's optimizer uses detailed knowledge of the underlying processor architecture to generate instruction sequences that complement that processor's instruction pipelining, branch prediction, and data-caching mechanisms. Of course, the optimizer tries to do this without changing the intended behavior of the code.

One difficulty with optimizers is that they operate on a small window of code. It's just not feasible for an optimizer to scan the entire body of code and take everything into account to optimize a `for` loop. By reducing the scope of what it looks at, the optimizer can occasionally generate code that doesn't do what you intended it to do. Consider the following example.

```
BOOL g_fExit = FALSE;   // a flag that indicates it's time to exit
// other variables and code here...

DWORD WINAPI ThreadProc (void *) {
    while (!g_fExit) { // see if it's time to exit
       // do something exciting...
    }
}
```

In this code, one or more threads loop around doing something useful as long as the global variable *g_fExit* has not been set to TRUE, which indicates that it's time to exit. This variable is set to TRUE elsewhere in the program by another thread when it's time for the threads to exit. This code works in debug builds because in debug builds the code generated to test the variable's value always refers to the contents of the variable in memory, as shown below; but it might not work in release builds.

```
; unoptimized code generated for while loop
LoopStart:
     cmp dword ptr [g_fExit], 0    ; compare the variable to FALSE
     jne ExitLoop         ; exit loop if flag variable != 0
     ; do something exciting...
     jmp LoopStart        ; go back to the start of the loop
ExitLoop:
```

When optimization is turned on, however, the compiler might generate code that looks like this.

```
; optimized code generated for while loop
mov esi, dword ptr [g_fExit]    ; fetch variable from memory
                                ; into a register
LoopStart:
    cmp esi, 0          ; compare the variable to FALSE.
    jne ExitLoop        ; exit loop if flag variable != 0
    ; do something exciting...
    jmp LoopStart       ; go back to the start of the loop
ExitLoop:
```

In this "optimized" code, the compiler fetches the value of the variable from memory into the ESI register before the start of the loop. This approach makes the references to the variable faster because it's more efficient to read, write, and test register contents than memory contents. If any code within the body of the loop were to set *g_fExit* to TRUE, the compiler would generate code to modify the ESI register, which in turn would cause the loop to exit just as intended. In this code, however, the body of the `while` loop never modifies *g_fExit*—that is done by another thread in the program. Now when that thread sets *g_fExit* to TRUE, it modifies the contents of the memory location where the *g_fExit* variable resides. Because the generated code here tests the value of a per-thread register (ESI), it doesn't notice that the value of the *g_fExit* variable has been changed; so the `while` loop will never stop. At run time, this problem looks like a hang, and the threads executing this "optimized" code will never acknowledge the request to exit.

The solution to this problem is very simple; the difficult part is realizing that the potential for a problem exists. In this situation, you can declare the *g_fExit* variable with the `volatile` keyword, as shown here.

```
BOOL volatile g_fExit = FALSE;
```

The `volatile` keyword instructs the compiler to assume that at any point in the program it is possible that another thread (or process, if the variable happens to be in shared memory) may modify the variable. For such variables, the compiler always generates code to refer to that variable in memory; it never generates code to cache that variable's value in a register. This keyword takes precedence over any optimizations that may otherwise be enabled. As compiler optimizers have become more intelligent, these types of glitches have become rarer; but they remain a very real possibility.

TIP

Use the `volatile` keyword to prevent optimization errors in multithreaded programs.

Preventing Resource Leaks

The C++ language can be a tremendous aid in preventing multithreading problems. One language feature provides more bang for your development buck when it comes to writing thread-safe code: destructors. The C++ language guarantees that the destructor will be called for any fully constructed automatic (local) object when it goes out of scope. In fact, this guarantee applies even in the presence of exceptions. Chapter 9, Debugging Memory, explored the role of destructors and smart pointers in preventing resource leaks. Destructors are just as powerful for writing thread-safe code. The idea is to use constructors and destructors to provide an automatically exception-safe way to acquire and release locks such as critical sections or mutexes. Consider the following example.

```
void DoSomething () {
    EnterCriticalSection(&g_cs);
    UseSharedResource();
    DoSomethingElse();
    LeaveCriticalSection(&g_cs);
}
```

In this example, a CRITICAL_SECTION variable *g_cs* is used to serialize access to a shared resource. Once the critical section is acquired, the code uses the shared resources, some other operations are performed, then the critical section is released before *DoSomething* returns. We need to make sure that the critical section is released, even in the face of exceptions. The way this code is written, the critical section is released only if no exceptions occur. You could put a guarded body around everything, but then you'd be doing something the hard way (in every similar situation throughout the program) that the compiler can do automatically.

By leveraging the C++ language, you use a more elegant solution in the form of an "auto lock" class. Such a class provides, at minimum, a constructor that acquires a particular kind of lock and a destructor that releases that lock. Here's what such a class might look like for a critical section.

```
class CAutoCritSec {
public:
    CAutoCritSec (CRITICAL_SECTION *pcs)
        : m_pcs(pcs) { // cache the naked pointer to the lock
        EnterCriticalSection(m_pcs);   // acquire the lock
    }
    ~CAutoCritSec () {
        LeaveCriticalSection(m_pcs);   // release the lock
    }
private:
    CRITICAL_SECTION *m_pcs;
};
```

This class allows you to rewrite the *DoSomething* function so that it is both thread safe and exception safe.

```
void DoSomething () {
    CAutoCritSec Lock(&g_cs);
    UseSharedResource();
    DoSomethingElse();
}
```

Now the critical section *g_cs* is acquired automatically whenever the *DoSomething* function is entered and the *Lock* constructor is called. Similarly, the *Lock* destructor ensures that the critical section is released when the end of the enclosing block is reached. In this case, the end of the block is the end of the *DoSomething* function. This behavior is true whether *DoSomething* returns normally or through an exception. You can also use block scopes to explicitly delineate areas of your code in which a lock should be held.

Use "auto lock" classes to ensure that locks are always released when a function exits, even when exceptions are thrown.

```
void DoSomething () {
    // ...statements that do not need to be protected by a lock...
    {
        CAutoCritSec Lock(&g_cs);   // lock claimed here
        UseSharedResource();
    } // lock released
    DoSomethingElse();
}
```

Thread Creation and Termination

A few issues related to the startup and shutdown of threads can lead to debugging headaches or subtle problems that are difficult to detect. None of these issues is particularly difficult to deal with, however. You simply need to be aware of the potential problems and code accordingly.

Beware of *TerminateThread*

Calling the *TerminateThread* API function should be considered a last resort when you are trying to shut down a thread. Unfortunately, many programmers consider *TerminateThread* the natural counterpart to the *CreateThread* API function. The thinking is "I created a thread, and now I need to shut it down. The *CreateThread* function returned a HANDLE to me. *TerminateThread* takes a HANDLE to a thread. Therefore, I'll use *TerminateThread* to stop and clean up my thread." It's difficult to fault that logic, but calling *TerminateThread* has a couple of undesirable side effects. The first problem is that the *Terminate Thread* function doesn't free the thread's stack (which is allocated by the *Create Thread* function), so calling *TerminateThread* guarantees that the program will leak memory.

The second problem with *TerminateThread* concerns DLLs. Whenever a thread is created within a process, Windows notifies every DLL in the process about the new thread by calling *DllMain* with a DLL_THREAD_ATTACH reason code. Many DLLs use this notification to allocate per-thread resources that are needed if that thread calls the DLL. Conversely, any time a thread exits, Windows notifies every DLL in the process by calling *DllMain* with a DLL_THREAD _DETACH reason code. The DLLs that maintain per-thread state can use this notification to flush any persistent information to disk or database, then release any resources that were acquired on behalf of that thread. If *TerminateThread* is used, however, the thread is immediately stopped and the DLLs aren't notified, again resulting in leaked resources.

The reason for this *TerminateThread* behavior is that Windows assumes you will use this function only in situations where the normal termination and cleanup procedures cannot be used, such as when the thread has gone into an infinite loop and is no longer responding to normal commands. In these situations, it's unlikely that Windows can successfully force such threads to change contexts and call a series of *DllMain* entry points, thus risking the stability of the process.

When it's time to stop a thread, the appropriate action is to request the thread to exit under its own power, performing any necessary cleanup on the way out. This request can take the form of a message posted to the thread, an event signaled using the *SetEvent* API function, or even something as simple as setting a Boolean variable. The controlling code that makes this request can then use the thread's handle in a call to *WaitForSingleObject* to wait until Windows confirms that the thread has exited its thread procedure. If you use a non-INFINITE timeout period to perform this wait, you will be able to identify "zombie" threads that have become unresponsive. Assuming you've waited a reasonable amount of time, *TerminateThread* might be the right choice if your call to *WaitForSingleObject* times out. I usually advise people to use what I call the Grand Jury Rule of Thumb for Thread Termination: If you want to call *TerminateThread*, be prepared to justify your actions to a jury of your Windows programmer peers. If it turns out to be justifiable "threadicide," so be it. But if you can't convince anyone that you took reasonable measures beforehand, you're in trouble.

TIP

Use *TerminateThread* only as a last resort because it can result in resource leaks.

Creating Threads

A more general issue related to thread initialization and cleanup stems from the use of the C Run-time Library, MFC, or any third-party libraries. The C Run-time Library and MFC both provide thread creation functions, and many programmers

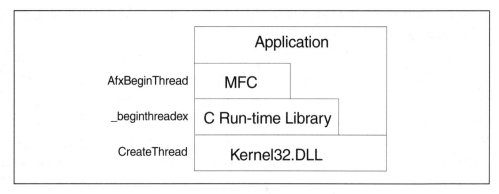

Figure 10.1   Thread creation alternatives

either don't know they exist or ignore them altogether. If you fall into either camp, you're destined to have some problems. Figure 10.1 shows the location of the various thread creation functions that a programmer might call.

All thread creation functions eventually call CreateThread, which is an API function provided by Windows. Each variation, however, provides an important "value-added" layer on top of the one below it. For example, the C Run-time Library _beginthreadex[1] function allocates some per-thread data, then calls *CreateThread*. However, _beginthreadex doesn't pass the program-defined thread procedure address into *CreateThread*. Instead, _beginthreadex passes the address of a thread procedure implemented within the run-time library itself. When Windows creates and starts a new thread, the run-time library's thread procedure is invoked. This function stores the pointer to the previously allocated per-thread data in thread-local storage and then sets up a guarded body around a call to the program-defined thread procedure using __try/__except. When the thread procedure returns, the run-time library calls _endthreadex, which cleans up and releases the per-thread data.

---

[1] There is also a function named _beginthread in the C Run-time Library, but its usage is quite different from the underlying *CreateThread* API function. For example, it's common to keep the thread handle that is returned and later use *WaitForSingleObject* to wait until the thread has completed shutting down, then possibly retrieve the thread's exit code. This technique is supported using _beginthreadex. If _beginthread is used, however, the thread handle is automatically closed when the thread exits, thereby rendering the saved thread handle invalid. In general, the _beginthreadex function is preferable.

If you call *CreateThread* directly and the new thread subsequently calls functions provided by the C Run-time Library, the run-time library is forced to bootstrap the required per-thread data the first time the thread calls a run-time library function. If you use the statically linked version of the C Run-time Library, the required cleanup procedures are bypassed because your thread exits directly back to Windows. It turns out that the DLL version of the run-time library is still able to perform the necessary per-thread cleanup because it receives the DLL_THREAD_DETACH notification like any other DLL. At this point it should be clear that if you use *TerminateThread*, those cleanup procedures will never be called. I should also mention that if a thread reaches a point where it wants to commit "suicide" instead of continuing to exit, the _endthreadex function should be used instead of the *ExitThread* API function. If you call *ExitThread*, you bypass all the C Run-time Library cleanup for that thread (unless you're using the DLL version of the run-time library, which can handle this scenario).

Aside from preventing resource leaks, it is important to use _beginthreadex instead of *CreateThread* if you are calling the C Run-time Library `signal` or `raise` functions. If you call `raise` from within a thread that was created using *CreateThread*, that thread incurs an unhandled exception. This is because support for signals is implemented by the C Run-time Library using Windows structured exception handling.

A similar situation exists in MFC. The MFC library provides two overloaded versions of a function named *AfxBeginThread*. One version takes a pointer to a thread procedure and the other takes an MFC run-time type information (RTTI) class structure of a class derived from *CWinThread*. Aside from these differences, *AfxBeginThread* provides some necessary value-added initialization and cleanup for threads that use MFC. As with the C Run-time Library, many MFC functions and classes assume the existence of per-thread state specific to MFC. If that state is not there (because *AfxBeginThread* wasn't used), you're likely to have trouble. As with the C Run-time Library, threads created using *AfxBeginThread* must return to MFC on exit so that MFC can perform any necessary cleanup before allowing the C Run-time Library to perform its cleanup. If a thread that was created with *AfxBeginThread* wants to commit "suicide," it's important that the *AfxEndThread* function be used instead of either _endthreadex or *ExitThread*. By not calling *AfxEndThread*, you're by-passing MFC's per-thread cleanup.

The best rule of thumb to use in thread creation is "when in Rome, do as the Romans." If you are using a library or framework, see what functions the library provides to create threads. If you use them, chances are you'll save yourself a lot of debugging hassles later on. If you're using multiple libraries, use the highest layer of value-added functionality.

> **TIP**
>
> Use the highest-level thread creation functions to prevent resource leaks and unhandled exceptions.

Terminating MFC Threads

I have one final suggestion on the use of MFC's *CWinThread* class and proper shutdown procedures. One version of the *AfxBeginThread* function takes a pointer to a thread procedure that you implement. This version behaves much like _beginthreadex in that it sets up some MFC-specific thread-local data, then calls the thread procedure. When the thread procedure returns, MFC goes through some shutdown procedures that I'll describe momentarily. This version also creates a *CWinThread* object and returns its pointer from *AfxBeginThread*. The other version of *AfxBeginThread* takes the RUNTIME_CLASS class struc-ture of your *CWinThread*-derived thread class, instantiates it using `new`, then calls the *InitInstance* method on that object, which you must override or the thread exits immediately. If *InitInstance* returns TRUE, MFC invokes the *Run* method, which most programmers don't override. The default implementation of *Run* executes a message pump until a WM_QUIT message is posted to that thread. When this event occurs, *Run* invokes the *ExitInstance* method and then proceeds with MFC's thread shutdown procedures.

Many MFC programmers have trouble getting these threads to shut down cleanly and knowing when that shutdown is complete. If you aren't using MFC, you have the thread handle returned by *CreateThread* or _beginthreadex. When you want to stop a non-MFC thread, you request it to exit using your favorite technique and then call *WaitForSingleObject* on the thread handle until Win-dows confirms that the thread has exited. The same basic procedure must be carried out when you're using MFC's thread creation mechanism, but the implementation is a little more involved due to MFC's added layer of abstraction. The questions to be addressed when shutting down an MFC thread are these:

- What is the best way to notify a thread that you want it to exit?
- How can you determine when Windows has confirmed that the thread has finished exiting?
- How do you obtain the thread's exit code once it has exited?
- What deletes the *CWinThread* object?

The best way to notify an MFC thread that you want it to exit depends on the version of *AfxBeginThread* you used. If you passed the address of a thread procedure to *AfxBeginThread*, you can use any shutdown technique you like. You can design your thread procedure so that it monitors a Windows event object or looks for a Boolean flag to get set. You could also design your thread procedure to run a message pump and look for a particular message that you post using *PostThreadMessage* (although if you want a thread with a message pump, you're better off using the other version of *AfxBeginThread*). If you use the version of *AfxBeginThread* that accepts a RUNTIME_CLASS class structure of a *CWinThread*-derived class and you're not overriding the *Run* member function, the correct way to tell the thread to shut down is to post a WM_QUIT message to that thread. From another thread, this can be accomplished by calling

```
pThread->PostThreadMessage(WM_QUIT, 0, 0);
```

If the thread wants to force itself to exit, it should call *PostQuitMessage*. In either case, MFC's implementation of *Run* exits its message pump when *PeekMessage* or *GetMessage* returns FALSE as a result of the WM_QUIT message, calls your *ExitInstance* method, and then continues to shut down.

The way to determine when an MFC thread has finished exiting is the same as with a non-MFC thread: Use *WaitForSingleObject* on the thread handle. The wrinkle is that the thread handle is hidden inside the *CWinThread* class. Since the handle is a public data member, you can access it directly; so that's not a problem. The only glitch is that the *CWinThread* destructor, which is called in the context of the thread that's being shut down, calls *CloseHandle* on the thread handle. If you're trying to use that thread handle in a call to *WaitForSingleObject*, the handle is invalid at this point, which causes *WaitForSingleObject* to return with a WAIT_FAILED error value. Depending on timing, the thread may or may not have finished exiting back to Windows yet. Since you no longer have a valid handle to the thread, you're incapable of determining its exit code.

The following function demonstrates the proper way to shutdown an MFC thread.

```
DWORD StopWinThread (CWinThread *pThread,
                        DWORD dwTimeout = INFINITE) {
    HANDLE hThread = 0;
    ::DuplicateHandle( GetCurrentProcess(), pThread->m_hThread,
                        GetCurrentProcess(), &hThread, 0, FALSE,
                        DUPLICATE_SAME_ACCESS );
    pThread->PostThreadMessage(WM_QUIT, 0, 0);
    ::WaitForSingleObject(hThread, dwTimeout);
    DWORD nExitCode = 0;
    ::GetExitCodeThread(hThread, &nExitCode);
    ::CloseHandle(hThread);
    return nExitCode;
}
```

Although error checking has been omitted for brevity, this function demonstrates the steps necessary to safely request a thread to exit, wait until Windows confirms that the thread has exited, and return that thread's exit code. Because the *CWinThread* destructor invalidates *m_hThread* with a call to *CloseHandle*, first call the *DuplicateHandle* function to get a new handle to the same underlying thread object, which increments the system-maintained reference count for that object. Then call the *PostThreadMessage* method on the thread object to initiate MFC's shutdown procedures for that thread. Next, call *WaitForSingleObject* using the duplicate thread handle to block until the thread finishes exiting. Once that's been confirmed, call *GetExitCodeThread* to obtain the exit code, close the duplicate thread handle, and return the exit code to the caller.

Deleting the thread object is pretty straightforward, although it's not obvious from the MFC documentation. By default, the *AfxEndThread* function calls a virtual member function defined in the *CWinThread* class named *Delete*. The default implementation of this function calls `delete this` if the *m_bAutoDelete* data member is TRUE. If you make no changes to the default settings, all your *CWinThread* objects self-destruct whenever *AfxEndThread* is called (either by you or by the MFC cleanup code). Consequently, in the *StopWinThread* function, you are assured that once *WaitForSingleObject* confirms that the thread has exited, the *CWinThread* object wrapping the thread has been deleted, and you don't have to (nor should you) delete the object.

If you don't want the *CWinThread* object to self-destruct, you have a couple of options. The simplest technique is to set *m_bAutoDelete* to FALSE anytime before requesting the thread to stop. You might do this within your *CWinThread*-derived class constructor or from another thread (it's a public data member). For example, you could use this technique to eliminate the need to call *DuplicateHandle* in the *StopWinThread* function. Here's an alternative implementation that accomplishes the same thing.

```
DWORD StopWinThread (CWinThread *pThread,
                     DWORD dwTimeout = INFINITE) {
  pThread->m_bAutoDelete = FALSE;  // disable self-destruction
  pThread->PostThreadMessage(WM_QUIT, 0, 0);
  ::WaitForSingleObject(pThread->m_hThread, dwTimeout);
  DWORD nExitCode = 0;
  ::GetExitCodeThread(pThread->m_hThread, &nExitCode);
  delete pThread;  // delete the MFC thread object
  return nExitCode;
}
```

Before the thread is asked to stop, *m_bAutoDelete* is set to FALSE. This causes the *Delete* member function to skip calling `delete` on the thread object. Since the *CWinThread* destructor is what invalidates the thread handle by calling *CloseHandle*, you can now safely use *m_hThread* in the calls to *WaitForSingle Object* and *GetExitCodeThread*. Once you've made sure the thread has exited and obtained its exit code, simply call `delete` to delete the thread object.

If you don't want the *CWinThread* object to self-destruct, your second option is to call *AfxEndThread* with a second argument of TRUE from within the context of the thread (remember, this function commits thread "suicide"). The documentation for *AfxEndThread* shows only a single *nExitCode* parameter to this function; but if you look at the prototype for *AfxEndThread* in its header file, you'll see that there is a second parameter named *bDelete* that defaults to TRUE. If you want the thread to exit right away without deleting the *CWin Thread* object, the thread can simply call the following:

```
AfxEndThread(exitCode, FALSE);
```

where the first parameter is the exit code for the thread and it can be any value you choose.

Understanding the Debugger

Aside from the development issues, it's important to understand exactly how the debugger interacts with a multithreaded program and with Windows. Often just knowing how the debugger works can make the difference between a successful debug session and a sleepless night of hair-pulling frustration. Understanding this interaction isn't as important when you're debugging a single-threaded program, but the debugging landscape is much different when multiple threads are involved. Knowing how all the players interact reduces the amount of time you spend with the debugger drawing incorrect conclusions and chasing phantoms.

TIP

Understanding how the debugger interacts with a multithreaded program prevents frustration and hair loss.

To begin with, there are generally two types of debuggers: application-level debuggers and system-level debuggers. Application-level debuggers are normal Windows applications that can be used to debug applications only (as opposed to kernel-mode drivers). What makes them debuggers is that they use a portion of the Windows API that is specifically intended for debuggers. The most notable feature of an application-level debugger is that when you break into the debugger, only the process that is being debugged and any processes it may have spawned are suspended. No other processes on the machine are affected. Visual C++ has an application-level debugger, which is the type of debugger I characterize here. However, system-level debuggers have a more intimate relationship with the kernel and usually include at least one kernel-mode driver component. You can use system-level debuggers to debug applications as well as drivers. When you break into a system debugger, every process on the machine (aside from the debugger itself) is suspended, including any kernel-mode threads. Such debuggers offer greater visibility into all aspects of system activity but are more intrusive to the operation of the machine as a whole. Microsoft's WinDbg and Compuware NuMega's SoftICE are good examples of system debuggers.

Debugger, Operating System, and Program Interaction

There are three ways to initiate a debugging session with Visual C++. The first, and probably most common, technique is to load a project workspace and choose the **Go** command in the **Build|Start Debug** menu. When you do this, Visual C++ uses the *CreateProcess* API function with the *dwCreationFlags* parameter set to include the DEBUG_PROCESS flag to launch your program. The second approach is to attach to a process that's already running. You can do this by choosing the **Attach to Process** command in the **Build|Start Debug** menu. This command causes Visual C++ to present a list of processes that you can choose from. After you make a selection, Visual C++ calls the *Debug ActiveProcess* API function, passing the process ID that you selected. Third, in Windows 2000 you can run the Task Manager, select the process you want to debug, and choose the **Debug** command in the context menu. In all cases, no matter how you attach the debugger to a program, one thing is the same: The debugger is welded to the "debuggee." There is no way to detach the debugger from a process. Once attached, there is a permanent link between the debugger and the program and there is no way to stop the debugging session without terminating the program. This is a limitation of the debugging API in Windows.

Windows debugging support uses an event-driven model. Once a debugger has attached to a program, it uses the *WaitForDebugEvent* API function to block until a debug event happens in the program. Whenever a debugging event occurs, Windows suspends all the threads in the program being debugged and passes the event to the debugger. At this point, the debugger handles the event as it chooses (for example, a breakpoint was hit, and the debugger must display the relevant source code). Once the event has been handled, the debugger uses the *ContinueDebugEvent* function to tell Windows to resume the program. At this point the program threads resume, and they continue execution. This process repeats until the debugging session terminates. Figure 10.2 illustrates the interaction of the principal players.

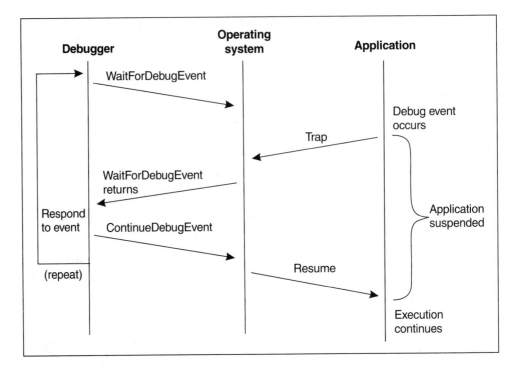

Figure 10.2   Debugger, operating system, and program interaction

From the moment a debug event occurs in the program until the debugger calls *ContinueDebugEvent* to resume the program, the program is completely suspended. So just what is classified as a debug event? Windows defines the set of debug events shown in Table 10.1, each of which causes the program to suspend and the debugger to be notified. Again, if any one of the events listed in Table 10.1 occurs in the process being debugged or in any process it may have spawned, the entire program is suspended and the debugger is notified. Only when the debugger has handled the event and called *ContinueDebugEvent* does the program continue to execute. For the programmer debugging a multi-threaded program, there are several very important implications of this process, most of which relate to the Heisenberg Uncertainty Principle.

Unexpected Thread Serialization

If you've survived at least one multithreaded project, you've learned that there's nothing like a release build running on a variety of platforms to test the correctness of your thread synchronization code. Most people understand that tim-

Table 10.1   Debug events received by *WaitForDebugEvent*

Event	Description	Typical Debugger Response
Exception	An exception was raised. Any processor-generated exception, such as a memory access violation, or programmer-generated exception (generated with *RaiseException, throw,* or *DebugBreak*) is passed to the debugger using this event type. Breakpoints are implemented using a breakpoint exception, so this is the event the debugger receives whenever a breakpoint is executed.	For first-chance notifications, log to output window and pass back to program. For last-chance notifications, break.
Thread start/exit	A thread was started or has exited.	Update internal list of threads, then continue.
Process start/exit	A process was launched or has exited.	Update internal list of processes, then continue.
DLL load/unload	A dynamic link library was loaded or unloaded.	Try to load debugging symbols for DLL, update internal list of loaded modules, convert "virtual" breakpoints that were set in the DLL before it was loaded into actual breakpoint, then continue.
OutputDebugString	The *OutputputDebugString* function was called to log some text in the debugger's output window.	Log string to output window, then continue.

ing can be significantly different between release and debug builds of a program due to compiler optimizations and the absence of debug code that's been conditionally compiled out of release builds. But why should the same debug build behave differently if you're running inside or outside control of the debugger? The answer has to do with the fundamental nature of the interaction between the debugger, Windows, and the program. Any time a debug event occurs, the program being debugged is suspended, and control is transferred to the debugger.

The most common debug event specific to debug builds is generated by the *OutputDebugString* API function. Most programmers use some type of trace statement to print diagnostic messages to the **Debug** tab of the Output window. When threads in a multithreaded program make calls to *OutputDebugString*, however, they're serialized on the same shared resource, namely, the debugger. If calls to *OutputDebugString* were not serialized, the debug output originating from different threads would become garbled and fairly useless. Therefore, threads that would otherwise run independently of one another when running outside the control of the debugger execute in lock-step fashion whenever more than one thread calls *OutputDebugString* simultaneously. If you're trying to diagnose a multithreading problem that's caused when the timing is just right, running the program from the debugger is almost certain to change the timing so significantly that the problem doesn't arise or maybe takes much, much longer to reproduce.

TIP

Calling *OutputDebugString* or any trace statement has the side effect of serializing threads, but only when the program is run from the debugger.

One solution is to define your own custom trace macro and have it conditionally compiled based on the presence of a preprocessor symbol other than _DEBUG. You don't necessarily have to roll your own implementation of a trace macro; you can simply define an alternate name for an existing trace macro. The following example illustrates the basic idea.

```
#ifdef DBGTRACEON
#define DBGTRACE(_exp) ATLTRACE(_exp)   // just use ATL's trace
                                        // mechanism
#else
#define DBGTRACE(_msg)
#endif
```

This macro allows you to create the debug build of your program with trace output compiled out, which eliminates the unwanted serialization of calling

OutputDebugString without abandoning the other benefits of using the debug build, such as debugging symbols, and assertion statements. Of course, if you were depending on trace messages to diagnose the problem, you've just removed your primary debugging aid. This is an excellent reason not to use trace statements as your primary debugging tool for multithreaded programs.

TIP

By conditionally removing trace statements using a symbol other than _DEBUG but leaving all other debugging support, you can improve your ability to debug multithreading programs.

Another approach can be useful in certain circumstances in which the trace output is important to the diagnosis of the problem: Use per-thread trace buffers instead of *OutputDebugString*. Each thread would have its own circular buffer in memory where trace messages are stored. Because each thread has its own buffer, locks need not be held while writing trace strings into the buffer. Because the *OutputDebugString* function is not being used to interact with a debugger, the program's timing is not affected by the act of tracing. Once the problem has surfaced, each thread's trace buffer can be displayed in the debugger or saved to disk for later viewing and analysis.

Thread Context Confusion

Let's examine what happens when a breakpoint exception occurs and you proceed to step through code to investigate. When a breakpoint is reached, an exception debug event is generated, and all threads in the process are suspended. You might look around, do some investigating, then give the **Go** command to continue until the next breakpoint. You might decide to single step through the code using both the **Step Into** and **Step Over** commands. When you single step, the debugger effectively places a temporary breakpoint on the next line of code, then resumes the program. At this point, all threads in the program run full speed until the next debug event occurs. The next debug event may or may not be the temporary breakpoint on the next line of code. If you're lucky, when the debugger regains control, you'll find yourself in a very different location in the code, which makes it obvious that you've changed contexts. If you're unlucky, when the debugger regains control, you'll find yourself at the next line of code or perhaps the next breakpoint a few lines away. This situation can be very confusing.

If you're debugging a multithreaded program and stepping through code that can be called by multiple threads, *you cannot assume that you're in the context of the thread you were in a moment ago.* If multiple threads can call the function you're stepping through, any one of them may have triggered the breakpoint. Depending on the commands you're using to step through code, the behavior may change. For example, if you have set breakpoints and are using the **Go** command to run the program until the next breakpoint, any thread may trigger one of your breakpoints. If you're using the **Step Into** and **Step Over** commands, Visual C++ sets a temporary breakpoint on the next line of code that fires only when the current thread executes that line of code. Even in this situation, however, when you use the **Step Over** command, only the thread you're currently in triggers *that* breakpoint. This doesn't prevent other threads from executing and possibly triggering other breakpoints. You must be aware of this behavior if you hope to avoid the inevitable confusion caused by a thread context switch.

TIP

When stepping through code that can be called by multiple threads, you cannot assume that you're in the context of the thread you were in a moment ago.

What can you do to avoid being confused by thread context switches? Do what pilots do to avoid confusion: Always keep one eye on the dials. For us, those dials are the Visual C++ debug windows. The following debug windows always display their information based on the current thread whenever you break into the debugger.

- The Watch window
- The Call Stack window
- The Variables window
- The Registers window

The best window to watch is the Variables window because you're likely to have that window visible already to monitor the values of local variables as you step through code. Imagine the worst-case scenario: You've set a couple breakpoints inside a function that can be called from many thread contexts. If the breakpoint is in a thread procedure, the Call Stack window won't be much help because the call stack looks the same no matter which thread triggered the breakpoint. Chances are good, though, that the local variables on the stack are different for each thread, so it's easy to detect a context switch if you notice that a variable's value suddenly changed even though you didn't execute any code that modifies it. The debugger provides an additional hint by drawing recently changed variable values in red, so you really only have to watch the red values to detect a context switch as you step through the code. If the breakpoint is not inside a thread procedure but inside a function called by many threads, the Call Stack window is likely to be different for each thread, thus reflecting the code path those threads took to reach the breakpoint.

TIP

Keep your eye on the Variables window values. If the values change to red unexpectedly, most likely you have detected a thread context switch.

However, this technique does not always work. Sometimes the local variable values don't differ from thread to thread, so they can't be used to determine the thread context. In this situation, your only recourse is to use the **Threads** command in the **Debug** menu. This command displays the Threads dialog box, which displays a list of threads currently executing inside the debugged process. The current thread has an asterisk in the far left column and is highlighted when the dialog box is first displayed. Unfortunately, this dialog box is modal, so you can't leave it floating above a source window or dock it at the edge of the workspace. Consequently, you must dismiss the dialog box before you can continue debugging.

TIP

You can use the Threads dialog box to determine the current thread, but it's a nuisance.

Unexpected Timeouts

Another insidious side effect of using a debugger stems from the fact that time doesn't stand still while the program is stopped in the debugger. This situation can adversely affect any threads that are making blocking system calls with any timeout period other than INFINITE. If such a thread happens to be blocked in the kernel waiting for some event to occur or for its timeout to elapse when you break into the debugger elsewhere, it's possible that the moment you proceed to execute the program the thread will timeout. This may happen because the time you spend looking around in the debugger, inspecting variables, analyzing the call stack, and scratching your head counts against the timeout specified by the thread. Timeout periods are measured in real time, not active processing time, so the clock is always running. If you break into the debugger while a thread is blocked, depending on the timeout period and how long you spend looking around in the debugger, it's possible that the block will timeout un-expectedly. Consequently, what might ordinarily be considered an extraordinary timeout condition can happen quite easily while debugging.

> **TIP**
>
> Timeout periods are measured in real time, not active processing time, so the clock is always running. Any time spent looking around in the debugger counts toward the timeout period.

Debugging Techniques

Now that we've explored the most common issues associated with multi-threaded development and have a firm understanding of how multithreaded programs interact with the debugger, let's look at some techniques for effective debugging in this hostile debugging environment.

Assessing the Situation

When you're dealing with a bug that is easily reproducible, it's not too difficult to zero in on the location of the buggy code. This is especially true if the bug is revealed by an unhandled exception because the debugger shows you where to investigate. Sometimes the domain of your program is quite large, however, and the bug you're hunting seems to show itself only when you're not looking. In these situations, it's useful to make a careful high-level assessment of the problem before you start looking at call stacks and registers in the debugger. Your goal is to determine the likelihood that the problem you're debugging is related to multithreading as opposed to some other problem, such as invalid user input.

If the problem appears to be related to timing, you might be able to focus on a smaller area within the code. Here are some questions you might ask yourself, as well as the clues the answers to those questions might provide.

- Is the bug reproducible using both debug and release builds? If not, you might be dealing with a race condition that is affected by the presence or absence of debug build code, such as assertions, trace statements, and other debugging code.

- Is the bug reproducible in the debugger? Given the often intrusive inter-action between the debugger and your program, bugs that occur only within the debugger or outside the debugger are a sign that you've got a timing-related problem that is exacerbated by the presence or absence of the debugger. Sometimes running a program outside the debugger speeds things up enough to uncover the bug. In this case, put your program through its paces outside the debugger and then attach the debugger to your program only after the bug surfaces. Conversely, some-times running the program within the debugger slows things down enough to uncover the bug. In this case, test your program from within the debugger.

- Does the bug occur only on a specific computer? A bug that surfaces only on a multiprocessor machine is a sure sign that you have a multithreading bug.

- What are the symptoms of the bug? Is an exception being thrown, such as an access violation? Or does the system appear to hang? Is the bug preceded by one or more first-chance exception notifications in the **Debug** tab of the Output window?

Answering these questions before you dive in probably won't reveal the exact source code that caused the bug, but the mental exercise might allow you to focus on a smaller set of likely causes. The answers might also give you a better idea of what to try first once you start using the debugger. For example, if the bug is preceded by one or more first-chance exception notifications, you might start by investigating those exceptions using the procedure described in Chapter 5, Using Exceptions and Return Values. Those exceptions might be pre-cipitating events that result in the bug.

TIP

> Before debugging multithreaded code, determine if the problem is build, debugger, system, or processor dependent. This information will give you a bet-ter idea of what to try first once you start using the debugger.

Getting Your Bearings

Assuming the nature of the bug is not obvious, once you start using the debugger, it's important to get your bearings before you start blindly trudging through the code. I prefer to approach the situation like a detective that has just walked onto a crime scene: Survey the scene without touching anything and build a mental picture of what happened. In a single-threaded program, this means looking at the call stack, inspecting the values of variables or registers, and looking at the source code. In a multithreaded program, you must also consider the other threads. Since much of the information available to you is per-thread data, such as the call stack, it's often enlightening to understand each thread's activities, starting with the current thread. What does the call stack look like for the current thread? Was an exception raised or is this thread blocked waiting for something to happen? If this thread crashed, what was it doing at the time?

If the thread was manipulating data that is shared by multiple threads, you must determine what those other threads are doing now. Use the Threads dialog box to switch to the other threads and look at each thread's current code location, call stack, variables, and registers. You might be able to identify another thread that is currently manipulating the same data the buggy thread was using. If you find such a thread, this indicates a thread synchronization problem, and it should pinpoint the area in the source code to investigate. Perhaps no critical section or mutex was used or the critical section or mutex that is supposed to be used wasn't acquired by one of the threads involved. The answers to these questions should put you back on the track to thread-safe code.

> **TIP** Use the Threads dialog box to examine other threads to see if any are manipulating the same data the buggy thread was using.

Watching the Thread ID in Windows 2000

If you are debugging on an Intel architecture platform in Windows 2000, a very useful thread identification technique is at your disposal. Chapter 7, Debugging with the Visual C++ Debugger, noted that the Visual C++ debugger has various pseudo-registers. The @TIB psuedo-register is a pointer to the thread information block. In the May 1996 of his "Under the Hood" column, Matt Pietrek documents the first several fields of this data structure. The most interesting TIB field for debugging multithreaded programs is the *threadID*, which is offset 0x24 bytes from the top of the TIB data structure. This field contains the systemwide unique thread ID for the current thread, which is the same value that would be returned if the thread called *GetCurrentThreadId*. Armed with this knowledge, it's easy to display the current thread ID by entering the expression "dw(@TIB + 0x24)" in the Watch window. This expression causes the Watch window to display the DWORD located at byte offset 0x24 from the top of the TIB for the current thread. This Watch expression eliminates the need to display the Threads dialog box, check the current thread, and dismiss the dialog box every time you want to double-check which thread context you're currently in. It also means you have to monitor only one expression in the Watch window while you're debugging.

TIP If you are debugging in Windows 2000, enter the expression "dw(@TIB + 0x24)" in the Watch window to monitor the current thread ID.

Watching the Thread ID in Windows 98

If you are debugging in Windows 98, you can use the TIB pseudo-register, but it's not quite as straightforward as it is for Windows 2000. In Windows 98, the TIB data structure doesn't include a *threadID* field, as it does in Windows 2000. Instead, the implementation of *GetCurrentThreadId* on Windows 98 returns a pointer to the calling thread's TIB XORed with an "obfuscator" value that is determined each time Windows 98 boots. It appears that this is a defensive measure to prevent programmers from getting their hands directly on a pointer to this important data structure. Because each thread has its own TIB, the TIB pointer is a systemwide unique number and can serve as a thread ID. By XORing a unique number with a constant value, the resulting number is still guaranteed to be unique; but it's no longer a pointer value.

Since you know that the @TIB pseudo-register points to the current thread's information block, you need only figure out the obfuscator value for the current boot of the machine. If you can determine the obfuscator value, you should be able to use a watch expression of "@TIB ^ obfuscator" to display the current thread ID at all times. There are two ways to determine the obfuscator value: (1) Walk through the disassembly of the *GetCurrentThreadId* function to determine where the obfuscator value is stored and dereference that address to retrieve its value, or (2) leverage the mathematical properties of the XOR operation. If you're comfortable with assembly language, the first approach is easy enough (you don't have to step through *GetCurrentThreadId* very far to find the obfuscator). In fact, I used this approach initially to figure out how Windows 98 determines the current thread ID. Once you know that Windows 98 just XORs the address of the TIB with a constant value, however, the second approach is the more elegant solution, doesn't require nearly as much effort or time, and requires no knowledge of assembly language.

The XOR operation has the property that if you calculate A XOR B = C, then computing C XOR B produces A, and computing C XOR A produces B. Since you know that the current thread ID is computed using @TIB XOR *obfuscator*, if you know the thread ID, you can determine the obfuscator's value by computing @TIB XOR *ThreadId*. The Threads dialog box on the **Debug** menu lists the thread IDs for every thread in the program, so you can pick any of those IDs to perform this calculation. At this point, you should be able to display the Threads dialog box, note the value of any thread ID shown in the resulting list, and then enter the expression "@TIB ^ *ThreadId*" in the Watch window to compute the obfuscator value. Unfortunately, Visual C++'s idea of where the TIB is located is off by eight bytes when running under Windows 98. Therefore, the actual recipe for finding an expression that can be entered in the Watch window to cause a persistent display of the current thread ID is as follows:

1. Display the Threads dialog box, and make a note of any thread ID in the list.
2. Enter the expression "(@TIB – 8) ^ *ThreadId*" in the Watch window. The resulting value is the *obfuscator* for this boot of Windows.
3. Enter the expression "(@TIB – 8) ^ *obfuscator*" in the Watch window. Each time the Watch window is evaluated by the debugger, this expression produces the ID of the current thread.

Because the obfuscator is computed each time Windows 98 boots, you must redo this quick procedure any time Windows is restarted. It's a simple procedure, however, so this isn't a barrier to success.

Setting Thread-specific Breakpoints

The most glaring omission from the Visual C++ debugging feature set for multi-threaded programs is the ability to set a breakpoint that is triggered only by a particular thread. Many other debuggers, such as WinDbg and SoftICE, support this feature, which allows you to set a breakpoint on a particular line of code, bring up the Breakpoints dialog box, and set a condition on the breakpoint to break only for a specific thread.

Although the debugger doesn't provide a user interface to set this kind of breakpoint directly, the @TIB pseudo-register can be used to configure a breakpoint so that it breaks only in the context of a given thread (or set of threads). To set a thread-specific breakpoint, evaluate the expression "@TIB" in the Watch window for the thread of interest to determine the thread's TIB address. Next, display the Breakpoints dialog box, select the breakpoint you'd like to qualify, and then click the **Condition** button. Now enter the expression "@TIB == *TIBAddress*", where *TIBAddress* is the value of the @TIB pseudo-register. From now on in this debugging session, this breakpoint breaks only for the specified thread. You can easily use a more sophisticated condition to test for a set of threads by using the TIB addresses for the threads of interest. Unfortunately, since TIB addresses vary between debugging sessions, you will have to reset these breakpoints whenever you restart the debugger.

Now for the bad news. This technique works on Windows 2000; on Windows 98, however, the same technique *should* work, but my tests showed the results to be unreliable. An alternative technique for Windows 98 is to check for a specific value of the FS register, which contains a unique selector for every running thread. My tests showed, however, that using @FS instead of @TIB in Windows 98 is just as unreliable. With luck, this problem will be resolved by a future Windows 98 or Visual C++ service pack, so don't hesitate to experiment on your own Windows 98 platform.

Naming Threads

If you have more than a few threads in your program, it can be difficult to remember that thread 0x0000073C is performing audio decoding while thread 0x0000071C is doing video capture. Pinpointing these two threads among a half dozen others displayed in the Threads dialog box can be time consuming and is error prone. Although creating a Watch window expression to display the current thread ID helps you detect thread switches while stepping through code, the thread ID itself doesn't convey any meaning. Luckily, there are two techniques you can use to assign a name to each thread. Neither of these is officially documented or supported, but both work reliably in Windows 2000 and Windows 98.

The first technique uses a field in the TIB at offset 0x14 called *pvArbitrary*. This field is not used by Windows and is available to programmers. By setting this field to point to a string, you can enter the expression "(char *)(dw(@TIB + 0x14))" in the Watch window to have a persistent display of the current thread's name.

The second technique for assigning a name to a thread was presented by Jay Bazuzi, a developer on the Visual C++ debugger team, at the 1999 Microsoft TechEd conference. It uses the *RaiseException* API function to throw a structured exception that is caught by the debugger. This exception associates a string with the given thread, so that when the Threads dialog box is displayed, the thread's name is displayed along with the thread ID and location in the code. This approach allows you to pinpoint a thread of interest quickly in the Threads dialog box without having to write down thread IDs and correlate them to thread activities in your program.

The following *SetThreadName* function combines both techniques into one function, which can be called in the context of any thread to assign it a name.

```
struct THREADNAME_INFO {
    DWORD    dwType;
    char     *pszName;
    DWORD    dwThreadID;
    DWORD    dwFlags;
};

BOOL SetThreadName ( char *pszName ) {
    BOOL fOkay = FALSE;
    // set the thread name in the TIB
    char **ppszThreadName = 0;
    __asm {
        mov eax, fs:[0x18]          // locate calling thread's TIB
        add eax, 0x14               // pvArbitrary is at offset
                                    // 0x14 in TIB
```

```
    // ppszThreadName = &pTIB->pvArbitrary
    mov [ppszThreadName], eax
}
if ( *ppszThreadName == 0 ) { // verify pvArbitrary isn't
                              // already in use
    *ppszThreadName = pszName; // set thread name
    fOkay = TRUE;
}


// set the thread name so that it shows in Threads dialog box
THREADNAME_INFO tni = {0};
tni.dwType = 0x1000;
tni.pszName = pszName; // name to assign to thread
tni.dwThreadID = -1;   // -1 indicates calling thread,
                       // can use any ID here

__try {
    RaiseException( 0x406d1388, 0, sizeof(tni) / sizeof(DWORD),
                    (DWORD *)&tni );
}
__except ( EXCEPTION_EXECUTE_HANDLER ) {
    fOkay = FALSE;   // the exception wasn't handled by
                     // the debugger
}
return(fOkay);
}
```

The first portion of this function uses inline assembly to locate the address of the *pvArbitrary* member within the calling thread's TIB. The address of this field is stored in the *ppszThreadName* local variable. Once this field is located, it is checked to see if it's already being used for another purpose. If this field isn't being used, *ppszThreadName* is dereferenced to set the *pvArbitrary* field to point to the thread's name, thus allowing it to be displayed persistently using the Watch window expression noted above. Since the string pointer passed to *SetThreadName* is stored directly in the TIB, make sure the storage for the string exists as long as the thread is alive. The string can be a literal, constant, global variable or it can be in the heap (as long as you don't free the string until after the thread exits).

After changing the TIB, a THREADNAME_INFO data structure is initialized to refer to the string name and its other fields are initialized to indicate to the debugger that you would like to assign a name to the calling thread. Once this structure is initialized, it is passed to *RaiseException* along with the exception code 0x406D1388. This exception tells the debugger to assign the given string name to the specified thread. Unlike other exceptions, this exception isn't reported by Visual C++ in the Output window and the exception filter is never evaluated. Once *RaiseException* returns, the thread name is displayed in the Threads dialog box in the **Location** column. Due to space limitations in the Threads dialog box, only nine characters (not counting the null-terminating character) are displayed. If your program is not being debugged, or support for this feature disappears, the unconditional exception filter (EXCEPTION _EXECUTE_HANDLER) guarantees that the exception never crashes the program. In this situation, the resulting exception is trapped and FALSE is returned to the caller.

To assign a name to a thread, just call *SetThreadName* at the start of every thread procedure. If you want to automate the use of *SetThreadName*, you can write a thread creation wrapper function that's appropriate for your environment. Having a persistent display of the thread name along with its ID greatly reduces the risk of context confusion while stepping through code. Similarly, it can save a lot of time to be able to pinpoint a thread of interest using the Threads dialog box without having to switch through several wrong threads until you find the right one.

> **TIP**
>
> Assigning thread names reduces the risk of context confusion while stepping through code and makes it easier to find the right thread.

Having a name associated with a thread can also improve the quality of trace messages or event log entries made by multithreaded programs. Many programmers augment their trace output to include the thread ID of the thread printing the message. By assigning names to threads, you can easily alter your trace macros to print the thread name as well as its ID by calling a *GetThreadName* function that's implemented as shown in the following code.

```
char *GetThreadName( void ) {
    char *pszName;
```

```
    __asm {
        mov eax, fs:[0x18]     // locate the caller's TIB
        mov eax, [eax + 0x14]  // read the pvArbitrary field
                               // in the TIB
        mov [pszName], eax     // pszName = pTIB->pvArbitrary
    }
    return(pszName ? pszName : "unknown");
}
```

This function locates the calling thread's TIB and extracts the *pvArbitrary* member. If this field is null, the literal "unknown" is returned so that your trace macro does not have to test the success or failure of this function.

Investigating and Diagnosing Hangs

If you're investigating a mysterious hang in a program, the process can be tough. If your program is going nowhere fast, what can you do in the debugger to determine the cause of the hang? Assuming you understand each thread's activities, the answer is to start by looking at the evidence. Once you've looked at the call stacks for all the threads in your program, look at the current code location of each thread. For example, if they are all stuck inside *WaitFor SingleObject* waiting for an event to be signaled, try to figure out which other thread is responsible for causing that event to be signaled and why that event hasn't happened yet. In Windows 2000, most deadlocks are characterized by all the threads being stuck deep within *Ntdll.dll*, as shown here for a thread that called *WaitForSingleObject*.

```
NTDLL!_ZwWaitForSingleObject@12:
    mov        eax,0C5h        ; EAX loaded with function # of
                               ; system call
    lea        edx,[esp+4]     ; EDX points to the arguments on the
                               ; call stack
    int        2Eh             ; Transition into kernel mode.
    ret        0Ch             ; ← thread's location shown here by
                               ; by debugger
```

This situation indicates that the thread has made a transition into kernel mode as a result of making a system call with the int 2Eh instruction. This means the thread in question is blocked somewhere in the kernel and hasn't had a chance to return. By looking at the call stack, you should be able to find the point in your source code that led to this situation. By knowing which kernel object this thread is waiting on and by considering how that kernel object affects all the other threads, you should be able to locate the problem. Unfortunately, there is no general step-by-step procedure for getting from the point where a single thread is blocked to the root cause of a deadlock. The fewer threads involved in a deadlock and the more familiar you are with the overall architecture of the program, the better your chances of diagnosing the root cause of the hang. There is no substitute for having a firm grasp of how the threads in your program are supposed to interact with one another.

Controlled Stepping

Sometimes you can't identify the cause of the problem simply by looking at call stacks. Just because some threads happen to be in the kernel when you break into the debugger doesn't necessarily mean that they'll never return. A simple experiment to try is to give the **Go** command and let the program run for a moment, then give the **Break** command to break back into the debugger. Now you can quickly look at all the call stacks to see if the threads are still stuck in the same location or if one or more threads are elsewhere. Repeating this exercise quickly a few times usually gives you a better idea of which threads are really stuck and which ones are still making progress.

TIP Use the **Break** command to help you determine if any threads are really stuck.

Often, the presence of many threads causes a lot of distracting activity while debugging, such as context switches that occur while you're stepping through code. If there's a particular thread you're interesting in stepping through, you can use the Threads dialog box to step in that thread without allowing other threads to run. After identifying a thread that you'd like to debug in isolation, display the Threads dialog box. If the target thread is the current thread, highlight all the other threads listed in the dialog box and click **Suspend**. Unfortunately, the Threads dialog box doesn't use a multiselection list box, so you'll have to select and suspend each thread individually. Now you can step through the program or run it at full speed. Only the threads that have not been suspended are allowed to execute.

TIP

Use the Threads dialog box to suspend other threads if you want to debug a thread in isolation.

One pitfall to be aware of before using this technique: Don't suspend the thread that the debugger indicates is the current thread (indicated by an asterisk in the left-hand column of the threads list). Doing so sometimes causes an artificial deadlock and results in the following message displaying in the **Debug** tab of the Output window.

```
DBG: break command failed within 3 seconds.
DBG: potential deadlock. Soft broken.
```

Unfortunately, it's easy to get yourself into this situation. For example, suppose there are four threads in your program. You want to step through thread B, but thread C is marked as the current thread in the Threads dialog box. You proceed to select and suspend threads A, C, and D so that you can follow thread B's activities without other threads getting in the way. Doing this may work, or it may result in the debugger-induced deadlock. Whether or not deadlock occurs is difficult to predict because it is governed by which debug event the debugger is relying on seeing next and whether or not the current thread plays a role in triggering that event. Avoiding the problem is easy: Select the target thread, click **Set Focus**, and then proceed to suspend all the other threads. This problem is easy to prevent, but it's frustrating to be hot on the track of a bug and make a simple misstep in the debugger that abruptly halts your investigation.

TIP

When suspending threads using the Threads dialog box, if the target thread isn't the current thread, use the **Set Focus** button to make the target thread current.

Debugging multithreaded programs is one of the most challenging activities a Windows programmer can undertake. The key to successful multithreaded debugging goes well beyond knowing which debugger commands to use.

Programmers who are successful at debugging multithreaded programs have the following capabilities going for them.

- A strong understanding of multithreaded development issues and how to develop thread-safe code
- An understanding of how the debugger works and the effect it has on a multithreaded program
- A vigilant awareness of the various pitfalls that can trip you up and cause you to head down the wrong investigative path

The information and techniques explored in this chapter should put you on the path to successful multithreaded debugging.

Recommended Reading

Asche, Ruediger. "Detecting Deadlocks in Multithreaded Win32 Applications." MSDN, January 11, 1994. Part One of a three-part series on deadlock detecting, this article introduces strategies for analyzing deadlock potential in a program.

Beveridge, Jim, and Robert Weiner. *Multithreading Applications in Win32: The Complete Guide to Threads*. Reading, MA: Addison-Wesley, 1996. Presents information on multithreading in Win32.

Burger, John. "A Lesson in Multithreaded Bugs." *Windows Developer Journal*, April 1998. Presents an introductory look at one developer's experience with ironing out the bugs in a multithreaded program running on a multiprocessor platform.

Cohen, Aaron, and Mike Woodring. *Win32 Multithreaded Programming*. Sebastopol, CA: O'Reilly, 1998. Focuses on multithreading in Win32, including coverage of the Win32 threading and synchronization APIs, exception handling in multithreaded programs, multithreading design advice, and how to leverage the C++ language to facilitate multithreaded development.

Pietrek, Matt. "Under the Hood." *Microsoft Systems Journal,* May 1996. Documents the TIB structure for Windows 95 and Windows NT.

Richter, Jeffrey. *Programming Applications for Microsoft Windows: Master the Critical Building Blocks of 32-Bit and 64-Bit Windows-based Applications*, 4th ed. Redmond, WA: Microsoft Press, 1999. Presents information on the Win32 API, including threads and thread synchronization.

Robbins, John. "Bugslayer." *Microsoft Systems Journal*, October 1998. Presents a deadlock detection utility library that can be used from within an application to log thread synchronization activities within a program for offline viewing after a deadlock occurs.

Chapter 11

COM Debugging

Debugging COM code is frustrating to many developers, especially if you are a relative newcomer to the Windows platform in general and COM in particular. Successfully working your way through a single bug often requires a broad range of knowledge and skills, including

- A solid understanding of operating system constructs, such as processes, threads, and DLLs
- A solid understanding of the rules associated with COM programming, such as reference counting, memory allocation, and threading
- Awareness of networking- and security-related details and their implications
- An understanding of the MTS/COM+ surrogate architecture
- Knowledge of how other products, such as Internet Explorer and Internet Information Server (IIS), host the code that you are trying to debug

Depending on your background and skills, this can make debugging COM code a daunting task. You probably won't need to master each item in the following list to debug every problem successfully. The exact skills and techniques required to solve a problem vary depending on the type of code you're writing and the environment it's running in.

Chapter Basics

Prerequisites

To keep this chapter focused on debugging techniques, as opposed to COM architecture and programming, it is assumed that you are already a functional COM programmer and more specifically, I assume you understand the fundamentals of interface-based programming with COM, the differences between in-process and out-of-process servers, what proxies and stubs are, and how self-registration works for DLL-based and EXE-based COM servers.

If you are deploying code within the MTS or COM+ run-time environment, we further assume that you understand what the term *context* means and how the MTS/COM+ run-time hosts your DLL within a surrogate process.

Terminology Used

So that we're all on the same page, here are definitions of some terms used in this chapter. These terms are standard nomenclature in most recent COM-related articles and texts, but I won't assume you and I have read the same set of materials. I use the term *base COM* to describe code that's being deployed outside of the MTS or COM+ run-time environment, as in *base COM DLL* or *base COM EXE*. I use the term *configured component* to describe a COM DLL that has been deployed within the MTS or COM+ run-time environment.

With respect to configured components, there are some differences between MTS, which is an add-on technology above base COM on Windows NT 4.0, and COM+, which is the unified COM-MTS infrastructure on Windows 2000. Some of the differences are superficial (for example, the surrogate process that hosts your code is called *Mtx.exe* on Windows NT 4.0 but *DllHost.exe* on Windows 2000), whereas other differences are more profound. When I discuss a technique that applies on both platforms or something that is only a superficial difference, such as the name of the surrogate EXE, I use generic terms such as *configured component*, *surrogate*, or *catalog* (when addressing configuration issues). When discussing a functional difference, I explicitly use the terms MTS and COM+ to refer to the Windows NT 4.0 and Windows 2000 environments, respectively.

Organization

This chapter is organized so that if you are not yet developing configured components, you can safely ignore the sections that are devoted to debugging issues specific to that environment. If you are developing configured components, don't skip the sections that discuss the base COM techniques. Many techniques described in those sections also apply to your world, and I do not repeat the discussions in the configured components sections.

DEBUGGING TECHNIQUES

Defensive COM Programming Practices

Since bug prevention is often the most effective form of debugging, it helps to look at various ways to prevent bugs in COM programs. For starters, what's wrong with the following code?

```
IShape *pShape;
IColor *pColor;
IGizmo *pToy;
HRESULT hr;
hr = CoCreateInstance(CLSID_Toy, 0, CLSCTX_ALL, IID_IColor,
                      (void**)&pShape);
hr = pShape->QueryInterface(IID_IColor, (void**)pColor);
hr = CoCreateInstance(CLSID_Toy, 0, CLSCTX_ALL, IID_IGizmo,
                      (void**)NULL);
```

The answer: it compiles. Each of these calls to *CoCreateInstance* and *Query Interface* has a bug that will cause problems at run time, but the bugs are not caught by the compiler. The first call to *CoCreateInstance* passed the wrong interface ID (that is, IID_IColor instead of IID_IShape). The call to *Query Interface* should have passed the address of the *pColor* variable (*&pColor*) rather than *pColor*. Finally, the second call to *CoCreateInstance* is downright ridiculous (a null pointer isn't too useful for retrieving [out] parameters). I've made two types of mistakes in my code. The first type of mistake is passing the wrong IID to a function that returns a new interface pointer. The second type of mistake—pointer problems—is a by-product of the fact that most functions that return interface pointers use an [out] parameter of type `void **`, thereby forcing the caller to cast and abandon any help from the compiler. Each of these problems can be addressed by making a slight change to the way code is written.

Leveraging the Compiler

In his book *Essential COM*,[1] Don Box presents a macro named IID_PPV_ARG that looks like this:

```
#define IID_PPV_ARG(Type, Expr) \
        IID_##Type, \
        reinterpret_cast<void**>(static_cast<Type **>(Expr))
```

---

[1] See Chapter 2, in the section Type Coercion and IUnknown

This macro solves both of the problems in the previous code without imposing any run-time cost. It allows me to rewrite my code like this:

```
IShape *pShape;
HRESULT hr;
hr = CoCreateInstance(CLSID_Toy, 0, CLSCTX_ALL,
IID_PPV_ARG(IShape, &pShape));
```

If you don't mind the odd appearance of the last two arguments to *CoCreate Instance*, this approach is ideal. First, the `static_cast` operator generates compiler errors for any type mismatch between the type name and pointer arguments you specify. This includes passing the wrong type name, such as IID_PPV_ARG(IColor, &pShape), as well as making a pointer mistake, such as IID_PPV_ARG(IShape, pShape). Both mistakes result in compiler errors, which are always preferable to run-time errors. The second benefit is that this technique does not result in any run-time overhead because everything is resolved at compile time.

Using __uuidof

Visual C++ 5.0 introduced the __uuidof keyword, which evaluates to the GUID associated with an object that has a `uuid` attribute. For example, the expression __uuidof(IShape) evaluates to the GUID associated with the interface *IShape.* So does __uuidof(pShape). This keyword allows you to write code as follows:

```
IShape *pShape;
HRESULT hr;
hr = CoCreateInstance( CLSID_Toy, 0, CLSCTX_ALL,
                       __uuidof(pShape), (void **)&pShape );
```

By writing your code this way, the correct IID is always passed to *CoCreate Instance,* even if you decide later to change the type of the *pShape* variable from *IShape* * to *IShapeEx* *. If you use IID_PPV_ARG, you'll need to change both the variable declaration and the place where you use the macro. The only drawback with this example is that we can still make a pointer error with the last argument to *CoCreateInstance.* However, the __uuidof keyword is also useful in situations where IID_PPV_ARG cannot be used. The most common example occurs when calling *CoCreateInstanceEx.*

```
IShape *pShape;
IColor *pColor;
HRESULT hr;
COSERVERINFO csi = {0};
MULTI_QI mqi[2] = { {&__uuidof(pShape), 0, 0},    // request IShape
                    {&__uuidof(pColor), 0, 0} }; // request IColor
hr = CoCreateInstanceEx(CLSID_Toy, 0, CLSCTX_ALL, &csi, 2, mqi);
```

> **TIP**
>
> Use __uuidof to retrieve the GUID associated with an interface type or variable.

Using *com_cast*

The problem used in Leveraging the Compiler resulted from the `void **` parameter many COM functions use to return [out] interface pointers variables. Even veteran C++ programmers who long ago rewired their brains to intrinsically understand pointers are not above occasionally dropping or adding an '&' character here and there. But because we are forced to cast expressions to `void **`, we abandon any help from the compiler. Macros such as IID_PPV_ARG are helpful, but their use is restricted to situations in which you're calling a function that has an IID argument immediately followed by a `void **` argument. If you're calling a function with a different signature (maybe the `void **` and IID arguments are reversed or other arguments appear between them), you'd need a separate macro that encapsulates only the two casting operations. Although this approach is possible, I use one that accomplishes the same thing without using the preprocessor and that looks like a C++ casting operator.

```
template< typename I >
void** com_cast( I **ppi ) {
    _ASSERTE (ppi != 0);
    return reinterpret_cast<void **>(ppi);
}
```

This template function is defined inline in a header file and allows me to write code as follows:

```
IShape *pShape;
HRESULT hr;
```

```
hr = CoCreateInstance( CLSID_Toy, 0, CLSCTX_ALL,
                       __uuidof(pShape),
                       com_cast<IShape>(&pShape) );
```

The last argument to *CoCreateInstance* has the appearance of a C++ casting operator and achieves the same result as the macro-based approach. The compiler performs a `static_cast` implicitly on the argument passed to *com_cast* and the template function performs a `reinterpret_cast`. In debug builds, using *com_cast* results in run-time overhead because a function call is made, unlike the IID_PPV_ARG solution. However, this has the benefit of allowing an assertion within the *com_cast* function. Given the usage model of IID_PPV_ARG, it cannot include an assertion. Because the release build of *com_cast* doesn't actually perform any work within its body (the assertion disappears and the cast is a compile-time check), no run-time overhead is incurred in production code.

> **TIP**
>
> Use `com_cast` to eliminate the dangers of casting `void**` [out] parameters.

Dealing with Reference Counting

Many C++ COM developers have heard the quip that C++ is the assembly language of COM. Beyond the relatively simple issues of dealing with pointers and the dangers of typecasting, there are many rules and idioms that COM programmers must follow. Programmers that use higher-level languages, such as Visual Basic, have the advantage of a run-time environment that follows these rules automatically. C++ developers do not have that luxury. The most frequent source of frustration for most C++ developers is reference counting.

When dealing with reference counting, if you want to program COM in C++ and not have bugs, you must use smart pointers. Debugging tools have not quite evolved to the point where C++ programmers can just run their project within a debugger and easily determine that they have failed to increase or decrease a reference count for a given interface pointer. Eventually, C++ tools will evolve to the point where there is such a run-time environment or our debugging tools can detect reference counting problems. If you are using a framework such as ATL, however, you have a set of smart pointer template classes available that encapsulates the COM reference counting rules for C++ developers.

Chapter 4 introduced ATL's support for tracing *QueryInterface* calls by defining _ATL_DEBUG_QI as well as *AddRef* and *Release* calls by defining _ATL_DEBUG_INTERFACES. These preprocessor symbols can be defined by component developers to cause ATL's relevant base classes to output messages to the **Debug** tab of the Output window each time *QueryInterface*, *AddRef*, or *Release* is called. If you're a component developer, the resulting information can help pinpoint a reference counting problem in your client's code. If you're writing client-side code, however, and are not calling a debug build component that has been built with these features enabled, you're in the dark.

This is when ATL's *CComPtr* and *CComQIPtr* template classes are useful. Both classes encapsulate the COM reference counting rules that C++ developers must follow. In Chapter 2 of their book *ATL Internals,* Brent Rector and Chris Sells provide a complete discussion of both *CComPtr* and *CComQIPtr*, so I won't repeat that discussion here. If you're not yet using ATL, these two template classes might be a good motivation to start. Because you may not have the luxury of integrating ATL into your existing code base, I present the seed of a smart interface pointer class here. This also allows me to write some code later in this section without making it specific to ATL.

In general, the goals of a smart interface pointer are as follows:

- To call *AddRef* on the encapsulated interface pointer as needed during initialization and assignment operations
- To *Release* the encapsulated interface pointer automatically before overwriting it during assignment
- To *Release* the encapsulated interface pointer automatically in the class destructor
- To have the same look and feel of a raw pointer

The following class provides a partial implementation of these requirements.

```
template< typename I >
class InterfacePtr {
public:
    InterfacePtr()
        : m_pi(0) {} // initialize encapsulated pointer to NULL
```

```
~InterfacePtr() {
    if( m_pi )
      { m_pi->Release(); } // release encapsulated pointer
    m_pi = 0;
}
I* operator -> () { _ASSERTE(m_pi != 0); return(m_pi); }
I** operator & () { return(&m_pi); }
operator = ( const InterfacePtr<I>& rhs ) { // assignment
    if( m_pi ) { m_pi->Release(); }
    m_pi = rhs.m_pi;
    if( m_pi ) { m_pi->AddRef(); }
}
operator = ( const I* p ) { // assignment
    if( m_pi ) { m_pi->Release(); }
    m_pi = p;
    if( m_pi ) { m_pi->AddRef(); }
}
private:
    I *m_pi; // the encapsulated "raw" interface pointer
private:
    InterfacePtr( const InterfacePtr<I>& init ); // not supported
};
```

Given this class, I can write code in the following style.

```
void UseSomeToys( IToy *pToy ) {
    InterfacePtr<IToy> pLocalToy;
    HRESULT hr;
    hr = CoCreateInstance( CLSID_Toy, 0, CLSCTX_ALL,
                           __uuidof(pLocalToy),
                           com_cast<IToy>(&pLocalToy) );
    if( SUCCEEDED(hr) ) {
        pLocalToy->DoSomething();
        pLocalToy = pToy; // releases pLocalToy.m_pi, AddRefs pToy
        pLocalToy->DoSomething();
    }
} // releases pLocalToy.m_pi
```

When the automatic (local) variable *pLocalToy* comes into scope, the class constructor initializes the encapsulated interface pointer to null. If I had attempted
to dereference *pLocalToy* before initializing it, the overloaded operator->
would detect the problem with an assertion and provide information that is
more useful than an unhandled exception message box.

By overloading the address-of operator (`operator&`), I can still use the expression &*pLocalToy* in my call to *CoCreateInstance*. (See Chapter 2 of Rector and Sells' 1999 book for a more in-depth discussion of the subtleties of implementing this operator.) Similarly, the overloaded assignment operator allows *pLocalToy* to be safely changed to refer to a new interface pointer (the one passed by the caller of *UseSomeToys*) while following the reference counting rules. Because the destructor takes care of releasing the interface pointer even in the presence of exceptions, the interface pointer is always released on return from *UseSomeToys*.

This example of a smart interface pointer class is a partial implementation because it doesn't completely handle all reference counting problems. For example, because `operator->` has been overloaded to return the raw encapsulated interface pointer, I can still call `pLocalToy->AddRef()`, although this will clearly throw a wrench in the reference counting maintenance the *InterfacePtr* class is trying to provide. The ATL smart interface pointer classes provide a full-featured implementation that addresses such issues. If you're using ATL but haven't yet embraced the smart pointer classes, it's very much worth the time to research them now. If you're not using ATL, please take the spirit of the *InterfacePtr* class with you into your own environment, but be sure to flesh out the implementation using ATL's *CComPtr* class as a guide.

Pinpointing Activation Failures

The final defensive COM development technique addresses the fact that any number of things can go wrong when you call one of COM's activation functions, such as *CoCreateInstance*, *CoCreateInstanceEx*, and *CoGetClassObject*. Consider what can go wrong with the call to *CoCreateInstance* in *UseSomeToys* above.

- The server may not be registered correctly.
- If the server runs out of process from the client, the proxy/stub for a given interface may not be registered correctly.
- If the server runs as a different user identity than the client, the client may not have launch or access permission to the server.
- If the server runs on a different machine, network authentication may fail.
- The ATL code doesn't list the CLSID in the class map (also known as BEGIN_OBJECT_MAP).

- The ATL code doesn't list an interface IID in the interface map (also know as BEGIN_COM_MAP).

This should serve as a diagnostic checklist when you're trying to debug a failure to activate a particular server. If you find yourself debugging activation failures often, you might consider committing this list to memory or photocopying this page and taping it to the side of your monitor. Better yet, you can embed this checklist in an activation function to use throughout your code instead of calling *CoCreateInstance*.

_CoActivateServer

The primary goal of _CoActivateServer_ is to embed the activation checklist in code, which will produce debug output messages that suggest where the problem might be. A somewhat superficial benefit to this function is that it supplies default arguments for some of the less frequently used parameters to *CoCreateInstance.* Here's the implementation[2] as it looks in debug builds (the release build version is defined later).

```
template< typename I >
HRESULT _CoActivateServer( CLSID clsid, I **ppi,
                           DWORD locality = CLSCTX_ALL,
                           const OLECHAR* pszServer = 0,
                           char *pszFile = 0, int nLine = 0 )
{
   *ppi = 0;
   // Step 1: try to activate server using class loader
   InterfacePtr<IUnknown> pUnkClassObject;
   COSERVERINFO csi = {0, const_cast<wchar_t*>(pszServer), 0, 0};
   HRESULT hr =
     CoGetClassObject( clsid, locality, &csi,
                       __uuidof(pUnkClassObject),
                       com_cast<IUnknown>(&pUnkClassObject) );

   if( FAILED(hr) ) {
     TraceActivateError(
       "CoGetClassObject", hr, pszFile, nLine,
     ">> Is the server registered?\n"
```

[2] This is inspired by an approach taken by Keith Brown in the programming exercises that accompany his excellent *Programming NT Security* course, which I teach for DevelopMentor. If you are an ATL developer, change all the references to the *InterfacePtr* class in this function to *CCcomPtr.*

```
      ">> Is the CLSID listed in the OBJECT_MAP?\n"
      ">> Is there a problem with authentication?\n"
      ">> Do you have launch permission?\n"
      ">> Do you have access permissions?\n" );
    return(hr);
}
// Step 2: acquire class loader's instantiation interface
InterfacePtr<IClassFactory> pcf;
hr = pUnkClassObject->QueryInterface(
        __uuidof(pcf),
        com_cast<IClassFactory>(&pcf) );

if( FAILED(hr) ) {
    TraceActivateError(
      "QI for IClassFactory", hr, pszFile, nLine,
      ">> Is there a problem with authentication?\n" );
    return(hr);
}
// Step 3: instantiate requested class, asking for IUnknown
InterfacePtr<IUnknown> pUnkServer;
hr = pcf->CreateInstance( 0, __uuidof(pUnkServer),
                          com_cast<IUnknown>(&pUnkServer) );
if( FAILED(hr) ) {
    TraceActivateError(
      "IClassFactory::CreateInstance", hr,
      pszFile, nLine,
      ">> Hmm...might have a corruption problem in "
      "one or more constructors.\n" );
    return(hr);
}
// Step 4: finally, ask for the requested interface
hr = pUnkServer->QueryInterface(__uuidof(I),com_cast<I>(ppi));
if( FAILED(hr) ) {
    TraceActivateError(
      "QI for interface", hr, pszFile, nLine,
      ">> Is the requested interface supported by"
          "the object?\n"
      ">> Is the IID listed in the COM_MAP?\n"
      ">> Did you register the proxy/stub DLL?\n"
      ">> Do you have access permission to the "
          "interface?\n" );
}
return(hr);
}
```

By taking a stepwise approach to activation, this function gives more specific feedback on the cause of a failure in the form of trace messages that are sent to the debugger using the *TraceActivateError* helper function (shown later in this section). The downside to this approach is that it results in more round-trips on the wire when the server being activated is on another machine. The release build version of *_CoActivateServer* eliminates the extra roundtrips. Here's an example of how *_CoActivateServer* is called.

```
IShape *pShape;
HRESULT hr;
hr = _CoActivateServer(CLSID_Toy, &pShape);
```

TIP *_CoActivateServer* pinpoints COM server activation failures in client code and provides suggestions for diagnosing the problem.

Since *_CoActivateServer* is a template function, implicitly parameterized by the type of the second parameter (*pShape* in this example), the compiler still detects any pointer mistakes and the correct IID is used automatically when *QueryInterface* is called.

In step 1, *_CoActivateServer* uses *CoGetClassObject* to attempt to activate the requested server, asking for the class loader's *IUnknown* interface pointer initially. If this fails, it's usually because the server hasn't been registered (so the CLSID isn't recognized by COM) or the ATL code doesn't list the requested CLSID in a class map. If the server runs out-of-process from the client and has not yet been started, this step also requires that the client be authenticated and have sufficient launch permissions for the server. Whether or not the server is already running or this activation request caused the server to be launched, the client must have sufficient access permissions. By asking for *IUnknown* at this point, you avoid any potential problems with unregistered proxy/stubs.

Step 2, which most programmers roll into step 1, is really just a sanity check designed to catch authentication problems. If step 2 fails, verify that the client can be authenticated to the server.

Step 3 should never fail. If you've made it past steps 1 and 2 successfully, a failure to call *IClassFactory::CreateInstance* usually means that something is catastrophically wrong with the server. First verify that the network cable is plugged in, then focus on the construction sequence for your implementation class. Because the implementation of *CreateInstance* typically boils down to calling `new` to instantiate a new instance of your C++ implementation class, a failure at this point usually indicates a memory problem in the constructor or code called by the constructor.

Step 4 asks the newly instantiated server object for the interface pointer that *_CoActivateServer* will return to the caller. This isolates any failures to *QueryInterface*. At this point, verify that the ATL code lists the requested IID in its interface map. Also verify that the required proxy/stub has been registered for the specified interface. If the object being activated resides in a configured component, make sure that the client has sufficient access permissions to the requested interface.

The implementation of the less exciting support function, *TraceActivate Error*, is shown here.

```
void TraceActivateError( char *pszFunc, HRESULT hr,
                         char *pszFile, int nLine,
                         char *pszHint ) {
    BOOL fOkay;
    char *pszMsg = new char[512];
    char *pszError = 0;
    fOkay = FormatMessageA( FORMAT_MESSAGE_FROM_SYSTEM |
                            FORMAT_MESSAGE_ALLOCATE_BUFFER,
                            0, hr, 0, (LPTSTR)&pszError, 0, 0 );
    wsprintfA( pszMsg, "%s failed:\n%s(%d): 0x%08x, %s%s",
               pszFunc, (pszFile ? pszFile : "unknown file"),
               nLine, hr,
               (pszError ? pszError : "unrecognized error\n"),
               pszHint );
    OutputDebugStringA(pszMsg);
    if( pszError ) LocalFree((HLOCAL)pszError);
    delete [] pszMsg;
}
```

This function looks up the specified HRESULT, and prints a message to the **Debug** tab of the Output window that includes the numeric value of the HRESULT, the text translation for that code, and the source file and line number of the caller's code where the failure occurred. Here's what the trace message looks like if the final call to *QueryInterface* within *_CoServerActivate* fails.

```
QI for interface failed:
unknown file(0): 0x80004002, No such interface supported
>> Is the requested interface supported by the object?
>> Is the IID listed in the COM_MAP?
>> Did you register the proxy/stub DLL?
>> Do you have access permission to the interface?
```

If a call to *_CoActivateServer* fails, this trace message provides some hints about what might have caused the failure. Note that the source file and line number of the caller are unknown in this example. This is because having to pass the source file name and line number to *_CoActivateServer* is cumbersome, so I explicitly passed only the first two parameters to *_CoActivateServer*, letting the compiler pass the defaults for the remaining parameters. Macros, however, provide an easy way to pass the source file name and line number to *_CoActivateServer*.

TRACE_ACTIVATE

If the default values for the *Locality* and *pszServer* parameters to *_CoActivate Server* are acceptable to you, the best way to leverage *_CoActivateServer* is to call it using a macro I call TRACE_ACTIVATE, which is shown here. (You can always define your own versions of this macro that allow you to specify different context flags, server host name, or both.)

```
#define TRACE_ACTIVATE(_clsid, _ppi) \
  _CoActivateServer( _clsid_ppi, CLSCTX_ALL, 0, _FILE__, __LINE)
```

This macro passes the file name and line number of the caller to *_CoActivate Server*, which results in trace messages that pinpoint the exact location in your code where the failure occurred. So if I now change my doomed call to *_CoActivateServer* to use this macro instead

```
IShape *pShape;
HRESULT hr;
hr = TRACE_ACTIVATE (CLSID_Toy, &pShape);
```

the resulting trace message looks like this:

```
QI for interface failed:
c:\dev\vc\FooClient\FooClient.cpp(32): 0x80004002, No such
interface supported
    >> Is the requested interface supported by the object?
    >> Is the IID listed in the COM_MAP?
    >> Did you register the proxy/stub DLL?
    >> Do you have access permission to the interface?
```

There are two advantages to having this extra information in the trace message. First, the exact location of the failure is recorded in the Output window, even if you are not single-stepping through the code, so you won't be wondering which call to _CoActivateServer failed. Second, the trace message is formatted so that if you double-click the trace message on the line where the file name and line number are displayed, Visual C++ automatically opens the identified file and locates the offending line of code.

_CoActivateServer and Release Builds

Since _CoActivateServer is defined inline in a header file, it's easy to provide a more efficient version that doesn't incur the added round trips that characterize the debug version. Here are the release build versions of _CoActivateServer and TRACE_ACTIVATE.

```
template< typename I >
HRESULT _CoActivateServer( CLSID clsid, I **ppi,
                           DWORD locality = CLSCTX_ALL,
                           const OLECHAR* pszServer = 0 ) {
    MULTI_QI       mqi = {&__uuidof(I), 0, 0};
    COSERVERINFO   csi = {0, const_cast<wchar_t*>(pszServer),
                          0, 0};
    HRESULT        hr;
    hr = CoCreateInstanceEx(clsid, 0, locality, &csi, 1, &mqi);
    if( SUCCEEDED(hr) ) {
        *ppi = reinterpret_cast<I*>(mqi.pItf);
    }
    else {
        *ppi = 0;
```

```
    }
    return(hr);
}
#define TRACE_ACTIVATE(_clsid, _ppi) \
    _CoActivateServer(_clsid, _ppi)
```

Debugging Base COM DLLs

Debugging base COM DLLs usually boils down to two activities: (1) verifying that you don't have a configuration issue, and (2) using the debugger effectively.

Configuration Issues

Before a client can successfully activate an in-process COM server, the server must be registered on the client's machine. Unfortunately, base COM does not provide an installation API that servers can use to inform the COM Service Control Manager (SCM) of their existence.[3] Instead, servers are expected to implement and export the well-known self-registration functions *DllRegister Server* and *DllUnregisterServer*. If you are having trouble activating a COM server, quickly run through the following checklist.

1. Has the server been registered on the client's machine?
2. Is the DLL in the directory where it was originally registered? Are you using the version of the DLL that you think you're using?
3. Can other clients activate the server?
4. If the DLL is being used in a multithreaded client, are the appropriate proxy/stubs registered?

Has the server been registered?

Servers are responsible for providing the self-registration functions, but that does no good if those functions are never executed. Installation scripts typically call the self-registration functions automatically; but if you are manually installing a COM DLL, it's up to you to run the Regsvr32 utility to register the server. If you are the author of the COM server being debugged or you have manually copied the DLL onto a new machine, be sure to run Regsvr32 before spending any time in the debugger. Because the ATL AppWizard generates a makefile that registers COM DLLs and EXEs at the end of the build, many developers simply forget that

---

[3] This statement assumes that, like the author, you do not consider using the registry API to modify someone else's area of the registry a proper installation API.

registration is an explicit step that must be performed on every machine the DLL is copied to, not just the machine on which the DLL was built.

Is the DLL in the directory where it was originally registered?

The CLSID for a given object is used by the COM SCM to determine where the server DLL resides. The simplest way to determine where the SCM believes the DLL resides is to use the Visual C++ OleView utility. To run OleView, choose the **OLE/COM Object Viewer** command from the **Tools** menu. Expand the **All Objects** entry in OleView, and locate the entry for the server you're trying to activate. If the server annotated its CLSID entry in the registry with a text-based name, you'll find the text name for the server in this list; otherwise, the raw CLSID will be listed. When you select the server entry, OleView displays the relevant registry entries for that server in the **Registry** tab of the property sheet on the right. The **LocalServer32** entry tells you where the SCM believes the DLL resides for the selected CLSID. Verify that the DLL is located at that location in the file system. If the DLL is moved from one directory to another, this entry in the registry may be pointing at the wrong location. If this is the case, reregister the DLL. Note that you can also use the registry editor to diagnose registration issues, but I find that using OleView is more informative and much less prone to error.

A variation of this problem occurs when you change from building one version of a DLL (say, the debug build) to another (say, the release build). If your build project doesn't include a post-build step that runs Regsvr32 automatically, the COM SCM doesn't know that you want clients to start using a different version of your DLL. This problem can also be fixed by reregistering your DLL.

> **TIP**
>
> Don't forget to register your COM DLL if you copy it to a different machine or move it to another directory, or use a different version.

Can other clients activate the server?

If everything seems to be in order but the client still cannot activate the server, right-click on the server entry in OleView and select **Create Instance**. This causes OleView to call *CoCreateInstance* on the server's CLSID, requesting the

IUnknown interface pointer. If OleView successfully activates the server, it will display the server entry in bold in the tree view and expand that entry to show the list of interfaces supported by the selected server. If the activation is successful, the problem is in the client code that is trying to activate the server; otherwise, the problem is in the DLL itself.

Are the appropriate proxy/stubs registered?

If the DLL is being used in a multithreaded environment, you need to make sure that the appropriate proxy/stubs are registered for any interfaces that the client is using. Proxies and stubs are required anytime a method call must cross an apartment boundary.[4] To verify that the appropriate proxy/stub is registered, run OleView and expand the **Interfaces** entry in the tree view. Make sure that each interface the server implements is listed. If an interface is missing from the list, the COM SCM won't know where to find the appropriate proxy/stub for that interface. If this is the case, you must find or build the proxy/stub DLL that is associated with your server DLL and register it using Regsvr32.

For each interface that is listed by OleView, look at the **Registry** tab on the property sheet. The CLSID of the proxy/stub implementation is listed, along with a LocalServer32 value that points to either a system DLL (for interfaces marked [dual] or [oleautomation]) or a custom proxy/stub DLL that you need to build and register in addition to the server DLL itself. If a custom proxy/stub DLL is being used, make sure that the proxy/stub DLL is found at the specified location. If it isn't, reregister the proxy/stub DLL. If the proxy/stub DLL is located where OleView says it should be, you've probably made a change to the IDL for that interface but forgotten to reregister the proxy/stub DLL. If this happened, rebuild and then reregister the proxy/stub DLL.

> **TIP** ▶
>
> If an interface pointer is being accessed across apartment boundaries and that interface is not marked [dual] or [oleautomation], you must build and register the proxy/stub DLL for that interface.

---

[4] Actually, proxies and stubs are needed anytime you cross a *context* boundary and cross-apartment access is just one example. With the advent of configured components, apartments are now subdivided into *contexts,* and whenever you cross one, a proxy/stub pair is necessary. If you're already developing configured components, you may already be aware of this issue.

Client-side Debugging Techniques

Debugging a base COM DLL is just like debugging a regular DLL except that the client code is letting the COM SCM call the *LoadLibrary* and *GetProcAddress* API functions. If you have the debugging symbols for a COM DLL, Visual C++ automatically loads them when the DLL is first activated in the client address space. Once you have an interface pointer into the DLL, single-stepping into a method call on that interface causes Visual C++ to step right into its source code. You don't have to do anything special to make this happen.

If you now set breakpoints in the DLL source code, Visual C++ will remember where those breakpoints are set. However, once you stop debugging and then start a new debugging session, Visual C++ will warn you that it cannot set the breakpoints that were in the DLL. To remedy this problem, you must have Visual C++ preload the debugging symbols for the DLL being debugged. To do this, give the **Settings** command in the **Project** menu. From the Project Settings dialog box, click the **Debug** tab, then select the **Additional DLLs** entry in the **Category** list box. Now enter the fully qualified path to the DLL in the list of modules. This causes Visual C++ to load the debugging symbols for the specified DLL whenever you begin a debugging session from the client project. This guarantees that the breakpoints you set in the DLL will remain valid across debugging sessions.

Server-side Debugging Techniques

Sometimes you know the client program isn't at fault. Maybe it was written and debugged long ago or perhaps you don't own the client source code (for example, you are writing an ActiveX component that's being called by Internet Explorer). In any case, you might want to initiate the debugging session from the server's project. To do this, choose **Settings** from the **Project** menu. From the Project Settings dialog box, click the **Debug** tab, then select the **General** entry in the **Category** list box. Enter the fully qualified path to the client executable in the **Executable for debug session** box, and enter any command-line arguments for the specified client program in the **Program arguments** box. Now when you start a debugging session, Visual C++ launches the program you identified, passing it any command-line arguments you have specified. This technique can be used to debug your C++ component in any environment.

When specifying the name of the executable to launch, you must include the fully qualified path to that program if the program doesn't reside in the working directory (which can be configured on the **Debug** tab). The debugger automatically attempts to load the debugging symbols for the program you selected and gives you a warning if it can't. That's not a problem because the debugger will still honor any breakpoints you set in the DLL project (as long as it has debugging symbols). Furthermore, Visual C++ provides a few shortcuts to selecting the executable to launch. If you are developing an ActiveX control and want to debug your component using the ActiveX Control Test Container, click the button immediately to the right of the **Executable for debug session** box and choose **ActiveX Control Test Container**. If you want to debug a component that is being called from script on a Web page, you can select **Default Web Browser** to specify the browser executable.

> **TIP**
> Use the **Executable for debug session** option on the **Debug** tab of the **Project Settings** property sheet to debug a base COM DLL that is called by a program you did not develop.

Debugging Initialization and Activation Code

If your server fails to activate and you are debugging from the client project, you must have the debugger preload the debugging symbols for the server DLL some time before it reaches the first activation request instead of waiting until the COM SCM calls *LoadLibrary*. Once the debugging symbols are loaded, you can set breakpoints in the server DLL. If you are debugging from the server project, you can set the breakpoints before starting the debugging session. In either case, the trick is to set the breakpoints at the right code to find activation problems. Here are the usual suspects.

- In *DllMain* if you're doing anything interesting there.
- In *DllGetClassObject* if you're trying to diagnose "class not registered" failures or other early activation errors. If you're using ATL to implement *IClassFactory,* the most likely problem is a missing entry in the class map, so check that first before using the debugger.
- The constructor for the C++ class that implements the requested interface. With ATL, most of the interesting initialization code is in *FinalConstruct.*

- The implementation of *QueryInterface* if you're trying to diagnose "interface not supported" errors. If you're using ATL to implement *IUnknown, QueryInterface* is implemented for you, so the most likely problem is a missing entry in the interface map.

Once your breakpoints are set, initiate the debugging session and follow through to the source of the trouble.

> To debug initialization or activation code, preload the debugging symbols for your DLL and set breakpoints before the client calls *CoCreateInstance* or any other activation function.

Debugging ATL Self-Registration Code

If you implemented *DllRegisterServer* yourself, debugging self-registration code is just like debugging any other function: Just set a breakpoint on *DllRegister Server* and start debugging. If you're using ATL, however, self-registration is taken care of by an ATL component called the registrar. The component registrar parses registry scripting files (RGS) that drive the self-registration process.

If you never modify the RGS file that the ATL AppWizard generates, you're not likely to run into trouble. The most notable case in which self-registration still fails, even though you never modified the RGS file yourself, is when you attempt to register a component while logged into Windows 2000 using an account that is not a member of the Administrator's local group. If *DllRegister Server* is failing, first double-check that you're using an administrator account.

If *DllRegisterServer* is still failing even though you're logged in as an administrator, you must determine exactly where the failure occurs in the registration process. The difficult way to accomplish this is to review the RGS script until you've figured out which part of the script the component registrar doesn't like. Luckily, ATL provides a verbose (and extremely useful) version of the component registrar, which you can invoke as follows:

1. Display the Project Settings dialog box and choose the Win32 Debug build target.
2. Click the **C/C++** tab and enter the symbol _ATL_STATIC_REGISTRY in the **Preprocessor definitions** box.

3. Click the **Debug** tab and set the executable for the debug session to the fully qualified path to RegSvr32 (*Regsvr32.exe* in the System folder).
4. Set the program arguments for RegSvr32 to ".\debug\YourDllName.dll".
5. Click OK to save these changes.
6. Rebuild your DLL. It will now use a statically linked version of the component registrar. This version of the component registrar is verbose and will tell you exactly which part of the RGS script it doesn't like or had trouble performing.
7. Start the debugger. You don't need any breakpoints set; you just want to have the debugger launch RegSvr32, which will invoke the *DllRegister Server* function. Let RegSvr32 run to completion.

Having done this, look at the **Debug** tab of the Output window. The verbose component registrar uses the *OutputDebugString* API function to display the contents of the RGS script as it is read from your DLL's resource database. Immediately after the RGS script in the Output window is a detailed narrative of what the registrar was doing and the results. If the registrar encountered any difficulties, such as invalid RGS syntax or other run-time errors, it tells you what the problem was. Address the problem and repeat this procedure until the registrar can successfully register your server.

TIP

Define the _ATL_STATIC_REGISTRY preprocessor symbol in your ATL projects to diagnose RGS script errors.

Debugging Base COM EXEs

Most of the time, debugging out-of-process COM servers boils down to diagnosing and correcting configuration issues. The majority of this section covers the most common configuration issues that affect COM programmers. When it comes to using the debugger, debugging base COM EXEs is almost identical to debugging a regular Win32 program. Just open the server project into Visual C++ (or attach Visual C++ to an already running server), set breakpoints, and start debugging. Beyond the basic debugging techniques, Visual C++ also provides an incredibly useful feature, called OLE RPC Debugging, that facilitates the process of stepping from a client program into a method call that's implemented in your server program. After exploring configuration issues, I'll explain how to leverage OLE RPC Debugging.

Configuration Issues

If you're building a typical out-of-process server executable, the diagnostic checklist you should run through before using the debugger is a superset of the items I listed in the previous section, Debugging Base COM DLLs. Here are some more configuration issues that you should verify when dealing with an out-of-process server.

1. Are the launch permissions on the server correct?
2. Are the access permissions on the server correct?
3. Is the identity of the server process set appropriately?
4. Is there an authentication problem?

Are the launch permissions correct?

The COM SCM automatically launches a server process when an activation request is made. Whether or not the client making the activation request is allowed to launch, the server process is configurable at the server location. To determine what the launch permissions are for a given AppId, run the DCOM Configuration utility (*Dcomcnfg.exe* in the System folder). Locate the appropriate AppId in the list of installed COM programs, click **Properties** and select the **Security** tab on the resulting property sheet. If the **Use custom launch permissions** option is selected, click the corresponding **Edit** button. The DCOM Configuration utility displays a dialog box that lists the security principals (individuals as well as groups) that are allowed to launch this server. If the client that's making the activation request isn't listed and is not a member of one of the listed groups, then it has not been allowed to launch the server. Either add the client principal to this list or run the client program using an account that has been granted launch permissions.

If the **Use default launch permissions** option is selected or the server isn't listed in the list of AppIds displayed by the DCOM Configuration utility, machine-wide defaults are being used to govern launch permissions for this server. Dismiss the application properties to return to the initial DCOM Configuration window. Select the **Default Security** tab, and then click the **Edit**

Default button that's listed for **Default Launch Permissions**. As with custom launch permissions, make sure that the client making the activation request is allowed to launch the server.

Are the access permissions correct?

Once the server process is running (whether or not the server was already started or launched as a result of an activation request by the calling client), access permissions are evaluated. Only clients that have been explicitly granted access permissions can invoke functions within a given server process. Access permissions can be set in two ways: using the registry and the DCOM Configuration utility or using the server code. To figure out exactly where the SCM is getting the access permissions from, apply the following logic (shown in pseudocode).

```
IF server is explicitly calling CoInitializeSecurity THEN
    SWITCH( first parameter to CoInitializeSecurity )
        CASE NULL:
            Everyone is allowed access permissions.
        END CASE
        CASE PointerToSecurityDescriptor:
            The DACL here governs security (registry is ignored).
        END CASE
        CASE PointerToIAccessControlImplementation:
            The COM SCM calls IAccessControl::IsAccessAllowed.
        END CASE
        CASE PointerToAppIdGUID:
            UsePermissionsFromRegistryForGivenAppId()5
        END CASE
    END SWITCH
ELSE
    IF server filename-to-AppId registry mapping exists THEN
        UsePermissionsFromRegistryForGivenAppId()[5]
    ELSE
        UseMachineWideDefaultsFromRegistryForAccessPermissions()
    END ELSE
END ELSE
```

---

[5] See the COM Security chapter of *Programming Windows Security*, by Keith Brown, for a detailed discussion of the frailties associated with this approach to access permissions.

The numerous possible reasons for calling *CoInitializeSecurity* can be overwhelming, but they boil down to knowing whether or not access permissions are being governed by information in the registry. If the server developer is passing a security descriptor or an *IAccessControl* interface pointer to *CoInitialize Security*, the server developer will have indicated what the access permissions are for the server. If you developed the server, you already know how you're calling *CoInitializeSecurity*. If you are using a server developed by another person, the only way to know what the server is doing is to consult with the server's developer. In all other scenarios, the COM SCM is consulting the registry to determine who is allowed access to the server.

If access permissions are being set through the registry, you can run the DCOM Configuration utility to view those permissions. As with launch permissions, view the server's security property page. If the **Use custom access permissions** option is selected, click the corresponding **Edit** button to find out who is allowed access to the server. If the **Use default access permissions** option is selected or the server isn't listed in the list of AppIds displayed by the DCOM Configuration utility, machine-wide defaults are being used to govern access permissions for this server. Dismiss the application properties to return to the initial DCOM Configuration window. Select the **Default Security** tab, and click the **Edit Default** button that's listed for **Default Access Permissions**. As with custom access permissions, make sure that the client calling in to the server is allowed access to the server.

Is the identity of the server process set appropriately?

When the COM SCM activates a server, it executes the program in the security context of a given security principal (by calling *CreateProcessAsUser* instead of *CreateProcess*). If you run the DCOM Configuration utility, display the property sheet for a particular server and select the **Identity** tab; you'll see that a COM server process can run using one of three identities:

- The interactive user
- The launching user (often referred to as "as activator")
- This user (often referred to as "a distinguished principal")

During debugging, servers should be configured to run as the interactive user. This allows assertions and any other forms of window-based feedback to be seen by the person sitting in front of the machine the server is running on. Since this person is usually you, this is almost always the behavior you want. Configuring a server to run as the activator almost never makes sense, but it is supported for backward compatibility. (MTS and COM+ do away with this option, allowing a server to be launched only as the interactive user or a distinguished principal.) The problem with this approach is that the SCM launches a unique copy of the server program for each client making activation requests, which doesn't scale well if there are a large number of clients. Another problem is that each copy of the server process is run in a unique and invisible window station, which means that if an assertion fails in the server, nobody can see the resulting message box and the server appears to be hung to any clients. For real-world deployment, servers should be configured to run as a distinguished principal. This approach is more scalable because all clients are connected to the same instance of the server process. The server process still runs in an invisible window station, however, so assertions and other forms of window-based user interfaces cannot be seen.

In addition to making assertions visible, there is another reason to configure a server to run as the interactive user. When the server calls *CoRegister ClassObject*, the SCM looks at the identity of the calling process and compares that to the configured "run as" identity of the associated CLSID. If there is a mismatch, *CoRegisterClassObject* returns CO_E_WRONG_SERVER_IDENTITY, thereby causing the server to fail. This isn't a problem when the SCM is launching the server process because the SCM launches the process using the appropriate "run as" identity. It is a problem if you are trying to debug the server by opening the server workspace, setting breakpoints, and then initiating a debug session. In this situation, the process identity for the server process is inherited from the Visual C++ process, which is running as the interactive user. If the server has been configured to run as anything other than the interactive user, *CoRegisterClassObject* is destined to fail.

> **TIP**
>
> Configure your server to run as the interactive user when you are debugging the server. Configure the server to run as a distinguished principal when you are deploying to the field.

Is there an authentication problem?

Even if all the previous configuration issues have been solved, one last hurdle must be overcome if the client and server processes are running on different machines: network authentication. When a client tries to connect to a server, the SCM enforces the launch and access permissions specified by the server. To support remote activation while maintaining the security of the server, the SCM creates a logon session locally on the server machine. The result of the logon session is an access token that represents the client's identity and can be used to grant or deny access to the server. For this logon to succeed, the client must be authenticated to the server. This means that the client must have an account either on the server's machine or on a domain controller that the server can access.[6] If there is no path of trust from the server machine to a domain controller that can vouch for the credentials being presented by the calling client, then authentication fails.

To determine if you have an authentication problem, run the Local Security Policy Microsoft Management Console (MMC) snap-in on Windows 2000 or the User Manager on Windows NT 4.0 and enable auditing of logon and logoff events for both successful and failed attempts. Now any attempt to log on to a machine (whether interactively or programmatically by the SCM on behalf of a client) results in an event being written to the Security event log on the server. You can then reattempt the access that's failing and review the event log to determine if the problem is related to authentication.

> **TIP**
>
> Audit logon and logoff events to help diagnose authentication failures.

One last note about authentication: In the typical scenario, a client attempts to acquire an interface pointer into a server, but this activity may fail due to authentication. If there is a callback relationship between the client and server whereby the server process makes outbound COM method calls back to the client process, the server must be authenticated to the client on the first such

---

[6] This is something of a simplification, but the details of network authentication are beyond the scope of this book. For details on network authentication, see *Programming Windows Security* by Keith Brown and *Network Security: Private Communication in a Public World* by Kaufman, Perlman, and Speciner.

method call. Consequently, if you're having callback problems, audit logon and logoff attempts on both the client and server machines.[7] Just because the client can call the server doesn't mean the server can call the client. Each party must grant the other party the appropriate access permissions.

TIP

When a callback relationship exists between two parties, both parties must have appropriate access permissions.

Client-side Debugging Techniques

The mechanics for debugging client-side code are basically the same whether the server being called is in-process or out-of-process. Visual C++ supports what it calls OLE RPC Debugging. When this feature is enabled and you single step into a method call that's implemented in a local EXE server, Visual C++ automatically launches a new copy of the debugger and attaches it to the server process. This new debugger instance breaks at the beginning of the method code that the client program just called. It's as if you were stepping into a method call implemented by a DLL in the client address space. In fact, when you step out of the method code, the original instance of Visual C++ (which is debugging the client program) is brought to the foreground and the instruction pointer is on the line of code after the method invocation you originally stepped into.

To enable OLE RPC Debugging, choose the **Options** command from the **Tools** menu, click the **Debug** tab, then select **OLE RPC Debugging**. To enable and use this feature, you must be running Visual C++ from an account that is a member of the Administrator's local group.

TIP

Enable OLE RPC Debugging to enable single-stepping across process address spaces from a client program into the server program.

---

[7] Having reached this point, you might be wishing you could disable security altogether. In fact, you can. Keith Brown keeps a security FAQ at *www.develop.com/kbrown* that explains exactly what to do. Furthermore, whereas security is enabled by default in base COM, it is *disabled* by default in MTS and COM+ until you decide to enable security.

Server-side Debugging Techniques

As I said earlier, debugging a COM executable is almost identical to debugging a Win32 program. Two techniques, however, do not always work the same in a COM server: *DebugBreak* and Just-in-Time debugging. The *DebugBreak* API function raises a breakpoint exception to the debugger. If no debugger is attached, Windows launches Visual C++ and attaches it to the program. In this regard, *DebugBreak* is handled just like any other exception. In a COM server, the stub that performs the call into your method implementation on behalf of a client traps any unhandled exceptions that occur within your method. This means that exceptions (including the one generated by *DebugBreak*) that occur within a COM method call do not cause the JIT debugger to launch. Instead, the client sees an HRESULT that indicates failure. Exceptions that occur *outside* the context of a COM method call (for example, in *WinMain* or in a worker thread you created in your server) are still trapped by Windows and passed to the debugger in the standard fashion. If you have already attached the debugger to your server, the debugger still sees first-chance exception notifications and responds accordingly.

> Stubs trap exceptions that occur within COM methods in the server, thereby reducing the usefulness of *DebugBreak* and Just-in-Time debugging in out-of-process COM servers.

Debugging Configured Components

Many programmers who first dip their toes into the waters of MTS/COM+ development feel like they have to relearn how to debug. I know I sure did. One difference is that configuration information is now split between the registry and the MTS/COM+ catalog. Another difference is that although you're still developing a DLL, the DLL is no longer loaded into the client address space (this assumes that you're developing *server packages* as opposed to *library packages,* which still run in the client address space). The good news is that debugging configured components is a relatively simple extension of the techniques you already know, with only a minor wrinkle here and there.

Configuration Issues

With the exception of security attributes, the configuration settings for base COM servers, such as CLSID mapping, threading model, and interface proxy/stub information, are still maintained in the registry. This was done for backward compatibility with base COM servers, but it means that we can't leave the "bad old days" of the registry behind us. Security settings, including identity, and all the new configuration options available for configured components are now stored in the MTS or COM+ catalog. This catalog provides a set of script-friendly COM interfaces that support enumeration, reading, and writing that installation programmers will appreciate. The catalog can also be read and modified graphically by using the MTS or COM+ Explorer. In general, diagnosing configuration issues in configured components is procedurally the same as for base COM EXE servers, except that you use the MTS or COM+ Explorer instead of the DCOM Configuration Utility. Nonetheless, several issues remain that need to be understood.

Do Not Self-Register Configured Components on Windows NT 4.0

In Windows NT 4.0, MTS is an add-on technology that was implemented without requiring any changes to the COM infrastructure. One side effect is that when you configure a DLL under MTS, the configuration process calls your self-registration entry point (*DllRegisterServer*) and spies on your calls to the registry API. This is how MTS discovers the CLSIDs for the various classes of objects your DLL may support. For each CLSID you support, MTS deletes the corresponding *InprocServer32* registry value and replaces it with a *Local Server32* value that tells the COM SCM to launch *Mtx.exe* with a command line identifying the MTS package of which your component is a member. This leaves clients unaware that the server DLL is now a configured component running in another address space.

If you subsequently reregister the DLL by running RegSvr32, however, your self-registration code restores the *InprocServer32* registry value, thus negating the MTS configuration procedure. The next time any client tries to activate the server and includes the CLTCTX_LOCAL_SERVER flag in its activation request, the COM SCM loads your DLL directly into the client's address space—which is not what you intended. ATL AppWizard-generated DLL projects (even when you select **Support MTS)** include a post-build step that automatically runs RegSvr32; therefore, the very next time you build your DLL, you undo the MTS registration.

There are two ways to remedy this situation. First, you can remove the post-build step from the project before you build the DLL. This is always a good idea. The second option is to run the MTS Explorer, right-click on **My Computer** in the **Computers** folder, and select **Refresh All Components**. This causes MTS to spy on your self-registration again and repair the registry. You can also execute the *Mtxregeg.exe* utility from a command shell. It's ironic that when you select **Support MTS** in the ATL AppWizard, the wizard adds a custom post-build step that warns you to run Mtxrereg. I imagine that Microsoft chose not to omit the RegSvr32 call for the sake of backward compatibility. In any case, there's no rule that you can't remove the RegSvr32 step yourself, which is what I recommend.

> For your configured components, remove the automatic self-registration custom-build step from ATL AppWizard-generated DLL projects.

Shut Down the Server before Making Configuration Changes

Be sure the server process isn't running when you make configuration changes. This may seem obvious, but the problem is that both MTS and COM+ keep the server process running even after the last client disconnects. Consequently, simply stopping the client program to make a server-side configuration change is insufficient. When the last client disconnects, the server process doesn't exit until no further activation requests have been made for about three minutes. This delay reduces server shutdown-startup thrashing. If you make a configuration change before the server process exits and then rerun the client, the configuration doesn't change.

Luckily, the solution to this problem is simple. After making the desired configuration changes, right-click on the server package in the MTS or COM+ Explorer and choose **Shut down**. This makes MTS/COM+ stop the server process. Any subsequent activation requests cause the COM SCM to relaunch the surrogate process for that package, picking up any configuration changes you may have made.

TIP

After making configuration changes to a configured component, use the MTS or COM+ Explorer to shut down the server package so that your changes take effect the next time the server is activated.

Client-side Debugging Techniques

Mechanically, debugging a configured component when you are working in the client project is the same as for base COM EXE servers. OLE RPC Debugging is still supported, but you must aid the transition from the client workspace into the server. When you single step into a method call on a configured component, Visual C++ still launches another copy of the debugger, attaching it to the surrogate process in which the component resides. This new copy of the debugger, however, stops a bit shy of the actual method implementation you were trying to step into, so you'll be looking at some disassembly for the surrogate process. To bridge the gap, open the source code file that contains the method you are stepping into, set a breakpoint, and then resume the debugger. The surrogate continues to execute until it reaches the breakpoint. If execution does not reach the method being called, it means the interceptor has rejected the method call (typically for security reasons) and returned to the client without ever invoking your component code.

Server-side Debugging Techniques

When it's not possible to initiate a debugging session by starting with the client workspace or when you want to debug the initialization code in a configured component, you must deal with the surrogate architecture directly. Again, the mechanics of debugging a configured component are the same as those for a base COM EXE, except that you no longer own the source code for the process that is hosting the component code. Because a COM-provided surrogate process hosts your server DLL, the procedure for prestarting your server or attaching Visual C++ to a running instance of your server is a little different for configured components.

Prestarting the Surrogate Process in the Debugger—Windows NT 4.0

Open the DLL workspace that contains the code you want to debug. Display the Project Settings dialog box and click the **Debug** tab. Set the executable program to the fully qualified path to *Mtx.exe* (in the System folder). Now set the command line arguments for *Mtx.exe* to */p:{package guid}*. You can determine the GUID for the package by right-clicking on the package in the MTS Explorer and selecting **Properties**. The GUID for the package is listed on the **General** tab. Now when you start the debugging session, the debugger launches *Mtx.exe,* which immediately loads your component DLL and then calls *DllGetClass Object* once for each CLSID your component supports. If you need to debug *DllGetClassObject*, set your breakpoints before initiating the debug session.

> You can prestart the MTS surrogate for your configured component by setting the debug executable for your DLL to *Mtx.exe,* with a command line option of */p:{package GUID}*.

Prestarting the Surrogate Process in the Debugger—Windows 2000

In Windows 2000, there are two ways to attach the debugger to the surrogate process for your DLL. First, you can follow the same procedure outlined above for Windows NT 4.0. There are just two differences in Windows 2000: (1) The surrogate program is *DllHost.exe,* not *Mtx.exe,* and (2) The command line for *DllHost.exe* is */ProcessId:{application guid}*, not */p:{package guid}*.

> Use the **Launch in the debugger** options for your package in the Windows 2000 COM+ Explorer to attach Visual C++ to the surrogate process whenever it is started.

The second option is to tell COM+ to activate the debugger for the surrogate automatically when the surrogate is initially started. Locate your COM+ package in the COM+ Explorer, select **Properties**, click the **Advanced** tab and select the **Launch in the debugger** option. When a client attempts to activate your server, the COM SCM launches Visual C++ using the appropriate command line for your package. As with the first technique, you can enter break-points and then start the server by initiating the debug session. If you want to prestart the server and set breakpoints before any clients attempt to activate your server, just right-click on the COM+ package in the COM+ Explorer and select **Start**.

Attaching to a Running Surrogate Process, or "Which Surrogate Am I In?"

Since every configured component runs inside a different copy of the surrogate executable, attaching the debugger to a component that's already running is no longer as easy as right-clicking on the program in the Task Manager and choosing **Debug**. Now you have to figure out which copy of *Mtx.exe* or *DllHost.exe* your component is hosted in. Here are the steps for determining the process to which you can attach.

1. Run the Visual C++ Process Viewer utility (*PView.exe*).
2. Select one of the surrogate process instances from the list of running processes.
3. Click the **Memory Detail** button.
4. In the Memory Details dialog box, pull down the **User Address Space for** list, which contains all the DLLs that are loaded into that copy of the sur-rogate process.
5. If you see your component DLL in this list, note the process ID of the sur-rogate, and attach the debugger to that process.
6. If you do not see your component DLL listed, repeat steps 2 through 4 until you discover the surrogate process hosting your component DLL.

Clearly, this procedure is a bit tedious if you have several MTS or COM+ packages running on a given machine. To make it easier to debug configured components, I've developed a tool that allows you to attach the debugger auto-matically to the correct instance of the surrogate process. This tool, called the DbgPak utility, can be found at *www.windebug.com*.

> **TIP**
>
> The DbgPak utility, available at *www.windebug.com,* automates the procedure of attaching Visual C++ to the running instance of *Mtx.exe* or *DllHost.exe* that is hosting your configured component.

Debugging Self-Registration Code

If you need to debug the self-registration code for a configured component, the easiest approach is to debug it before you configure the DLL to run in MTS or COM+. Just follow the steps listed in Debugging Base COM DLLs, earlier in this chapter. Once you've ironed out the self-registration issues, configure the component to run under MTS/COM+. This approach is much, much easier than trying to configure MMC as the debugging executable for your DLL, starting a debug session, loading the MTS/COM+ component snap-in into MMC, creating the server package, and then adding the DLL in question to the package.

TIP

Debug self-registration problems before configuring your DLL in MTS or COM+ by specifying Regsvr32 as the debug executable that Visual C++ should launch.

Debugging Base COM DLLs That Are Called from ASPs

If you are writing base COM DLLs that are being called from script running within an Active Server Page (ASP), your code is being called from a configured component. When Microsoft's Internet Information Server processes a request for an ASP, it activates a configured component called the Web Application Manager. This component performs activation and method call requests being made by scripts on that ASP. Because the Web Application Manager component is configured in MTS/COM+, your base COM DLL will execute in the context of a surrogate process.

Attaching the debugger to the right surrogate process in this scenario is a matter of determining which server package will be used to host your component. The Internet Services Manager allows you to control the degree of isolation that encapsulates requests to a given directory on your Web site. Depending on how you configure a particular virtual directory, your component will be executed either directly within the IIS process or in another address space.

Debugging Components Called from ASP—Windows NT 4.0

The property page for a given virtual directory contains an option called **Run in a separate address space (isolated)**. If this option is not selected, your component will run within the IIS address space (*Inetinfo.exe*). To debug your component, attach Visual C++ to *Inetinfo.exe,* load the symbols for your DLL, set breakpoints, then use a web browser to view the ASP that calls your component. If the virtual directory is configured to run in a separate address space, use the MTS Explorer to locate the package named **IIS—{*website//virtual directory name*}** and note the package's GUID. At this point, you can follow the procedure outlined earlier for prestarting the surrogate process in the debugger using the server package GUID you just determined.

Debugging Components Called from ASP—Windows 2000

In Windows 2000, the property page for a given virtual directory contains an option called **Application Protection**, which can be set to one of the following values.

- Low (IIS Process)
- Medium (Pooled)
- High (Isolated)

The setting you choose governs which server package will host your component. If Application Protection is set to Low, find the package GUID in the COM+ Explorer for **IIS In-Process Application**. If Application Protection is set to Medium, find the package GUID in the COM+ Explorer for **IIS Out-Of-Process Pooled Applications**. If Application Protection is set to High, find the package GUID in the COM+ Explorer for **IIS—{*website//virtual directory name*}**. At this point, you can follow the procedure outlined earlier in the chapter for attaching Visual C++ to the running surrogate process in the debugger using the server package GUID you just determined.

I hope that this survey of the COM debugging landscape helps give you some direction. After applying these techniques a few times, you should be able to zero in on the points of failure in your system more quickly. The sooner you can pinpoint the problem, the sooner you can remove the bug and be on your way.

Recommended Reading

Box, Don. *Essential COM*. Reading, MA: Addison-Wesley, 1998.   Introduces the core concepts and programming model of COM, along with advice on typical programming mistakes and how to prevent them.

Brown, Keith. *Programming Windows Security*. Boston, MA: Addison-Wesley, 2000. Provides a comprehensive look at the security architecture and programming models in Windows, including a chapter devoted to COM security.

Kaufman, Charlie, Radia Perlman, and Mike Speciner. *Network Security: Private Communication in a Public World*. Englewood Cliffs, NJ: Prentice-Hall, 1995. This book, which is not specific to Windows, presents information on various network authentication protocols.

Rector, Brent, and Chris Sells. *ATL Internals*. Reading, MA: Addison-Wesley, 1999. Provides a comprehensive look at ATL programming, with detailed information on using ATL's smart interface pointer classes.

Chapter 12

Desperate Measures

When you get stuck while debugging, you must sometimes take unusual measures. This chapter presents several alternative debugging techniques to use when your normal debugging process isn't finding the bug.

First, it's important to specify exactly what I mean by a desperate measure. I will start by stating what a desperate measure is not: A desperate measure is not the same as a last resort. These are not necessarily techniques to try when you have abandoned all hope and can't think of anything else to do. Rather, try these when you need to deviate from your normal debugging process. For example, the first two suggestions are to restart Windows and perform a complete rebuild of your program. These techniques are out of the ordinary because you don't restart Windows and do a complete rebuild every time you find a bug. When debugging, if Windows or any other program starts to exhibit erratic or unexpected behavior, I immediately stop what I am doing and restart Windows; quite often, that fixes the problem. Thus, restarting Windows clearly isn't a last resort; in fact, it might be one of the first things I do.

> **TIP**
>
> Consider these desperate measures when you get stuck, but remember that a desperate measure is not a last resort.

One of the dictionary definitions of *desperate* refers to employing extreme measures in an attempt to escape defeat or frustration. If you define *extreme* as something out of the ordinary, this definition fits here. You need to use desperate measures when there is something about the bug or its circumstance that makes it unlikely that your standard debugging approach is going to find the problem. In such cases, the cause of the bug might not be in your code at all. Rather, the cause could be external to your code, such as a problem with the system configuration or the hardware. Sometimes the cause is a bug in Windows itself; sometimes the problem is some type of system corruption or running out of system resources. On occasion the "bug" isn't even a bug; rather, the program is behaving correctly but unexpectedly, and those expectations are wrong. In circumstances like these, you can spend a great deal of time tracking down a bug in your code when the bug isn't even in your code.

A word of caution: You should have a justification before using any measures that cast blame away from your code. As stated in Chapter 1, The Debugging Process, some programmers are too eager to blame their colleagues, their compiler, or Windows itself for their bugs. Don't play the blame game, and don't go into denial. Although it is possible that external factors are the cause of the problem, it is more courteous and productive to assume that the problem is in your code and cast suspicion on other factors only after finding compelling evidence that the problem isn't in your code. Your inability to find the bug in your code after a quick check is not compelling evidence. However, once you begin to collect evidence that the problem may not be in your code, using such measures is appropriate and can save you a lot of time and frustration.

Checking the Easy Stuff

Here are some things to try that are easy to do and require little justification. When debugging, the instant you say to yourself, "Wait a minute, that doesn't make any sense," it's time to consider these steps.

Restart Windows

You should restart Windows whenever you see Windows or any other program start to exhibit erratic or unexpected behavior. The Windows system may be corrupted, or it may have run out of resources. The cause could be a bug in your program, a bug in another program, or even a bug in Windows itself; but whatever the problem or cause, restart Windows to eliminate the state of the operating system as a factor in your debugging effort.

Completely Rebuild Your Program

Although Visual C++ does a remarkable job of compiling only the modules it needs to, things sometimes get out of kilter and your program must be completely rebuilt. For example, the Visual C++ Edit and Continue feature can sometimes result in problems because it doesn't perform any prelink or post build steps, which results in a bad build if your program requires these steps. Do a complete rebuild whenever your program starts to exhibit erratic or unexpected behavior or if the Visual C++ compiler fails with an internal compiler error. For example, your program might start to crash when performing tasks that used to work and whose source code hasn't been changed. Not being able to set breakpoints on valid source code locations is a good sign that something is out of synch. First you might want to delete your project's *Debug* and *Release* folders to ensure that the rebuild is complete. Always delete the *Debug* and *Release* folders and perform a complete rebuild after upgrading your compiler. If you believe your program or the debugger is behaving in a way that doesn't make sense, do a complete rebuild to eliminate the build as a factor in your debugging effort.

Reset the Visual C++ Environment

I once had a program crash during debugging when I stepped into *WinMain*. Specifically, I set a breakpoint at the start of *WinMain*, ran the program to the breakpoint, and then did a single step, which crashed the program. Because no global variable initialization was involved, my code was nowhere in sight. The problem? An errant breakpoint expression I set in the Breakpoints dialog box. When I cleared all breakpoints, the problem immediately went away.

Visual C++ has some extraordinary capabilities, but these features may lead to bizarre problems. If your program is behaving strangely, try clearing all breakpoints, clearing or hiding the Watch window, and checking the Project Settings dialog box for recent changes. These steps should remove any unexpected behavior caused by the Visual C++ environment.

Using Your Head

Of course, you should always use your head: Sleepwalking through a debugging session isn't likely to be productive. When you are stuck, though, it really pays to work smarter, not harder. Here are some techniques for making sure your brain is fully engaged.

Don't Depend on the Debugger

One place where programmers tend to get stuck is with trying to reproduce a problem using the debugger. Although the debugger is usually your most powerful and productive debugging tool, this is true only if you are able to reproduce the problem in a reasonable amount of time. If you can't reproduce the problem, it's time to start thinking about tracking down the problem using other techniques. Don't become overly dependent on the debugger.

You might not be able to reproduce a problem using the debugger for a variety of reasons. The most insidious of these relates to the Heisenberg Uncertainty Principle (discussed in Chapter 1), whereby the presence of the debugger itself changes the behavior of your program, thus making some types of bugs impossible to reproduce.

It is important to remember that you don't have to witness the bug with the debugger to understand what is happening. Instead of directly witnessing the crime with the debugger, it may be more productive to reconstruct the crime scene using circumstantial evidence. Since you have the source code and you know how it is supposed to work, you can determine how the code really works by executing the relevant portions of it in your head. Of course, you can supplement your circumstantial evidence by instrumenting your program with debugging aids, such as assertions, trace statements, and log files. Once you have gathered enough information, you can often track down the bug using deductive and inductive logic or with creative thinking, as discussed in Chapter 1, The Debugging Process.

Understand the Program

Regardless of whether you are using a debugger or not, you need to understand how the program works. This includes knowing its goals, its design, its components and their relationship, and its core technologies. Attempting to debug a program that you don't really understand is likely to be unproductive or even harmful.

The best way to understand a program is to walk through its source code and its documentation (there is documentation, isn't there?) and learn how it works. Then walk through the code again, but this time analyze it with respect to the bug. Determine how the bug could possibly happen, then try to determine which specific code could be the cause. For each possible cause, compare the behavior you would expect to the actual behavior and eliminate some possibilities. Finally, walk through the remaining code carefully and look for the problem.

I find that if I try hard enough and perhaps run a few tests, I can isolate many bugs by walking through the code without the debugger. It's hard work; but if you're stuck, it's rarely a waste of time. Even if you don't find the bug, at least you obtain a better understanding of the program and the problem, and you might determine a better way to find the problem. Furthermore, making an effort to understand the program will help you determine where the problem isn't, which in turn helps you focus your effort where the problem is.

Work through Test Cases

Sometimes code is just too complex to understand completely. For example, I worked on a program that performed complex graphical transformations. To display the data, I had to scale and zoom the data within the document, then rotate and scroll the data, then change its origin within the view. (Really.) Although it is easy enough to understand any one or two of these transformations, I found it impossible to think about three or more transformations simultaneously. So how do you understand such a program enough to find the bugs? Well, you can't; but what you can do is work through individual test cases. For example, you can debug the code by taking a single point, such as the upper left-hand corner, and walking through the code to see how the single point is transformed. If the code is simply too complex to think through abstractly, debug the problem by working through a few strategic test cases.

TIP

If the code is too complex to think through abstractly, debug the problem by working through a few strategic test cases.

Try a Different Approach

If you are stuck, stop and think. Ask yourself why you are stuck. Have you overlooked something? Have you made an incorrect assumption? Are you trying the same unproductive approach over and over again? Have you become so focused on accomplishing some insignificant task that you have lost sight of the big picture? If so, stop what you are doing and consider trying a different approach to help get you moving again, even if that movement doesn't immediately appear to be the right direction. Even if you try something that appears to be a waste of time, the failed effort might provide valuable information or even reveal the right approach. (Thomas Edison is famous for using this technique in discovering the incandescent light bulb. However, he is also famous for not getting much sleep.)

Rechecking Your Assumptions

You make many assumptions during the debugging process, especially when you receive bug information indirectly through a bug report. When you get stuck, it is a good idea to review your assumptions and convince yourself that they are valid. If you have made invalid assumptions, chances are you are looking for the bug in all the wrong places.

Assumptions about the Bug

Here are the typical assumptions one makes about a bug.

- **There actually is a bug.** Occasionally a "bug" really is a feature. For example, suppose you fixed a bug that resulted in receiving an error message for good data. Now suppose you receive the error message again. Based on your previous experience, it is easy to assume that the bug is still there and that the error message is incorrect; but it's possible the error message is correct and the data really is bad. This assumption would result in you wasting time trying to remove a bug that doesn't exist. I've fallen into this trap on more than one occasion. Programs sometimes work the way they are supposed to, even when previous experience suggests otherwise.

- **The bug hasn't already been fixed.** Bugs are often reported more than once. Sometimes fixing one bug fixes another bug. Other times bugs are fixed by other programmers. As a result, you sometimes try to debug a problem that has already been fixed; so be aware of this possibility when you can't reproduce a bug. Bugs don't go away by themselves, however, so you should never assume a bug has been fixed. Rather, verify that it has been fixed by reviewing the bug database and the appropriate files in the source code control system.

- **The bug report is correct.** Bug reports are sometimes incorrect, incomplete, or misleading. When you suspect a bug report problem, don't be afraid to ask for a clarification or more information.

- **The test program or script is correct.** If a bug was detected by a test program or test script, there is a possibility that the test itself has a bug. Keep this in mind if you can't reproduce a bug reported by a test program or script.

- **The bug can be reproduced.** Sometimes a bug isn't really a bug but a symptom of system corruption. Other times a bug can be reproduced only with a specific version of Windows, possibly requiring a specific service pack. Thus, it is important for testers to try to reproduce the bugs they find and report the specific version of Windows they are using.

Assumptions about the Program

Here are the typical assumptions made about a Windows program.

- **The source code is correct.** Be sure you have checked out the right version of the source code. This mistake is especially easy to make if there are several versions of the program.

- **The compilation is correct.** Be sure you are using the right version of the compiler with the right compiler and linker settings. Compiler options such as /Zp (struct member alignment) are especially prone to cause nasty bugs. You can easily review the compiler and linker settings by opening the project's DSP file using a text editor (be sure to open it in Visual C++ as a text file). From the editor, you can compare the current compiler and linker settings to the base settings. You can also compare the debug build settings to the release build settings.

- **The build process is correct.** Make sure the build process is using the right files and is successfully performing all the necessary steps. Make sure that you are using the right library versions, for example, that the debug build is using debug libraries, the release build is using release libraries, or the MFC and the C Run-time Libraries are either both dynamic or both static.

- **The Windows system components are correct.** Be certain you are debugging with the right version of Windows. Unfortunately, checking this assumption isn't as simple as it might seem because there are several versions of Windows and some Windows APIs are distributed with the Internet Explorer. For example, look at the Requirements section of any of the shell functions in the MSDN documentation, such as the *SHGetSpecialFolderPath* API function. It's scary.

- **The third-party components are correct.** Be sure that any third-party components required by your program have been installed and registered.

- **The Windows registry is correct.** All the registry settings required by your program must be correct. If the program requires environment variables (hopefully, it doesn't), review them as well.

- **The program options are correct.** Windows programs typically have many options. Some programs also have several different modes, both at the user interface level and internally. Not surprisingly, some bugs can be reproduced only with the correct combinations of options and modes, a fact that is easy for both programmers and testers to overlook.

- **The data is correct.** The data required by your program must be available and correctly formatted. Make sure your program is using the data you think it is using, not some old version or test version of the data.

- **The setup program is correct.** Be sure the setup program correctly installs your program by copying the right files to the right locations and making the right registry settings. If not, all bets are off.

- **The peripherals are correct.** If your program is having trouble with a peripheral, ensure that the peripheral is correctly installed, connected, turned on, enabled, and properly functioning. For example, if you are having a problem printing to a specific printer, make sure the printer is plugged in, turned on, properly connected, and correctly installed. Then try the printer self-test to make sure the printer is working correctly and that it has ink and paper.

Most of the time you can take these assumptions for granted, especially when you have been working with the same program for a while. However, if you are debugging with a computer or other hardware you don't normally use or you are debugging a program you haven't touched in some time, it's a good idea to verify these assumptions when things stop making sense. Note that any conclusions based on faulty assumptions are likely to be wrong. Keep in mind also that a program can malfunction in many ways that don't require defects in the code.

TIP

A program can malfunction in many ways that don't require defects in the code.

Checking the Obvious

Sometimes you can get stuck simply by overlooking a detail that, in retrospect, should have been obvious. What is considered obvious is always retrospective; that is, you never consider something obvious while you are overlooking it.

Here are some obvious details to check.

- **Review the compiler warnings.** Compile at the /W4 warning level and look at all the warnings. Also, occasionally build using a release build: the Visual C++ compiler does a much better job of detecting the use of uninitialized local variables with release builds than with debug builds because this is situation is checked for during optimization.

- **Enable MFC trace statements.** Trace statements in MFC can be disabled by running the Visual C++ Tracer program. Run Tracer to make sure they are enabled.

- **Look at the trace statements.** Review the trace statement output to look for clues. Unfortunately, trace statement output is a bit too easy to overlook.

- **Examine the new code.** Run the Visual C++ WinDiff utility (or an equivalent) to determine all the recent code changes, then carefully review these changes either manually or with the debugger. New problems are more likely to be found in new code. The WinDiff utility allows you to compare entire directories, so you can find all the code changes in a matter of seconds.

- **Check the build.** The specific compiler and linker options you are using for a build may be a factor in the bug. Display the **Program Settings** dialog box, and carefully review all the settings for both the debug and release builds. You can also check for build problems by creating both debug and release builds and comparing their behavior. Although different behavior can suggest a build problem, it may imply a bug in the code. The differences between debug and release builds and how they affect bugs is discussed in Chapter 7, Debugging with the Visual C++ Debugger.

- **Check the components.** Make sure you are debugging the components you think you are. If you load a DLL workspace in Visual C++ and then specify an executable for your debugging session, that executable is guaranteed to be used but the DLL loaded in the workspace is not. Rather, the executable uses the first matching DLL it finds in the Windows file search sequence. (The Windows file search sequence is documented with the *LoadLibrary* API function.) Similarly, the COM *CoCreateInstance* function uses the server it finds in the registry, regardless of what you have loaded in your workspace. You can determine the exact components used by a program in Visual C++ using the **Modules** command in the Debug menu.

- **Check the system.** Examine the system to make sure that resources are available, including GDI resources, memory, and hard disk space. The available hard disk space affects the available memory because the hard disk is used for the virtual memory swap file. You can quickly determine the system state by running the Microsoft System Information utility. If any system resources are low, take the appropriate action to make more available. Of course, check all peripherals to make sure they are turned on and plugged in.

Checking the Code

It's possible that the problem is simply a silly mistake in the code (it wouldn't be the first time that has happened). Review the relevant code and verify that it is

- Calling the correct functions
- Using the correct function parameters in the right order
- Using the correct function calling convention (for example, always use `__stdcall` (or CALLBACK) for window and dialog procedures)
- Using the correct variables
- Using the correct variable types
- Using the correct variable qualifiers, such as `const` and `volatile`
- Initializing all variables and data members
- Zeroing freed pointers and handles
- Using the correct parentheses
- Using the correct logic, such as not having dangling `else` clauses
- Using header files for declarations shared across files and not declaring `extern` variables
- Using correct casting
- Not having unintended side effects
- Exception safe

In addition, make sure you have reviewed the comments in the relevant code. Sometimes code is actually well documented.

Checking the System

The possibility always exists that a bug is either caused by the system or is system dependent. Were Windows programs largely self-contained, as MS-DOS programs are, system-related bugs would be far less likely. Once you combine the different base versions of Windows and the different versions of all the various system DLLs, there is ample opportunity for system configuration problems that result in bugs.

The first clue of a system-related problem is the program's behaving differently on different computers. For example, your program may crash on one machine but work fine with all the others. When this happens, look for trends. Try the program on several different computers. Does the program behave differently with Windows 2000 than it does with Windows 98? Is the program even compatible with both versions? Are service packs a factor? Is the version of Internet Explorer (which often installs system DLLs) a factor? Is the problem limited to a single computer? Are drivers a factor? Does program behavior change when you run in Windows Safe Mode? Every test you make provides more information to help narrow down the problem.

If the problem occurs only with computers that don't have a recent service pack, apply the latest service pack to one of those computers and verify that the bug is gone. If this works, you're in luck: Until you determine otherwise, you can assume the problem lies in Windows itself and make your software require the service pack. This is an assumption, however: sometimes system changes don't add or remove bugs from the system but reveal latent bugs in a program. It is usually a good idea to make sure your development computer has the latest version of Windows, Internet Explorer, and Visual C++, with the latest service pack for each. This measure reduces the likelihood of getting sidetracked by other people's bugs. Do make sure that some test machines don't have the latest software, however, so that you can track down system-dependent problems.

The Microsoft System Information utility is useful in tracking down other types of system-related problems. Suppose the bug happens only with a single computer, which suggests a system problem. To check for this, try running all the relevant tools in the **Tools** menu of System Info. The following are some particularly helpful diagnostic tools.

- **Windows Registry Checker** checks for registry corruption
- **Version Conflict Manager** finds and restores out-of-date system files, which were most likely replaced by rogue setup programs
- **System File Checker** verifies the integrity of the system files
- **ScanDisk** checks the hard disks for errors
- **DirectX Diagnostic Tool** checks the various DirectX files and drivers

Suppose that the problem doesn't seem to be related to service packs or any sort of system corruption; there is a good possibility the problem is a DLL conflict. For example, I worked on a program that functioned properly with all the computers in the office except two. After disproving a wide variety of hypotheses, I decided to look for a DLL conflict. By comparing the versions of the DLLs used by the program on the computers that worked to those of the computers that didn't work, I found that the computers that didn't work had the same versions of *Advapi32.dll* and *Oleaut32.dll*. Replacing these files made the problem go away. As it happens, those rogue system files were installed by a beta version of a Microsoft SDK. Not cool! Apparently somebody at Microsoft didn't eat quite enough of their own dogfood. (The "eat you own dogfood" principle requires that a software company use its own software for its own needs while it is in development. That way, if there are any problems, the company should see them first and fix them before the product is released to the marketplace.)

You can use the following somewhat tedious technique for comparing DLLs across computers.

1. Run the Microsoft System Information utility.
2. Export the results to a file using the **Export** command in the **File** menu.
3. Run the program using the Visual C++ debugger.
4. Determine the program's dependent DLLs using the **Modules** command in the Debug menu. Alternatively, you can determine the dependent DLLs using the Visual C++ Dependency Walker utility (in *Common\Tools\ Depends.exe*).
5. Open the exported system information in a text editor. Extract the lines related to the program's modules.
6. Load the module list into a spreadsheet and print it. (Note that the information is tab delimited.)
7. Compare the program modules with those on other computers. Check the version numbers, file dates, file sizes, and paths.

If the existence of the bug correlates to using a specific set of DLLs, you probably have a DLL conflict. If the file paths aren't consistent, you might have multiple versions of the file installed and your program may not be using the one you expect. Welcome to DLL Hell.

A somewhat less labor-intensive way to get similar information is to use the Windows 98 version of Dr. Watson (discussed in Chapter 6, Debugging with Windows). Unfortunately, you can't get program module information from Dr. Watson unless the program crashes, so this approach won't work if your program is stable. (You can, however, change the code to make it crash intentionally: Just enable Dr. Watson, have your program crash, then run Dr. Watson to view the system snapshot information. Select the **Advanced View** command in the **View** menu, then select the **Modules** tab, which has the version, path, file date, and address information for all the program modules.)

Finally, I must reiterate my usual warning. Having your program behave differently on different versions of Windows doesn't necessarily imply a system problem. There may still be a bug in your code. Windows 2000 and Windows 98 use substantially different code bases, so a buggy program is likely to behave differently. In fact, unless you can resolve the problem with a service pack, by fixing a system problem, or by removing a DLL conflict, you should assume the problem is in your code. At the very least, checking the system and failing to find a system problem will give you confidence that your debugging effort is well placed. It may also give you more information to help find the problem.

Double-checking the Documentation

Although I find that the MSDN documentation is quite good, two traps are easy to fall into. The first trap is that some of the documentation is very old. Many documents have a section at the head that reads "The information in this article applies to: . . ." Always read that section! Make sure that the document is relevant to what you are doing. Some documents discuss issues related only to Windows 3.1, but this may not be obvious unless you read that section.

TIP
Be careful when reading MSDN documentation. Some of it is very old.

The second trap involves checking the Requirements section of the Windows API documentation when using new or unfamiliar API functions. The new shell and common control APIs (in *Comctl32.dll*, *Shell32.dll*, and *Shlwapi.dll*) are particularly hazardous because they require specific versions of Windows *and* Internet Explorer. To avoid surprises, choose a target version of Windows and define the _WIN32_IE symbol to enforce compatibility with your target version. For example, to be compatible with all versions of Windows 95 and Windows NT 4.0, define the _WIN32_IE macro as follows before including the shell and common control header files.

```
#define _WIN32_IE  0x0400
...
#include <shlobj.h>
#include <shlwapi.h>
#include <commctrl.h>
```

Note that _WIN32_IE is set to 0x0500 by default, which requires Windows 2000 and IE 5.

TIP
Define the _WIN32_IE macro to ensure compatibility with your target version of Windows.

Using Other People

It is admirable to be self-sufficient and able to bail yourself out of your problems, but at some point you should consider asking someone for help. After all, needlessly wasting your time on a problem you can't solve isn't all that admirable. Although you don't want to be overly dependent on others, when you are genuinely stuck, ask a knowledgeable colleague for help.

Why It Works

Different people have different expertise and experience, so it shouldn't be surprising that asking other people can help you solve your problem. What is surprising is how often this happens without the other person saying much of anything. Sometimes the other person can help you solve your problem by giving little more than a grunt or two. It is possible that this is some form of primal nonverbal communication, but it often happens that merely articulating your approach to the bug and your reasoning behind it is enough to reveal the problem.

> **TIP**
>
> Articulating your approach to the bug and your reasoning behind it may be enough to reveal the problem.

This happens for several reasons. When you are explaining something to someone, you are generally more self-conscious than usual. Verbalizing a problem forces you to identify your assumptions and justify them—something you don't always do on your own. You also have to justify the steps you took, as well as the steps you didn't take; you can't gloss over your assumptions or overlook obvious details. Consequently, any faulty logic becomes readily apparent. Talking to a colleague makes you look at the problem from another point of view and try to explain things in a way that makes sense from the listener's perspective—again, something you don't often do on your own.

In *The Practice of Programming* (Addison-Wesley, 1999), Brian Kernighan and Rob Pike tell a story of a university computer center that kept a teddy bear near the help desk. Anyone needing help first had to explain their problem to the bear before getting help from a human counselor. As long as the students made a serious effort to explain their problems, I'm sure the bear was quite helpful.

When to Ask

The hardest thing about asking for help is determining the right time to ask. If you ask too late, you have wasted a lot of your time. Ask too early and you can be wasting other people's time. When asking for help, be considerate of others. Show that you value their time by making a sincere effort not to waste it.

When asking for help, be considerate. Show that you value other people's time by making a sincere effort not to waste it.

Using Newsgroups

As an alternative to asking someone in person, you could post your question on a developer's newsgroup on the Internet. Deja.com has several debugging-related forums. Use the same courtesy in posting questions to a newsgroup as you would in asking questions in person. Don't waste people's time, even if you don't know them; and be sure to do your homework first. Make a sincere effort to solve the problem on your own, then make an effort to see if a similar problem has already been posted. It's remarkable to see how often the same questions are posted over and over again. These newsgroups have excellent search capabilities. Use them.

Here are some tips for posting a debugging question.

- Be specific about your program. Supply enough information so that readers can understand what you are doing. Give a description of what the program does, how it is built, and what components it uses. Give the compiler version, including the service pack, plus any relevant compiler options. Indicate the version of Windows you are running, including the service pack. If using MFC, state whether your program uses the DLL or the static library. Also state whether your program is single threaded or multithreaded. Give any other relevant details.

- If your program is multithreaded, indicate the type of thread (worker thread, UI thread) and which function (such as *CreateThread, _beginthreadex,* or *AfxBegin-Thread*) was used to create the thread. Is the thread created in a *DllMain* function? Describe how the thread is shut down. Also describe the code the thread executes: Does it call C Run-time Library functions, MFC functions, or COM interfaces? If it calls COM interfaces, how does it get the interface pointers? Is it in a single-threaded or multithreaded apartment? If it's in a single-threaded apartment, is it pumping messages properly and at all times? How does timing affect the problem? How does the program's behavior differ with debug and release builds? Does it differ when run from within the debugger versus stand alone? With single versus multiprocessor machines? Give any other relevant details.

- Be specific about the problem. Supply enough information so that readers can understand what the problem is and the specific activity that caused the problem. Did the program crash? If so, don't just say it crashed. Describe how the program crashed and what you did to make it happen. Did it crash with an unhandled exception? If so, which kind of exception? Did an assertion fail? If so, what did the assertion say? Did a Windows API fail? If so, what was the error code returned by *GetLastError*? What was on the call stack?

- Be concise. Reduce the problem to its simplest form. If you can show a simple code fragment (preferably less than 20 lines) that demonstrates the problem, be sure to post that as well. Don't post pages and pages of code.

- Be clear. Proofread your question before you post it, and make sure that it says what you want and that it makes sense.

- Put some effort into your Subject line by making it both descriptive and brief. A good subject line is more likely to receive a response and more likely to be helpful to others. Subject lines like "Here's a weird one" or "HELP!!" don't encourage reading.

- Demonstrate that you have done your homework. Describe what you have done to track down the bug and the results of your work.

- Make sure you post your question to an appropriate newsgroup forum.

To be a good newsgroup participant, you also need to return any favors you receive. Consider these ideas.

- Post the final outcome. For example, suppose someone suggests trying three different approaches, and you find that one approach finds the bug, but the other two don't. Your work is now done, but your newsgroup thread isn't. Don't leave the thread hanging unresolved. Post the final results of your debugging effort so that others can benefit.

- Help others by answering their questions. Try to answer at least as many questions as you ask.

Here are some practices to avoid in newsgroups.

- Unless you are posting to a beginner's forum, don't post a question that could be readily answered by quickly searching MSDN or by reading a few pages of an introductory book. Don't post questions just because you are too cheap to buy a book.

- Don't be profane.

- Don't get personal.

- Don't be too cute.

- Don't present bogus challenges, such as, "I bet none of you geniuses can solve this one. . . ." Although you want to present your question in a way that encourages people to answer, this particular tactic doesn't work.

- Don't make statements such as, "HELP!!! If I don't figure this out by tomorrow, I'm going to lose my job!" no matter how urgent your problem is. Statements like this appear more amateurish than sympathetic, so you won't evoke much sympathy. If you get any response at all, most likely it will consist of reasons you should consider a career change.

- Don't post the same question simultaneously to multiple newsgroup forums. This is very inconsiderate. Think about it: If you post a question to five forums, the efforts of four of those groups will be wasted. Many people monitor multiple forums, and seeing the same posting tends to upset them. These tend
to be the people with the most expertise—the ones you want to answer your questions.

It's fair to say that people who participate in newsgroups are willing to help you help yourself, but they're not willing to do your work for you. Be considerate, be courteous, and be patient, and you will get your questions answered.

Here is an example of a bad newsgroup question (with a typical response) and an improved version.

Bad question: *I created a program, but when I run it I receive a "Failed to create empty document" error. What should I do?*

A typical response, if the question gets any response at all: *Create a debug build, set a breakpoint, trace through the code, find the bug.*

The following improved question is both more specific and shows that you've done your homework.

I created an MFC SDI program a while ago and it used to work fine, but now when I run it in Windows 95 (any service pack), I receive a "Failed to create empty document" error in a message box at program initialization. I am using

Visual C++ 6.0, SP3. I traced through the code; but the problem seems to be internal to MFC, specifically within *CSingleDocTemplate::OpenDocumentFile.*

Interestingly, I tested the program with Windows 98 and Windows 2000 and it works fine. Furthermore, it also seems to work in Windows 95 as long as IE 4.0+ is installed. I rebuilt the program using Visual C++ 5.0 and it also works in all platforms, even without IE. I then checked MSDN, without luck. It appears that Visual C++ 6.0 is the key factor.

Has anyone else seen this problem? Any suggestions?

Stop Living Dangerously

Now it's time to 'fess up. OK, admit it—to get your project done quickly, you've cut a few corners. You tried to get away with living dangerously; but it didn't work this time, and now you must pay the price. Rather than spending two weeks finding a bug, why not invest a couple days in bug-proofing your code so that bugs will come to you?

Here is a summary of the most effective techniques for bug-proofing your code.

- Develop an assertion strategy and use it.
- Develop a trace statement strategy and use it.
- Develop an exception strategy and use it.
- Compile using the /W4 warning level, and fix all the compiler warnings.
- Compile using the /GZ compiler option to detect uninitialized variables and stack problems.
- Instrument the debug heap to display useful source code information and dump data in a readable format.
- If using MFC, really implement the *AssertValid* and *Dump* functions for your *CObject*-derived classes.
- Use the C++ `auto_ptr` smart pointer template class or similar class to prevent memory leaks.
- Program defensively.
- Rewrite any sloppy, hastily written code that you know is full of bugs.

If you've cut some corners and now have bugs you can't get rid of, stop living dangerously and take the time to do things right. You'll be glad you did.

Bibliography

Asche, Ruediger. "Detecting Deadlocks in Multithreaded Win32 Applications." MSDN, January 11, 1994.

Asche, Ruediger. "Rebasing Win32 DLLs: The Whole Story." MSDN, September 18, 1995.

Bates, Rodney. "Debugging with Assertions." *C/C++ Users Journal,* January 1992.

Beveridge, Jim, and Robert Weiner. *Multithreading Applications in Win32: The Complete Guide to Threads.* Reading, MA: Addison-Wesley, 1996.

Box, Don. *Essential COM*. Reading, MA: Addison-Wesley, 1998.

Brown, Keith. *Programming Windows Security.* Boston: Addison-Wesley, 2000.

Burger, John. "A Lesson in Multithreaded Bugs." *Windows Developer's Journal,* April 1998.

Cargill, Tom. *C++ Programming Style.* Reading, MA: Addison-Wesley, 1992.

Cline, Marshall, Greg Lomow, and Mike Girou. *C++ FAQs,* 2nd ed. Reading, MA: Addison-Wesley, 1999.

Cohen, Aaron, and Mike Woodring. *Win32 Multithreaded Programming.* Sebastopol, CA: O'Reilly & Associates, 1998.

DiLascia, Paul. "C++ Q & A." *Microsoft Systems Journal,* July 1999.

DiLascia, Paul. "C++ Q & A." *Microsoft Systems Journal,* November 1998.

DiLascia, Paul. "C++ Q & A." *Microsoft Systems Journal,* April 1997.

DiLascia, Paul. "Meandering Through the Maze of MFC Message and Command Routing." *Microsoft Systems Journal,* July 1995.

Fong, Earl. "Being Assertive in C/C++." *C/C++ Users Journal,* June 1997.

Kaufman, Charlie, Radia Perlman, and Mike Speciner. *Network Security: Private Communication in a Public World.* Englewood Cliffs, NJ: Prentice-Hall, 1995.

Kernighan, Brian W., and Rob Pike. *The Practice of Programming.* Reading, MA: Addison-Wesley, 1999.

Kernighan, Brian W., and P. J. Plauger. *The Elements of Programming Style,* 2nd ed. New York: McGraw-Hill, 1978.

Lippman, Stanley B., and Josée Lajoie. *C++ Primer,* 3rd ed. Reading, MA: Addison-Wesley, 1998.

Maguire, Steve. *Writing Solid Code: Microsoft's Techniques for Developing Bug-Free C Programs.* Redmond, WA: Microsoft Press, 1993.

McConnell, Steve. *Code Complete: A Practical Handbook of Software Construction.* Redmond, WA: Microsoft Press, 1996.

Meyers, Scott. *Effective C++: 50 Specific Ways to Improve Your Programs and Designs,* 2nd ed. Reading, MA: Addison-Wesley, 1998.

Meyers, Scott. *More Effective C++: 35 New Ways to Improve Your Programs and Designs.* Reading, MA: Addison-Wesley, 1996.

Microsoft Corporation. *Microsoft Press Computer Dictionary,* 3rd ed. Redmond, WA: Microsoft Press, 1997.

Microsoft Corporation. *Microsoft Windows 2000 Server Operations Guide.* Redmond, WA: Microsoft Press, 2000.

Myers, Glenford J. *The Art of Software Testing.* New York: Wiley, 1979.

Pietrek, Matt. "A Crash Course on the Depths of Win32 Structured Exception Handling." *Microsoft Systems Journal,* January 1997.

Pietrek, Matt. "Peering Inside the PE: A Tour of the Win32 Portable Executable File Format." *Microsoft Systems Journal,* March 1994.

Pietrek, Matt. "Remove Fatty Deposits from Your Applications Using Our 32-bit Liposuction Tools." *Microsoft Systems Journal,* October 1996.

Pietrek, Matt. "Under the Hood." *Microsoft Systems Journal*, September, November 1999.

Pietrek, Matt. "Under the Hood." *Microsoft Systems Journal,* February, June 1998.

Pietrek, Matt. "Under the Hood." *Microsoft Systems Journal,* October 1997.

Pietrek, Matt. "Under the Hood." *Microsoft Systems Journal,* May 1996.

Pirsig, Robert M. *Zen and the Art of Motorcycle Maintenance: An Inquiry into Values.* New York: William Morrow, 1974.

Plooy, Ton. "A dbwin Utility for Win95." *Windows Developer's Journal,* December 1996.

Rector, Brent, and Chris Sells. *ATL Internals.* Reading, MA: Addison-Wesley, 1999.

Richter, Jeffrey. *Programming Applications for Microsoft Windows: Master the Critical Building Blocks of 32-Bit and 64-Bit Windows-based Applications,* 4th ed. Redmond, WA: Microsoft Press, 1999.

Robbins, John. "Bugslayer." *Microsoft Systems Journal,* February, June, August, October, December 1999.

Robbins, John. "Bugslayer." *Microsoft Systems Journal,* April, June, October 1998.

Robbins, John. "Bugslayer." *Microsoft Systems Journal,* December 1997.

Robbins, John. "Introducing the Bugslayer: Annihilating Bugs in an Application Near You." *Microsoft Systems Journal,* October 1997.

Rosenberg, Jonathan B. *How Debuggers Work: Algorithms, Data Structures, and Architecture.* New York: Wiley, 1996.

Rosenblum, Bruce D. "Improve Your Programming with Asserts." *Dr. Dobb's Journal,* December 1997.

Schmidt, Robert. "Handling Exceptions." MSDN.

Stout, John W. "Front-End Bug Smashing in Visual C++ and MFC." *Visual C++ Developers Journal,* November 1996.

Stroustrup, Bjarne. *The C++ Programming Language,* 3rd ed. Reading, MA: Addison-Wesley, 1997.

Sutter, Herb. *Exceptional C++: 47 Engineering Puzzles, Programming Problems, and Solutions.* Reading, MA: Addison-Wesley, 2000.

Thielen, David. *No Bugs! Delivering Error-Free Code in C and C++.* Reading, MA: Addison-Wesley, 1992.

Tucker, Andrew. "A DBWin32 Debugger for Windows." *C/C++ Users Journal,* October 1996.

Index

A

B

bad_alloc exception, 206
bad_cast exception, 206
bad_typeid exception, 206
bargaining stage, 3
base addresses
    displaying virtual in Watch window, 296
    in MAP files, 236
    preferred base virtual, 219–220
    rebasing DLLs, 221–224
base classes
    broad as alternative to casting, 62
    CException, 171
    classifying exceptions by, 194
    destructors and resource leaks, 70
    exception, 194
    for exceptions, 181
base COM. *See also* COM
    definition of, 468
    DLLs called from ASPs, 501–502
    EXE debugging, 488–495
Bazuzi, Jay, 460
_beginthread, 440
_beginthreadex, 440, 441
Big Endian, 234
Bind utility, rebasing DLLs and, 224
bit masking, 50–51
blame, 25–27
block scopes, 437
BlueSave utility, 264
Blue Screen of Death (BSOD)
    in bug reports, 10
    debugging Windows 2000, 263–264
    saving information on, 10, 264
Boolean expressions, code location breakpoints and, 309–310
Boolean variables
    in assertions, 80
    using, 52
Box, Don, 469–470
box of death, 211, 212
Break at box, 308, 309
Break command, 464
Break Execution command, 121, 306–307

breakpoints
    Additional DLLs and, 287
    advanced expressions, 308–309
    on API functions, 312–313
    change verification with, 22
    code location, 307, 309–312, 318
    complex statement lines and, 43
    condition expressions, 307–308
    data, 307, 313–315
    debugging message problems with, 343–345
    debugging symbols and, 316
    debugging with, 306–318
    determining if debugger stops at, 307–308
    expression problems, 316
    expressions, 307–308
    guaranteeing valid in DLLs, 485
    how Visual C++ sets, 317–318
    memory allocation, 394
    message, 307, 315
    in multithreaded programs, 451–453
    problems with, 315–318
    reasons for failure to set, 317–318
    setting, 306
    setting in Disassembly window, 291
    setting in release builds, 279
    setting temporary, 306–307
    setting thread-specific, 459
    supported by the Visual C++ debugger, 267
    system code, 312–313
    in Watch window function calls, 295
    for WM_MOUSEMOVE, 342–343
breaks, taking, 20
break statements, deselecting GDI objects and, 405
BSOD. *See* Blue Screen of Death
.bss, 222
"Bug of the Month" column, 26
bug report forms, 7–11, 329
    information on, 7–8
    instructions for, 9–11
bug reports, 329
bugs. *See also* debugging; prevention of bugs
    analyzing information on, 4, 12–20
    assuming they exist, 24–25, 510

DumpBin utility
    comparing file timestamps in, 287
    viewing PE file internals with, 220–221
Dump Symbol Table, 256
dump virtual function, 137–138
dynamic_cast, 61–62, 63–64
DYNAMIC_DOWNCAST macro, 64
Dynamic Link Library. *See* DLLs

E

@EAX, 297, 298
EAX register, 228, 229, 244
    addresses in Dr. Watson files, 255
    @ prefix with, 297
@EBP, 298
EBP register, 228–229, 244–245
    in debug build, 412
@EBX, 298
EBX register, 228
@ECX, 298
ECX register, 228
.edata, 222
@EDI, 298
EDI register, 228, 244
Edit and Continue, 268
    debugging with, 321–325
    limitations of, 323–324
    Program Database for, 276
    setting execution point in, 323
    setting up, 322–323
    tips for, 324–325
    using, 323
Edit Code, 318
@EDX, 298
EDX register, 228, 244
E_FAIL, 153
@EFL, 298
EFLAGS register, 228
EFLGS values, 244
/EHa compiler option, 185
    asynchronous exception model and, 170
E-INVALIDARG, 153
@EIP, 298
EIP register, 228

elimination, process of, 16
ellipsis catch handler, 172, 186, 187–189
Enable tracing option, 364
_endthreadex, 440–441
EnterCriticalSection API function, 427
enum, preferring to #define, 46–47
E_OUTOFMEMORY, 153
equality operator, 71–72
equals sign, in AutoExpand, 303–304
error codes
    API, 214–217
    displaying in error messages, 216–217
    mapping of, 215
error handling
    assertions and, 121
    bugs from incorrect, 161–163
    exceptions for, 161, 165–206
    return values for, 159–160
    strategy, 164–165
    trace statements vs., 130
    Windows, 213–217
error messages
    displaying error code in, 216–217
    exceptions, 204–205
errors
    data, 166
    definition of, 166, 168
    file system, 166
    memory, 166
    network, 166
    peripheral, 166
    user, 166
@ERR pseudo-register, 297–298, 298
    debugging with, 214, 215
    GetLastError values in, 339
@ES, 298
ES register, 228, 244
@ESI, 298
ESI register, 228, 244
@ESP, 298
ESP register, 228–229, 244
E_UNEXPECTED, 153
European Space Agency (ESA), 161–163
EXCEPTION_ACCESS_VIOLATION, 174
exception base class, 194

F

false assumptions, 19
file comparison utilities, 21–22
file names
    in context operator, 293–294
    displaying source code in debug heap, 370–372
    and line number in Crash Dialog box, 243
    truncated by assert, 85
file system errors, 166
FinalConstruct, 486
Find in Files command, 22
    C-style casts and, 62
findstr.exe utility, 312, 313
F12 key, 333
flight control software, 161–163
Float.h, 54
floating-point errors
    exceptions from, 206
    exceptions in Windows, 219
floating-point overflow, 166, 174
floating-point stack, monitoring in Registers window, 289
floating-point variables, 54
FormatMessage, displaying error codes with, 216–217
frame pointer omission (FPO), 229–231, 272
    bugs from, 230–231
free, 46, 48
_FREE_BLOCK, 360
FromHandle, 348–349
@FS, 298
FS register, 228
full-screen programs, 320
function name breakpoints, 309
function parameter assertions, 107–108
function prototypes
    calling conventions and, 231–233
    declaring, 230
    FPO and, 230–231
    mismatches, 411–413
    mismatches of, detecting, 272
function return corruption, 410–411

functions
    assembly language calling conventions, 231–233
    assertions and private vs. public, 105–106
    calling in Watch window, 294–296
    detecting dynamically called, 263
    displaying calls in Call Stack window, 290–291
    exception handling by, 182–183
    freeing resources with, 184
    identifier name selection for, 38–40
    inline vs. #define macros, 46
    input checking with assertions, 101
    logic assertions, 110–111
    not changing names of, 29
    output checking with assertions, 101
    parameter assertions, 107–108
    resolving overloaded, 309
    specialized as alternatives to casting, 63
    that crash on return, 347
    thread stack frame after entering, 229
    tracing failure of, 149
    tracing incorrect input for, 148–149
    uniform code alignment and, 44
    viewing return values of, 339
    virtual, in constructors, 69

G

garbage in/garbage out, 119
GDI. *See* graphics device interface
GetAsyncKeyState API function, 331
    debugging mouse handling with, 342–343
GetCurrentThreadId, 457
    obfuscator values and, 458
GetDocument function, 63
GetLastError, 159, 168, 214
    checking values of, 339
    monitoring value in, 215
    setting error code in, 214–215
GetMessage, VERIFY macro and, 91
GetNextObject function, loop statements and, 66
GetObject, VERIFY macro and, 91
GetObjectType API function, 126
GetProcAddress, 485
/GF compiler option, Edit and Continue and, 276

g_fExit, 435–436
Girou, Mike, 70, 77, 390, 391
GlobalAlloc/GlobalFree functions, 355, 356–357
GoGetClassObject, activation failures, 475–476
Go To Code command, 290–291
Go To Disassembly command, 279
Go To Source command, 291
Grand Jury Rule of Thumb for Thread Termination, 439
graphics device interface (GDI)
    batch processing, 341
    objects, deleting, 398–399, 403
    resource and cleanup functions, 399–400
    resource leaks, 353–354
grief, stages of, 3–4
@GS, 298
GS register, 228
guard bytes, 414
GUIDs, _uuidof to retrieve, 470–471
/GX compiler option, synchronous exception model and, 170
/GZ compiler option, 72–73
    catching release-build errors with, 277
    detecting function prototype mismatches with, 412
    variable initialization with, 49

H

handles
    initializing, 56
    reasonableness of, 383
hangs, investigating and diagnosing, 463–464
header files, 48
HeapAlloc, throwing exceptions from, 213–214
HeapAlloc/HeapFree functions, 355
HeapCreate, throwing exceptions from, 213–214
HeapReAlloc, throwing exceptions from, 213–214
HeapWalk API function, 357
Heisenberg Uncertainty Principle, 13, 27–28
    depending on the debugger and, 508
    drawing code and, 340–341
    mouse handling code and, 342–343
    multithreaded programs and, 448

trace statements and, 131, 152–153
    value of remote debugging with, 320
Hexadecimal Display option, 288, 293, 299
hex dumps, reading, 234
hierarchical lock acquisition, 429–431
horizontal coupling, 36
HRESULT, 480
Hungarian notation, 40–43, 79
    standard prefixes from, 42
hypotheses, 17–18

I

.idata, 222
identifier names
    abbreviations as, 38–39
    generic, 39
    joke, 39
    random, 39
    selection of, 38–40
    similar, 39
idiv, 227
_IGNORE_BLOCK, 360
IID_PPV_ARG, 470–471
IIDs
    passing wrong, 469
    _uuidof keyword and, 470–471
IIS. *See* Internet Information Server
illegal instruction, 166
image file header, 220
image optional header, 220
imul, 227
inc, 227
incremental development, 25
inductive logic, 16–18
Inetinfo.exe, 502
infinite recursion, 408–410
INFINITE timeouts, 453–454
information gathering, 5–12
    bug report forms, 6–12
    on bug reproduction, 7
    no information as information and, 19–20
    from testers, 6–12
initialization
    by constructors, 67–68
    debugging base COM DLL, 486–487

N

unsigned values against signed, 53
using test cases, 509
which build to use for, 281–282
.text, 222
Thielen, David, 100, 128
thiscall, 231, 232, 407
THIS_FILE, MFC ASSERT macro and, 89–90
thrashing, 497–498
threadID, 457
Thread Information Block. *See* TIB
Thread Local Storage (TLS) arrays, 299
threads
    context confusion with, 451–453
    creating, 439–442
    definition of, 420
    handling of, 420–421
    naming, 459–463
    setting breakpoints on, 459
    suspending, 465
    synchronization, difficulty of debugging,
        27–28
    termination of, 438–439, 442–446
    unexpected serialization of, 448–451
    zombie, 439
thread-safe programs, 421
    bug nonreproducibility in, 432–433
    deadlock prevention in, 428–431
    optimization problems in, 433–436
    race condition prevention in, 425–428
    resource leak prevention in, 436–438
    writing, 425–438
Threads dialog box
    determining current thread with, 453
    examining data manipulation in, 456
    suspending threads in, 465
thread stacks
    assembly language, 228–229
    debugging, 406–413
    function prototype mismatches and, 411–413
    function return corruption and, 410–411
    infinite recursion and, 408–410
    large automatic variables and, 408
    problems with, 407–408
    stack overflow exceptions, 406–407
    Windows calling conventions, 407

Thread start/exit, 449
ThrowFunction, 189
throw statements, 171
    exceptions and, 169–170
@TIB pseudo-register, 299, 456–457
    obfuscator value in, 457–458
    thread-specific breakpoints in, 459
TIB (Thread Information Block)
    addresses in Dr. Watson files, 253
    definition of, 420
    displaying structure in the Watch window, 299
    FS register pointer to, 228
timeouts
    INFINITE, 428–429
    preventing deadlock and, 428–429
    unexpected in multithreaded programs,
        453–454
TLS. *See* Thread Local Storage arrays
.tls, 222
tools, knowledge of, 28
tooltip code, 345
_tprintf, 159–160
TraceActivateError, 478, 479–480
TRACE-ACTIVATE macro, 480–482
    release build version of, 481–482
trace buffers, 451
TraceEnabled, 350
TRACE macro, 134–135
    buffer size, 154–155
    source code, 143–144
TRACEn macro, 135
Tracer utility, 135–136, 350
trace statements, 5, 129–157
    ANSI C++ Run-time Library, 132–133
    ATL, 140–141, 144–145
    cerr, 132–133
    characteristics of, 130
    clog, 132–133
    compared with assertions, 131
    _CoServerActivate, 480
    custom, 145–146
    DBWIN-like utilities with, 154, 156
    Debugger Replacement Model with, 152–153
    Debugger Supplement Strategy, 147–152
    debug report macros and, 155